Gender Hierarchy in the Qur'ān

Medieval Interpretations, Modern Responses

This book explores how medieval and modern Muslim religious scholars (*'ulamā'*) interpret gender roles in Qur'ānic verses on legal testimony, marriage, and human creation. Citing these verses, medieval scholars developed increasingly complex laws and interpretations upholding a male-dominated gender hierarchy; aspects of their interpretations influence religious norms and state laws in Muslim-majority countries today, yet other aspects have been discarded entirely. Karen Bauer traces the evolution of these interpretations, showing how they have been adopted, adapted, rejected, or replaced over time, by comparing the Qur'ān with a wide range of Qur'ānic commentaries and interviews with prominent religious scholars from Iran and Syria. At times, tradition is modified in unexpected ways: learned women argue against gender equality, or Grand Ayatollahs reject sayings of the Prophet, citing science instead. This innovative and engaging study highlights the effects of social and intellectual contexts on the formation of tradition, and on modern responses to it.

Karen Bauer is a research associate in Qur'ānic Studies at the Institute of Ismaili Studies in London. Her publications include articles on the Qur'ān, the genre of *tafsīr*, and gender, as well as an edited volume entitled *Aims, Methods and Contexts of Qur'anic Exegesis (2nd/8th – 9th/15th Centuries).*

For My Parents

Cambridge Studies in Islamic Civilization

Other titles in the series are listed at the back of the book.

Gender Hierarchy in the Qurʾān

Medieval Interpretations, Modern Responses

KAREN BAUER

CAMBRIDGE
UNIVERSITY PRESS

CAMBRIDGE
UNIVERSITY PRESS

32 Avenue of the Americas, New York NY 10013-2473, USA

Cambridge University Press is part of the University of Cambridge.

It furthers the University's mission by disseminating knowledge in the pursuit of education, learning and research at the highest international levels of excellence.

www.cambridge.org
Information on this title: www.cambridge.org/9781107041523

First published 2015

A catalogue record for this publication is available from the British Library

Library of Congress Cataloguing in Publication data
Bauer, Karen.
Gender hierarchy in the Qur'an : medieval interpretations, modern responses / Karen Bauer.
pages cm. – (Cambridge studies in Islamic civilization)
Includes bibliographical references and index.
ISBN 978-1-107-04152-3 (Hardback)
1. Sex role–Religious aspects–Islam. 2. Qur'an–Criticism, interpretation, etc.
3. Qur'an–Criticism, interpretation, etc.–History. I. Title.
BP134.S49B38 2015
297.1′2283053–dc23 2015010542

ISBN 978-1-107-04152-3 Hardback

Contents

Acknowledgements

This book owes a lot to a number of people, but Michael Cook deserves special mention. He supported the project from its first iteration, gave me many invaluable comments on various drafts, and encouraged my trips to Iran and Syria. Patricia Crone's support was also instrumental in bringing this book about. Her willingness to discuss the topic and honest feedback greatly improved my writing and my work, and her recent impatience has spurred on the completion of this project. I would also like to thank David Hollenberg, Robert Gleave, Andrew Rippin, and Behnam Sadeghi, who commented on earlier drafts of parts of this book, and the anonymous reviewers for their helpful feedback. Abdeali Qutbuddin and Husain Qutbuddin helped me find and understand Fāṭimid Ismāʿīlī sources. Russell Harris, of the Institute of Ismaili Studies, made the beautiful maps. Will Hammell and Kate Gavino of Cambridge University Press facilitated publication. Most of all, this work would not have been possible without the generosity, patience, and goodwill of my interview subjects, from whom I learned so much.

In order to conduct the interviews in Syria and Iran, I had both practical and financial help. For my trip to Syria in 2004, I received a grant from the Princeton Institute for International and Regional Studies. I would especially like to thank Huda al-Habash, who took me under her wing for intensive study sessions in Damascus. When I returned to Syria in 2005, I was befriended by Mariam Roncero, who went to great lengths to help me.

My trip to Iran in 2011 was enabled by the sponsorship of Mofid University and funding from the British Academy Small Grants Programme. The arrangements made by Mofid University ensured the success of my trip, and I am grateful for the generosity of my colleagues there for arranging my visa, housing, room in the library, and interviews. I owe special thanks to Dr Majid Rezaei, director of the Center for Qur'ānic Studies, and Mr Hedayat Yousefi, then deputy for the director of the Center for Human Rights Studies (now Chief of Staff for the Office of the President and faculty member of the Department of Political Science), for their professionalism, generosity, patience, and kindness during my stay in Iran. More recently Mr Yousefi was a great help when I needed to get back in touch with all of my interview subjects. I would also like to thank Dr Hamed Shivapour and Mrs Fatemeh Muslimi, both of whom accompanied me to interviews (and added to them!), and Fatemeh for her work translating the interviews in Persian. Miss Behnaz Hajizadeh shared her apartment in Tehran and accompanied me to interviews there. This book would not be what it is without the research I conducted in Iran, and I would particularly like to thank the then–Vice Chancellor of Mofid University, Dr Seyed Masoud Moosavi Karimi, for agreeing to sponsor my trip.

Finally, I would like to thank my husband Peter, who has been very supportive and who has done more than his fair share of the housework while I have been completing this project, and our son Simon, for being such a delight.

Although I have sought to present the views of my sources accurately in quotes and text, the analysis of these views is mine alone, and as such may not represent the opinions of my interview subjects. Nor does this work represent the views of the institutions that have supported me financially or through their sponsorship. I have had much helpful advice and feedback on this work, but neither interview subjects nor colleagues bear any responsibility for its mistakes.

A Note on Names and Transliterations

I have used the common, shortened version of medieval authors' names in text. These short names are used for alphabetisation in the bibliography. A fuller version of the name is also provided in the first footnote and the bibliography.

I have maintained transliteration for modern names in Arabic. Many of my Iranian interview subjects have a preferred spelling of their name in English, which I have followed. In some cases I provide the fully transliterated name on the first mention, and in the bibliography.

Transliteration is alphabetic, rather than phonetic, with some common exceptions.

Introduction

In his interpretation of the punishment for recalcitrant wives, the exegete, jurist, and historian Muḥammad ibn Jarīr al-Ṭabarī (d. 310/923) came up with a novel solution for an exegetical problem. The problem, as al-Ṭabarī saw it, was that the Qur'ān seemed to go against men's legal rights in marriage. The punishment for recalcitrant wives outlined in Q. 4:34 is that the husband should *admonish them, shun them in the beds, and beat them. And if they obey you, seek not a way against them.* From this portion of the verse, it is clear that husbands have recourse to three steps, and that each step is predicated on the wife's continued disobedience. What bothers al-Ṭabarī is the middle step, which I have translated as *shun them in the beds*. For him, a wife's disobedience consisted of her refusal to have sex with her husband, so shunning this recalcitrant wife in bed is hardly a punishment at all; in fact, such a wife wants precisely to be left alone. This did not sit well with al-Ṭabarī, who, incidentally, never married. He reasoned that the earliest exegetical authorities must have missed the point in their interpretations of the verse's words, particularly *wa'hjurūhunna*, which I have translated above as 'shun them'.[1] Al-Ṭabarī

[1] Abū Ja'far Muḥammad b. Jarīr Al-Ṭabarī, *Jāmi' al-bayān 'an ta'wīl āy al-Qur'ān*, eds. Maḥmūd Muḥammad Shākir and Aḥmad Muḥammad Shākir (Cairo: Dār al-Ma'ārif bi-Maṣr 1950–60), v. 8, pp. 307–8 (at Q. 4:34). I return to this interpretation in Chapter 5. It is also discussed at greater length in my dissertation, Karen Bauer, 'Room for Interpretation: Qur'ānic Exegesis and Gender', PhD Dissertation, Princeton University, 2008, and mentioned in Manuela Marín, 'Disciplining Wives: a Historical Reading of Qur'ān 4:34', *Studia Islamica* (2003): 5–40, at pp. 24–5, and Ayesha Chaudhry, *Domestic Violence and the Islamic Tradition: Ethics, Law, and the Muslim Discourse on Gender* (Oxford University Press, 2013), pp. 78–9.

referred to the 'speech of the 'Arabs', by whom he means the Bedouins, to interpret the Qur'ān from a perspective that is closer to its original milieu than al-Ṭabarī's own milieu of urban Baghdad.

The first of the three meanings of this word in Arabic, he says, is that 'a man avoids speaking to another man, which means he repudiates and rejects him'.[2] The second meaning is the 'profusion of words through repetition, in the manner of a scoffer'.[3] The third possible meaning is one that had not been suggested by any earlier exegete. It is 'tying up a camel, i.e., its owner ties it up with the *hijār*, which is a rope (*ḥabl*) attached to its loins and ankles'.[4] For al-Ṭabarī, only the third solution fits the bill. After cautioning husbands that they should never do this to an obedient wife, al-Ṭabarī advises: 'If they refuse to repent of their disobedience, then imprison them,[5] tying them to their beds, meaning in their rooms, or chambers, in which they sleep, and in which their husbands lie with them'.[6]

Sa'diyya Shaikh, a modern feminist interpreter, is outraged by al-Ṭabarī's interpretation. She points out that it 'epitomises oppressive and abusive gender relations'.[7] For her, this interpretation embodies everything that is wrong with the medieval tradition, and against which she, a modern Muslim woman, must struggle to gain equality. But modern feminists are not the only ones to express their dismay at al-Ṭabarī's suggestion that husbands should tie their wives up to force them to obey. Although al-Ṭabarī was a well-respected scholar, in this instance his own scholarly community treated him with scorn: 'this is a deviant interpretation, and it is doubly so considering God's words *in the beds*, because there are no ropes (*ribāṭ*) in bed',[8] says al-Ṭūsī (d. 459/1066), an Imāmī Shī'ī exegete. According to the Shāfi'ī al-Māwardī (d. 450/1058), the narrative that al-Ṭabarī used to support his view contains 'no proof of his interpretation rather than another'.[9] The most involved rebuttal comes from the Mālikī jurist and exegete Ibn al-'Arabī (d. 543/1148). He is astonished, and addresses al-Ṭabarī personally through the two centuries that separate them: 'What a mistake, from someone who is so

[2] Ibid., v. 8, p. 306 (at Q. 4:34). [3] Ibid. [4] Ibid., v. 8, p. 307 (at Q. 4:34).
[5] *Istawthaq min*, according to Dozy, is 'imprison'.
[6] Al-Ṭabarī, *Jāmi' al-bayān*, v. 8, p. 309–10 (at Q. 4:34).
[7] Sa'diyya Shaikh, 'Exegetical violence: nushūz in Qur'ānic gender ideology', *Journal for Islamic Studies*, 17 (1997): 49–73, at p. 65.
[8] Abū Ja'far Muḥammad b. Ḥasan Al-Ṭūsī, *al-Tibyān fī tafsīr al-Qur'ān*, ed. Mu'assasat al-Nashr al-Islāmī (Qom: Jami'a al-Mudarrisīn, 1992), v. 4, p. 451.
[9] Abū 'l-Ḥasan 'Alī b. Muḥammad Al-Māwardī, *al-Nukat wa'l-'uyūn*, ed. Sayyid b. 'Abd al-Maqṣūr b. 'Abd al-Rahīm (Beirut: Dār al-Kutub al-'Ilmiyya, 1992), v. 1, p. 483.

learned in the Qur'ān and the behaviour of the Prophet (*sunna*)! I am indeed amazed at you, [al-Ṭabarī], at the boldness with which you have treated the Qur'ān and *sunna* in this interpretation!'[10] These scholars do not question al-Ṭabarī's sources or methods; Ibn al-ʿArabī replicates his method of picking and choosing among *ḥadīth*s, performing linguistic analysis, and rejecting some early views in favour of others. To find the true meaning of the verse, Ibn al-ʿArabī reinterprets the reports of early authorities, obscuring their differences in order to find the one 'correct view', while chastising al-Ṭabarī for having missed it: 'And it is indeed strange that, with all of al-Ṭabarī's deep studies into the science [of the Qurʾān] and into the language of the Arabs, he has strayed so far from the true interpretation! And how he deviates from the correct view!'[11] Since Ibn al-ʿArabī does not object to al-Ṭabarī's method as such, it must be that the substance of his interpretation shows his incorrect use of that method. He has obtained an unacceptable result.

For these medieval interpreters, hierarchies in society and family life were natural and fair; all of al-Ṭabarī's medieval critics defend the gender hierarchy and assert that men should have the right to punish their disobedient wives. But even though they accept the premise, they sometimes struggle with the boundaries of a just hierarchy. They do not describe a husband's control as unbounded, unconditional, or absolute. Al-Ṭabarī's proposition for correcting a disobedient wife overstepped the mark: he went beyond the meaning and intention of the verse.

The responses cited here highlight much that is important in the genre of Qurʾānic interpretation (*tafsīr*): the early exegetical authorities, in theory, trump later interpreters like al-Ṭabarī, but in turn, their views can be reinterpreted; there is room for many conflicting views, but not every view is tolerated; respected works by respected scholars are read across the boundaries of legal schools; and the correct interpretation is bounded by common practice, common understanding, and ideas of right and wrong. Medieval interpretations of the gender hierarchy shed light on what these scholars considered to be good, just, and correct in their societies.

Today, the Qurʾānic gender hierarchy poses a different problem for religious scholars (*ʿulamāʾ*).[12] Their tradition takes hierarchy for granted.

[10] Muḥammad b. ʿAbd Allāh Abū Bakr Ibn al-ʿArabī, *Aḥkām al-Qurʾān*, ed. ʿAlī Muḥammad al-Bajawī ([Cairo]: ʿĪsā al-Bābī al-Ḥalabī, 1967), v. 1, p. 418 (at Q. 4:34).

[11] Ibid.

[12] I use the term *ʿulamāʾ* to refer to religious scholars who have been trained in the traditional sources. However, when possible, I differentiate between different types of scholars, particularly the *mufassirūn* (exegetes/interpreters) and *fuqahāʾ* (jurists).

But for many believers, the very notion of hierarchy is outdated: modern ideas of fairness are often based on the ideal of equality. Sa'diyya Shaikh's reaction to al-Ṭabarī's interpretation is representative of many modern Muslims' struggles with the hierarchical and male-orientated medieval tradition. Squaring the medieval tradition with modern notions of fairness and egalitarianism is a challenge for both conservative and reformist *'ulamā'*. For conservatives, the challenge is to prove that the patriarchal system outlined in the Qur'ān's hierarchical verses is appropriate today, in a time when many women are able to be educated, earning, and socially equal to men. Reformists support gender egalitarianism. For them, the challenge is to reinterpret the plain sense of these verses, to explain away centuries of interpretation, and to justify the correctness of their rereading. Through discussions of the gender hierarchy, *'ulamā'* today indicate their adherence to a larger set of interpretative values, involving the role of tradition, reinterpretation, and human reasoning.

Not all Qur'ānic verses on women are hierarchical. Some verses affirm that believing men's and believing women's prayers and good deeds will be rewarded; others name specific women as either good or bad examples to all believers. As believers, women and men alike can either do good or go astray. They each seem to be responsible for their own spiritual destiny regardless of sex. Verses about the nature of the relationship *between* men and women in the world, however, draw distinctions between the sexes, and I argue that this distinction is hierarchical. Four such 'difficult' verses are the core of this study. Q. 4:1 deals with the creation of the first humans, widely understood to be Adam and Eve. Q. 2:228 and Q. 4:34 speak of the marital hierarchy: men's 'degree' over women, the necessity of wifely obedience, and the husband's right to punish his recalcitrant wife. Q. 2:282 refers to a woman's testimony as half of a man's testimony, which raises the question of the worth of a woman's word and of her mental abilities.

The following pages examine the content of these verses and their context in the Qur'ān, and trace how the *'ulamā'* have interpreted them through time, from the earliest interpretations to the most recent, living interpretations, in the form of interviews with *'ulamā'* from Iran and Syria.[13]

[13] My focus on the *'ulamā'* in the Middle East and Iran, who write in Arabic and Persian, differentiates this book from much of the important recent work which examines the Qur'ān and tradition from a modern feminist lens, or which incorporates the interpretations of feminists writing in English. See, for instance, Kecia Ali, *Sexual Ethics and Islam: Feminist Reflections on Qur'an, Hadith, and Jurisprudence* (Oxford: Oneworld, 2006); Asma Barlas, *'Believing Women' in Islam: Unreading Patriarchal Interpretations of the*

Through their views on women's role in marriage, creation, and testimony, the *ʿulamāʾ* define their stance towards tradition and reinterpretation. In turn, their views on both women and interpretation are determined not only by a textual heritage, but by their own social, intellectual, cultural, and political circumstances. The portrayal of women in these texts may reveal more about their (male) authors' own attitudes towards hierarchy than it does about women's actual social position: women are portrayed as the proper subjects of an idealised, just male rulership in medieval texts, and today the Qurʾān's verses on women have become an axis of reformist–conservative debate over the place of traditional social, political, and legal structures in the modern world. In this book, the gender hierarchy becomes the lens through which to explore the Qurʾān and its interpretation, the links between medieval and modern interpretations, and the effect of social and intellectual context on the production of religious knowledge.

MEDIEVAL INTERPRETATIONS, MODERN RESPONSES

The notion of tradition is immensely important for the *ʿulamāʾ*, and their grounding in tradition differentiates them from other groups who interpret the Qurʾān.[14] I use 'tradition' to refer to aspects of the medieval social and intellectual heritage: the Qurʾān and its interpretation, *ḥadīth*s, historical narrations, law, and custom. As others have noted, religious thinkers often reference an idea or impression of tradition, rather than a concrete reality.[15] However, although the *ʿulamāʾ* regularly draw on this rhetorical notion of 'tradition', certain aspects of tradition are more than just a rhetorical notion: they are traceable. 'Tradition' partially consists of

Qur'an (Austin: University of Texas Press, 2002); Ayesha Chaudhry, *Domestic Violence and the Islamic Tradition*; Aysha Hidayatullah, *Feminist Edges of the Qur'an* (Oxford: Oxford University Press, 2014); Sa'diyya Shaikh, 'A Tafsir of Praxis: Gender, Marital Violence, and Resistance in a South African Muslim Community', in *Violence Against Women in Contemporary World Religions: Roots and Cures*, ed. Daniel Maguire and Sa'diyya Shaikh (Cleveland, OH: Pilgrim Press, 2007), Amina Wadud, *Qur'an and Woman: Rereading the Sacred Text from a Woman's Perspective* (Oxford: Oxford University Press, 1999, reprint edition).

14 Qasim Zaman takes the view that this attitude towards tradition separates the *ʿulamāʾ*, as a scholarly class, from other groups in society, such as the Islamists (including the Salafīs) and modernists, who, on the whole, have the attitude that tradition is not necessarily needed in order to understand Islam. Muhammad Qasim Zaman, *The Ulama in Contemporary Islam: Custodians of Change* (Princeton, NJ: Princeton University Press, 2002), p. 10 ff.

15 For instance, Chaudhry, *Domestic Violence and the Islamic Tradition*, p. 16.

specific interpretations that are passed from generation to generation, and yet continually reinterpreted, appropriated, and repurposed through time as the *ʿulamāʾ* engage with their intellectual legacy in changing circumstances. In the example given in the previous section, al-Ṭabarī records, but then rejects, the early authorities' views of *shun them in the beds*. These early interpretations were revived and defended by his detractors, reformulated entirely by Ibn al-ʿArabī, and ultimately judged by a modern feminist. It is possible to trace particular elements of tradition and show precisely how they have been adopted, adapted, or rejected through time.

Scholars of history and religious studies have long acknowledged that the past is subject to appropriation and reinterpretation. In a context where many Muslim countries base aspects of their laws on medieval sources, the appropriation of tradition has important implications for women's rights. The most restrictive interpretation of women's rights is often equated with the most traditional. This popular perception is sometimes reflected in the language used to describe the range of interpretations among today's *ʿulamāʾ*. Ziba Mir-Hosseini describes three types of clerics she encountered in Qom, Iran, in 1997, which she labels the traditionalists, the neo-traditionalists, and the modernists. By 'traditionalist', she means a cleric who adheres strictly to pre-modern Islamic law. The 'neo-traditionalists' adapt traditional rulings for today's times, accepting that a certain amount of change is inevitable in Islamic law, and that circumstances must determine understanding. The 'modernists', not bound by medieval laws, boldly advocate new interpretations of traditional sources.[16] The 'traditionalist' label is adopted by the *ʿulamāʾ* themselves.[17] Such terminology is no accident: it plays directly into the question of authenticity. As Zaman says: 'The *ʿulamāʾ* ... are hardly frozen in the mold of the Islamic religious tradition, but this tradition nevertheless remains their fundamental frame of reference, the basis of their authority and identity'.[18] By adopting the label 'traditionalist', conservative *ʿulamāʾ* are portraying themselves as the authentic, authoritative *ʿulamāʾ*, those who truly represent the past.

[16] Ziba Mir-Hosseini, *Islam and Gender: The Religious Debate in Contemporary Iran* (Princeton: Princeton University Press, 1999), pp. 18–19.

[17] Ibid., p. 17: 'The clerics I came across in Qom fell into two broad categories: adherents of the pre-revolutionary school, now referred to as Traditional Jurisprudence (*feqh-e sonnati*); and those who promoted what they referred to as Dynamic Jurisprudence (*feqh-e puya*)'.

[18] Zaman, *The Ulama in Contemporary Islam*, p. 10. He returns to this point later in the book, for instance, p. 180.

These categories represent real differences between the interpreters. However, the terms 'traditionalist' and 'modernist' are problematic when used to describe modern conservative and reformist *ʿulamāʾ*: they can imply that only progressive or reformist readings are modern, and that the most conservative interpretation always emerges from the tradition. Yet neither of these assumptions is true. For instance, when I interviewed the Grand Muftī of Syria, Aḥmad Ḥassoun, in 2005, he told me that he had a new initiative to train women to be *muftīs* for other women.[19] A *muftī* is a person qualified to issue valid opinions on the law; unlike the opinions of a judge, a *muftī*'s judgment is non-binding. He presented the initiative to train women as *muftīs* as a reinterpretation of tradition in women's favour, and a way of involving them in legal authority. It is a reinterpretation of medieval law, but not in the direction of equality. According to almost all Sunnī schools of law in the medieval period, women were allowed to be *muftīs* for both women and men. The modern rereading, which restricts women's activities to other women, and to 'women's issues' such as menstruation and childbirth, does not grant women the same leeway that they were granted in medieval law.

Conservatives and reformists approach tradition in different ways.[20] The primary aim of conservative *ʿulamāʾ* is to preserve particular interpretations of past laws; but they pick and choose, use modern justifications, and sometimes create entirely new laws. Reformists seek to reinterpret past laws by rereading traditional sources. These varied approaches to tradition lead to practical differences between conservative and reformist interpretations on women. Conservatives explain the continued necessity of a gender hierarchy by saying that the Qurʾānic verses indicate differences in men's and women's innate characteristics and minds. To justify this today, they refer to scientific arguments about the natural differences between men and women. Reformists argue against the hierarchy by asserting that the Qurʾān's hierarchical verses were addressed to a specific time and place. Both groups claim tradition as

[19] This initiative is also reported in 'Women Want Female Muftis', *Institute for War and Peace Reporting*, Syria Issue 16 (2 September 2008), accessed online at: http://iwpr.net/report-news/women-want-female-muftis; no author listed.

[20] Suha Taji-Farouki puts this nicely: 'Tradition is recruited either to legitimise change, or to defend against perceived innovations and to preserve threatened values'. Suha Taji-Farouki, 'Introduction', in *Modern Muslim Intellectuals and the Qur'an* (Oxford: Oxford University Press in association with the Institute of Ismaili Studies, 2004), pp. 1–36, at pp. 1–2.

their keystone, but they also use modern tools, arguments, and reasoning to re-examine and re-interpret their tradition.

Through time, the *'ulamā'* have formed their views, in part, as a response to their particular intellectual context. Intellectual context includes textual genre, an interpreter's legal school, his personal opinion, his forebears, and his intended audience: teachers, students, and peers. It also includes the named sources of his interpretation, the Qur'ān and *ḥadīth*. Each of these aspects of intellectual context affect interpretations in different ways. Kecia Ali describes the importance of genre with regard to legal texts. She points out not only that the jurists 'use specialized terminology and rely on a wealth of assumed knowledge', but also that 'the rhythms or modes of argument characteristic of legal texts shaped the jurists' views'.[21] As in the juridical texts described by Ali, works of interpretation have their own language, methods, and lines of argumentation. Authors within each genre are involved in particular discursive contexts.

The context of intellectual jockeying can have a profound effect on discussions of 'women's status'. Often, a statement that seems integral to women's status is presented as a part of a wider argument, for instance, for or against a particular school of Qur'ānic reading, law, or grammar. Arguments that can seem vehemently to defend or deny women's rights, for instance their right to testify in court or to assume judgeship, may be primarily rhetorical attempts to discredit rival schools of law or interpretation. This type of argumentation leads to real differences in interpretations; but it is important to investigate the intellectual context of these arguments in order to understand their nature, particularly since ideas of women's rights have changed so radically in the modern age. A modern reader might assume that certain statements or rulings – such as the ruling that a single woman could testify to the live birth of a child – was an argument for, or at least towards, equality. But what a modern reader might regard as a natural corollary of a certain statement or law was by no means natural for its medieval author: they explained that women's testimony was only accepted out of necessity. In the classical period and beyond, the idea of sexual equality in the worldly realm seems to have been absent. In the worldly realm, hierarchies were the norm, and statements about women's rights were made with the underlying presupposition of the justice of these worldly hierarchies.

[21] Kecia Ali, *Marriage and Slavery in Early Islam* (Cambridge, MA: Harvard University Press, 2010), p. 25.

STRUCTURE & SOURCES

This project started as a study of medieval Muslim interpretations of the gender hierarchy. I was curious to know whether, in the medieval interpretations of the Qurʾān, there was any notion of gender egalitarianism akin to the feminist notions common today (the short answer is no). To research this question, I undertook a study of the interpretation of three Qurʾānic verses, primarily in medieval works of exegesis (*tafsīr al-Qurʾān*). That project became my PhD dissertation on sixty-seven medieval interpretations of verses on creation and marriage – now, in a modified form, Chapters 3 and 5 of this book.[22] However, as I was working on my dissertation, it became apparent to me that these interpretations were shaped by certain types of constraints.[23] In order to undertake a deeper exploration of exactly what I was reading, I expanded the scope: this study includes the important question of women's testimony, goes outside the genre of *tafsīr*, and is based on both medieval and modern sources, drawing on both the earliest available Islamic source – the Qurʾān itself – and the most recent, in the form of interviews with the *ʿulamāʾ*. The following pages detail the structure of the book, as well as expanding on my use of Qurʾān, medieval and modern written *tafsīr*, and interviews as source material.

This book is divided into three main parts: Testimony, Creation, and Marriage. Testimony focuses on interpretations of Q. 2:282, *call to witness two of your men, and if there are not two men, then a man and two women, so that if one of the two women errs, the other can remind her*. Many *ʿulamāʾ*, both medieval and modern, attribute the difference in testimony between men and women to a difference in their minds. I have chosen to open the book with this issue since the question of mental equality is at the basis of the gender hierarchy as a whole. Creation discusses the creation of the first woman in the Qurʾān and its interpretation, centring on the interpretation of Q. 4:1, *fear your Lord, who created you from a single soul, and from it created its mate*. Medieval exegetes considered Eve, and by extension all women, to be secondary creations. Modern interpreters view men and women as equal in their

[22] Karen Bauer, 'Room for Interpretation: Qurʾānic Exegesis and Gender', 2008.

[23] Jane Dammen McAuliffe, 'The Genre Boundaries of Qurʾānic Commentary', in *With Reverence for the Word: medieval scriptural exegesis in Judaism, Christianity, and Islam*, ed. McAuliffe et. al., Oxford: Oxford University Press, 2003, pp. 445–461.

created form. This fundamental transformation in references to women, from a discourse of inherent inequality to one of inherent equality, amounts to a change in consensus among the *'ulamā'*. Underlying this change in discourse is a tectonic shift in notions of correctness, orthodoxy, and the sources of authority. Marriage describes how the *'ulamā'* interpret verses that raise ethical issues around the nature of and reasons for the marital hierarchy. The verses at the centre of this discussion are Q. 2:228 and Q. 4:34. Q. 2:228 is about men's and women's rights: *women have rights like their obligations according to what is right, and men have a degree over them.* Q. 4:34, which today is one of the most controversial verses in the Qur'ān, reads:

> Men are *qawwāmūn* [in charge/supporters/maintainers] over women, with what God has given the one more than the other, and with what they spend of their wealth; so the good women are obedient, guarding for the absent with what God has guarded, and those from whom you fear *nushūz* [ill conduct/disobedience], admonish them, abandon them in the beds, and beat them; and if they obey you, do not seek a way against them, for God is mighty, Wise.

Ethical notions are tested by a verse that orders wifely obedience regardless of considerations of the husband's piety, and allows a husband to beat his recalcitrant wife. This part of the book addresses the effect on interpretation of ethics, social mores, and truths taken for granted.

The interpreters see each of these verses as a part of a whole picture: the arguments they make about one verse are predicated on those they make about the others. So, thematically, all of the parts of this book are interrelated; but in terms of overall argument, each also builds on the last. Testimony broadly examines the way that generic conventions shape a discourse. Creation focuses on the development within, and sources for, one genre, that of *tafsīr*. Marriage focuses on the ethics of interpretation, describing how ethics, social mores, and culturally taken-for-granted arguments can influence interpretation, and how as these notions change through time, so does interpretation. Together, these parts document a subtle shift in the authorities cited in the medieval genre of *tafsīr*, from a genre that relied almost exclusively on the reports of early exegetical authorities, to one that relied much more heavily on reports attributed to the Prophet himself. Another shift in authoritative sources occurs in the modern period, when *ḥadīth*s are frequently dismissed or discounted, and science is used to frame and explain interpretations.

While it is possible to examine the trajectory of *tafsīr* and law on gender without ever really engaging with the text of the Qur'ān, each part of this book begins with a modest reading and contextualisation of the verses in question. I focus on the Qur'ān in part because it is so central to the *'ulamā'* today. Non-Qur'ānic sources of authority shift through time: the *'ulamā'* readily admit that disciplines such as *tafsīr* and *fiqh* are a human creation, and therefore fallible; even the collections of *ḥadīth* include non-authentic material. The Qur'ān is the unchanging core.

My Qur'ānic reading is an attempt to get at the 'plain sense' of the verses by comparing them with other Qur'ānic verses with similar themes, content, and vocabulary. By 'plain sense' I mean the most straightforward reading that can be gleaned from the Qur'ānic context. Taking into account other verses of a similar theme or those that use similar language, what was the likely meaning of this verse? Interpretations vary; However, the *'ulamā'* presume that verses with similar themes work together to form a coherent whole, despite a scattered placement or piecemeal presentation. I believe that most *'ulamā'* would disagree with postmodern theories of interpretation that state that the text is empty, or that it gains meaning solely through interpretation. For the *'ulamā'*, it is not empty; they work with words and a text that they believe has an inherent meaning, which they must understand clearly as a part of the act of interpretation and response. By undertaking to understand the plain sense of the Qur'ān, I share their fundamental assumption that there is meaning inherent in the text.

A prominent component of this study is its diachronic element: it is a study of how interpretation develops through time. Each of the three main parts of the book has a medieval chapter that examines the Qur'ān and medieval interpretations of specific verses, and a modern chapter, including written *tafsīr*, the oral interpretations of the *'ulamā'* given to me in interviews, and references to their books. By 'medieval', I mean, essentially, the entire precolonial period, from the earliest interpretations in the 8th century through around 1800. The following paragraphs address the issue of change and development within the medieval period and between medieval and modern texts.

Scholars of medieval *tafsīr* have long acknowledged that this genre develops through time, and that, just as it was never static, the genre was never monolithic. There were different types of works, written for different audiences: short, medium, and long works of varying levels of difficulty.[24] The genre has certain characteristics: it is inclusivist, home to

[24] Walid Saleh, *The Formation of the Classical Tafsīr Tradition: The Qur'ān Commentary of al-Tha'labī (d. 427/1035)* (Boston: Brill, 2004); Karen Bauer, 'I Have Seen the People's

more specialised branches of knowledge; it is often polyvalent, meaning that it includes many, sometimes conflicting, interpretations; and it is first and foremost the record of the views of certain early authorities.[25] The importance of these early authorities goes back to the origins of *tafsīr* in their teaching sessions.[26] The earliest exegetical authorities are in some ways akin to the founders of legal schools, in that almost all subsequent works refer, obliquely or overtly, to their views.

These works were written in a way that seemed simply to record and preserve the views of the earliest authorities and the Prophet. Yet they not only preserved, but also modified and even erased past interpretations. The term 'stratigraphy' has recently been applied to historical writings in Islamic studies.[27] Stratigraphy, originally the name for a branch of geology, studies the layering of rock. When applied to historical texts, this term refers to the layering of meaning and interpretation: one story or interpretation can be retold in many different ways, with layers of detail added in subsequent generations. Used in this sense, the term stratigraphy can describe the continual accretion of meanings in the genre of *tafsīr*. Through time, interpretations built up in layers, and the very process of building up could also impose new meanings on the text and on earlier interpretations. This is how Ibn al-ʿArabī treated the views of the early authorities in the example cited at the beginning of this Introduction. Rather than acknowledging that the views of the earliest authorities were incompatible, he reinterpreted disagreement so that it became agreement, thus imposing new meanings on the earliest authorities' words.

Antipathy to this Knowledge: The Muslim Exegete and His Audience 5th/11th–7th/13th Centuries', in *The Islamic Scholarly Tradition: Studies in History, Law, and Thought in Honor of Michael Allan Cook*, ed. Ahmed, Sadeghi, and Bonner (Leiden: Brill, 2011), pp. 293–314, especially pp. 295–9.

25 C. H. M. Versteegh, *Arabic Grammar and Qur'ānic Exegesis in Early Islam* (Leiden: Brill, 1993), p. 61 and pp. 63–95; Norman Calder, 'Tafsīr from Ṭabarī to Ibn Kathīr: Problems in the Description of a Genre, Illustrated with Reference to the Story of Abraham', in Hawting and Shareef, *Approaches to the Qur'ān* (New York: Routledge, 1993), pp. 101–38.

26 Claude Gilliot, 'A Schoolmaster, Storyteller, Exegete and Warrior at Work in Khurāsan: al-Ḍaḥḥāk b. Muzāḥim al-Hilālī (d. 106/724)', in *Aims, Methods and Contexts of Qur'anic Exegesis (2nd/8th–9th/15th c.)*, ed. Karen Bauer (Oxford: Oxford University Press in association with the Institute of Ismaili Studies, 2013), pp. 311–92.

27 Sarah Bowen Savant, *The New Muslims of Post-Conquest Iran: Tradition, Memory, and Conversion* (Cambridge: Cambridge University Press, 2013), p. 17.

The accretion of interpretation in the genre of *tafsīr*, and its repurposing, is complicated by considerations both practical and stylistic. We know that patterns of citation/accretion were fragmentary. When writing a work of *tafsīr*, authors would selectively pick and choose from previous works, usually without crediting the original author. But we know very little about the practical mechanisms that enabled such picking, choosing, and selective accretion of tradition. Walid Saleh has claimed that the whole tradition is available to exegetes at any moment; thus picking and choosing is up to the exegete alone.[28] However, the idea of the availability of the entire tradition discounts the way that book production, distribution, and preservation worked in the medieval Islamic world. Not all books were widely distributed or kept intact. In one of the only library catalogues that exist for the medieval Islamic world, many of the works of *tafsīr* are partial.[29] Fragmentary patterns of citation might reflect not only an author's choice, but also practical considerations of which works were available to him and in what state.

While it is important to explore the variations in interpretation specific to particular genres or authors, it is no less important to attempt to understand the wider context of these variations, and to investigate the likely presuppositions of their authors. That the gender hierarchy was considered natural in the medieval period is apparent in legal rulings, such as that for the blood-money payment in the case of killing: 100 camels for men, 50 for women. It was also widespread in *ḥadīth*s, one of which asserts that woman was created 'crooked', from a rib of Adam, while another claims that women are deficient in rationality and religion.[30] Men in these *ḥadīth*s are the model: they are complete humans, while women are defective. These *ḥadīth*s are often reinterpreted today; but in the medieval period, they were taken at face value. In their view of women as unequal, subservient, and deficient, medieval Muslim interpreters are on common ground with medieval interpreters from other world religions, particularly Judaism and Christianity. Medieval Jewish interpretations of the Biblical verse Genesis 3:16, *to the woman he said, 'I will make your pains in childbirth severe; with labour you will give birth to children, and your desire shall be for your husband, and he shall rule over thee'*, are similar to Medieval

[28] Walid Saleh, *Formation*, pp. 14–15.
[29] See Bauer, 'I Have Seen the People's Antipathy to this Knowledge'.
[30] These *ḥadīth*s are discussed in further depth, with source citations, in Chapters 1 and 3.

Islamic interpretations of Q. 4:34.[31] Although I describe important differences in opinions between medieval interpreters, their interpretations are always bounded by certain common presuppositions.

Theoretically, 'modern' interpretations could date from around 1850 onwards. Muslim intellectuals of the 19th century were deeply engaged in larger societal debates about women's place in society, the relationship between science and revelation, religion as an expression of cultural values, and the relationship between 'the West' and 'the East', which are all central themes for the contemporary *'ulamā'* in this study. But within the genre of *tafsīr*, the first 'modern' work, meaning one that deals with these themes at length, and in a new way, is the *Tafsīr al-Manār* of the Egyptian Muhammad 'Abduh (d. 1905) and his student Rashīd Riḍā (d. 1935). They were deeply influenced by the colonial encounter and sought to engage with the modern ideas and ideals that were matters of widespread discussion in their day. In the words of J. J. G. Jansen, 'Before Abduh the interpretation of the Koran was mainly an academic affair. Commentaries were written by scholars for other scholars . . . to this kind of scholarly exegesis Abduh objected on principle'.[32] 'Abduh intended his commentary for a wider public, as a solution to the problems of the day.[33] It is these modern aims, ideals, and ways of writing that form a break from the medieval texts, which nevertheless exert a strong influence on most modern interpretations.

In the modern period the audience for, and methods used in, these works have changed. With the advent of mass literacy, many more people are reading works of *tafsīr* than in the past. Whereas in the medieval period such works might have been used as scholarly references by preachers, and then summarised and condensed into arguments suitable for a mass audience, today some of the most prominent and popular works of *tafsīr* (such as *Tafsīr al-Manār*) are themselves collected sermons. The boom in audience has resulted in a different way of writing. No longer is polyvalence common: now, the norm is to present one

[31] Ruth Roded, 'Jews and Muslims [Re]Define Gender Relations in their Sacred Books: *yimshol* and *qawwamun*', in *Muslim-Jewish Relations in Past and Present: A Kaleidoscopic View*, eds. Camilla Adang and Josef (Yousef) Meri, Studies on the Children of Abraham Series (Leiden: Brill, forthcoming), and 'Jewish and Islamic Religious Feminist Exegesis of Their Sacred Books: Adam, Woman and Gender' (forthcoming). Muslim interpreters also refer to the pain of childbirth as a punishment for women.

[32] J. J. G. Jansen, *The Interpretation of the Koran in Modern Egypt* (Leiden: Brill, 1974), pp. 18–19.

[33] Ibid., p. 19.

unified conclusion, an argument, rather than a number of possibilities. Following from the work of ʿAbduh, there is also a strong feeling that modern works must address pressing social concerns. Concurrently, women's rights have become a pressing social concern in a way that they were not in the medieval period.

These modern ways of writing and thinking have a striking effect on interpreters' descriptions of the gender hierarchy. Today's *ʿulamāʾ* have, on the whole, jettisoned all talk of women's inferiority. The language of equality pervades texts from the modern period, even when the *ʿulamāʾ* do not advocate legal equality between the sexes. Another common feature of modern interpretation is the recourse to science. An example of these trends is to be found in modern interpretations of women's testimony. Some modern conservative interpreters assert that the medieval rulings on women's testimony should remain today. But rather than justifying these rulings by saying that women are deficient in rationality, as did medieval interpreters, they claim that women and men can reason equally well, but that modern science proves that women and men have different mental strengths. As opposed to this approach, modern reformists assert that medieval rulings on women's testimony should be overturned, and that scientific proof is on their side. They claim that science proves that men's and women's minds are equal and that they should have equal testimony in all or most cases, and that this equality is deeply embedded in the spirit of the Qurʾānic verse, if not in its wording.

My analysis of the gender hierarchy shows not only development, but important elements of continuity between medieval and modern works in the genre. As I have mentioned, the pre-modern genre of *tafsīr* was a scholarly venture: works were often written for specific levels of scholar, or for scholars with particular interests or sets of interests. Writing a *tafsīr* was one way for an author to prove his scholarly credentials. In the modern period, although they address a wider audience, authors still write works of *tafsīr* to prove their scholarly credentials. Like pre-modern works, modern works of *tafsīr* relate directly to their precursors within the genre, citing or quoting previous works, with or without attribution. While modern authors have different aims for their works, and this is expressed in their methods and their engagement with various types of sources, they nevertheless still choose to write this type of work to demonstrate their familiarity with the tradition. I thus argue that the genre of *tafsīr* in the modern period is one that is both conservative and circumscribed. Modern works of *tafsīr* do not represent the whole range of modern interpretations of the Qurʾān.

The circumscribed nature of the genre of *tafsīr* was one of the main reasons that I decided to incorporate interviews into my source pool, which led to my travels to Syria (2004 and 2005) and Iran (2011). My transcription of the Iran interviews ran past 150 pages; these pages were to become the core of the modern chapters in this book. By interviewing the *'ulamā'*, I was able to get beyond the constraints of *tafsīr* texts, while still remaining within the bounds of tradition.

When I spent three months in Syria in 2004, I was in graduate school, and this project was in its formative stages. I was fortunate to be able to conduct interviews with some of Syria's leading clerics at the time: Member of Parliament Muḥammad al-Ḥabash, Grand Muftī Aḥmad Ḥassoun, and popular preacher Sa'īd Ramaḍān al-Būṭī. Unfortunately, I conducted these interviews using a tape recorder with poor sound quality, and my transcriptions were of only limited use to me years later while writing the final iteration of this project. But the experience of being in Damascus and hearing living, interactive interpretations had an indelible effect on my work and thought.

While there, I attended the mosque lessons of Ḥannān al-Laḥḥām, who preached to other women in the basement of a mosque in Damascus. She had just published a work of *tafsīr* of *Surat al-Baqara* (the second chapter of the Qur'ān), which she taught in her lessons. But far from the dry, medieval-sounding interpretations that were presented in the book, her lessons were interactive question-and-answer sessions with a group of lively, engaged women. She brought the text to life, elaborating on the written interpretation and speaking to the current concerns of her audience. Suddenly, through her, I gained some insight into Islamic scholarly circles of learning, and the world beyond the textual tradition. Even in mosque sessions with less interactive methods, such as those of Hudā al-Ḥabash at the Zahra mosque, the audience was deeply engaged as the teacher made the text relevant to their daily lives. It was my Syrian experience that led me to pursue a trip to Iran to complete the research for this book.

When I went to Iran in 2011, I learned that the very concerns that motivated my work were also central for some of the *'ulamā'*. Like me, they meditated on the relationship between the text and its context, between medieval interpretations and the modern world, and between culture and interpretation. In interviews, I was thus able to ask not only about an interpreter's view, but also about why he or she took that view. Although my interview subjects often gave me books that they had written, the interviews went beyond their written words. For instance, in her book on women's rights, Dr Fariba ʿAlasvand barely touched on the issue of women's testimony. But in our interview, she explained why she believes that women's and men's testimony should be counted differently in most cases, and also explained the scientific theories upon which she draws as proof.

As a non-Muslim trained in the 'orientalist' tradition, I embodied a particular type of audience for my interview subjects. The trope of West versus East looms large in modern texts and in my interviews on the issue of women's rights and the marital hierarchy. For some of the *ʿulamāʾ*, discussing these verses with me was not just arguing an academic point: it was defending their religious culture against my secular one. In this conservative-minded dynamic, a defence of the status of women in the family and society is a synecdoche for the defence of traditional Eastern cultural values against Western incursion. For some conservative clerics, feminism is seen as the hallmark of the West; to argue for a form of patriarchy is to argue for cultural authenticity. Yet my readings and interviews revealed few simplistic arguments against equality. Instead, almost all modern interpreters embrace some aspects of equality while rejecting others. And while many *ʿulamāʾ* defend patriarchal systems in various forms, some argue against them: rather than asserting that the patriarchal model is the only culturally authentic model, reformists use narratives from the past and present to argue for gender equality.[34] To take one example, Grand Ayatollah Yusuf Saanei asserted that Q. 4:34 describes particular social circumstances: for the Qurʾān's original audience, husbands were in charge of wives. Today, not all marriages conform to the description in the Qurʾān; according to him, marriage does not have to be hierarchical.[35]

The interviews in Iran provided a valuable counterpoint to my Syrian interviews, by highlighting broad elements of similarity and difference between modern Sunnī and Imāmī Shīʿī interpreters. One area of similarity was the substance and nature of conservative interpretations. Often, Sunnī and Imāmī Shīʿī conservatives used the same or very similar arguments. However, Sunnīs and Shīʿīs approach their sources of interpretation differently, particularly *ḥadīth*s. While Sunnī interpreters were likely to preserve *ḥadīth*s by explaining, justifying, or reinterpreting them, Shīʿīs

[34] It is well recognised that historical contextualisation is the main method by which reformists reinterpret the Qurʾān. See, for instance, Manuela Marín, 'Disciplining Wives: A Historical Reading of Qurʾān 4:34', p.7.

[35] Grand Ayatollah Saanei's views on Q. 4:34 are described in Chapter 6.

were more likely to dismiss *ḥadīth*s irrespective of whether they had been transmitted from Sunnī or Shīʿī authorities. Shīʿī interpreters on the whole accepted the use of human reason (*ʿaql*) as a means of critiquing *ḥadīth*s and deriving the law, and some accepted human reason as a basis for the law and interpretation. Thus, the sources and methods of Sunnīs and Shīʿīs differ even when the substance of their interpretations is quite similar. In writing about my interviews, I highlight these methods, particularly the interpreters' own views of the role of tradition versus that of human intellect. In this way, the subject of women sheds light on the approaches that the *ʿulamā'* take to Qur'ānic interpretation as a whole.

There are a number of caveats on the conclusions to be drawn from interviews. Like texts, interviews are intended for a particular audience; and, whether as a representative of the West, as an academic, as a non-Muslim, or as a woman, my presence shaped the answers I was given. There are limits on what is presented in interviews, just as in texts. In the words of Mir-Hosseini, about her own interviews: 'As with any other debate in the Islamic Republic in the 1990s, there were limits that cannot be transgressed, and I was never sure how far I could go'.[36] In both Iran and Syria, I could very much relate to her feeling of unspoken limits and boundaries on what could, and could not, be expressed. Because of my focus on the Iranian interviews, the modern chapters are slanted towards the Shīʿī perspective. I have used my interviews and textual studies to draw comparisons between the views of Sunnī and Shīʿī *ʿulamā'*, but such comparative work in gender studies is still in its infancy.

Finally, it is possible to read too much into the 'conservative' and 'reformist' labels I have chosen for the *ʿulamā'*. There is undoubtedly a relationship between politics and interpretation in some sense, but an individual's perspective on gender does not necessarily correlate with his political views.[37] In this book, the labels 'conservative', 'neo-traditionalist', and 'reformist' point to the substance of an *ʿālim*'s interpretation on gender issues, and are not intended to convey political affiliation. Regardless of these caveats, the interviews shed light not only on how the *ʿulamā'* respond to the concerns of a secular outsider, but also on the limits of the textual sources which are commonly the sole basis of analysis in the field of Qur'ānic studies.

[36] Mir-Hosseini, *Islam and Gender*, p. 19; she elaborates on the implications of this on pp. 277–8.
[37] Ibid., p. 276.

THEORETICAL AND PRACTICAL PERSPECTIVES ON THE INTERPRETATION OF THE QUR'ĀN

This book is, in part, a meditation on the nature of Qur'ānic interpretation. To conclude the Introduction, I now describe some of the theoretical considerations that bind the interpreters studied here.

Gadamer's ideas about historical consciousness are relevant to the study of Islamic interpretation, because he speaks about the relationship between the historian and the past; seemingly like the Muslim interpreter of the Qur'ān, the historian seeks to obliterate self and to return to a past time. But, according to Gadamer, such obliteration is impossible. 'Even in those masterworks of historical scholarship that seem to be the very consummation of the extinguishing of the individual', he says, 'it is still an unquestioned principle of our scientific experience that we can classify these works with unfailing accuracy in terms of the political tendencies of the time in which they were written'.[38] The interpreter of the Qur'ān presents 'truth' by calling forth past witnesses, as does Gadamer's historian. In this case, those witnesses include the Prophet's *ḥadīth*s, the interpretations of his Companions, grammatical analysis, and the interpretation of past exegetes. But like Gadamer's examples of historical works, works of Qur'ānic interpretation are rooted in particular times. The present always shapes the interpretation of the past. According to Gadamer, it is our present concerns and hopes that make the past real for us.[39]

My analysis is predicated on the idea that context influences interpretation. But it was not always taken for granted that context must have an influence on the interpretive venture, and that therefore interpretation is time-bound and changeable; many of the interpreters in this study attempt to abide by theories of interpretation developed in the classical period by al-Ṭabarī and others. In classical interpretive theory, the ultimate sources of Qur'ānic commentaries lie in the past and are timeless: the language of the Qur'ān itself, the *ḥadīth*s of the Prophet and his Companions. These timeless sources in some ways imply an essentially stagnant and unchanging venture of interpretation. A basic template of the idealised sources of

[38] Hans-Georg Gadamer, 'The Universality of the Hermeneutical Problem', in *Hermeneutical Inquiry, Vol. 1: The Interpretation of Texts*, by David E. Klemm, the American Academy of Religion: Studies in Religion, No. 43 (Atlanta, GA: Scholars Press, 1986), pp. 179–91, at p. 181.

[39] As he says, 'History is only present to us in light of our futurity' (Ibid., p. 183).

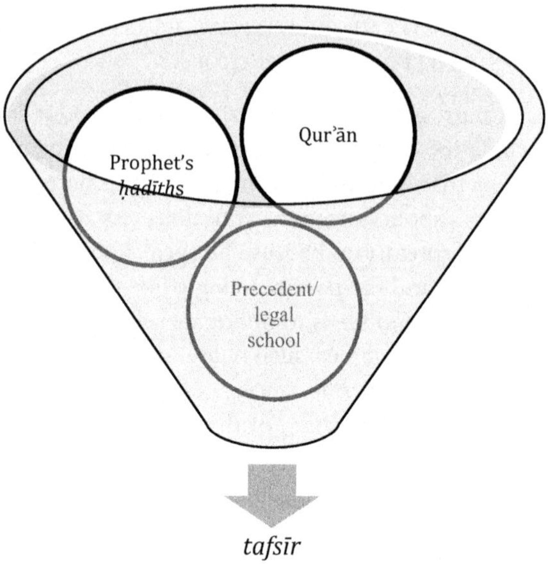

FIGURE I.1: A Simple (or Simplistic) Template for the Theoretical Sources of Interpretation

Qur'ānic commentary might look like Figure I.1, which includes the words of the Qur'ān, *ḥadīth*s on the authority of the Prophet, his Companions, and their Followers, and the interpreter's own legal school and precedent from exegetical authorities.

Figure I.1 is an idealisation, and in this depiction, the theoretical sources of interpretation remain constant. Exegetes through time have recognised that these sources are not unmediated, and they differentiate their own contribution by describing their methods of interpretation; but even with methodological development, these theoretical sources remain unchanging. The aim of the exegete, as in the theory of Gadamer, is the extinction of the individual self, and the return to a mythologised past time.

The overall development of theories of Qur'ānic interpretation has not been the subject of a sustained study; but it is likely that, like interpretations themselves, the theory of interpretation depicted in Figure I.1 developed through time and emerged in conversation with alternate and competing theories.[40] I base this observation primarily on analogy with

[40] Cf Gilliot, 'The Beginnings of Qur'ānic Exegesis', in Andrew Rippin, ed., *The Qur'ān: Formative Interpretation* (Aldershot: Ashgate, 1999), pp. 1–27.

recent studies of legal theory (*uṣūl al-fiqh*). Though the genres of exegesis (*tafsīr*) and law (*fiqh*) are separate, it is not unreasonable to suppose that legal and exegetical theories developed in similar ways, or that their authors share certain concerns. David Vishanoff has shown that what came to be accepted as classical Sunnī legal theory was not inevitable and that it evolved after the jurist al-Shāfiʿī (d. 204/820).[41] In legal theory, the Sunnī approach emerged in debates with the Muʿtazilī and Shīʿī approaches. One key point of difference between the Sunnī approach and the Imāmī Shīʿī approach (as each was eventually formulated) lies in the acceptance or rejection of the use of human reasoning in the derivation of law. It is worth saying a few words about these differences in legal theory, because the tension between transmitted text (*naql*) and human reasoning (*ʿaql*) which is central to the discussion of Islamic law also affects the interpretation of the Qurʾān, and indeed this tension endures throughout the history of interpretation. This division came to be described by the interpreters themselves as *tafsīr bi'l-maʾthūr* and *tafsīr bi'l raʾy* (exegesis according to transmission, and exegesis according to opinion).

This is not the place to enter into an in-depth discussion of *uṣūl al-fiqh*. But broadly speaking, after an initial period of development, most Sunnīs came to accept certain sources of law and interpretation, including *ḥadīth*s and analogy.[42] In general, Sunnīs do not accept the use of human reasoning (*ʿaql*) as an independent source of law, although some Ḥanafīs, particularly those under the influence of the rationalist Muʿtazilī school of thought, accept *istiḥsān*, which has been translated as 'subjective reasoning'.[43] In distinction to the majority of Sunnīs, Imāmī Shīʿī *ʿulamāʾ* accepted human reasoning as a source of law.

Gleave writes about the emergence of the proof of rationality (*dalīl al-ʿaql*) as a source of Shīʿī law in the medieval period. He describes how the Muʿtazilīs held it as a 'central tenet' that 'human reason, without the aid of revelation from God, could discover certain truths'.[44] This Muʿtazilī

41 David R. Vishanoff, *The Formation of Islamic Hermeneutics: How Sunni Legal Theorists Imagined a Revealed Law* (New Haven, CT: The American Oriental Society, 2011).

42 See, for instance, Shāfiʿī's *Epistle on Legal Theory*, the chapter on Subjective Reasoning, in which he says 'opinions given on the basis of anything other than a report or analogical reasoning are impermissible', al-Shāfiʿī, *Epistle on Legal Theory*, ed. and trans. Joseph Lowry (New York: New York University Press, 2013), p. 363.

43 Ibid.

44 Robert Gleave, *Inevitable Doubt: Two Theories of Shīʿī Jurisprudence* (Leiden: Brill, 2000), p. 87.

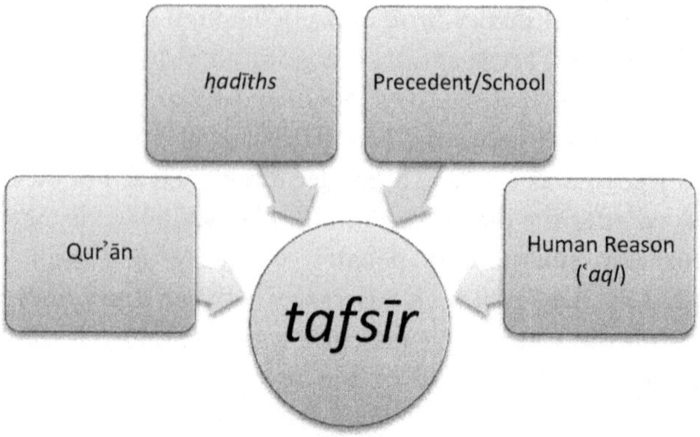

FIGURE I.2: The *Uṣūlī* Approach in a Nutshell

doctrine was passed on to some Sunnī schools and most Shīʿa, particularly in the Buyid period (334/945–447/1055). Thus, 'those Shīʿa who held that morally (or legally) relevant information could be derived from reason were compelled to add *ʿaql* (reason) to *naql* (transmitted revelatory texts) as a means of obtaining knowledge'.[45] After the introduction of Muʿtazilite doctrine into Shīʿī thought, this doctrine developed through time, culminating in the work of ʿAllāma al-Ḥillī (d. 726/1325). He overtly accepted the use of *ijtihād* (independent reasoning by a qualified jurist), rather than just reliance on the words of the Imāms.[46] The jurists who held the doctrine of acceptance of human reasoning in some form were called Uṣūlīs. The Uṣūlī approach to the sources of law might be depicted in a simple diagram such as Figure I.2.

Akhbārism, which developed as a response to Uṣūlī doctrine, is a school of thought more akin to the mainstream Sunnī model. For Akhbārīs, human reason is misleading: transmitted texts are necessary for humans to understand which actions are good and evil.[47] This doctrine may have developed in the 17th century with the work of Muḥammad Amīn Astarābādī (d. 1036/1627), who explicitly rejected the use of *ijtihād*, or it may have developed considerably before then, closer to the time of ʿAllāma al-Ḥillī.[48] In a nutshell, Uṣūlīs accept the use of *ʿaql* as a means of deriving the law, and even as a source of law; Akhbārīs, on the whole, reject it.

[45] Ibid. [46] Ibid., p. 4. [47] Ibid., chart on p. 185. [48] Ibid., p. 6.

The medieval Uṣūlī–Akhbārī attitudes towards the use of human reason in interpretation roughly correlate with the modern reformist–conservative groupings I have described. Many reformists explicitly accept the use of their own reason in deriving the law, or even as a basis for the law. Many conservatives follow Akhbārī methods, particularly insofar as these methods correlate with the Sunnī sources of interpretation outlined herein. In the latter ideology, transmitted texts take priority.

However, just as there is some crossover in reformist and conservative methods and interpretations, there is also crossover between reason and revelation as sources of law or interpretation. Among Uṣūlīs, the areas in which knowledge could be obtained through *ʿaql* were disputed, particularly around the question of whether reason could determine 'legally relevant knowledge',[49] or in other words, the type of knowledge on which laws are based. Uṣūlī doctrine holds that human rationality can determine good and evil independently of the Lawgiver, but that there is a correlation between the assessment of human rationality and God's law.[50] Therefore, for the Uṣūlīs (and some Akhbārīs), human reason has the ability to recognise good and evil independently of the Lawgiver, but most Uṣūlīs also say that rationality agrees with God's law. Modern reformists who accept the use of reason, like pre-modern Uṣūlīs, generally assert that their reasoning leads them to the same conclusions as those in the revealed texts. Some, however, allow that human reason can go beyond the transmitted text or the Prophet's example.

But does theory matter? As Vishanoff says, 'The discipline of legal hermeneutics ... represents not a record of some interpretive process whereby Islamic law was actually brought into being, but a choice to imagine Islamic law in a certain way'.[51] It is worth investigating whether theory says more about the process of imagining ideal sources than it does about the realities of the interpretative process.

Sadeghi's study of the relationship of law to the binding texts proposes a model in which there are three main sources for law: canon (by which he means Qurʾān and *sunna*), received law, and the jurist's contemporary conditions and values; all of these are moderated by the individual jurist's hermeneutical-methodological approach.[52] Thus, he argues, the text of

49 Ibid., p. 183–4.
50 Ibid., see the chart on p. 185, which has been sourced from Muẓaffar Riḍā, *Uṣūl al-fiqh*.
51 Vishanoff, *The Formation of Islamic Hermeneutics*, p. 258.
52 Behnam Sadeghi, *The Logic of Law Making in Islam: Women and Prayer in the Legal Tradition* (Cambridge, MA: Cambridge University Press, 2013), pp. 1–39, especially at p. 12 and p. 21.

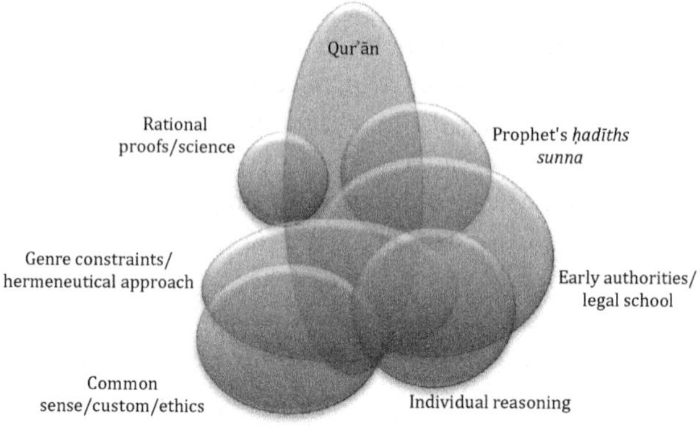

FIGURE I.3: A Basic Template of Early Interpretation

Qur'ān and *ḥadīth*s do not determine law, which is usually determined by received law; but even received law is moderated by other factors.[53] Sadeghi's findings are in some ways analogous to what I have found to be the mechanisms of interpretation in *tafsīr*. Received interpretation is highly important, but it is affected by the exegete's hermeneutical approach, conditions, values, and individual reasoning.

It may be impossible to account for everything that influences interpretation, but I would propose a general model that accounts for the fluidity of the venture of interpretation. In Figure I.3, the Qur'ān, *ḥadīth*, and legal school/precedent have been joined by an exegete's individual reasoning, genre constraints, social custom/common sense/ethical considerations, and recourse to rational or scientific proofs. In the model depicted in Figure I.3, the mechanism of interpretation is not fixed and static: it is dependent on many factors. An interpreter's theoretical approach matters, but it is not the only determinant of interpretation. Figure I.3 depicts a basic template of the actual source of interpretation for the early works of interpretation, including al-Ṭabarī and those who preceded him.

The relative weight given to each factor in this basic template depends on the individual; yet, as I show in the following chapters, there are broad trends in the use of these sources through time. Theoretically, the sources of exegesis are static and rest ultimately on the sayings of the Prophet; but

[53] Ibid., p. 5.

in practice, the earliest interpreters put the greatest weight on early exegetical authorities, rather than on sayings that they trace directly to the Prophet. These early authorities are often Successors (those who transmitted on the authority of Companions) who had some connection to the Companion Ibn ʿAbbās. Through time, their interpretations still underlie much of what is said in the genre of exegesis, but in the classical period sayings attributed directly to the Prophet are cited much more frequently. Everything else stays relatively constant: each interpreter incorporates these elements as he sees fit. In the modern period, particularly among the Shīʿa, much greater weight is given to rational and scientific proofs. Basic templates for the classical and modern approaches are depicted in Figures I.4 and I.5. Notably, gender has been left out of

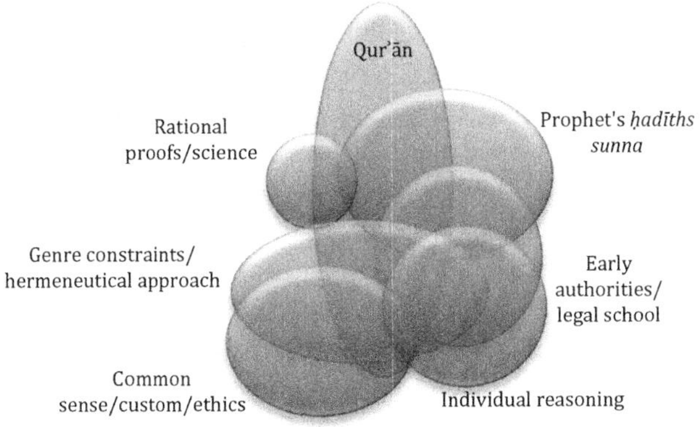

FIGURE I.4: Basic Template of Classical Interpretation

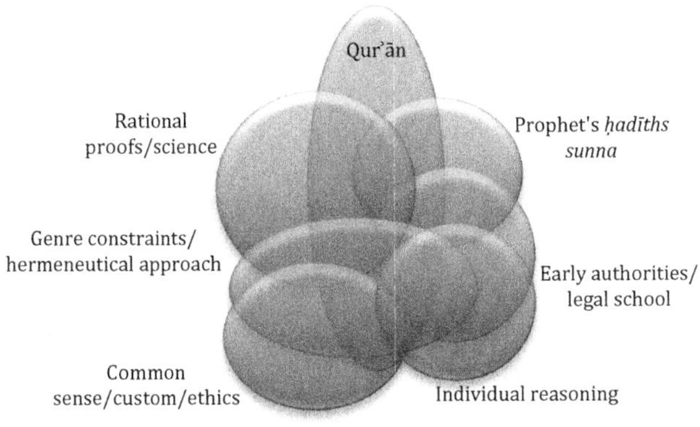

FIGURE I.5: Basic Template of Modern Interpretation

these basic templates; but it should be considered as a part of cultural context: in the genre of *tafsīr*, the authority to interpret has until very recently been held by men, and only those men educated in a specific system as *mufassirūn*. Muslim feminists such as Amina Wadud have pointed out that medieval *'ulamā'* took for granted the patriarchal mores of their societies, and that they read these into the Qur'ān.

I have called Figures I.3, I.4, and I.5 'basic templates', rather than 'models' because a model can predict an outcome, whereas these figures represent a much more fluid system: certain elements are likely to take precedence, but much is left to the preferences of the individual author.

What do these fluid templates mean for the Qur'ān? Can we say, like Stanley Rosen, that 'there is no difference between the written lines of the text and the blank spaces between them'?[54] Previously, I referred to Gadamer's notion that social context must affect interpretation. The effect of context goes right back to the origins of the genre of *tafsīr*. Versteegh argues that the genre of *tafsīr* started in oral teaching sessions, in which the expert helped the believers apply the Qur'ānic dictates to their own daily lives.[55] In this way, the interpreters sought to influence social practice. But the question is the extent to which it worked the other way around: how did social practice affect interpretation? The interpreters studied here sometimes use social arguments to justify their interpretations – such as the assertion of al-Zamakhsharī (d. 538/1143) that it is ethical to expect wives to do the housework, because it is the common practice. I argue that social conventions can and do shape exegetes' notions of right and wrong; moreover, today the gender hierarchy has become an issue bound up with both politics and cultural identity, and it is almost impossible not to see this as having some effect on its interpretation.

Intellectual context is no less important. Early exegetical authorities and subsequent generations of interpreters within the genre are the interlocutors in an ongoing conversation about the true meaning of these verses, and through time the *'ulamā'* have formed their interpretations as a part of this conversation. Occasionally, as in the case of Ibn al-'Arabī's words to al-Ṭabarī, they address their long-deceased colleagues directly, personally, as though through scholarly attentiveness and close reading they had become bosom friends. The interpretive stance of the *'ulamā'* is always taken against the backdrop of the medieval textual

[54] Stanley Rosen, *Hermeneutics as Politics* (Oxford: Oxford University Press, 1987), p. 161.
[55] Versteegh, *Arabic Grammar*, pp. 63 ff.

tradition. As will become obvious in the following pages, understanding the medieval heritage is necessary for understanding the modern religious discourse of women's rights and roles.

Ultimately, because the *ʿulamāʾ* commonly agree on a certain 'plain sense' reading of the Qurʾān, to some extent the Qurʾān does determine its own interpretation. The *ʿulamāʾ* are bound by historical antecedents and the plain sense meaning up to a certain point of uncomfortability, sometimes resolving this by saying that the rulings do not seem fair, but must be obeyed.[56] But when the plain sense of the Qurʾān violates the interpreters' deeply held beliefs, they sometimes use hermeneutical strategies to interpret the Qurʾān away. There is always interplay between the words of the Qurʾān and the social and intellectual contexts of interpretation. This interplay is not straightforward, particularly when it comes to the question of *ḥadīth*s mitigating the words of the Qurʾān, or to the question of determining what the Qurʾān means versus what it says. For the very nature of *ḥadīth*s as authoritative sources changed through time, and meaning is a slippery concept, bound up not only with what the Qurʾān says, but what it intends, the discovery of which is at the heart of the venture of interpretation.

[56] In speaking of the exegetes' 'uncomfortability', I am indebted to Behnam Sadeghi, 'The Structure of Reasoning in Post-Formative Islamic Jurisprudence (Case Studies in Ḥanafī Laws on Women and Prayer)', PhD Dissertation, Princeton University, 2006.

TESTIMONY

1

Women's Testimony and the Gender Hierarchy

The case of Mukhtar Mai is famous in Pakistan. In 2002, she was raped by four men from a powerful family in her village, with the full knowledge of at least ten others, including the village elders. A local Imām preached against the incident in his Friday sermon and brought a court case on her behalf; a protracted legal battle ensued, a battle that was followed by millions. The story received widespread national and international media coverage. It fascinated the nation and the world for many reasons; but one of the most controversial aspects of the case within Pakistan is one of the least reported by international papers: it had to be tried as terrorism, rather than rape, for Mukhtar Mai's own testimony to be accepted. At the time when the case was brought, rape was counted as 'forced adultery' in Pakistan's laws and was tried according to the court's interpretation of the Islamic law on adultery. According to that interpretation, a woman's testimony alone could not stand, even if she herself was the victim of the rape.

Following this incident, human rights activists campaigned successfully for changes to the laws on women's testimony in cases of rape.[1] Some

[1] Mukhtar Mai's case was said to have led to legislation in which rape is prosecuted as a criminal offence, and thus a woman is now treated as an eligible witness to her own rape. But in their 2011 ruling in which they overturned the conviction of the alleged rapists, the Pakistani Supreme Court pointed out that acceptance of a sole woman's testimony 'is not an absolute rule'. (Ruling of the Supreme Court of Pakistan on the case of Mukhtar Mai, Criminal Appeals No. 163 to 171 and S.M. Case No. 5/2005, p. 41 (point 27), dated 19 April 2011. Accessed online at: http://www.supremecourt.gov.pk/web/user_files/File/Crl.P.163_to_171_S.M.C.5_2005.pdf, last accessed 20 August 2014). They required DNA evidence, which had not been collected by the police and therefore was not available.

resist these changes, believing that Islamic law legislates for four male witnesses in adultery and rape. However, the Qur᾿ān contains no direct ruling on this issue: it never mentions rape, the sex of the four witnesses is not specified in cases of adultery, and women's testimony is permitted in other arenas. The case of Mukhtar Mai thus raises the question of the relationship between the Qur᾿ān and the legal and interpretational edifice that supposedly rests on the text, as well as that of the influence of medieval interpretations on modern law, practice, interpretation, and understanding. In this chapter, I consider why and how medieval laws and interpretations on women's testimony formed. I analyse the Qur᾿ān, the earliest interpretations in the genres of law (*fiqh*), *ḥadīth*, grammar, and *tafsīr*, which shows the state of the field at a time when the issue of women's testimony was hotly contested, and finally the development of interpretations in *tafsīr* of the classical and post-classical periods. In Chapter 2, I examine how these medieval interpretations have been reinterpreted in the modern period.

This chapter has three principal arguments that affect our consideration of how medieval interpreters dealt with the gender hierarchy in the one verse of the Qur᾿ān that mentions women's testimony specifically, Q. 2:282. First, interpretations of women's testimony develop through time in a discourse only somewhat related to the Qur᾿ān's verses. The Qur᾿ān is not the only, nor even the main, source for these interpretations. Second, genre considerations deeply affect the way authors wrote about women's testimony. As the genres developed, so did their methods and source citation. Finally, it is difficult to know what a medieval author or a set of authors really thought about women. While there is no doubt that in the medieval period women were commonly considered to be less intelligent than men, the particular rulings that grew up around this general belief are varied and diverse. Some schools presumed that women's testimony was generally allowed, and that Q. 2:282 imposed limits on it; others presumed that women's testimony was generally disallowed, and that Q. 2:282 allowed it as an exceptional case. These arguments seem to indicate real variation in authors' beliefs about women's abilities. Yet it is often difficult to gauge the extent to which such arguments represent a real division on gender, and the extent to

Despite Mai's doctor's statement that she had been raped, and the semen that had been found on her clothing, the evidence was not ruled as sufficient to convict the thirteen men, but was seen only as evidence of a sexual encounter with one man, which, according to the Supreme Court Justices (and against Mai's testimony), may have been consensual.

which they are simply a manifestation of ongoing doctrinal rivalries. Do interpreters have widely varying opinions of women's abilities, or are they just scoring points in a fierce debate?

An underlying premise here is one that I alluded to in the Introduction, which is that considerations other than gender may affect an author's discussion of the gender hierarchy. What can seem like an argument for women's rights may have its motivation in external political or legal concerns – broadly, in an interpreter's social context. This is a point made, albeit in different terms, by Wilferd Madelung in his article 'Shiʿi Attitudes towards Women as Reflected in Fiqh'.[2] He writes that 'the motivations of the deviation of Imāmī from Sunni law derived, in one way or another, from typically Shiʿi concerns'.[3] In other words, concerns such as succession rights affected the law of inheritance because the Shīʿī doctrine was that the Prophet's lineage was carried through his daughter. What seems to be a law supporting women's rights must thus be seen in its larger context: women may be the secondary concern of the jurists or exegetes whose primary concern is upholding particular doctrinal positions. Of course, an unintended consequence is still a consequence: there are real variations in law and interpretation. But these combined factors mean that it is not really relevant to study 'women's status' or discourses on women divorced from considerations of time, place, and genre. Context is crucial, particularly given the somewhat ambiguous message of the Qurʾān itself.

WOMEN'S TESTIMONY AND THEIR INTELLECTUAL CAPACITY IN THE QURʾĀN

The Qurʾān is a text in which much is taken for granted. Vague allusions have meaning, but that meaning can be obscure. Most of the key verses on testimony do not mention the sex of the witnesses explicitly; the one verse to speak of women's testimony directly is Q. 2:282, which deals with the contracting of debts. Therefore, read without the accretion of juridical opinion or *ḥadīth*s, the verses on serious crimes do not present a straightforward denial of women's participation. Given the Qurʾān's oral culture, the fact that the early jurists interpreted certain verses to refer solely to

[2] Wilferd Madelung, 'Shiʿi Attitudes towards Women as Reflected in Fiqh', in *Society and the Sexes in Medieval Islam*, ed. Afaf Lutfi Sayyid-Marsot (Malibu, California: Undena Publications, 1979), pp. 69–79.

[3] Ibid., p. 75.

men may in itself be evidence that the verses referred to men. Read alone, however, the text of the Qur'ān is often ambiguous on the question of women's testimony.

In the Qur'ān, references to witnessing and bearing witness to moral deeds are numerous: God is a constant witness, his Messenger is a witness over the people, and people are witnesses over each other (Q. 2:143). Only a handful of verses describe specific worldly transactions that require a set number of witnesses. In these, the number of witnesses varies from two to four, but the sex of the witnesses is not mentioned. For instance, Q. 5:106, on bequests, specifies only *two just persons from among you* (*ithnāni dhawā 'adlin minkum*). The other verses are: Q. 4:6, on handing over the property of orphans (two witnesses); Q. 4:15, on lewdness (four witnesses); and Q. 24:4, on the accusation of fornication (four witnesses). Additionally, a cluster of verses, Q. 24:6–8, deals with the accusation of fornication in the absence of witnesses. Women's chastity is the prime concern of the fornication/lewdness verses, for example: *for those of your women whom you suspect of lewdness, call to testify against them four* (Q. 4:15); *and those who accuse chaste women and do not produce four witnesses, lash them with eighty lashes* (Q. 24:4). Women are the object of these verses, and the implication is that men are addressed; but the sex of the witnesses is not overtly specified. Are these witnesses male? From the syntax of these verses, it is difficult to say. But for centuries, jurists and exegetes have ruled that the witnesses in cases of fornication and adultery must be male. In turn, those rulings led to rulings such as the one in Pakistan, in which Mukhtar Mai's own word was not sufficient to prove rape.

The worth of a woman's word is made explicit only twice in the Qur'ān. The first occurrence is in Q. 2:282, which deals with the contracting of a debt. In its plain sense reading, the verse makes women's testimony half of men's and attributes a possibility of error to women that is not attributed to men: *Call to witness from among your men two witnesses; but if there are not two men, then one man and two women from among those who are pleasing witnesses, so that if one of the two women errs, one of the two may remind the other*. In this verse, when two men are not available to testify, they can be replaced with a man and two women. This could indicate not only that a woman's word is worth half of a man's word, but also that women's testimony alone – without men – is unacceptable. Q. 2:282 is the only verse to specify the worth of a woman's word to a third party, not involving the woman herself and her husband.

The second verse to mention the value of a woman's word explicitly is Q. 24:8, in which a woman's word is given equal weight with a man's word; however, testimony in this verse does not refer to third parties, but rather to a dispute between the testifying woman and her husband. This verse enables her to defend herself against an accusation of adultery. Q. 24:8 is part of a verse cluster (Q. 24:6–9) describing *liʿān*, which is the procedure for accusations of fornication in the absence of witnesses. In this procedure, the husband may swear to his wife's infidelity and the wife may defend herself against an accusation of fornication. Although these verses give a woman's oath the same weight as a man's, the outlook of the text is still androcentric:[4] women's chastity, not men's, is the object of question and scrutiny:

> [A]nd as for those who accuse their wives and have not witness except themselves, let the testimony of one of them be four testimonies, [swearing] by God that they are solemnly telling the truth, and yet a fifth, invoking the God's curse if he should lie; and it shall avert the punishment from her if she swears four times that what he says is false, and the fifth [oath] that the wrath of God be upon her if he speaks the truth.
>
> (Q. 24:6–9)

According to these verses, when a man wishes to accuse his wife of adultery without witnesses, he may swear five times to her adultery, with the fifth invoking God's curse for lying, but the wife may defend herself by also swearing five times. If she does so, then she is considered innocent. Allowing a woman's word about her own chastity protects her from possibly false accusations on the part of her husband. This case, therefore, differs from the type of impersonal testimony described in Q. 2:282.

Women's mental capacity is never discussed explicitly in the Qurʾān. Q. 4:5 may refer to women's intellects: it tells men not to give their property to those *weak of understanding* (*sufahāʾ*), but rather to clothe them and provide for them as necessary. But it is not entirely clear who is meant by the term *sufahāʾ*: the verses before and after this one refer to both wives and orphans. On balance, the term seems to refer to the orphans, since the following verse states that when they marry, the

[4] The observation that women are the 'they' and men are the 'you' in the text of the Qurʾān has been made by Farid Esack in his work 'Islam and Gender Justice: Beyond Simple Apologia', in *What Men Owe to Women: Men's Voices from World Religions*, ed. John C. Raines, Daniel C. Maguire (Albany: SUNY Press, 2001), pp. 187–210, at p. 195; Kecia Ali borrows the term 'androcentric' from secondary sources on Rabbinic literature, and aptly uses it to describe the Qurʾān. Kecia Ali, *Sexual Ethics and Islam*, p. 112.

guardian should then release the property to them.[5] In later texts, women were described as 'foolish': in al-Ṭabarī's *History*, for instance, a narrative is quoted to say that Eve was created wise, but then was made foolish (*safīha*). However, within the Qur'ān the term *sufahā'* is used to describe people in general, not just women – for example, in Q. 2:13, 2:142, 2:282, 6:140, and 7:66. While women may have been considered to be naturally somewhat foolish, it is by no means clear that Q. 4:5 is meant as a reference to them.

In the remainder of this chapter, I focus on interpretations of Q. 2:282, the single verse in the Qur'ān to mention explicitly women's testimony to third parties, and to imply that women's minds may not be the same as men's.

Q. 2:282 IN THE EARLY SOURCES: SPECIALISED GENRES OF DISCOURSE

The intention of this section is to present a global picture of the state of the interpretation of this verse in a period when it was debated and discussed intensely, and to explore the nature of these debates in works of grammar, *tafsīr*, *ḥadīth*, and *fiqh* from the earliest texts through the first half of the 10th century, highlighting the differences that existed between individual interpreters and between genres. There are three key points here: despite real diversity among them, no interpreter considered women equal to men; social circumstances may have influenced these interpretations; and genre matters. In this period, no one genre represents the totality of the picture of discourse on this verse. While *tafsīr* and grammar are closely interrelated genres, the discourses in *fiqh*, *tafsīr*, and *ḥadīth* remain separate, and only *ḥadīth* mentions women's inferiority. Authors in any one genre doubtless took the discourse in other genres for granted; but in the earliest period, form certainly follows function, and the disjuncture between genres is one concrete illustration that each was intended to fulfil a specific function.

[5] Q. 4:3–6 reads: *If you fear you will not deal justly with the orphans, then marry those women that please you, two, or three, or four; but if you fear you will not do justice between them, then one and those that your right hand possesses. That is more suitable that you may not incline. And give the women their dowries graciously; but if they give anything of it to you willingly, then ye are welcome to absorb it* [lit.: eat it]. *Do not give those weak of understanding* (sufahā') *your property which God has given you to as a support, but feed and clothe them from it, and speak to them according to what is right. Test the orphans until they marry, then if you perceive that they have sound judgment, release their property to them.* [Trans. based on Pickthall]

Although the Qur'ān was somewhat ambiguous about women's worth in testimony, *ḥadīth*s were less so. One *ḥadīth* in particular, which I term the 'deficiency *ḥadīth*', probably contributed to jurists' and exegetes' understanding of Q. 2:282: it states that a woman's testimony is worth half of a man's because of their deficiency in reason (*ʿaql*). Therefore, unlike the Qur'ān, early *fiqh*, *tafsīr* or grammatical works described later in this section, this *ḥadīth* explains the reasoning behind the rulings in terms of women's innate nature:

> The Messenger of God went out to the prayer at Aḍḥa or Fitr and passed some women. So he said 'O group of women! Give alms, for I have seen you are the majority of the inhabitants of the fire!' The women said 'Why, O Messenger of God?' He said, 'You curse frequently, you are ungrateful to your husbands (*takfurna al-ʿashīr*), and I have not seen anyone more deficient in reason and religion (*nāqiṣāt ʿaql wa-dīn*), leading astray the mind of the upright man, then you women'. So they said 'What is the deficiency in our reason and our religion, O Messenger of God?' He said, 'Is not the testimony of the woman like half of the testimony of the man?' They said 'Yes, it is'. He said: 'So that is a consequence of the deficiency in her mind. And is it not [the case] that the menstruating woman does not pray or fast?' They said 'Yes, it is'. He said: 'That is a consequence of the deficiency in her religion'.[6]

This *ḥadīth*, found in the *Ṣaḥīḥ* of al-Bukhārī, is a clear statement of women's innate deficiencies as compared with men. It assigns a clear, gendered cause to Q. 2:282; furthermore, women's deficiencies in this world have an effect on their standing in the next: they are the majority of the inhabitants of Hell. It clearly denies the notion of women's equality with men on mental and religious levels.

For many today, this *ḥadīth* makes little sense: women do not fast while menstruating because they are told not to do so in law, so it seems somewhat unfair to punish them for obeying this ordinance. Yet this *ḥadīth* seems to have been widespread: versions or parts of the deficiency *ḥadīth* appear several times in the 'sound' (*ṣaḥīḥ*) works of al-Bukhārī, Abū Dawūd, and Ibn Mājah. A shortened version, with the same chain of transmission, is found in Bukhārī's chapter on women's testimony: 'It is narrated on the authority of Abū Saʿīd on the authority of the Prophet that he said: "Is not the testimony of the woman like half of the testimony of the man?" The women said: "Yes". He said: so that is a consequence of

[6] Al-Bukhārī, *Ṣaḥīḥ*, in *Mawsūʿat al-ḥadīth al-Sharīf: al-kutub al-sitta: Ṣaḥīḥ al-Bukhārī, Ṣaḥīḥ Muslim, Sunan Abī Dawūd, Jāmiʿ al-Tirmidhī, Sunan al-Nasāʾī, Sunan Ibn Mājah*, ed. Ṣāliḥ b. ʿAbd al-ʿAzīz Āl al-Shaykh (Riyadh: Dār al-Salām lil-nashr wa'l-tawzīʿ, 1999), p. 26 (*Ṣaḥīḥ al-Bukhārī, Kitāb al-ḥayḍ*, 6: *Bāb tark al-ḥāʾiḍ al-ṣawm, ḥadīth* 304).

the deficiency in her intellect (*'aql*)'.[7] This version, which does not tell the whole story, is clearly shortened in light of the longer version found earlier in the book in the context of menstruation. But the versions in other works include slight variations. For instance, a version in the *Sunan* of Abū Dawūd omits the beginning of the story, and a single woman questions the Prophet.[8] The chain of transmission is also different from the version in al-Bukhārī. The chapter in which this *ḥadīth* is found is entitled 'Indications of the excess of faith and its deficiency'; this *ḥadīth* is therefore being cited as a proof of a natural deficiency in women's faith. A version in Ibn Mājah, also on the authority of 'Abd Allāh b. 'Umar (as in Abū Dawūd's version), includes minor variations, omitting the 'upright men' and adding a woman's somewhat plaintive question, 'what is it about us, O Messenger of God? (*mā lana, yā Rasūl Allāh?*)'.[9] Again, the chapter title (the chapter on 'the torments of women') is suggestive of women's status in these texts.

The numerous versions of the *ḥadīth* could indicate that it was a part of popular preaching and storytelling. It was, perhaps, well known and often repeated in different iterations and taken for granted by jurists and exegetes. The female interlocutor in the *ḥadīth* may well have voiced widespread questioning about the fairness of this verse and others that favoured men over women; at the same time, the *ḥadīth* serves to justify laws that go further than the Qur'ān in privileging men over women and husbands over wives.

The storytelling aspect seems especially prominent in the version attributed to the Shī'ī Imām al-'Askarī. This version of the *ḥadīth* is from a compilation of *ḥadīth*s on various verses of the Qur'ān. Although it is a later compilation, it may represent oral interpretations of the verse from an early period, and thus verges into the milieu of popular storytelling. In this version, the *ḥadīth* breaks in the middle (represented here by ellipses) for several pages of dialogue about the merits of the Prophet's

7 Ibid., p. 210 (*Ṣaḥīḥ al-Bukhārī, Kitāb al-shahadāt, Bāb Shihādat al-nisā'*, 12, *ḥadīth* 2658).

8 Abī Dawūd, *Sunan*, Ibid., p. 1565 (*Bāb ziyādat al-imān wa-naqṣānuhu*, 15, *ḥadīth* 4679). This version of the *ḥadīth* reads: 'It was narrated to us on the authority of 'Abd Allāh b. 'Umar that the Messenger of God said "I have not seen women more deficient in intellect (*'aql*) nor religion, who can lead astray reasonable men, than you." The woman said "what is the deficiency in intellect and religion?" The Prophet said "As for the deficiency in intellect, the testimony of two women is for the testimony of one man, and as for the deficiency in religion, one of you women eats during Ramaḍān and spends days without praying."'

9 Ibn Māja, *Sunan*, Ibid., p. 2717 (*Kitāb al-fatn, Bāb fitan al-nisā'*, *ḥadīth* 4003).

family and the Imāms; the digressive nature of the *ḥadīth* adds to the sense that it is a representation of popular preaching:

In testimony, two women equal a single man, and when there are two men or a man and two women, then judgment can be passed on their testimony. The Commander of the Faithful said: we were with the Messenger of God while he was reminding us of His Exalted words *two of your men shall testify.*[10] He said: your free men, not your enslaved men. For God almighty has taxed slaves with service to their masters, and has exempted them from witnessing and delivering testimony. They [who testify] should be just Muslims, for God Blessed and Almighty has honoured just Muslims with the acceptance of their testimony, and that stems from the worldly honour towards them, and from their worldly rewards before they reach the afterlife. Then a woman came, and she stopped in front of the Messenger of God, and said:

'By my father, you, and my mother: O Messenger of God, I am a delegate to you from the women, and no woman heard of this, my trip to you, but that she was made happy by it. O Messenger of God, indeed God, blessed and exalted, is the lord of men and women, and the creator of men and women, and the rewarder of men and women, and indeed Adam is the father of men and women and indeed Eve is the mother of men and women, so why is it that two women are in place of one man in testimony and inheritance?'

The messenger of God replied: 'O woman! Indeed that is a judgment from the King. He does not oppress, nor does He deal unjustly, nor does He take sides, nor does that which has been prevented from you advantage Him, nor does what He has granted to you cause Him deficiency. He organises the matter according to His knowledge, O woman, because you women are deficient in religion and rationality'.

She asked: 'O Messenger of God, what is our deficiency in religion?'

He said: 'Indeed one of you sits half of her lifetime without praying due to menstruation, and you swear a lot, and you deny the blessings, and one of you may dwell with a man for ten years and more, while he is good to her, and kind to her, and if he is incapable of spending for one day, or he quarrels with her, she says to him "I have never seen any good from you at all!" This is not from the women [themselves], but from their creation, and those deficiencies that afflict one of them are a severe trial to her, for her to endure. Thereby, God increases her rewards, so rejoice'.

Then the Messenger of God said to her 'There is no wicked man, but that there is a woman who is more wicked than he; nor is there a good woman but that a good man is better than she. So God has not made woman and men equal at all, except for that equality which God granted for Fāṭima towards ʿAlī, and He attached her to him, and she is a woman better than all of the women of the generations.[11]

[10] Quoted references to Q. 2:282 in Chapters 1 and 2 are italicized but not otherwise identified.

[11] Al-ʿAskarī (attrib.) *Tafsīr al-Imām Abī Muḥammad al-Ḥasan b. ʿAlī al-ʿAskarī*, ed. ʿAlī Āshūr (Beirut: Dār Iḥyāʾ al-Turāth al-ʿArabī, 2001), pp. 512–14.

He said: 'When one of the two errs from her testimony, and she forgets it, then one of them reminds the other of it, so the two of them stand in in delivering the testimony. God made the testimony of two women equal that of one man, due to the deficiency in their intellects and their religion'. Then he said, 'O women, you have been created deficient of intellect (*nāqiṣāt al-ʿuqūl*) so guard against mistakes in testimony, for God has made the reward great for those men and women who remember testimony'.[12]

The female protagonist in this version is more eloquent than in other versions: she reminds the Prophet of the entirely equal human status of men and women, as the descendants of Adam and Eve. But the Prophet replies that this is God's justice, not done for the sake of oppression, or of taking sides, but rather due to women's and men's natural, innate strengths and weaknesses.

The only woman who ever came close to equalling a man, according to this *ḥadīth*, is Faṭima, the daughter of the Prophet. God granted her a special dispensation so that she would be equal to ʿAlī b. Abī Ṭālib, her husband, the father of Ḥasan and Ḥusayn. The *ḥadīth* is interesting for many reasons. It combines various Sunnī versions and elaborates on them; additionally, it has a distinctly Shīʿī interpretative flair, with the references to Faṭima and ʿAlī, and their descendants in the omitted section. It is more elaborate than the other traditions attributed to the period; this probably indicates it is from a later source.

A succinct *ḥadīth* is attributed to ʿAlī b. Abī Ṭālib in the collection of his sermons, *Nahj al-Balāgha* (the peak of eloquence). This *ḥadīth* seems somewhat more vitriolic than Sunnī versions: it refers to women's 'evil'. It was presumably said in anger, since the title of the *ḥadīth* is: 'after the Battle of the Camel, concerning the disparagement of women'. The Battle of the Camel was the famous clash between the Prophet's widow ʿĀʾisha and his son-in-law ʿAlī over the leadership of the community, which ʿĀʾisha lost. In response ʿAlī is reputed to have said:

O people! Indeed women are deficient in faith, deficient in shares, and deficient in mind (*ʿuqūl*). As for the deficiency in their faith, they sit apart from prayer and fasting during their menstruation. As for the deficiency in their minds, the testimony of two women is like the testimony of a single man. And as for the deficiency in their shares, their inheritance is half of the inheritance of men. So fear women's evil, and beware [even] of the good ones. And do not obey them concerning what is right, so that they do not covet what is wrong (*wa lā tuṭīʿūhunna fīʾ l-maʿrūf ḥatta lā yaṭmʿna fīʾ l-munkar*).[13]

[12] Ibid., p. 528.

[13] ʿAlī b. Abī Ṭālib (attrib.), *Nahj al-balāgha ṭabʿa jadīda munaqqaḥa bimakhṭūṭa al-iskorīyal, jamaʿahu wa nassaqa abwābahu al-Sharīf al-Rāḍī*, ed. ʿAbd Allāh Anīs

This *ḥadīth* is similar in its themes to the Sunnī versions, in that women's deficiencies in religion and mind are mentioned, but there are also important differences. Rather than religion (*dīn*), this *ḥadīth* speaks of women's faith (*īmān*); but it also speaks of two other legal situations ignored by the Sunnī *ḥadīth*s: inheritance, and commanding right and forbidding wrong. The *ḥadīth* instructs men not to obey women in what is right (*al-ma'rūf*) lest they should lead them astray, although in Q. 9:71 both sexes are told to command right and forbid wrong.[14] Like some of the other *ḥadīth*s here, this *ḥadīth* has hallmarks of responding to popular discourse and also of acting as a post-facto explanation for legal rulings.

While *ḥadīth*s such as the 'deficiency *ḥadīth*s' may have been a part of common knowledge, taken for granted by religious scholars, the genres of *tafsīr*, grammar, and law each have a specific focus within the scholarly milieu. In this period, they do not even refer to the *ḥadīth*s discussed previously.

The influential early grammarian al-Farrā' (d. 207/822) has much to say on the grammatical complexities of Q. 2:282, and how it can be understood or explained in oral teaching sessions. This interpretation at times reads as an instruction manual for the *'ulamā'* teaching the verse: 'If you wish', he asserts, 'you may say: "then it is a man and two women (*fa-huwa rajulun wa-' mra'atāni*)"'; here he adds the pronoun *huwa* to the verse in order to clarify its meaning.[15] He points out that some may read this phrase *if there are not two men, then a man and two women should testify*.[16] Such directions give some indication of the intended audience of al-Farrā''s book of grammar: it was not written for a general audience, but for learned men who would go on to teach or read his work to the general public. In a later period, authors of *tafsīr* described their intended audience as scholarly, rather than popular.[17]

The phrase *if one of the two errs* is supplied with a lengthier explanation. The problem here is the term that I have translated 'if', spelled *'-n*.

al-Ṭabbā' and Muḥammad Anīs al-Ṭabbā' (Beirut: Mu'assasat al-Ma'ārif, 2004), p. 133 (Sermon 78).

[14] For other references to women commanding right and forbidding wrong, see Michael Cook, *Commanding Right and Forbidding Wrong in Islamic Thought* (Cambridge: Cambridge University Press, 2000).

[15] Yaḥyā b. Ziyād al-Farrā', *Ma'ānī al-Qur'ān*, ed. Aḥmad Yūsuf Najātī and Muḥammad 'Alī Najjār (Cairo: al-Hay'a al-Miṣriyya al-'Āmma lil-Kitāb, 1980), v. 1, p. 184 (at Q. 2:282).

[16] Ibid.

[17] Karen Bauer, 'I have seen the people's antipathy to this knowledge'.

In the majority reading of Q. 2:282, the word used is not *in* ('if'), it is *an* ('that'). In other words, in a plain sense reading the verse states 'that one of the two errs the one will remind the other', which is difficult to understand; furthermore, *in* and *an* are followed by different grammatical constructions. Al-Farrā' explains that the word may be read *an* or *in*; in both cases there is a grammatical problem that involves technical stratagems. When it is read as *in*, the first part of the clause must be divorced from the second; when read as *an*, the reader must understand it through the technical device of anteposition/antecedent and postposition (*taqdīm wa-ta'khīr*) 'so the condition and the answer have become like one word'.[18]

He explains that, although the verse's grammar is convoluted, the meaning is straightforward: 'its meaning – and God knows best – is that the two women testify in the place of one man, so that the reminder can remind the forgetter when she forgets'.[19] With this statement, al-Farrā' finds a way to reconcile the difficult grammatical structure of the verse with a simple, common sense, explanation of its meaning. Without the grammatical addenda, this went on to become the most widespread explanation for the verse in the genre of *tafsīr*. The popularity of this interpretation is due not only to the exegetes' esteem for al-Farrā', but also to the elegance of his solution for this problematic verse.

The earliest *tafsīr* interpretations of Q. 2:282 tend to focus on meaning and grammar, although not necessarily in the same detail as the grammarian al-Farrā'. So, for instance, Muqātil b. Sulaymān's (d. 150/767) interpretation of Q. 2:282 simply says that the witnesses must be 'pleasing (*marḍiyyan*), whether man or woman';[20] he glosses the 'error' as 'forgetting', and explains the phrase on women's testimony thus: 'He says the one woman who has preserved what the two of them saw reminds the other'.[21] Similarly, al-Qummī (d. c. 308/919) simply clarifies: 'meaning, that if one of the two forgets, then the other will remind'.[22] Both of these early works of *tafsīr* are therefore simple, straightforward readings of the meaning of the verse.

Al-Ṭabarī's interpretation of Q. 2:282 breaks the mould. It is long, intricate, and involved. In this work, the integral nature of *tafsīr* as a genre

18 Al-Farrā', *Ma'ānī al-Qur'ān*, v. 1, p. 184. 19 Ibid., v. 1, p. 184.
20 Muqātil b. Sulaymān, *Tafsīr Muqātil b. Sulaymān*, ed. 'Abd Allāh Muḥammad Shihāta (Cairo: al-Hay'a al-Miṣriyya al-'Āmma lil-Kitāb, 1979), v. 1, p. 229 (at Q. 2:282).
21 Muqātil b. Sulaymān, *Tafsīr*, v. 1, p. 229 (at Q. 2:282).
22 'Alī b. Ibrāhīm al-Qummī, *Tafsīr al-Qummī*, ed. al-Ṭayyib al-Musawī al-Jazā'irī (Najaf: Maṭba'at al-Najaf, 1996), v. 1, p. 94.

incorporating other sub-genres becomes apparent. The two most important sub-genres represented in al-Ṭabarī's interpretation of this verse are grammar and variant readings (*qirā'āt*), but his grammatical discussion is barely more than what has already been given by al-Farrā'. What seemed to interest al-Ṭabarī more was the question of the variant readings.

The existence of variant readings is an important aspect of the context of this verse and the intellectual milieu of the 10th-century Islamic lands. Readers usually agree on the orthography of the verses, but they often diverge on vowelling. The variant readings of Q. 2:282 probably arose because of the grammatical difficulty alluded to by al-Farrā': the particle spelled *'-n*. One group reads this as *an*, while the other reads it as *in*. Al-Ṭabarī describes a well-known geographical split between the readings of this verse: the first reading, which he follows, is held by the 'majority of the Hijāzīs, and the people of Medina, and some of the Iraqis'; this reading holds that *'-n* is vowelled with a *fatḥa*, becoming *an*; the subsequent words 'err' and 'remind' are in the subjunctive.[23] The meaning is that if one of the two women errs, the other will remind her. A second reading, ascribed to al-A'mash (d. 147 or 148/764–5), reads *in* instead of *an*. For al-A'mash, this is information about 'what one of the two women will do if the other one forgets ... the reminder will remind the forgetter'.[24] The two variant readings listed here, therefore, do not represent substantial differences in doctrine or meaning of the verse: they consider the question of the vowelling and grammatical case of words, rather than their meaning.

The readers formed distinct schools, and around the period of al-Ṭabarī, certain readings became standard. Al-Ṭabarī himself stresses the importance of sticking with the canonical variants, and of not deviating from them:

> We have chosen that reading due to the consensus of proofs from the ancient readers and the recent ones about it. The isolation of al-A'mash and those who follow his reading is because, with it, he has isolated himself. And it is not permissible to leave a reading that Muslims have followed, and which is pervasive among them, for another [non-canonical reading].[25]

The reason al-Ṭabarī mentions the importance of sticking with the canonical variants is because another reading that he cites is not canonical. It is a reading ascribed to Sufyān b. 'Uyayna (d. 198/814), who was not a

[23] Al-Ṭabarī, *Jāmi' al-Bayān*, v. 6, pp. 62–3 (at Q. 2:282).
[24] Ibid., v. 6, p. 64 (at Q. 2:282). [25] Ibid., v. 6, p. 65 (at Q. 2:282).

recognised Qur'ān reader. Not only did his reading differ from the recognised, canonical variants, it also had implications for the meaning of the verse. In this reading, rather than one woman reminding the other (*tudhakkir*), she makes her like a man (*tudhkir*). It is worth quoting this interpretation at length, because it is another example of an interpreter going too far, and giving an interpretation that is recorded by tradition, only to be dismissed:

Another [within this group] reads *tudhakkir* like that, except that he puts a *sukūn* on the *dhāl*, and they remove the *shadda* from its *kāf* [*tudhkir*]. By reading that like that, the adherents of this reading differ among themselves concerning the interpretation, and they read it thus: some of the interpreters turn it so that it means one of the two makes the other one a man by virtue of the collection of the two of them. The meaning is that her testimony, when it is joined with the testimony of her friend, is permitted as the testimony of one male is permitted in debts, on the grounds that the testimony of each one of the two of them singly is not permitted in the matters of debt to which they are permitted to testify, unless the two of them agree on one testimony. At that moment the testimony of the two of them is in the place of the testimony of one male. So each of the two, according to the doctrine of those who interpret it with this meaning, makes her friend with her into a man. And they refer to the saying of the Arabs: 'so-and-so has made his mother a man', i.e., she gave birth to him, a male, and she became a male through him ... and this is the doctrine that is narrated on the authority of Sufyān b. 'Uyayna, that he ascribed to it. That is narrated on the authority of Abū 'Ubayd al-Qāsim b. Sallām that he said: 'It was narrated on the authority of Sufyān b. 'Uyayna that he said "the reading of His words is not *fa-tudhakkir iḥdāhumā al-ukhrā* from 'reminding (*dhikr*)' after forgetting; rather, it is from 'maleness (*dhakar*)', with the meaning that if she testifies with the other one the testimony of the two of them becomes like the testimony of the male.[26]

In Sufyān's reading, women are not the same as men; but in the circumstance that the two of them are put together, the one makes the other like a man. As I will describe in the next section, this interpretation was rejected roundly by subsequent generations of exegetes, and one of the reasons that they rejected it was on the basis that women's testimony is not equal to men's testimony even when two women are together, and that women are not like men. However, al-Ṭabarī does not reject the interpretation on gendered grounds. Instead, he asserts that this interpretation goes against the scholarly consensus and does not makes sense. As he says, 'The one of the two who errs in her testimony is, at that moment, doubtless more needful of reminding than the other is of being made like a man'.[27] He then develops a plausible explanation for Ibn

[26] Ibid., v. 6, pp. 63–4. [27] Ibid., v. 6, pp. 66–7.

ʿUyayna – perhaps it refers to her strength, for describing something as 'male' is a manner of speaking that can be applied when someone is strong in something or good at it. If this were what Ibn ʿUyayna meant, then his reading would be acceptable. But, even if that were what he meant, nobody else reads the word in the way that Ibn ʿUyayna does.[28] Consensus therefore plays a key part in al-Ṭabarī's rejection of Ibn ʿUyayna's reading. Certain variants are acceptable, others are not. Although al-Aʿmash's reading was isolated, it was still an acceptable variant, unlike Ibn ʿUyayna's.

Al-Ṭabarī's explanation about the logic of the correct interpretation has much to do with common sense, and little to do with gender. He does not say that women cannot be like men – instead, he uses a logical argument: the forgetful woman would need reminding more than the other woman would need to be made like a man. Al-Ṭabarī's work therefore differs from that of later interpreters. Classical-era authors, whose work I describe in the next section, cite gender as a key reason why 'making like a man' does not work as an explanation for the term.

Although we cannot know why al-Ṭabarī did not use gender to explain the term, it may be that he was operating within the boundaries of the genre in his time. Al-Ṭabarī's *tafsīr* plays a prominent part in my analysis in this volume; in his explanation of these verses, he never describes women as inferior to men in the ways that later authors of *tafsīr* do. However, his silence on the matter of women's rationality in his *tafsīr* does not amount to a declaration of equality with men. As I mentioned previously, in his *History*, for instance, he cites an account of Eve's creation in which she was created wise, but God made her foolish after she tempted Adam.[29] His silence on women's abilities in his *tafsīr* indicates that he was working within the boundaries that he considered appropriate for his genre: in the *tafsīr* of his period, consensus and grammar were all-important for determining the correct interpretation.

Although he was working within certain genre constraints, al-Ṭabarī's interpretation incorporates other genres with a direct link to *tafsīr*: grammatical works and *qirāʾāt*. It is likely that the genre of grammar grew out of *tafsīr*,[30] and although the influence of *qirāʾāt* on *tafsīr* has not been

[28] Ibid., v. 6, p. 67.

[29] In this account, God says: '*wa-an ajʿaluhā safīha wa-qad kuntu khalaqtuha ḥalīma*', al-Ṭabarī, *Taʾrīkh al-rusul wa'l-mulūk* [*Annales*], ed. M. J. De Goeje (Leiden: Brill, 1964, prima series), v. 1, p. 109.

[30] Versteegh, *Arabic Grammar and Qurʾānic Exegesis*, p. 65.

investigated, it is likely that readings were also an important element in the emergent genre of *tafsīr*. *Tafsīr* was meant to incorporate all types of linguistic knowledge about the meaning of the Qurʾān. Notably absent from al-Ṭabarī's interpretation of Q. 2:282, as well as that of other exegetes, is direct influence from works of *fiqh* and *ḥadīth*. These genres developed separately, with authorities, methods, and aims distinct to those found in *tafsīr*. It is to works of *fiqh* that we now turn.

In the following pages, I outline some of the basic disagreements among early jurists on women's testimony. This brief survey of early views highlights how discussions are shaped, in part, by contestation and rivalry between nascent schools and individual jurists, in part by common practice, and only in part by the words of the Qurʾān. There are two main juridical positions, which involve different interpretations of the nature of Q. 2:282: that of those who interpret Q. 2:282 to be an exception, and thus only allow women's testimony in monetary cases and cases where men are not present, and that of those who interpret Q. 2:282 to be a general premise regarding women's testimony, and therefore allow two women to testify along with one man in most cases. Within these two basic positions there are many nuanced disagreements between the jurists on specific points where women can and cannot testify.

The followers of Abū Ḥanīfa permit women's testimony in almost every case, but women's testimony is not permitted at all in matters of crimes against God (*ḥudūd*) or retaliation (*qiṣāṣ*). For Ḥanafīs, women's testimony is usually only accepted with a man (so: two men, or a man and two women, but not four women); but they accept women's testimony alone when men were not usually present, such as the birth of a live child.

Other schools and interpreters went further than the Ḥanafīs and permitted women's testimony even in *ḥudūd* cases. They include the Ẓahirīs, who according to Ibn Ḥazm allowed women's testimony at the rate of two women to one man in every type of case,[31] and the early jurists ʿAṭāʾ b. Abī Rabāḥ of Mecca (d. 114) and Ḥammād b. Salama of Basra (d. 167), who allowed two women to testify in place of one of the four men in *ḥudūd* cases.[32] According to the Fāṭimid Ismāʿīlī Nuʿmān b. Muḥammad, known as al-Qāḍī al-Nuʿmān, women's testimony is

[31] See Karen Bauer, 'Debates on Women's Status as Judges and Witnesses in Post-Formative Islamic Law' *The Journal of the American Oriental Society* 130.1 (2010): p. 6, n. 15.

[32] 'It is narrated on the authority of ʿAṭāʾ and Ḥammād that the two of them said "the testimony of three men and two women is permitted [in cases of *ḥudūd*] because the decrease in the number of men is by one, and in his place are two women, just as in monetary transactions"', Abū Muḥammad ʿAbd Allāh Ibn Qudāma, *al-Mughnī*, ed.

acceptable in marriage, property, and areas where only women have knowledge; furthermore, it seems that their testimony could be accepted in *ḥudūd* cases, along with the fifty-fold oath on the trustworthiness of the female witness (a process known as *qasāma*): 'The testimony of women in cases of murder is suspicious, so with it pronounce *qasāma*'.[33] According to one text, al-Qāḍī al-Nuʿmān accepts two women's testimony with three men in cases of unlawful sexual intercourse (*zinā*), but not that of four women and two men: 'When three men and two women testify to unlawful intercourse (*zinā*), stoning is obligatory. But the testimony of two men and four women is not accepted in *zinā*'.[34] Although none of these jurists accept women's testimony as equal to men's, they show that not all schools of law entirely prohibited women's testimony in cases of *ḥudūd*.

Other early jurists and nascent schools were far more restrictive in their general approach, although in some areas they may have allowed women's testimony in areas that the Ḥanafīs did not. Al-Shāfiʿī (d. 204/820) is almost entirely negative about women's testimony, both in rulings and in tone. It is not clear if that negativity is due to a harsh view of women per se, or if it is due to his desire to discredit rival interpretations. In his description of when women can and cannot testify, he does not mention women's shortcomings; instead, he concentrates on those areas where his doctrine differs from that of other prominent jurists. Rather than focusing on elements that were presumably taken for granted among the interpreters, such as women's capacity, he explains the reasoning behind the contested elements of his rulings. For instance, al-Shāfiʿī says that a man must be with the female witnesses, and that his oath is not permitted. This puts him at odds with the view of Mālik (d. 179/795), who says it is permitted to accept a man's oath with the two women's testimony. Perhaps because of this disagreement, al-Shāfiʿī explains why his position is correct: God says in Q. 2:282 that the man should testify with the women, and that they stand in the place of another man.[35]

Mahmūd ʿAbd al-Wahhāb Fāyid (Cairo: Maktabat al-Qāhira, 1968), v. 10, p. 130 (*Kitāb al-Shahādāt*, issue 8368). I owe this reference to Hossein Modarressi.

33 Nuʿmān b. Muḥammad, known as al-Qāḍī al-Nuʿmān, *Daʿāʾim al-Islām wa-dhikr al-ḥalāl wa'l-ḥarām wa'l-qaḍāyā wa'l-aḥkām*, ed. Āṣif ʿA. A. Fayḍī (Beirut: Dār al-Aḍwaʾ n. d.), v. 2, p. 514.

34 Nuʿmān b. Muḥammad, *Mukhtaṣar al-āthār lil–Dāʿī al-ajall sayyidnā al-Qāḍī al-Nuʿmān b. Muḥammad*, [no named editor] (Surat, India: al-Jamīʿa al-Sayfiyya, 2004) [1425 a.h.]. I owe thanks to Husain Qutbuddin for sending me the relevant pages of this text.

35 Muḥammad b. Idrīs al-Shāfiʿī, *al-Umm*, ed. Muḥammad Zuhrī al-Najjār (Beirut: Dār al-Maʿrifa, [198-?]), v. 7, p. 47.

On another debated point, al-Shāfiʿī says that in cases where women testify alone, it is necessary for four of them to testify; the other schools disagree about this number: in the Ḥanafī school, for instance, one single woman can testify in such cases. Here too, al-Shāfiʿī explains his reasoning: God put two women in place of a man, so when they are alone, there must be four of them instead of two male witnesses.[36]

But why could or could not women testify alone, without men: was their word considered to be equal to men's? Al-Shāfiʿī and other early jurists assert that the acceptance of women alone is only due to men's absence in specific circumstances. Thus, the acceptability of women's testimony alone is not because women's word is valued equally to men's, but rather because there is no other choice of witness. Ron Shaham, who has studied the acceptability of women's expert testimony, argues that the word of midwives, in particular, was accepted because there was no other choice.[37] His study indicates that there is a relationship between customary practice and law: apparently men never attended births, so jurists were forced to accept women's word in this instance.

Mālik b. Anas, eponym of the Mālikī school of jurisprudence, says that accepting women's testimony in certain instances is due to customary practice:

> Mālik said: the testimony of women is not permissible in slander and what resembles it either. This is one of the matters on which judges differ, and the common practice (*mā maḍā min al-sunna*) is that the two women [alone] can testify to the live birth of the child (*istihlāl al-ṣabiy*), from which follows his inheritance. Therefore he inherits, and his inheritance is for whomever inherits from him if the child dies, even though there is no male, nor an oath, with the two women who testified, and even though it may have been a very large amount of money in gold. As for silver (*wariq*), pasture (*al-ribāʿ*), enclosed property (*ḥawāʾiṭ*), and slaves (*raqīq*) and other monetary things like that, even if two women testified to a single dirham, or more or less than that, nothing of the testimony of the two of them would be effective, nor would it be accepted unless a single male witness was with them, or an oath, Mālik says.[38]

Taken at face value, the issue of women's testifying alone reveals something about the common practices of the time. Birth was something only

[36] Ibid., v. 7, p. 47.

[37] Ron Shaham, 'Women as Expert Witnesses in Pre-Modern Islamic Courts', in *Law, Custom, and Statute in the Muslim World: Studies in Honor of Aharon Layish*, ed. Ron Shaham (Leiden: Brill, 2007), pp. 41–65, at p. 64.

[38] Mālik ibn Anas, *al-Muwaṭṭā*, [no named editor] (Lichtenstein: Thesaurus Islamicus Foundation, 2000), p. 277 (*Kitāb al-aqḍiya*).

seen by women, not men; therefore, it was necessary to have women testify to the live birth of a child, although it potentially involved large sums. However, in monetary matters that men do see, such as slaves, houses, property, and the like, women could not testify without men to any sum. The acceptance of women's testimony at all here seems somewhat grudging.

Common practice could explain much about this reluctant acceptance of women's testimony. Because of the prevailing legal culture of rejecting women's testimony, for instance in Jewish law, most schools may have presumed that women's testimony was rejected except in cases where the Qur'ān clearly specified that it could be accepted. The prevailing legal culture could be one of the reasons why most jurists following the Shāfiʿī, Mālikī, and Ḥanbalī schools ruled against women's testimony in most cases. Mālik is open about attributing his own ruling on this issue and others to common practice.[39] The Ḥanafīs and Ẓāhirīs operated instead on the presumption that Q. 2:282 could be applied to other cases, and thus presumed that women's word was accepted in most cases according to the Ḥanafīs, or all cases according to the Ẓāhirīs. The rulings of the major schools persisted, but the explanations for them changed through time. The cultural explanation favoured by Mālik was soon left behind in favour of more complex and involved legal theorising.

THE CHANGING PARADIGM OF WOMEN'S TESTIMONY IN CLASSICAL *TAFSĪR*

This section describes a paradigm shift in discussions of women's testimony in classical *tafsīr*. In the previous section, I showed that the earliest works of *tafsīr* were limited in their focus. They included grammar, variant readings, basic 'meaning', and the interpretations of past exegetical authorities. Notably, they did not usually include lengthy *ḥadīth*s or references to *fiqh*, nor did they include any explanations of women's innate inferiority. As I describe in this section, in the 4th/10th century, interpretation is still divided between sub-genres under the umbrella of '*tafsīr*'; but in the 5th/11th century, *fiqh* and *ḥadīth* entered into *tafsīr*

[39] This explanation is also attributed to Mālik on other matters: 'It is narrated of Mālik, on the authority of al-Zuhrī, that he said: "the common practice (*maḍḍat al-sunna*) is that the testimony of women is not permissible in *ḥudūd* nor in marriage and divorce"'; another version mentions '*ḥudūd* or *qiṣāṣ*', [no named author or editor], *al-Mawsūʿa al-Fiqhiyya* (Kuwait: Wizārat al-Awqāf wa'l-shuʾūn al-Islāmiyya, 1992), v. 16, p. 227 (*Shahāda*, 29). I owe this citation to Hossein Modarressi.

in a more systematic way. Thus, ideas about women's deficiency that were once limited to *ḥadīth*s on the Prophet's authority became a part of *tafsīr* as the genre developed; concurrently, it became commonplace to offer some explanation for why the verse said what it did, rather than restricting the focus solely to the verse's meaning, grammar, and variant readings. This expansion of what was included in interpretations reflects the expanding nature of *tafsīr*, particularly in the 5th/11th century: it was becoming a catch-all genre, which would include the basic elements from all of the sciences brought to bear on any one particular verse. By the end of the 5th/11th century, the gender hierarchy began to take centre stage in these interpretations.

In the 4th/10th century, there were three separate tracks of interpretation in what is now broadly known as the genre of *tafsīr*. Each of these tracks followed different sub-genres. Works of *Maʿānī al-Qur'ān* were written by grammarians and focused on grammar. In his interpretation, al-Zajjāj (d. 311/923) cites the grammarian Sībawayh, and al-Naḥḥās (d. 388/949) cites the deviant interpretation of Sufyān b. ʿUyayna.[40] Neither of these explains why the verse says what it does. The second track was the juridical track, found in the *Aḥkām al-Qur'ān* of al-Jaṣṣāṣ (d. 370/982). Al-Jaṣṣāṣ was a jurist: his surviving works include a work on *uṣūl*, a commentary on Ḥanafī law, and a book of *Adab al-Qāḍī*. His *Aḥkām al-Qur'ān* is perhaps the first explanation of the legalities of women's testimony in the format of a *tafsīr*.[41] He describes, for instance, the legal controversy over permitting women's testimony in cases other than monetary, and then explains his own view:

> The plain sense of this verse is that it indicates the permissibility of women's testimony in all contracts [...] and it indicates the permissibility of women's testimony in cases other than monetary, and on the authority of [...] the Prophet, 'the testimony of the midwife is permitted', although birth is not monetary, and her testimony is permitted against another, and that indicates that women's testimony is not limited to monetary matters.[42]

[40] Ibrāhim b. Sarī al-Zajjāj, *Maʿānī al-Qur'ān*, ed. ʿAbd al-Jalīl ʿAbduh Shalabī (Beirut: Manshūrāt al-Maktaba al-ʿAsriyya, 1973), pp. 363–4; Abū Jaʿfar al-Naḥḥās, *Maʿānī al-Qur'ān*, ed. Muḥammad ʿAlī al-Ṣābūnī (Mecca: Umm al-Qurā University Press, 1988), v. 1, pp. 317–19.

[41] I have not had access to older works of *Aḥkām al-Qur'ān*, and therefore am unable to assess the extent to which al-Jaṣṣāṣ's work represents a development within that sub-genre.

[42] Aḥmad b. ʿAlī Abū Bakr al-Jaṣṣāṣ, *Aḥkām al-Qur'ān*, ed. ʿAbd al-Raḥmān Muḥammad (Cairo: al-Maṭbaʿa al-Bahiyya al-Miṣriyya, 1928 [1347]), v. 1, pp. 596–8 (at Q. 2:282).

Here al-Jaṣṣāṣ includes *ḥadīths* about women's status, and disregards the subjects typical of earlier works of *tafsīr*, such as grammar and variant readings. His work, a typical representative of the sub-genre of *Aḥkām al-Qur'ān*, was an attempt to bring elements of *fiqh* and *ḥadīth* into the format of a work of *tafsīr*.

The third stream of interpretation is found in the works entitled '*tafsīr*'. The *Tafsīr al-Qur'ān* of Ibn Abī Ḥātim al-Rāzī (d. 327/938) focuses on the interpretations of early exegetical authorities such as Muqātil b. Ḥayyān, Ibn 'Abbās, and Sa'īd b. Jubayr. Interestingly, in this work these exegetical authorities give interpretations on the Qur'ān's legal applications: the 'man and two women' may testify in the case of debts, and four women do not count, only a man and two women.[43] But exegetical authorities are also cited giving basic explanations of the meaning: al-Ḥasan al-Baṣrī, al-Ḍaḥḥāk, Sa'īd b. Jubayr, Rabī' b. Anas, and al-Suddī are all cited in order to say that to 'err' is to forget. These authorities also give some details about the reminding.

These three distinct types of interpretation found in works with different titles indicate that in the mid-4th/10th century, *tafsīr* itself may have been a type of sub-genre that could include grammar and variant readings, but that above all relied on the interpretations of early exegetical authorities for a basic sense of the Qur'ān's meaning. It is notable that even authors whose main expertise was in other fields adhered to the genre conventions of *tafsīr* when writing a work in that genre. Abū 'l-Layth al-Samarqandī (d. 375/985), for instance, is primarily known as a jurist and wrote many works of *fiqh*; but in his less-well-known work of *tafsīr* he does not cite the *fiqh* on women's testimony. Instead, he gives a simple gloss of the meaning of the verse and alludes briefly to its variant readings.[44] He chose to stay within the genre boundaries of *tafsīr*, although his knowledge surely encompassed the legal rulings on the verse and its legal implications. It seems that each of these sub-genres were recognised by some as being substantially different: in his *fihrist*, Ibn

[43] 'Abd al-Raḥman Muḥammad Ibn Abī Ḥātim al-Rāzī, *Tafsīr al-Qur'ān al-'Aẓīm*, ed. As'ad Muḥammad al-Ṭayyib (Mecca: Maktabat Nizār Muṣṭafā al-Bāz, 1999), v. 2, p. 561 (at Q. 2:282).

[44] Abū 'l-Layth Naṣr b. Muḥammad al-Samarqandī, *Tafsīr al-Samarqandī al-Musammā Baḥr al-'Ulūm*, ed. 'Alī Muḥammad Mu'awwad, 'Ādil Aḥmad 'Abd al-Mawjūd, and Zakarīyā 'Abd al-Majīd al-Nūtī (Beirut: Dār al-Kutub al-'Ilmiyya, 1993), v. 1, pp. 237–8 (at Q. 2:282).

al-Nadīm (d. 990) lists works of *Ma'ānī al-Qur'ān* and *Aḥkām al-Qur'ān* under separate headings from *Tafsīr al-Qur'ān*.[45]

It is not until the work of al-Tha'labī (d. 427/1035) that all of the basic elements of interpretation from both *fiqh* and *tafsīr* are incorporated systematically into one work. In his gloss on Q. 2:282, al-Tha'labī includes grammatical analysis, variant readings, and *fiqh*. He thus represents a distinct turning point in the development of the genre. *Tafsīr* is now inclusive: it becomes an all-encompassing genre with porous boundaries, rather than one specialised sub-genre among others. Many of his predecessors in the field of *tafsīr* had lived and worked in the region of Khūrāsān, and the whole region was known as a centre for exegetical learning, in the way that other regions were known as centres of law, grammar, or variant readings. The leap forward represented by al-Tha'labī's work is therefore the culmination of a long line of regional exegetical development.

Al-Tha'labī's interpretation begins with a definition of the 'men' who can testify. Immediately, he refers to prominent legal authorities such as Mālik, al-Shāfi'ī, and Abū Ḥanīfa – jurists, rather than grammarians:

> *Two of your men* meaning free, mature, not slaves or youths and not free unbelievers. This is the position of Mālik, al-Shāfi'ī, Abū Ḥanīfa, Sufyān, and the majority of the jurists. Ibn Shīrīn and Shurayḥ allowed the testimony of slaves, and that is the doctrine of Anas b. Mālik. And some jurists have allowed their testimony in inconsequential matters.[46]

The references to named legal authorities mark a change from the earlier definitions of the 'two men' in works of *ma'ānī* and *tafsīr*. Al-Zajjāj, for instance, simply says that the two men are 'of your faith (*min millatikum*)'.[47] He therefore clarifies the meaning of 'your men', without referring to a legal discussion of the matter or naming any jurists. The difference is even more striking when one compares this text with an earlier work of *tafsīr* that names authorities. Like al-Tha'labī, Ibn Abī Ḥātim al-Rāzī was a Shāfi'ī, and from the same region. But Ibn Abī Ḥātim's method of interpretation and source citation differs markedly from that of al-Tha'labī: 'my father told me, on the authority of Aḥmad b.

[45] Ibn al-Nadīm, *Fihrist*, trans. Bayard Dodge as *The Fihrist of al-Nadim* (New York: Columbia University Press, 1970), v. 1, pp. 75–6 (for *ma'ānī* and *tafsīr*) and p. 82 (for *aḥkām al-Qur'ān*).

[46] Abū Isḥāq Aḥmad al-Tha'labī, *al-Kashf wa'l-Bayān 'an tafsīr al-Qur'ān*, ed. Abū Muḥammad b. Āshūr et al. (Beirut: Dār Iḥyā' al-Turāth al-'Arabī, 2002), pp. 292–3.

[47] Al-Zajjāj, *Ma'ānī al-Qur'ān*, v. 1, p. 363 (at Q. 2:282); al-Naḥḥās has 'from the people of your faith (*min ahl millatikum*)' (al-Naḥḥās, *Ma'ānī al-Qur'ān*, v. 1, p. 317, at Q. 2:282).

ʿAbd al-Raḥmān, on the authority of his father, on the authority of Rabīʿ b. Anas *if there are not two men then a man and two women* refers to debts'.[48] In Ibn Abī Ḥātim's narration, family networks and exegetical authorities such as Rabīʿ b. Anas are emphasised. Al-Thaʿlabī instead echoes the style of early works of *fiqh* by providing a summary of the rulings on this matter, citing early legal authorities, rather than exegetical ones.

Al-Thaʿlabī continues in the legalistic vein by describing the situations in which women's testimony is permitted according to different schools. The following quotation shows the extent to which al-Thaʿlabī's discourse resembles that in the earliest works of *fiqh*, cited previously:

> *And if there are not two men* meaning if there are not two male witnesses *then a man and two women* or, then a man and two women should testify. There is consensus among the jurists that the testimony of women is permitted with men in monetary matters (*māl*), but they differ in matters other than monetary. Mālik, al-Awzāʿī, al-Shāfiʿī, Abū ʿUbayd, Abū Thawr, and Aḥmad [Ibn Ḥanbal] do not permit it except in monetary matters. Abū Ḥanīfa, Sufyān, and their colleagues permit two female witnesses with the man in everything with the exception of *ḥudūd* and *qiṣāṣ*. [. . . .] The testimony of women is permitted alone without a man with them in four contexts: the hidden parts of women, what is sinful concerning the private parts of women which, in a free woman, includes all of her body except her face and hands, and among slave women what is between her navel and her knees; and in breastfeeding, in parentage, and in [testifying to] a live birth. There is no contrary opinion on any of that except in breastfeeding, and Abū Ḥanīfa goes so far as to say that the testimony of women alone is not permitted in it except with the testimony of two men, or a man and two women.[49]

Like early *fiqh*, and unlike early *tafsīr* and grammar, al-Thaʿlabī here discusses the different schools of *fiqh* on women's testimony, outlining the cases in which women can testify alone. However, this legal-minded interpretation differs from contemporary discussions in works of *fiqh*. To give an example for comparison, the jurist Ibrāhīm b. ʿAlī al-Shīrāzī (d. 476/1083), who was a Shāfiʿī like al-Thaʿlabī, explains the ruling on women's testimony alone with reference to the deficiency *ḥadīth* and Q. 2:282. He says that women's testimony alone is acceptable only because certain things are not witnessed by men, and that it is only established with the proper number of witnesses:

> Fewer than four women is not acceptable, because the least number of acceptable witnesses is two men and the testimony of two women is worth the testimony of

[48] Ibn Abī Ḥātim al-Rāzī, *Tafsīr al-Qurʾān al-ʿAẓīm*, v. 2, p. 561 (at Q. 2:282).
[49] Al-Thaʿlabī, *al-Kashf waʾl-Bayān*, v. 2, p. 293.

> one man. The proof of this is the words of the Almighty: *if there are not two men, then a man and two women.* So the two women stand in place of the single man. ʿAbd Allāh b. ʿUmar, may God be pleased with him, narrated that the Messenger of God said: 'I have not seen people more deficient in religion and rationality, who can conquer the minds of sensible men, than you women'. The woman said: 'O messenger of God, what is the women's deficiency in reason and religion?' He said: 'as for the deficiency in reason, the testimony of two women is like the testimony of a single man, and this is the deficiency in reason; and as for the deficiency in religion, one of you spends nights without praying and eats during the month of Ramaḍān, and this is due to her deficiency in religion'. Therefore in this [property], the testimony of two men is acceptable, and the testimony of a man and two women, because if the testimony of women alone were permitted then the men would not need to be mentioned.[50]

Women's deficiencies take centre stage in al-Shīrāzī's explanation, but only insofar as these deficiencies explain why the Shāfiʿī ruling in *fiqh* is correct. Al-Shīrāzī justifies his requirement for four women using Q. 2:282 and the *ḥadīth* that says that two women equal one man in testimony. This version of the *ḥadīth* does not match exactly any of the ones from the *Ṣaḥīḥ* works I cited previously. After this passage, al-Shīrāzī goes on to describe each of the instances in which women's testimony alone is permissible, and all of the other cases of women's testimony. Al-Thaʿlabī's work of *tafsīr* has a decidedly different emphasis. Rather than replicating the intricate discussions from the *fiqh* of his own time, al-Thaʿlabī summarises the main rulings.

Following his summary of *fiqh*, al-Thaʿlabī turns to grammatical discussions, as is common in works of *tafsīr*. He describes the different readings of al-Aʿmash and Ḥamza, and provides Qur'ānic parallels to explain why the meaning of 'err' is actually 'forget'. Although his methods are reminiscent of al-Ṭabarī's, their exact interpretations are not the same. While al-Ṭabarī did not provide any grammatical exemplar-poetry in this instance, al-Thaʿlabī does. Al-Thaʿlabī was not much interested in the variant reading of Sufyān b. ʿUyayna to which al-Ṭabarī had dedicated so much time and effort. He dismisses it summarily: 'It is said on the authority of Sufyān b. ʿUyayna that he said that it is from "male", meaning that she, when she testifies with the other one, her testimony becomes like the testimony of a male. I say that this doctrine does not please me, because it disregards the forgetting, but God knows best'.[51] As Saleh has stated, the work of

[50] Ibrāhīm b. ʿAlī Abū Isḥāq al-Shīrāzī, *Al-Muhadhdhab fī fiqh al-Imām al-Shāfiʿī*, ed. Muḥammad al-Zuḥaylī (Damascus: Dār al-Qalam, 1996), v. 5, p. 635 (at. Q. 2:282).
[51] Al-Thaʿlabī, *al-Kashf wa'l-Bayān*, v. 2, p. 295 (at Q. 2:282).

al-Ṭabarī was not the base point for al-Thaʿlabī's *tafsīr*: he went well beyond it.[52] As we shall see in Chapter 5 of this book, al-Thaʿlabī also incorporated many lengthy *ḥadīth*s in his work that were absent from al-Ṭabarī's *tafsīr* and others.[53] It is clear that al-Thaʿlabī meant to change the field of *tafsīr*.[54]

The effect of al-Thaʿlabī's inclusivist policy was immediate, and the expectation of that *fiqh* should be incorporated was not limited to al-Thaʿlabī's teachers and students. For instance, after a lengthy discussion of the verse's grammar and a brief summary of certain elements of its *fiqh*, the Imāmī al-Ṭūsī, mentioned in the introduction, explains why he doesn't include further details of juridical rulings on the verse:

> We have already explained the issue of female witnesses, and its details as to what is acceptable and unacceptable, and the rulings on the testimony of women and slaves and others, in our books [of *fiqh*] *al-Nihāya* and *al-Mabsūṭ*, so there is no sense in prolonging our discussion of it here.[55]

Al-Ṭūsī's reference to his other work emphasises that, although *fiqh* could be included in *tafsīr*, the generic boundaries still matter. His interpretation references exegetical and grammatical authorities: al-Ḍaḥḥāk, al-Suddī, and Rabīʿ from the former group; Sībawayh, al-Farrāʾ, and Abū Bakr al-Fārisī (d. 377/987) from the latter. He cites the Muʿtazilī author of a *tafsīr* al-Rummānī (d. 386/996), whom he names in his introduction as an inspiration, and whose work is, in large part, the basis for al-Ṭūsī's. As quoted by al-Ṭūsī, these authorities give explanations typical of the genre, for instance, that the error is actually forgetting. He goes into some detail in the debate over whether *ʾ-n* should be read as *an* or *in*. Any reference to women's inherent nature and why they might be counted as less than men in testimony is missing from al-Ṭūsī's interpretation. Notable here is his response to the controversy over the interpretation of Sufyān b. ʿUyayna, which said that one of the women makes the other like a man. Al-Ṭūsī is unique in that he seems defend Sufyān b. ʿUyayna, by supporting the view that the two women together become like a man:

> A group say: Sufyān b. ʿUyayna is mistaken in his interpretation, because if the one of the two forgets, the other one would not make her like a man. But this is worth nothing (*wa-hādhā laysa bi-shayʾ*) because the meaning of 'make her like a man' is that she becomes, with her, in the place of a man

[52] Saleh, *The Formation of the Classical Tafsīr Tradition*, p. 10.
[53] For more on al-Thaʿlabī's incorporation of *ḥadīth*s, see Ibid., pp. 191–8.
[54] For a detailed discussion of al-Thaʿlabī's aims, see Ibid.
[55] Al-Ṭūsī, *al-Tibyān*, v. 3, p. 531 (at Q. 2:282).

because it makes the two of them further from forgetting when they are joined together after the reminding.[56]

This defence of Sufyān, like previous attacks on him, does not refer to women's natures. But that is not because al-Ṭūsī believed women and men to be the same. In his interpretation of Q. 4:34, al-Ṭūsī says: 'Men are in charge of women's discipline and upbringing because God made men superior to women in reason (*'aql*), and judgment (*ra'y*)'.[57] It is likely that al-Ṭūsī took men's mental superiority over women for granted when he interpreted this verse on women's testimony; he had no need to mention it here.

Al-Wāḥidī (d. 468/1075), a student of al-Tha'labī's, was the first exegete to mention women's deficient intelligence specifically in relation to this verse. He wrote three works of *tafsīr*, the most scholarly of which is *al-Basīṭ*.[58] It is in *al-Basīṭ* that Q. 2:282 is explained thoroughly. Although al-Wāḥidī was a Shāfi'ī and al-Ṭūsī was an Imāmī Shī'ī, these near-contemporaries share interpretive elements. However, they diverge in their assessment of the interpretation of Sufyān b. 'Uyayna, which, for al-Wāḥidī, stands for the idea that women can be made like men. For him, this interpretation disregards the inherent differences between the sexes and the legal precepts that follow from these differences:

The majority of the exegetes are of the opinion that this is remembering after forgetting, except what is narrated on the authority of Sufyan b. 'Uyayna that he said concerning His words *one should remind the other* i.e., make her like a man, meaning that when she testifies with the other, her testimony becomes like the testimony of a man. This was also narrated on the authority of 'Umar and Ibn 'Alā' .... The exegetes deny this interpretation and consider it weak because even when women have reached [physical] maturity they are not mature (*law balaghna mā balaghna*), and if there is not a man with them then their testimony is not accepted; and even when a man is with them the matter is like this ... and if adding one woman to another made them like a man, then the testimony of the two women would be in place of the testimony of a man in all circumstances.[59]

[56] Ibid., v. 3, p. 528 (at Q. 2:282). [57] Ibid., v. 4, p. 449 (at Q. 4:34).

[58] For more on al-Wāḥidī, see Saleh, 'The Last of the Nishapuri School of Tafsīr: Al-Wāḥidī (d. 468/1076) and His Significance in the History of Qur'anic Exegesis' *Journal of the American Oriental Society* 126.2 (April–June 2006): 223–43, and 'The Introduction of al-Wāḥidī's Baṣīṭ: An Edition, Translation, and Commentary', in Bauer (ed.) *Aims, Methods, and Contexts of Qur'ānic Exegesis*, pp. 67–100.

[59] Al-Wāḥidī, Abū' l-Ḥasan 'Alī b. Aḥmad, *al-Basīṭ*, MS Nuru Osmaniye, 236, p. 366. My thanks to Walid Saleh for giving me a copy of the relevant pages of this MS many years ago.

Al-Wāḥidī's assertion that women are in a permanent state of pre-pubescence with regard to witnessing is a defence of the Shāfiʿī doctrine, which is against women's testimony in all matters except monetary. Other categories of person who do not have full rights to testify include slaves and children. By comparing women with children, al-Wāḥidī justifies the Shāfiʿī doctrine of generally disallowing women's testimony. If women could be made like men, he says, their testimony would be allowed in all matters. Al-Wāḥidī also cites a source as saying that women have a 'deficiency in remembering when compared with men'.[60] These arguments, based on women's innate natures, defend the restrictive Shāfiʿī position against the more open Ḥanafī position, which allows women's testimony in all matters except *ḥudūd* and *qiṣāṣ*.

After al-Wāḥidī, it becomes common to explain this verse by citing women's inferiority. The Mālikī jurist Ibn al-ʿArabī whose refutation of al-Ṭabarī was described in the introduction, writing in his work of *Aḥkām al-Qurʾān*, lists six ways in which men were made superior to women. Unlike that in the work of al-Wāḥidī, this discussion is not tied to any particular reading, previous interpretation, or legal ruling; it is an excursus of sorts. As the first full-length explanation of the gender hierarchy, I quote at length:

> God Most High made men superior to women in six aspects:
>
> The first is that he was made as her origin, and she was made as one of his limbs, because she was created from him as God Almighty mentions in His book.
>
> The second is that she was created from the most crooked of his ribs, the Prophet said: indeed woman was created from the most crooked rib, and if you go to straighten her out, you will break her, while if you wish to enjoy her, then enjoy her with her crookedness. And it is said: breaking her is divorcing her.
>
> The third is the deficiency of her religion.
>
> The fourth is the deficiency of her mind (*ʿaql*). In the *ḥadīth* we find: 'I have not seen anyone more deficient in rationality (*ʿaql*) and religion, leading the prudent man astray, than you women'. The women said: 'O Messenger of God, what is the deficiency in our religion and our reason?' He said: 'Is it not so that one of you stays nights without fasting nor praying, and the testimony of one of you is half the testimony of a man?'
>
> The fifth is the deficiency in her share in inheritance. God Almighty said: *for the man, the share of two women* [Q. 4:11].
>
> The sixth is that her strength is deficient, so she does not fight, and there are no shares [of booty] for her. And all of this has wisdom.
>
> If it is said: how can deficiency be attributed to them when it is not something they have done? We say: this is God's justice. He puts down what He wills and elevates what He wills, He performs what He wishes, He praises and He blames.

[60] Ibid., p. 365.

He shall not be questioned about what He does, but they shall be questioned [Q. 21:23]. This is because He created the creation in their places, and organized them in their levels, and clarified that to us. So our knowledge and our faith is in Him, and we submit ourselves to Him.[61]

There was near universal consensus in this period that Adam and Eve were the parents of humankind, and that Eve was created from Adam. Ibn al-ʿArabī says the first woman's creation from a man means that women in general are inferior to men, created as subsidiary beings and from a crooked rib. At their very essence, women are on unequal footing with men, who are the primary creation. (For more on the creation of the first woman in the Qurʾān and interpretation, and how this creation was used to justify the gender hierarchy, see Chapter 3.) The third and fourth reasons for women's inferiority to men are based on the deficiency *ḥadīth*. The fifth reason is Qurʾānic: women's lesser inheritance. The final reason is that women are not as strong as men physically, which means that they do not fight in jihad and receive booty the way that men do. Ibn al-ʿArabī ends by saying that although it might seem unfair to blame women for their deficiencies, it is God's will and must not be questioned, for which he quotes a Qurʾānic verse and an aphorism that is quite close to Psalm 75:7, *It is God who judges: He puts one down and exalts another*. The admonition not to question one's unfair lot in life was surely a common trope in medieval societies. Ibn al-ʿArabī's interpretation represents a summation of the reasoning that was probably taken for granted by many of the jurists and exegetes of his time. But it is important to note that we do not know if the reasons he gives for women's decreased testimony are actually the reasons that earlier jurists and exegetes would have mentioned, had they been asked. These might well be the reasons for the rulings, or they might equally be ex post facto explanations for the rulings.

This work marks a change from the earlier work of *Aḥkām al-Qurʾān* by al-Jaṣṣāṣ in both substance and style. Although Ibn al-ʿArabī focuses on the legal rulings, he also includes linguistic analysis and general explanations of the reasoning behind the verse. Thus, this is much more a work of *tafsīr* than the earlier *Aḥkām* work, and it reflects the contemporary climate of genre inclusiveness.

Fakhr al-Dīn al-Rāzī (d. 606/1209), a Shāfiʿī, is another exegete who explains the reasoning behind the verse. He first refers to supposed physical differences between women and men taken from Ancient Greek medicine:

[61] Ibn al-ʿArabī, *Aḥkām al-Qurʾān*, v. 1, pp. 253–4 (at Q. 2:282).

If one of the two errs, the one will remind the other: The meaning is that forgetfulness dominates women's nature because of the excess of coldness and moisture in their physical constitutions. Joining together the two women renders the forgetfulness further from the mind than the forgetfulness that overcomes one single woman. The two women take the place of a single man, so that if one of the two of them forgets, the other will remind her. And this is the intended meaning of the verse.[62]

According to Fakhr al-Dīn, the intention of the verse is to join together two women so that they are able to overcome their natural forgetfulness, brought about by the excess of coldness and moisture in their bodies (the import of this explanation, taken from Ancient Greek medicine, will be discussed at greater length in Chapter 5).

Not only does he blame women's physical constitutions for their mental deficiencies, but Fakhr al-Dīn takes a gendered approach to a grammatical problem in Q. 2:282. The problem is that the particle *ʾ-n* is vowelled as *an* in the majority reading of the Qurʾān, but *an* means 'that'. So the plain sense would be 'a man and two women, that one of the two women [should] err, the one shall remind the other'. This seems to mean that God intended the woman to err. But why would God have intended an error? The earliest exegetes, and the majority of subsequent exegetes, interpreted *an* synonymously with *in*, meaning '*if* one of the two women errs'. But later exegetes questioned whether it might not have the plain sense meaning of *an* after all. Al-Wāḥidī seems to solve this problem by saying that this particle refers to the fear of error.[63] Al-Ṭūsī takes a more traditional approach: he cites the interpretations of the grammarians Sībawayhi and al-Farrāʾ, siding with the former.[64] Fakhr al-Dīn takes *an* at face value. He claims that the error is intentional:

We say that there are two goals here. The first of them is reaching the testimony, and that is not reached except when one of the women reminds the other one. The second is the clarification of the superiority of men over women, so that it will be clear that two women taking the place of a single man is just in this matter, and that is not attained unless one of the two women errs. Since each of these matters, I mean the testimony and the clarification of the superiority of men over women, is intended, and there is no way to that except through the error of one of the two of them and the reminding of the other, there is no harm in making these two issues required.[65]

[62] Fakhr al-Dīn al-Rāzī, *al-Tafsīr al-kabīr*, ed. ʿAbd al-Raḥmān Muḥammad (Cairo: Maṭbaʿat al-Bahīya, 1938), v. 7, p. 122 (at Q. 2:282).
[63] Al-Wāḥidī, *al-Basīṭ*, pp. 355–6 (at. Q. 2:282).
[64] Al-Ṭūsī, *Tibyān*, v. 3, p. 527 (at Q. 2:282).
[65] Fakhr al-Dīn al-Rāzī, *al-Tafsīr al-kabīr*, v. 7, p. 122 (at Q. 2:282).

Part of the intention of the verse, according to Fakhr al-Dīn, is to show that men are superior to women, and this will not happen unless one of the women errs. Error is required; otherwise, two women taking the place of one man might not be considered just.

Both Fakhr al-Dīn al-Rāzī and Ibn al-ʿArabī address the issue of the fairness and justice of Q. 2:282. Ibn al-ʿArabī attributes the difference between men and women to women's innate deficiencies. Although these deficiencies are not their fault, women still bear the burden and are not counted equally with men. Fakhr al-Dīn al-Rāzī similarly says that God meant for women to err because otherwise men and women might be considered equal. For each of these interpreters, God's word must be considered the highest justice, even when that justice is not obvious to human reason. There is a strong implication that women's deficiencies might seem unjust, which in itself is interesting. When they discuss marriage, many sources also address the question of how women's lot can possibly be a fair one (this is addressed in Chapter 5).

The sophisticated arguments and debates brought to Q. 2:282 by Fakhr al-Dīn al-Razī and Ibn al-ʿArabī follow a long period of evolution in the genre of *tafsīr*. In this time, the paradigm for the interpretation of the verse shifted. By the 6th/12th century, exegetes from almost all schools of law seem to follow the new pattern of explaining the verse with reference, even brief, to *fiqh* rulings on women's testimony and to the ostensible reasons behind the verse, namely women's deficiencies. For example, the Imāmī al-Ṭabrisī (d. 548/1153) asserts, 'This is because forgetfulness overcomes women more than it overcomes men'.[66] The Ḥanbalī Ibn al-Jawzī (d. 597/1200) cites the same source as al-Wāḥidī: 'Abū ʿAlī says: the school [of interpretation] of Ibn ʿUyayna is not strong, because even when women are mature, they are not mature, and their testimony is not allowed unless a man is with them'.[67]

One exception to this general rule is the *Kashshāf* of the famous Muʿtazilite al-Zamakhsharī, who followed Ḥanafī *fiqh*. Al-Zamakhsharī does not mention women's deficiencies in his explanation of Q. 2:282. In other words, he breaks from the basic 12th-century

[66] Abū ʿAlī al-Faḍl b. al-Ḥasan al-Ṭabrisī, *Majmaʿ al-bayān li-ʿulūm al-Qurʾān*, ed. Muḥammad Wāʿīẓzādeh al-Khurāsānī (Tehran: Muʾassasat al-Hudā, 1997), v. 2, p. 275 (at Q. 2:282).

[67] Abū ʾl-Faraj Ibn al-Jawzī, *Zād al-masīr fī ʿilm al-tafsīr*, [no editor listed] (Beirut: al-Maktab al-Islāmī, 1964), v. 1, p. 338 (at Q. 2:282).

paradigm followed by exegetes from other schools of law. This omission might support the thesis that the Ḥanafīs, because of their comparatively relaxed rules on women's testimony, did not attribute deficient *ʿaql* to women in their works of *tafsīr*. However, it is difficult to attribute much importance to al-Zamakhsharī's exceptionalism without further Ḥanafī comparisons. The relative absence of such comparisons is perhaps because the genre of *tafsīr* in his time was dominated by the Shāfiʿī school.

While the early trends in exegesis were not entirely forgotten, in the classical and post-classical period a gendered discourse emerged to explain even the grammatical points of the Qurʾān. This new pattern may represent a change in society's attitudes towards women, but concurrently the shift represents a changing idea of what was allowed within the genre of *tafsīr*. *Tafsīr* was expanding to include brief summaries of all different types of knowledge. The incursion of *fiqh* and the inclusion of more *ḥadīth*s on the Prophet's authority are the most obvious examples of this shift. Intriguingly, it is likely that elements of popular preaching, which were never far from a genre that emerged originally from popular mosque lessons, shaped these interpretations. If so, it gives pause to wonder how women in mosque lessons or preaching sessions may have addressed the seeming unfairness, and been addressed (or rebuked) in turn by the likes of Ibn al-ʿArabī and Fakhr al-Dīn al-Rāzī.

LATE MEDIEVAL *TAFSĪR*: THE STRATIGRAPHIC ACCRETION OF INTERPRETATION

In the post-classical and early modern period, the paradigm shift that occurred in the classical period is not repeated: the basic pattern for interpreting the verse had been set. But authors still exercised a considerable amount of individual choice in their interpretations. The examples that follow highlight how exegetes pick and choose from tradition, but they also show how it is possible to use picking and choosing to create new interpretations. In short, these are examples of the stratigraphic accretion of interpretation that I alluded to in the Introduction.

The *tafsīr* of the Mālikī Andalusian interpreter Abū Ḥayyān al-Gharnāṭī (d. 745/1353) is a good illustration of the way in which an individual exegete's choice affects the contours of his interpretation. More than any *tafsīr* I reviewed from this period, this work delves deeply into the intricacies of *fiqh* discussions on women's testimony. He includes many variant interpretations attributed to early legal and exegetical authorities, going well beyond the major school eponyms. After several pages that resemble works of *fiqh*, he includes interpretations accrued from *tafsīr*, including a quote from Fakhr al-Dīn al-Rāzī, with some alterations:

> [God] said *if one of the two errs* and the meaning is that forgetfulness is predominant in women's natures, because of the excess of coldness and moisture. Bringing together two women makes forgetfulness further in the mind from the forgetfulness that overcomes one woman. So the two women stand in the place of the single man, so that if one of the two forgets the other will remind her. In this is a proof of the superiority of men over women.[68]

This excerpt is but a small fragment of the many pages that Abū Ḥayyān devotes to the *fiqh* and grammar of the verse. Nevertheless it is illustrative of a basic pattern of picking and choosing in interpretation. Here Abū Ḥayyān seems to replicate Fakhr al-Dīn al-Rāzī's interpretation, but it is not an exact replication by any means. The crucial point for Fakhr al-Dīn was that the error was intended in order to demonstrate that women are inferior to men. That controversial element of intentionality, which involves God causing error to occur, is missing from Abū Ḥayyān's interpretation. The palatable aspects of Fakhr al-Dīn's interpretation are retained, whereas its unsavoury aspects have been discarded. But in the process of discarding the unsavoury elements, Abū Ḥayyan has also discarded the very rationale behind this interpretation: the intentionality is central to the fairness of making women's testimony less than a man's. In Abū Ḥayyān's hands, the question of fairness does not enter in.

Inequality between the sexes seems to be taken for granted in these sources; but its exact boundaries, and the reasoning behind it, were open for discussion. The Ḥanbalī jurist Ibn Qayyim al-Jawziyya (d. 751/1350) wrote a chapter on this matter entitled 'Wisdom concerning the equality of women with men in some rulings, and not others'. Ibn al-Qayyim was one of the most famous students of the radical reformer Ibn Taymiyya (d. 728/1328), who advocated going back to the original sources and shedding much of the accretion of interpretation that had happened throughout Islamic history.[69] In his two-page-long excursus on the question of gender equality, Ibn al-Qayyim says that men and women have

68 Muḥammad b. Yūsuf Abū Ḥayyān al-Andalusī, *al-Baḥr al-Muḥīṭ*, ed. ʿĀdil Aḥmad ʿAbd al-Mawjūd, et al. (Beirut: Dār al-Kutub al-ʿIlmiyya, 1993), v. 2, p. 366 (at Q. 2:282).

69 This theme runs through his *Muqaddima*. For example, see his critique of Ibn ʿAṭiyya, in Ibn Taymiyya, *Muqaddima fī ʿuṣūl al-tafsīr*, [no named editor] (Kuwait: Dār al-Qur'ān al-Karīm, 1971), pp. 23–4.

equality in their bodily acts of worship, but not in certain legal matters such as testimony, inheritance, blood money, and the manumission of slaves. This is an unusual passage in that it cuts to the heart of the very issue of equality and inequality. According to Ibn Qayyim al-Jawziyya, the only reason that some acts of worship are not obligatory for women is when such an act would entail their mixing with men, which would be unseemly. Testimony, however, is a matter in which women and men differ because of their inherent mental differences. Ibn al-Qayyim claims that the Qur'ān itself refers to women's weak minds; this is his interpretation of the error attributed to women in Q. 2:282. In the following passage, he explains the broad reasons for the areas of equality and inequality between the sexes:

As for His doctrine that there is equality between men and women in bodily acts of worship and in matters that transgress against God (*ḥudūd*), while He made her half of him in blood money, testimony, inheritance, and the manumission of slaves, this is also an aspect of the perfection and subtlety of His law and His wisdom. Women and men share in the matter (*maṣlaḥa*) of the bodily acts of worship and in the matter of divine punishment; and the needs of one of the two sexes for these things are like the needs of the other sex for them. It is not proper to have differences between the two of them except when a difference exists in those matters that are more properly differentiated, such as Friday and communal prayers. The obligation of these is confined to men, not women, because women are not the kinds of people who go out mixing with men. Likewise, there is a difference between them in the undertaking of jihad, since women do not do that. But there is equality between them in the necessity of performing *ḥajj* because of the necessity for the two sexes of its benefits, and in the obligation of almsgiving, fasting, and ritual purification. As for testimony, woman has only been made half of a man in it. The wisdom of this the Powerful Wise One indicates in His book, and it is that the woman is weak in reason (*'aql*), having little exactness when she recollects. God has made men superior to women in their minds (*'uqūl*), understanding, preserving information, and exactness; so a woman, in those things, cannot assume the place of a man. Forbidding her testimony entirely would entail the loss of many rights and would be an impairment to her, so the best way is to join the minds together ... and the testimony of two women together takes the place of the testimony of one man.[70]

According to Ibn Qayyim al-Jawziyya, the only reason that women are not obligated to attend Friday and communal prayers, or to perform *jihād*, is that it is unseemly for them to mix with men as would be required

[70] Shams al-Dīn Abū 'Abd Allāh Ibn Qayyim al-Jawziyya, *I'lām al-muwaqqi'īn 'an rabb al-'Ālamīn*, ed. Ṭāhā 'Abd al-Ra'ūf Sa'd (Cairo: Maktabat al-Kuliyyāt al-Azhār, n.d.), v. 2, p. 168.

in these situations. That exempts them from certain acts that fall in the category of 'worship', although generally women are equal with men in these areas. In matters that require the use of the mind, however, the difference exists because women's minds do not equal men's minds. He goes on to say that women's blood money is different from men's because they have a different value in society and that men get more inheritance because they support women and are superior to them.[71] For a medieval jurist, then, these are the reasons behind the laws. For a modern scholar reading the texts, the picture is more complex. The earliest jurists, who set forth these rulings, did not explain matters in the same way as Ibn Qayyim al-Jawziyya, and did not include chapters on the question of the equality of the sexes. As in other cases discussed here, the reasons mentioned by Ibn al-Qayyim may well represent the true reasons behind the laws. But equally, they may simply be ex post facto explanations for laws that long pre-dated Ibn al-Qayyim and that arose from the particular circumstances of their own time.

SUMMARY AND CONCLUSION

Given the Qur'ān alone, interpretations of women's testimony could have taken a number of paths. But the Qur'ān was never read alone, contextless, without supplementary material or widespread, taken-for-granted knowledge. To a certain extent *ḥadīth*s serve to justify the jurists' rulings in the face of Qur'ānic ambiguities. Yet, despite their seeming centrality to these discussions, the precise role of *ḥadīth*s is not entirely clear, and seems to have shifted through time. At times, what is put forth as a *ḥadīth* seems instead to be a record of popular preaching, reflecting common concerns. At times *ḥadīth*s seem to be explanations for legal rulings. Whether pre- or post-dating the laws themselves, these *ḥadīth*s justify a general approach to women's testimony, but even in the *ḥadīth*s that seem to have a very negative attitude towards women, women's word is valued at half a man's word. From the text of the *ḥadīth*s reviewed here, it is unclear why women would be prohibited from testifying at all in certain matters. The *ḥadīth*s therefore do not seem to have determined the precise formulation of these laws, which may have been based on the judgment of the earliest jurists.

[71] Ibid., v. 2, p. 169.

In this chapter, I have focused particularly on the ways in which genre plays a role in shaping the nature of discussions on women's testimony. In the earliest works, only the genre of *ḥadīth* addressed the question of women's mental capacity as compared with men's: a prominent set of *ḥadīth*s attributes women's disadvantage in testimony to their mental deficiency. The deficiency *ḥadīth*s may have been taken for granted by authors of works in other genres, but they were not cited. In early works of *fiqh*, the discussion centres on the proper limits of women's testimony, rather than the reasons for the rulings. In *tafsīr* and grammatical works, the issue is how the verse could and should be read and understood in terms of vowelling, grammar, oral teachings, and variant readings, both from experts in that field, and from other recognised sources whose un-canonical readings were transmitted. In the period of Ṭabarī and before, the 'why' of the verse is not addressed, even when the question of women's similarity with men is raised, as in the interpretation of Sufyān b. ʿUyayna.

Early interpreters' omission of women's deficiencies is not sufficient evidence to assert that they considered women and men to be equal. Each genre was meant to include certain types of knowledge; different genres were platforms for different types of interpretive enterprise. In pre-10th-century works, grammar was at the heart of the interpretive venture that was *tafsīr*. The style of writing and argumentation of this period reflect elements of both the social and intellectual context. Social practice was an acknowledged source for certain authors, while the intellectual context, particularly inner-genre debates, shaped authors' arguments.

There is marked development between 10th-century *tafsīr*, which gave no explanation for the reason for men's and women's testimony being treated differently, and 11th- and 12th-century *tafsīr*, which attribute the difference to women's deficiencies, with some even addressing the question of why it is fair for women to have been created deficient. This change in the discourse on women was accompanied by technical changes in the way the genre was written and in the sources of authority cited in the genre. The genre of *tafsīr* was changing rapidly in the classical period in both form and function. With the increasing sophistication of the madrasa system, these works were intended for various levels of audience, and they were probably used in a variety of ways: as sourcebooks for preachers; as teaching texts for students in both open and closed teaching sessions; as personal guides for the literate. By the 11th century, there is often much generic crossover: *fiqh* and *ḥadīth* discussions enter into *tafsīr*. What might, therefore, have been taken for granted in an earlier period is spelled out, and *tafsīr* texts begin to speak about women's mental deficiencies. In this period, Sufyān's reading is attacked on the basis that it does not make sense for women and men to be considered equal. Although the Prophet's words had always ostensibly been a source for interpretation, the citation of his words became increasingly important as proof of the correctness of interpretations. The shift to the citation of sound *ḥadīth*s among some exegetes, described further in Chapters 3 and 5, is an important marker of the changing nature of authoritative sources through time.

The gradual introduction of women's deficiencies into the genre of *tafsīr* raises a question for the modern reader of these texts: Was there a change in exegetes' attitudes towards women between the early and the later period? It is certainly possible that the emergence of statements about women's deficiencies in these texts reflects changes in society. But on the basis of evidence in works of *tafsīr* alone, it is difficult to draw any firm conclusions about any large-scale change in attitudes towards women. The technical development of the genre as described must account for at least some of the change in the gender discourse in these texts. And the very nature of the genre makes it difficult to prove that it is a record of social changes (with certain exceptions, discussed further in Chapter 5). *Tafsīr*, originally the reports of the preaching of certain authorities, became heavily associated with the region of Khurāsān and the with the Shāfiʿī legal school. Discussions in this genre are influenced by these regional and legal affiliations, with their authors jockeying to justify their own position against that of rival interpreters or legal schools. Explanations for rulings in classical works may or may not represent their actual cause: such explanations may represent ex post facto justifications, rather than the underlying reason for a ruling.

Despite the difficulties of attempting to assess social change through works of *tafsīr*, there can be no doubt that social mores, common ideas, and common concerns played a part in the formation of both the original rulings and later interpretations. *Tafsīr* was meant, in part, to answer the questions of an audience: How could it be fair that women's word is worth half a man's? No doubt some thought this undervalued female testimony, while others thought it overvalued it. But if women were deficient in rationality, then why did they have spiritual responsibilities similar to men? Although the majority of exegetes simply took inequality for granted, several explained why such inequality was fair, just, and according to God's will. Such interpretations may reveal more, however, about the worldview of the interpreters than they reveal about the Qur'ān.

2

Modern Rereadings of Women's Testimony

In the medieval period, one might expect certain laws to discriminate against women's participation in the public sphere; however, for many people nowadays notions of fairness are predicated on the idea that all are treated equally under the law. The case of Mukhtar Mai referred to in Chapter 1 is an example of what is at stake in discounting a woman's word. For many Muslims today, it is difficult to imagine how justice can be served if women cannot testify to crimes, even those crimes that have been perpetrated against them. But most modern *ʿulamāʾ* do not grant women and men equal rights to testify in all arenas. I argue that the limitations they put on women's testimony are directly related to medieval rulings.

In what follows, I describe three approaches to Q. 2:282 that emerged in my reading and interviews; these echo the categories established by Ziba Mir-Hosseini. In the conservative approach, which is the approach in written *tafsīr* and many of my interviews, the core rulings on women's testimony were retained from widespread medieval interpretations, but the justifications were modern, often incorporating references to scientific findings. The reformist approach is opposed to the conservative approach. Rather than seeking to maintain medieval juridical rulings, the reformists seek a direct engagement with the sources of rulings, the Qurʾān and the Prophet, or, in the case of Shīʿī interpreters, the Imāms. Shunning the rulings of medieval *fiqh*, the reformists assert that women's and men's testimony is equal in all arenas. A third way is the blending of conservative and reformist: the neo-traditionalist approach, in which the *ʿulamāʾ* are open to reinterpreting some aspects of women's right to testify while retaining some elements of the traditional rulings against their testimony.

All of these approaches to women's testimony are shaped by both intellectual and social context, particularly since laws on women's rights have formed a crucial issue in the self-definition of both governmental regimes (as 'secular' or 'religious', for instance) and members of the *ʿulamāʾ* (as 'reformist' or 'conservative'). This is not the place for a thorough analysis of the relationship between state law and religious law in the various countries that are home to the *ʿulamāʾ* studied here; that would be the subject perhaps of another book. But a few words may give some sense of the context of these debates.

With the advent of the modern nation-state, many Muslim nations for the first time codified certain aspects of what is now vaguely known as 'Islamic law'. The process of codification changed the very nature of the legal process, which had been shaped by dissent and discussion, and was ultimately predicated on the judgment of the jurists and judges. In the pre-codification period there was no single 'law'; 'the law' as applied very much depended on the circumstances, including not only the legal school of the judge but also his own interpretation of that school's view. There were always dissenting views even within schools. Codification did not necessarily circumscribe the debates between the *ʿulamāʾ* that occur outside of the courts – the type of debates described in the next section – but it did mean that the court was obliged to follow one interpretation of the law. Both in those nations where state law is a form of Islamic law, and in those that follow secular law, dissenting *ʿulamāʾ* risk arguing against the state itself, which can have consequences. Modern jurists' and exegetes' opinions on women's testimony are therefore embedded in a larger arena of contestation and collusion among various actors within the ranks of both *ʿulamāʾ* and state over the nature of law and its application. It is important to bear in mind that while the relationship between tradition and modern conservative interpretation is in a sense causal, it is not inevitable: there may be complex sociopolitical reasons why the *ʿulamāʾ* seek to preserve particular interpretations of the law while disregarding others.

WRITTEN *TAFSĪR* ON WOMEN'S TESTIMONY: A CONSERVATIVE AND CIRCUMSCRIBED GENRE

This section consists of a brief survey of modern written works of *tafsīr* on the subject of women's testimony. My argument about these works is that, despite their authors' diverse interests, they are conservative and do not represent the variety and complexity of the modern discourse.

By 'conservative' here, I mean that authors within this genre are reluctant to advocate interpretations that are essentially new. Although the explanation for the ruling might be modern, this modern explanation justifies the traditional legal ruling on women's testimony. So the interpretation is not entirely 'traditional'; it is modern, but the core of the interpretation, its essence, remains as one of the accepted interpretations from the medieval period. Thus, the interpretations described here rely heavily on the medieval tradition of interpretation, even while they add to and amend what can be considered to be acceptably within the genre of *tafsīr*.

As I remarked in the Introduction, the genre of *tafsīr* is conservative precisely because it is, by its very nature, a repository of tradition and a bastion of traditionalism. Jansen uses an imaginary exercise to describe modern Qur'ānic interpretation. He asks his reader to imagine the exegetes 'working together in a large circular reading room, somewhere in the middle of Cairo'.[1] They view the Qur'ān from different perspectives: some seek to incorporate science, others to resist such innovation; but they all 'use the same reference library', going back to the same medieval commentaries, dictionaries, and works about the Qur'ān.[2] This shared source pool and close connection between the *'ulamā'* is one way of understanding the similarity between these works; it is also an indication of the purpose and nature of the genre in the modern period. When an *'ālim* decides to write such a work, part of his ambit is to demonstrate his familiarity with particular works within the tradition, even if he himself is a reformist. Thus, genre matters even in the modern period: any attempt to access the entire modern discourse through works of *tafsīr* would fail miserably; this genre is circumscribed and represents particular trends in thinking and reasoning.

The conservatism of the genre was not a foregone conclusion. At one time, it seemed that the genre of *tafsīr* might become a platform for reformist discourse. In the *Tafsīr al-Manār*, Muḥammad 'Abduh and Rashīd Riḍā argue against following traditional interpretations. On the question of women's testimony, the authors assert that it is incorrect to attribute women's diminished testimony to something inherent in women as a sex: 'Some have given as proof the makeup of women, asserting that the error or forgetfulness is due to their deficiency of rationality and religion, and others give as proof that women have excess moisture in

[1] Jansen, *The Interpretation of the Koran in Modern Egypt*, p. 6.
[2] Ibid., pp. 6–7.

their physical constitution ... but this is not convincing'.[3] Instead, according to ʿAbduh and Riḍā, women's diminished testimony is because they do not work outside of the home. In matters to do with the household, a woman's testimony counts as much as a man's; however, in financial matters and so forth, it is worth half of a man's. ʿAbduh and Riḍā accept that some foreign women do have experience in financial matters; however, because this is a minority, and the law is for the majority, the two-for-one ruling stands.[4] Although this interpretation preserves traditional rulings, it seems to open up the door to changing the interpretation based on current circumstances; nowadays, when women work with men in the public sphere, their testimony could count equally with men's. However, the reformist tendencies of *Tafsīr al-Manār* were not to have a lasting effect on the genre of *tafsīr*.

Later 20th-century interpreters within this genre typically incorporate, appropriate, and give modern glosses to medieval interpretations. An example is the interpretation of the former Grand Muftī of Egypt and Shaykh of al-Azhar, Muḥammad al-Ṭanṭāwī (d. 2010):

> The testimony of women with men is permitted according to the Ḥanafīs in monetary matters, divorce, marriage, the return after divorce, and everything except for crimes against God (*ḥudūd*) and those involving retaliation (*qiṣāṣ*). According to the Mālikis it is permissible in monetary matters and personal affairs, and is not permitted in rulings that affect the body such as *ḥudūd*, *qiṣāṣ*, marriage, divorce, and the husband's right to invoke his wife's return after divorce. Then He clarified the reason for the two women standing in place of one man in testimony, saying *if one of the two errs, the other will remind her*. Al-Qurṭubī says: the meaning of 'err' is forget, and error in testimony is forgetting a part of it and remembering a part, and the person who remains confused is erring. And the meaning: we have made two women in place of a single man in testimony, guarding against one of them forgetting, because each of them will remind the other. Because woman, on account of her overpowering emotions and the intensity with which she is affected by events, may imagine what she has not seen. It is therefore wise to have another woman with her by way of reminding of the truth, which they have between the two of them.[5]

Al-Ṭanṭāwī's interpretation could be verbatim from medieval sources, except for the final lines, which, instead of saying that woman's

[3] Muḥammad ʿAbduh and Rashīd Riḍā, *Tafsīr al-Qur'ān al-ʿaẓīm, al-maʿrūf bi-Tafsīr al-manār*, ed. Samīr Muṣṭafā Rabāb (Beirut: Dār Iḥyā' al-Turāth al-ʿArabī, 2002), v. 3, p. 109 (at Q. 2:282).

[4] Ibid., v. 3, pp. 109–10 (at Q. 2:282).

[5] Muḥammad al-Ṭanṭāwī, *Tafsīr al-wasīṭ lil-Qur'ān al-karīm* (Cairo: Dār al-Maʿārif, 1992), v. 1, pp. 648–9 (at Q. 2:282).

rationality is deficient, say that her emotions may overpower her rational sense, causing her to 'imagine what she has not seen'. Thus, like medieval authors, al-Ṭanṭāwī still refers to woman's mind – and indeed an element of irrationality – to justify the ruling; however, his explanation does not include the value judgment of woman's 'deficiency', or say that woman has less rational sense than man; rather, he implies instead that she has more emotions than man. Whereas medieval authors clearly stated that men are better than women, modern authors describe 'differences'. Conservatives' attempt to use neutral language to describe women's abilities, language that does not mention irrationality by name or (as I show later in the chapter) even denies it outright, is entirely modern. Aside from this modern justification, al-Ṭanṭāwī relies on the medieval jurist and exegete al-Qurṭubī and on a basic summary of the positions of two legal schools. Al-Ṭanṭāwī's approach incorporates medieval interpretations and rulings, providing them with a new explanation.

Sometimes such new explanations indicate mainstream currents of thought and debate at the time. For instance, the *tafsīr* published in Egypt in 1962 by Muḥammad Maḥmūd Ḥijāzī, a scholar at al-Azhār, begins as a medieval work might, and then includes a modern reference to women's work within the house:

> *If there are not two men, then a man and two women from those witnesses who are pleasing to you* on account of their religiosity and their justness, and the law has only put two women in the place of one man out of fear that one of the two might make a mistake, so the second will remind her. This is due to the paucity of exactness in women with regards to financial matters, and the paucity of their interest in the likes of that, because woman has the natural disposition for work within the house and its milieu, and bringing up children, and therefore her memory of financial transactions is weak.[6]

This interpretation was evidently somewhat influenced by the *tafsīr* of Muḥammad ʿAbduh and Rashīd Riḍā, for it says that women's lack of experience in financial matters leads to their reduced testimony in that sphere; but here the door is not really open for reinterpretation because, unlike ʿAbduh and Riḍā, Ḥijāzī locates the reason for this lack of experience firmly in women's natural inclination towards child rearing.

Some interpreters back up the view of natural disposition by referring to modern scientific findings. The Imāmī Muḥammad Karamī says: 'we may infer from this verse that woman is weaker at remembering than

[6] Muḥammad Maḥmūd al-Ḥijāzī, *Tafsīr al-wādiḥ* (Cairo: Maṭbaʿat al-Istiqlāl al-Kubrā, 1962–69), v. 3, p. 27 (at Q. 2:282).

man, and that is considered from a natural point of view because of the deficiency of the weight of the woman's brain'.[7] By citing science, he draws on objective facts (men's brains are heavier than women's) in order to justify a conclusion (women do not remember well) that is not supported by the scientific evidence. This is a common method, to which I return later.

The approach of finding new rationales to justify a traditional core interpretation is by far the most common method of interpretation in modern *tafsīr*. In the course of my research within the genre of *tafsīr*, I was unable to find even one example of a work that reinterpreted women's right to testify: all upheld the core medieval rulings, while replacing medieval justifications for the laws with modern ones. The following is a partial list of authors who take this approach: Muḥammad ʿAlī Ṭāhā al-Durra and Saʿīd Ḥawwā, both Syrians who were in the Muslim Brotherhood;[8] Syrian academic and member of the *majlis al-iftāʾ* Wahba al-Zuhaylī;[9] the Tunisian Ibn ʿĀshūr;[10] and the Imāmī Shīʿī scholars Muḥammad Javād Balāghī al-Najafī (d. 1933), Muḥammad Jawād Maghniyya,[11] ʿAllāmah Ṭabāṭabāʾī, Grand Ayatollah Naser Makarim Shirazi,[12] and Grand Ayatollah ʿAbd Allah Javadi Amoli.[13] Not all of these authors were always conservative per se: as we will see in the case of the creation of Eve, Ṭabāṭabāʾī is not closed to new interpretations and displays acute reasoning when describing why his interpretation is correct. But his interpretation of Q. 2:282 encompasses very little of the innovative thought of which he is capable; it consists of

[7] Muḥammad Karamī, *Al-Tafsīr li-kitāb Allāh al-munīr* (Qom: Al-Matbaʿa al-ʿIlmiyya, 1982), v. 1, p. 369 (at Q. 2:282).

[8] Muḥammad ʿAlī Ṭāhā al-Durra, *Tafsīr al-Qurʾān al-karīm wa-iʿrābuhu wa-bayānuh* (Damascus: Dār al-Ḥikma, 1982), v. 2, p. 68; Saʿīd Ḥawwā, *al-Asās fī ʾl-tafsīr* (Beirut: Dār al-Salām, 1975), v. 1, p. 661.

[9] Wahba al-Zuhaylī, *al-Tafsīr al-munīr fī ʾl-ʿaqīda waʾl-sharīʿa waʾl-manhaj* (Damscus: Dār al-Fikr, 1991), v. 1, p. 661.

[10] Muḥammad al-Ṭāhir Ibn Āshūr, *Tafsīr al-taḥrīr waʾl-tanwīr* (Tunisia: al-Dār al-Tunisiyya lil-Nashr, [1900?]), v. 3, p. 105–12.

[11] Muḥammad Jawād Maghniyya, *Tafsīr al-kāshif* (Beirut: Dār al-Malāyīn, 1968), v. 1, pp. 445-7.

[12] Nāṣir Makārim al-Shīrāzī (Makarim Shirazi), *al-Amthal fī tafsīr kitāb Allah al-munzal* (Beirut: Muʾassasat al-Biʿtha, 1990), v. 2, pp. 255-6.

[13] ʿAbd Allāh Javadi Āmoli, *Tasnīm tafsīr al-Qurʾān al-karīm*, ed. Muḥammad Ḥusayn Alhā Zādeh (Qom: Markaz Nashr Isrāʾ, 2007), pp. 627–45 (not contiguous); Muḥammad Javād Balāghī al-Najafī, *ʾAlāʾ al-raḥmān fī tafsīr al-Qurʾān* (Qom: Maktabat al-Wijdān, 1971), v. 1, pp. 248–9; ʿAllāmah Sayyid Ḥusayn Ṭabāṭabāʾī, *al-Mizān fī tafsīr al-Qurʾān* (Qom: Muʾassasat al-Imām al-Muntaẓar, 2004), v. 2, p. 440.

a grammatical explanation of the phrase '*if one of the two should err, the one will remind the other*' (Q. 2:282).[14]

It is my contention that the nature of the genre is at least partially responsible for this limited discourse. For the modern *ʿulamāʾ*, writing a work of *tafsīr* is a way of expressing familiarity and affiliation with the tradition; therefore, it is somewhat natural that traditional interpretations for the most part prevail, particularly in points of law. However, it could be that the verse also does not lend itself well to reinterpretation. It is an explicitly legal verse, with a clear statement of inequality between the sexes. Sadeghi argues that although laws can and do change through time, such change only happens when there is overwhelming pressure.[15] Within the ranks of the *ʿulamāʾ*, the pressure tends to be to preserve rulings rather than to discard them. The traditionalism evident in written works of *tafsīr* is also evident in the interviews of conservative clerics, whose views I describe in the next section.

THE CONSERVATIVE VIEW: MEN AND WOMEN ARE EQUAL, EXCEPT FOR THEIR BODIES AND MINDS

Before I met Dr Fariba ʿAlasvand, I had heard about her: an acquaintance mentioned her regular attendance at Dr ʿAlasvand's immensely popular lessons. My acquaintance told me that I could trust what I heard from Dr ʿAlasvand because she was the foremost authority on women's issues in Qom. For Dr ʿAlasvand does not just have popular appeal, she is a prominent figure in the scholarly world in Qom. She is on the scientific board of, and teaches at, the Center for Studies and Research for Women, a conservative think tank on women's issues; concurrently, she is a professor at Jāmiʿat al-Zahrā, which is the women's seminary in Qom, and she is the author of several books. She is learned in primary source texts and is fluent in Arabic, the language in which we spoke. We met in the lecture hall of the Center for Studies and Research; despite her hectic schedule, she was extremely generous with her time and we spoke for two full hours about her interpretation of the Qurʾān and women's status.

[14] Ṭabāṭabāʾī, *al-Mizān fī tafsīr al-Qurʾān*, v. 2, p. 440.

[15] Sadeghi, *The Logic of Law Making in Islam*, p. xii: '[T]he primary constraint [on the law] was imposed by the need for legal continuity: normally a law would not change, even if it failed to mirror new social values, as long as it did not become intolerable or highly undesirable'.

During the interview, Dr ʿAlasvand immediately referred me to one of her books, which she proceeded to give me, entitled *Critique of the Convention of Elimination of all Forms of Discrimination Against Women* (*Naqd konvensiyūn rafʿ kuliyya-i ashkāl tabʿayiḍ ʿalayhi zanān*).[16] The Convention of Elimination of all forms of Discrimination Against Women (CEDAW) is a treaty adopted in 1979 by the United Nations General Assembly. Ratifying states must agree to end legal discrimination against women and to treat men and women equally under the law. Iran is not a signatory; Dr ʿAlasvand's written critique of CEDAW explains why, in her view, the Convention contravenes Islamic law and human nature. The basic message of the book is that legal difference between men and women in Islamic law is not necessarily discrimination. She argues that difference is beneficial rather than harmful. That is because, according to her, Islamic legal provisions reflect the natural differences between the sexes.

The *Critique* includes a few pages on women's testimony, in which she summarises the Imāmī Shīʿī *fiqh* on women's testimony, according to the Marjaʿ al-Ḥurr al-ʿĀmilī (d. 1104/1693), who was a prominent Akhbārī. In ʿAlasvand's analysis, women's testimony can be divided into four different types of cases: cases in which women's testimony is accepted without men; cases in which the testimony of one woman is valid against that of four men; cases in which women's testimony, whether alone or with men's, is not accepted; and cases in which women's testimony is accepted along with men's.[17] She gives a brief explanation of each type of case: the first has to do with areas in which women specialise, such as the birth of a live child. Like the medieval source Mālik b. Anas, cited in Chapter 1, ʿAlasvand points out that testifying to the birth of a live child may have important implications for inheritance. This case rates an entire paragraph; thus, she emphasises the importance of women's testimony alone, without men. The second case, in which a woman's testimony may contravene that of four men, is in a case of adultery (*zinā*); this is when a woman can swear to her own innocence of the crime as a part of the *liʿān* procedure described in Chapter 1. The third case, in which women's testimony is not accepted at all, is in *qiṣāṣ*, *ḥudūd*, and divorce. And the fourth case, when women's testimony is accepted along with men's, is in monetary matters.[18] Notably, her source for these rulings is a

[16] Fariba ʿAlasvand, *Naqd konvansiyūn rafʿ kuliyya-i ashkāl tabaʿyiḍ ʿalayhi zanān* (Qom: Markaz-i Mudīrīyat Ḥawzah-yi ʿIlmīya, 1382/2004).

[17] Ibid., pp. 84–5. [18] Ibid., p. 85.

pre-modern jurist of the Akhbārī school; although she does not go into detail, she replicates these pre-modern rulings without question. What is modern about this summary is the emphasis that is placed on women's right to testify alone. While the framing of the rulings has shifted away from the medieval texts, the substance has not.

In her book, Dr ʿAlasvand did not clarify why women's testimony does not count equally to men's in all cases. In the interview with me, however, she explained that a woman's physiology is her defining feature. Women's hormonal cycles affect even basic decisions: buying shoes, sitting for exams. Thus, women need to look at themselves first as women, and organise their lives around this principle:

DR FARIBA ʿALASVAND: Being a woman is a reality, and we need to take everything into account from this framework. First it is necessary to see yourself as a woman, and from there take everything else into consideration. For instance, the issue of menstruation is very important, and you must plan for it. Now it has been established that for three weeks out of the month, women are under the influence of pre-menstrual tension.

KAREN BAUER: Three weeks!

FA: For three weeks you are involved with that and for only one week you are relaxed.

KB: Have you noticed that? I have never noticed that. Maybe for one week.

FA: No, only one week you can be completely relaxed. But three weeks out of every month a woman is involved with this [hormonal shift]. Scientists have counted two thousand signals to indicate this. This affects all of women's issues. You cannot, for instance, buy shoes when you are menstruating, because the size of your feet may change. Or you may feel uncomfortable because of having to take a test at the university. So it affects everything that has to do with women, everything in your life. You should consider the reality of the differences between women and men and then make a programme to deal with it. You should not think that women and men are equal and then not take our differences into consideration. We must look into the framework in which men and women differ, and then take these differences into consideration.[19]

[19] Fariba ʿAlasvand, Personal Interview, Qom, Iran, 8 June 2011.

For Dr ʿAlasvand, the physiological differences between the sexes show that equality is a myth; treating men and women the same is unfair to women. Only by being treated as women, with a different set of rules, can women feel truly relaxed and free. According to her, these physiological aspects are an advantage rather than a disadvantage. Yet to ignore them leads women into a state of being oppressed. As she says, 'it is a mistake for women to say that they wish to have equal rights to testify with men. No. God has in this way disentangled us from a difficult responsibility, by not forcing us to do this'.[20] Her assertion that unequal testimony is an aspect of God's care and protection marks an important shift away from the medieval discourse, which attributed it to women's deficiencies. And, in another shift from the medieval discourse, *ḥadīth*s are entirely absent from her discussions of women's testimony in both book and interview. She framed the medieval rulings within an entirely modern scientific discourse.

Indeed, science is at the heart of Dr ʿAlasvand's argument, which rests on her claims about women's hormonal balance and other measurable physiological signals. The reason that women cannot testify equally with men, she explains, is also established through science: 'we have scientific proof that women pay more attention to details, so they remember less. There is more likelihood that they will forget, because they pay attention only to details'.[21] Thus, as in medieval texts, women's minds are the root of their inability to assume full weight in testimony. But unlike medieval interpreters, Dr ʿAlasvand does not say that women's minds are less able than men's minds, or that they are 'deficient'. She concurrently insists on their equal value and their intrinsic differences. In her words: 'This does not mean that one is flawed and the other is flawless; it means that women and men have different functions, and so this is actually perfection for each of them'.[22] For her, the unequal rulings on women's testimony are beneficial for women; the burden is lightened on them.

To prove the scientific credentials of her claims, Dr ʿAlasvand referred me to the book *Why Men Don't Listen and Women Can't Read Maps*, by Allan and Barbara Pease, pop psychologists whose works have been translated into 33 languages and have sold millions of copies throughout the world. On her recommendation, I bought this book. It was immediately obvious why this work had so much resonance for the conservative *ʿulamā'* (and indeed for conservative Christians in the West

[20] Ibid. [21] Ibid. [22] Ibid.

who advocate traditional familial roles). Pease and Pease begin their book with a simple statement reminiscent of the words of Dr ʿAlasvand: 'men and women are different. Not better or worse – just different'.[23] They do not discuss the equality of the sexes, saying that this is a 'political or moral' question; however, they strongly assert the differences between them and claim to base their findings on neuroscience. The book describes women's detail-orientated vision, and men's superior night vision, in terms of the structure of the eye.[24] Mr Zibaei Nejad, Ḥujjat al-Islām wa'l-Muslimīn,[25] director of the Center where Dr ʿAlasvand works, quotes the findings of Pease and Pease on the differences between men's and women's eyes in order to justify the ruling that women cannot testify to having seen the new moon, which signals the beginning and end of Ramaḍān. In doing so, he uses science to back up a pre-modern legal ruling in the Imāmī school:

> One reason that women cannot testify about the moon is that women's eyes are capable of receiving more visual signals than men's. So women can see in a wider range; and as for men, they have better tunnel vision and can focus on things that are small and far away, particularly in darkness. Therefore, their testimony in seeing the moon is acceptable. Allan and Barbara Pease who have written this book say that women are better drivers during the day, but men are better at night because of these differences in their eyesight. Testimony about seeing the moon is because men have better tunnel vision, whereas women have better peripheral vision.[26]

Allan and Barbara Pease probably never imagined that their arguments would be used by conservative clerics in Iran to justify women's testimony not being counted equally to men's in court. But for Dr ʿAlasvand and Mr Zibaei Nejad, their work embodies the central idea of the conservative worldview on gender: men and women, while equal as humans, are essentially different in body and mind.

The work of Pease and Pease has the added appeal that it is written in the West. These authors are from a society where the sexes have equal rights; however, they still insist on the intrinsic differences between the sexes. Their books are a part of a global trend in popular science: detailed scientific studies are appropriated to make assertions that often go well beyond the conclusions of their academic authors. The science of sexual differences is a major bestseller in the West, where it is billed as

[23] Allan and Barbara Pease, *Why Men Don't Listen and Women Can't Read Maps* (London: Orion, 1999), p. xvii.

[24] Ibid., pp. 20–7.

[25] This is a ranking in the hierarchy that is just below Ayatollah.

[26] Zibaei Nejād, Personal Interview, Qom, Iran, 28 May 2011.

relationship self-help. It is hardly surprising that this literature has been picked up by religious conservatives to justify traditional roles for men and women. While authors of popular science have appropriated neuroscientific findings to make broad and general statements about the sexes that were probably never intended by the scientists who produced the studies, pop science is in turn appropriated in ways equally unintended by its authors, by groups who have an interest in justifying social or legal differences between the sexes. In Iran, works like this lend credence to the conservatives' view that the differences between the sexes in Islamic law reflect innate, unchanging characteristics. Because these characteristics are not bound to particular circumstances, the laws based on them are also timeless, and not subject to change or reinterpretation.

Dr ʿAlasvand's emphasis on the determining power of women's natural characteristics raises the question of her own position as a religious authority. Dr ʿAlasvand uses her empowered position to reaffirm a male-dominated social and legal structure, one that excludes women from certain aspects of testimony and judgeship, and that sees women's primary responsibility as being in the home. Yet, for Dr ʿAlasvand, a gendered social hierarchy is positive, not negative: it takes into account the sexes' natural characteristics. Furthermore, this conservative legal structure does not prevent women from all forms of religious authority or public empowerment. Some women have become *mujtahida*s, which means that they are entitled to exercise *ijtihād*, or independent interpretation of the law. Dr ʿAlasvand is working within the Qom *hawza* (Shīʿī seminary) to attain a higher rank for herself. 'Reaching the level of *ijtihād* has been one of my goals since I began to study in the *hawza*', she told me, 'and there is nothing preventing any woman from reaching this rank, but she must, herself, be able to bear the difficulties. For women, this will be more difficult than their role at home'.[27] She does teach men, when there is a need. And she pointed out to me that she has attended and contributed to the lessons of many prominent Ayatollahs: 'I always put forth my suggestions and my theses to others, whether they be men or women, in learned gatherings and study sessions. Some of the *marājiʿ* have affirmed the truth of what I observed and supported me in oral disputation, such as Ayatollah Khurasānī, Ayatollah Makarim Shirazi, Ayatollah Misbah, Ayatollah Jawadi Amoli, and the Supreme Leader Ayatollah Khameini'.[28] All of the men she names are prominent

[27] Fariba ʿAlasvand, personal email correspondence, 10 June 2014.
[28] Ibid. I will return to the question of women's authority in Chapter 6.

conservative Grand Ayatollahs or Sources of Emulation (*marājiʿ*), and participating in their study sessions gives her a much greater chance of recognition in her own right.

Despite their ability to rise within the ranks of the Imāmī Shīʿī *ʿulamāʾ* to a certain point, the highest rankings, such as Ayatollah, Grand Ayatollah, and Marjaʿ have eluded women. One reason for this is that they are not allowed to be spiritual leaders of both men and women according to classical Imāmī doctrine. In order to gain rank in Imāmī Shīʿī practice, an *ʿālim* needs to have not only a distinguished record of teaching and learning, but also a wide personal following. When a woman's audience consists solely of other women, as is the case for the vast majority of female scholars (*ʿālimas*) and mosque leaders, then half the general populace and most of the *ʿulamāʾ* are excluded. Even if they were not theoretically prevented from rising in the religious hierarchy, homosocial spaces of learning present structural obstacles for women who might wish to do so. A female-only audience enables conservative women to have authority without necessarily challenging the power structure of traditional male religious authority.

I chose to focus on Dr ʿAlasvand here precisely because she is such a good representative of the conservative view of women's testimony, regardless of her gender. Her main method of interpretation was to justify pre-modern laws with modern rationales, which, as I have mentioned, is a typical conservative approach. Notably, there is much in common between Shīʿī and Sunnī conservative methods and interpretations. According to most Shīʿī and Sunnī conservatives alike, women are prone to forget their testimony; forgetfulness was the most common interpretation of 'err' in the pre-modern sources, and therefore it is not surprising that the notion of forgetfulness is carried over into modern conservative discourse. But the exact descriptions of this forgetfulness differ between individual interpreters.

A related justification is that women's minds differ from men's. The Syrian Sunnī Wahba al-Zuhaylī, professor at the College of Islamic Law at the University of Damascus, is much closer to the medieval sources in his explanation. He cites both women's minds ('lack of exactness, paucity of attention, and their forgetfulness'), and also their lack of experience in monetary matters ('their information is limited and they have little experience').[29] He goes on to explain that even though today

[29] Wahba al-Zuhaylī, *al-Tafsīr al-munīr*, v. 3, pp. 110–11 (at Q. 2:282).

women work outside of the home, the ruling is for the majority; these exceptions do not change the rule.[30] Whereas al-Zuhaylī almost exactly echoes medieval texts, most modern interpreters couch mental differences in slightly more modern language. One of these is Grand Ayatollah Muhammad 'Ali Gerami.

I met with Grand Ayatollah Gerami, a welcoming and charming gentleman who had once been a student of 'Allāmah Ṭabāṭabā'ī's, in an immaculately clean office in the heart of Qom's old quarter. In perfect Arabic, and with a lot of good humour, he explained to me exactly why men are superior to women. Although he echoes the sentiment from medieval texts – that women's place beneath men is justified by mental differences – he denies that women are deficient in *'aql*, which was one of the common justifications used by medieval authors:

> Women – and I think you know this – are more sensitive and emotional than men. One might say of a particular man that he has no rationality (*'aql*) and that he is emotional, and it is possible for you to say that a particular woman is not at all emotional. But these are exceptions. With regards to the majority, women are much more emotional than men. The effects of this emotionality comprise various problems. If a woman were to be a judge, her emotions would enter into her judgment. If a woman wants to imprison a criminal, her emotions would enter into that decision. Women are more emotional than men, and this can cause problems. We do not say that women's rationality (*'aql*) is less than that of men – by the will of God, you have picked that up. No, women's *'aql* is not less than that of men. But women's emotions are stronger than men's emotions, and they have a greater effect on women's *'aql*.[31]

Ayatollah Gerami's argument is an example of how the medieval discourse of women's inferiority has been subtly modified today, in order to deny inferiority but uphold the basic idea of mental difference. I often asked conservative clerics about why women do as well as men at university, but cannot be in positions of authority. For Grand Ayatollah Gerami, women and men have the same intellectual abilities, but women's emotions can overpower their rational minds. This interpretation denies women's deficiency while upholding the doctrines that were justified through that deficiency. The theory of women's emotions overpowering their rational minds, which we encountered earlier in the interpretation of al-Ṭanṭāwī, has been present in modern *tafsīr* since at least the time of Sayyid Quṭb (d. 1966). It arose repeatedly in my interviews with Shī'ī

[30] Ibid., v. 3, p. 111 (at Q. 2:282).
[31] Muhammad 'Ali Gerami, Personal Interview, Qom, Iran, 14 June 2011.

clerics in Iran in 2011 and Sunnī clerics in Damascus in 2004. Exegetes cited various different types of source to prove their case. Since there were no sources in the medieval tradition that made this point – the medieval sources often deny mental equality between the sexes – the most common modern method of asserting the difference was on the basis of scientific and/or medical study. The Syrian Sunnī Dr Muḥammad Saʿīd Ramaḍān al-Būṭī asserted that his view has a medical basis:

> We have studied psychology, and we have a medical degree. Women have more tender emotions than men, and men have fewer tender emotions than women. Men's spiritual transparency and gentleness of heart, is less than the woman's, whereas the man is more rational (*ʿaqlāniyya*). We studied this issue in educational psychology and these words are said by an American doctor: 'I would not be happy except with a husband who has deeper thoughts than me, that is what makes me happy'. This is a reality that you need not read about, you may see it from experience. As for the man, if he sees that his wife is more emotional than himself, he is happy with that and takes comfort in her tender characteristics, and the woman is not comfortable, nor happy, except with a man who is smarter than she.[32]

Al-Būṭī, who was arguably the most popular Syrian cleric when I undertook research there in 2004, was highly respected for being both learned and moderate. His view was widely perceived to be the middle way, neither overly reformist nor overly conservative, and yet based on tradition. His statement exemplifies his approach. He cites his medical degree as well as outside sources to prove that the general position of a gender hierarchy in the medieval texts is correct and based on science and nature. Actually, he is subtly shifting the interpretation from the medieval texts, which routinely say that women are inferior to men. This enables him to maintain the core pre-modern doctrine (men have rights that women do not), while asserting that the doctrine is, and has always been, compatible with modern norms.

In the interview, he is referring to research he published in his book *Women: Between the Tyranny of the Western System and the Mercy of the Islamic Law.*[33] As is indicated by the title, the book is clearly a denouncement of the 'Western System'. But rather than demonising all things Western, al-Būṭī claims examples from the West to prove his point,

[32] Muḥammad Saʿīd Ramaḍān al-Būṭī, Personal Interview, Damascus, Syria, September 2004.

[33] Muḥammad Saʿīd Ramaḍān al-Būṭī, *Women: Between the Tyranny of the Western System and the Mercy of Islamic Law*, trans. Nancy Roberts (Damascus: Dār al-Fikr, 2003).

such as the example of the American doctor.[34] Although he claims to base his opinion on medical research, his ultimate source is common sense and cultural norms. The difference between men and women is something that he says I 'need not read about' – it is obvious from experience.

The inflexibility of conservative *'ulamā'* on most aspects of women's testimony is in part because the issue of women's testimony has become a key point on which *'ulamā'* identify themselves as conservative or reformist. The conservatives begin from the premise of unchangeability in laws on women, and they refashion the justifications for the laws around this principle. This premise of unchangeability sometimes creates contradictions in their interpretations. Wahba al-Zuhaylī's position is typically contradictory: women cannot testify because they have a lack of experience, but even if they should gain this experience, the ruling would not change. Al-Būṭī puts forth an argument about change and constancy in testimony laws in *Women: Between the Tyranny of the Western System and the Mercy of the Islamic Law*. This argument is more involved than Zuhaylī's, but it is also contradictory.

Al-Būṭī begins by framing his argument in a typically modern manner, stating that actually men and women are equal. It does not matter whether a witness is a man or a woman, he says; there are two main points in testimony: reliability and knowledge.[35] According to al-Būṭī, women are not allowed to give testimony in crimes, 'due to the infrequency with which women tend to deal with such crimes, including murder and the like',[36] because women would naturally run away or faint at the sight of a violent crime. So their testimony is disallowed in this instance, while it is granted full weight in matters in which women specialise, such as childbirth. Al-Būṭī's initial statement that men and women are exactly alike in testimony, which is entirely modern and based on the ideal of gender equality, is therefore undermined by his argument that women's inherent nature does not permit testimony in certain areas.

Al-Būṭī admits that in some areas, the rulings on testimony might change on account of changing circumstances. A man's word may be accepted in childbirth if a male doctor attends the birth; a woman's word may be accepted in pharmacology.[37] But certain modern practices go

[34] For instance, he says that when he visited the New York Stock Exchange, it was dominated by men, which explains why women's testimony is worth half of a man's testimony in financial matters (*Women: Between the Tyranny of the Western System and the Mercy of Islamic Law*, p. 216).

[35] Ibid., pp. 213–14. [36] Ibid., p. 215. [37] Ibid., p. 220.

against 'a fixed Islamic ruling or principle', and when that is the case, the practice should change rather than the ruling. Women's testimony on violent crimes is based on just such a fixed ruling:

> It is important to realize that if a certain modern practice is, by its very nature, in violation of some fixed Islamic ruling or principle, then it cannot serve as a basis for rulings relating to the acceptability of testimony by people who take part in this practice. After all, if a given practice or custom is itself invalid, then anything which is based on it would likewise be invalid. For example, someone might state that in societies, which have developed the custom of accepting women on the police force, women's testimony should be accepted in cases involving violent crimes. However, this argument cannot be accepted in view of the fact that the Lawgiver does not sanction the adoption of such a practice in the first place and, as a consequence, He would not sanction rulings which arise from it. The reason for the unacceptability of a woman's being employed as a police officer, or in other similar positions, is that the nature of the work involved in such a position holds the potential of robbing her of her femininity, which is a great injustice not only to the woman, but to the man as well, since it robs him of the inscrutable, God-given delight in 'woman as woman'.[38]

Al-Būṭī's argument is that certain types of ruling can change, but that others are based ultimately on unchanging prescriptions from the Lawgiver. One might expect that the fixed notions referred to by al-Būṭī are those mentioned specifically in the Qurʾān, but this is not the argument he gives. His argument is that the fixed and unchanging element is women's natural essence. It is women's inherent nature that must not be denied or transgressed; to do so would be unfair for both men and women. That is why he says that having female police officers is not sanctioned by the Lawgiver, when clearly such matters were not mentioned in the Qurʾān. The rulings in the book only give proof of women's essence. Women's unchanging essence can then be generalised to prove that Islamic laws are correct, even those laws not mentioned in the Qurʾān.

When I interviewed him in September 2004, al-Būṭī accepted that certain elements of a ruling could change according to time and place; he said that the rational human understanding of the Qurʾān is continually evolving.[39] At the time, I was very excited by this proof of his flexibility towards medieval interpretations. However, as his book makes clear, only limited development of laws is possible. In the passage quoted, core elements of the medieval rulings preventing women's testimony remain. Yet the rulings preventing men's testimony in the birth of children

[38] Ibid., p. 221–2.
[39] Interview with Saʿīd Ramaḍān al-Būṭī, Damascus, Syria, September 2004.

are changeable. Social custom has enabled change in one part of the law, because male doctors commonly attend births these days, but social custom does not affect the other part of the law, which will not permit women's testimony even when they have experience and expertise. Although conservative *ʿulamāʾ* adhere to core interpretations from medieval laws, and almost uniformly justify these laws based on the sexes' innate characteristics, ultimately there is some arbitrariness about which elements of the medieval core are retained and which are discarded. Or, perhaps to put it more strongly, because 'women's rights' is a defining issue for conservatives and reformists, for conservatives like al-Būṭī it is possible to change the laws on testimony in favour of men, but not in favour of women.

The argument that human nature itself prevents women from giving reliable testimony is one that is inherently challenged by legal systems in which women's testimony is accepted in all instances. When I went to Iran in 2011, I questioned some of the *ʿulamāʾ* about whether Muslim women in England could testify on an equal basis with men since the customs and laws in England permit women's testimony. This question was a way of assessing a cleric's openness to the ruling changing according to circumstance. Grand Ayatollah Makarim Shirazi, a highly respected conservative cleric and an author of a work of *tafsīr*, answered that a woman should follow her religious law rather than the secular law of the land. Thus, a Muslim woman in Britain may only testify if giving testimony is a necessity and it would cause hardship for her to resist; if she could avoid it, she should follow her religious law and refrain in cases where her testimony was not acceptable religiously.[40]

By giving her testimony alone, according to Makarim Shirazi, a woman might err due to her emotionality; when he was asked for the source of the information that women are more emotional than men, he replied: 'This is apparent. It is an obvious reality and everyone can see its effects in the society'.[41] It is common to appeal to an idea of common sense against testable hypotheses. Mr Zibaei Nejād, for instance, answered using the modern science of intelligence quotients:

> You may say that some IQ tests show that women and men have the same memory. My answer is that they do not have the same memory in the specific circumstances in which they are going to testify, because they are emotional and their sentiments may affect their memory.[42]

[40] Makarim Shirazi, Personal Interview, Qom, Iran, 25 June 2011. [41] Ibid.
[42] Zibaei Nejād, Personal Interview, Qom, Iran, 28 May 2011.

Western science here stands in for Western equality; for conservatives, it is not tenable because it would mean reinterpreting the medieval core laws. This is precisely why arguments about women's innate nature take precedence; arguments that rely on circumstantial evidence, such as the argument that women have less experience in certain matters, could admit the possibility of change. And although many conservatives admit change in 'non-essential' matters, such as men testifying to the birth of a live child, or, as we shall see in Chapter 6, the degree to which a husband is allowed to chastise his wife, for a variety of reasons women's testimony is considered to be a part of the unchanging core, rather than the changing periphery.

REFORMISTS: A NEW *FIQH*

The reformists are open to reinterpreting the law. They begin not from the premise of unchangeability, but from the premise of change and development. Reformists recognise that *tafsīr* and *fiqh* are disciplines that develop through time, and that these texts are shaped by the circumstances of their authors. On the subject of women's rights, one of the most vocal proponents of this view in Iran is Mr Mehdi Mehrizi, Ḥujjat al-Islām wa'l-Muslimīn. As I mentioned earlier, Dr Fariba ʿAlasvand had been introduced to me as the foremost authority on women's issues in Qom. Mr Mehdi Mehrizi was introduced to me in the same way – but this introduction came from another prominent reformist. Just as Dr ʿAlasvand speaks for many conservatives, so too does Mr Mehrizi speak for many reformists on the subject of women's issues.

I met Mr Mehrizi at his office in the Library of Ḥadīth in Qom. He says that, read correctly, the Qurʾān guarantees women equal rights to testify with men. He explains why he cannot rely on received *fiqh*:

> The fundamental problem and the main doubt is connected with the opinion of the jurists, not with the Book or the *sunna*, because what is mentioned in them is some of the general opinions, some of which are specific to one time and particular circumstances . . . and the proof that the results which the jurists reach on the basis of returning to the Book and the *sunna* are something different from the source of the Book and the *sunna*, is that the jurists present, on some issues, opinions and views that are completely opposed, to the extent that some of them make certain matters obligatory, while others forbid these matters.[43]

[43] Mehdi Mehrizi, *Masʾalat al-marʾa: dirāsāt fī tajdīd al-fikr al-dīnī fī qaḍiyyat al-marʾa*, trans. (into Arabic from Persian) ʿAlī Mūsawī (Beirut: Markaz al-Ḥaḍāra li-Tanmiyat al-Fikr al-Islāmī, 2008), pp. 265–66.

Mr Mehrizi observes that the jurists frequently disagree on basic premises in the law and about whether certain behaviours are acceptable; therefore, he asserts, law cannot actually be considered to represent the Qur'ān and the *sunna*: it is a product of the jurists' own opinions and of their time and place. 'There is no doubt', he says, 'that the social circumstances in which the jurists live affects their thought'.[44] He sees law as a living construct that is continually evolving.

The title of his book, *The Problem of Woman: Studies in Renewal of Religious Thought on Women's Issues* (*Mas'alat al-mar'a: dirāsāt fī tajdīd al-fikr al-dīnī fī qaḍiyyat al-mar'a*), indicates that he believes in renewal and change, rather than finding new justifications for medieval interpretations. His method is to re-examine the sources of law, particularly *ḥadīth*s that indicate women's place in society. Thus, he does not abandon the idea that sacred history, tradition, and religious law are binding for believers. Instead, he believes in renewing and reinterpreting the sources of religious law. Independent reinterpretation of the sources leads him to draw conclusions entirely different from the medieval jurists studied in Chapter 1 or the conservative clerics described in this chapter.

Because Mr Mehrizi is not bound to follow pre-modern rulings, he argues for women's testimony to be counted equally with men's in all arenas. He bases his opinion on the content of Q. 2:282, on events in its historical milieu, and on a grammatical discussion. Each of these in some way relates to the traditional sources of Qur'ān, history, and *fiqh*.

In his analysis of the content of the verse, he asserts that the subject of the verse is not women's testimony per se. It is about the writing down of testimony in order to protect the rights of the parties concerned in a debt.[45] According to him, it is a mistake to use this verse to speak about women's testimony in all arenas.

He uses historical examples to argue against strict limitations on women's testimony. It is clear, he says, that women's testimony was accepted among the Shī'a in the earliest period, because Fāṭima, the Prophet's daughter, testified that her father had bequeathed to her the oasis of Fadak, and her word was believed:

In the *Kitāb al-Kāfī*, there is a *ḥadīth* regarding the incident of Fadak. This was an incident that occurred in which there was a difference between Fāṭima and Abū Bakr. Fāṭima went to Abū Bakr and claimed that Fadak was hers. She went, not [her husband] 'Alī, and said that Fadak is ours, and Abū Bakr judged in favor of Fāṭima. This *ḥadīth* exists in *al-Kāfi*. If Fāṭima did not believe, and Abū Bakr did

[44] Ibid., p. 267. [45] Mehdi Mehrizi, Personal Interview, Qom, Iran, 9 June 2011.

not believe that the testimony of women was worth that of half of a man, then how is it possible that the testimony of women is not counted equally?[46]

Mr Mehrizi argues that because the *ḥadīth* exists in the well-respected *ḥadīth* collection *al-Kāfī*, it shows that these early authorities took women's testimony for granted. He asks how it could it be possible to include the *ḥadīth* in this collection if women's word were worth less than man's word. Rather than simply saying that *fiqh* is time-bound, therefore, he says that historical examples prove his point and that jurists through time have gotten it wrong.

Dr Mehrizī's next type of explanation is grammatical. The grammatical explanation engages both the words of the verse and also ideas in the theory of law. He focuses on the problematic term *ʾ-n*. As I described in Chapter 1, medieval interpreters had many theories about the way to deal with this particle, for although I consistently translate it as '*if* one of the two women errs', the literal translation is '*that* one of the two women errs'. Mr Mehrizi takes the literal interpretation of the term, and says that the term *an* is giving a cause (*ʿilla*) for the second woman's testimony. Here he refers to the legal theory of the ruling and its causes. He asserts that the ruling (*ḥukm*) of two women for one man rests on this cause/proof of the term 'that' (*an*). Therefore, only in a case *when* (not 'if') a woman does not remember the testimony does he allow that a second woman can be brought. According to him, this cause is not inevitable but circumstantial: 'if we were to look at a group of Bedouin, we might find a woman who does not enter into financial matters, and we can examine the situation to see if she will make a mistake'.[47] When the cause (the forgetfulness of the particular Bedouin woman) is removed, so is the effect. Therefore, for him, the verse speaks about the testimony of men and women as equals:

> But if the situation and the time changes, then the cause (*ʿilla*) changes and the ruling (*ḥukm*) changes. *When one of them errs, the other will remind her*, but when one of them does not err – for instance, today many women work in banks, many women are directors of factories, and the woman of this day and age does not differ from the man with regards to financial matters. So the verse makes things easier in this matter.[48]

Mr Mehrizi therefore rests his argument on grammatical analysis, but he also takes into account the changing times and historical circumstances of the verse. His interpretation uses traditional elements and methods to grant women and men equal rights to testify in all cases.

[46] Ibid. [47] Ibid. [48] Ibid.

History is at the heart of Mr Mehrizi's defence of women's rights. Many of his historical examples are from Shī'ī sources, and involve 'Alī b. Abī Ṭālib. In one, he describes a battle between the Persian forces commanded by the daughter of Chosroes (*bint Kisrā*) and the Islamic forces commanded by Khalīd b. Ka's. When they captured her, they brought her to 'Alī, who offered to marry her to his son Ḥasan. However, she refused, saying that she would not marry anyone but 'Alī himself. A relative of hers came to ask for her hand, but 'Alī said that she could choose for herself.[49]

For Mr Mehrīzī, the main sources of law are the Qur'ān and *sunna*, whereas for the conservatives a core source of today's law is the received law. But basing his reinterpretation on the *sunna* poses some problems: he must deal with uncomfortable *ḥadīth*s, such as the 'deficiency *ḥadīth*' mentioned in Chapter 1. His argument against the deficiency *ḥadīth* rests primarily on history as well. He mentions five main points against this *ḥadīth*, which I paraphrase here: (1) the version mentioned in the *Nahj al-balāgha* (a collection of speeches attributed to 'Alī b. Abī Ṭālib) was limited to a specific circumstance; (2) the narrations about women's deficient religion and rationality contradict the Qur'ān because the Qur'ān clarifies that the reason for the lack of equality between men and women in testimony is due to the forgetfulness, which women fall into, not due to a deficiency in their minds;[50] (3) this narration goes against reason (*'aql*); (4) the deficiency in rationality in the narrations does not indicate a substantial difference between men and women, but rather refers to the circumstances and milieu; and (5) This narration was propagated by some of the enemies of Fāṭima, the daughter of Muḥammad.[51] Three of these points refer to historical circumstances, while two of them indicate that the use of reason is appropriate to critique *ḥadīth*s.[52] The overall thrust of the argument is that at the time when the Qur'ān was revealed, women were not as involved in certain types of business, and were therefore likely to be forgetful; furthermore, it was in the interests of those who were against Fāṭima's inheritance claims to discount the testimony of women altogether.

In his argument against the deficiency *ḥadīth*, Mr Mehrizi therefore uses some *ḥadīth*s to counter others. This is possible because certain *ḥadīth*s, such as the deficiency *ḥadīth*, have long been used to justify legal

[49] Mehdī Mehrīzī, *Mas'alat al-Mar'a*, p. 234. [50] Ibid., p 240.
[51] These points are paraphrased from Ibid., p. 240.
[52] I return to the reformist doctrine of using reason against *ḥadīth*s in Chapter 4.

rulings against women; jurists do not cite *ḥadīth*s that may present the historical circumstances in a different light. He is a reformist, but his methods are in some ways similar to those of the medieval jurists. Like medieval jurists, Mr Mehrizi is picking and choosing; just as they did, he discounts information that goes against his notions of propriety. By dismissing the deficiency *ḥadīth*, and particularly by attributing the former palatability of the *ḥadīth* to historical circumstances, he prepares the way for his argument that the rulings themselves need to be renewed.

NEO-TRADITIONALISTS: OPEN TO REINTERPRETATION FROM A BASE IN TRADITION

Mehdi Mehrizi's view is unusual even among reformist *'ulamā'*. Far more common is the neo-traditionalist view: many aspects of testimony can be reconsidered, but some elements of the traditional rulings are preserved. Like the reformists, neo-traditionalists start from a premise of openness to reinterpreting the Qur'ān and medieval legislation, but they still ultimately refer to medieval *fiqh* and use it as their base point. This is the method of Grand Ayatollah Saanei, for whom the issue of women's testimony is of great importance: his son Fakhr al-Din Saanei has written a book about his views, *The Testimony of Women in Islam: a Legal Reading, an Exposition of the Theory of the Great Marja', Grand Ayatollah Yusuf al-Saanei.*[53]

Yusuf Saanei was born into a clerical family in 1937 and had a traditional education. He moved to Qom in 1951 and became a star pupil in the *hawzeh* system there. In 1955 he began studying with Ayatollah Khomeini, and continued to study with him until 1963. In the post-revolution government, Ayatollah Saanei became the State Prosecutor-General and was a member of the Council of Guardians and the Supreme Judicial Council.[54] He ended his time in government and returned to the *hawza* in 1984.

Grand Ayatollah Saanei adheres to the principle of dynamic *fiqh* (*fiqh-i pūyā*), which was developed by his teacher, Ayatollah Khomeini. Dynamic *fiqh* means that, when deriving the laws, one must take into account time (*zamān*) and place (*makān*). There is a difference between

[53] Fakhr al-Din Saanei, *Shahādat al-mar'a fī l-Islām qirā'a fiqhiyya, 'arḍ li-naẓariyyāt al-marja' al-kabīr samāḥat Āyat Allāh al-'Uẓmā al-Shaykh Yūsuf al-Ṣāni'ī* (Qom: Manshūrāt Fiqh al-Thaqlayn, 2007) (1428).

[54] Ziba Mir-Hosseini, *Islam and Gender*, p. 144.

this approach and the approach that says that the laws themselves can change; instead of changing the law, in dynamic *fiqh* a new ruling is imposed in response to changing circumstances.[55] Many of the reformist clerics I interviewed in Iran referred obliquely or directly to the principle of dynamic *fiqh*.

Grand Ayatollah Saanei has a commanding presence; he has a sharp wit and a powerful rhetorical style, which was apparent in our interview. He chose to address the question of women's testimony, and their intelligence, first. He was one of the few Grand Ayatollahs to attempt to establish common ground with me, to show that he understood the perspective of sexual equality:

> The problem is this: two women have been put in the place of one man. In the instance when both women and men see and hear something, and men and women both see as well as each other, one man is enough. But if a woman sees and hears the same thing, then two of them are needed in place of one man. Their sight is like one [man]. Their hearing is like one [man]. Their perception is the same. This is a certainty. Their understanding is like that of a man, and so why are two women put in place in one man? Why does Islam do this to women, putting two of them in the place of one man? I am restating the problem to show that I understand it well. If one understands the problem, it is much easier to answer it.
>
> According to scientific method, the difference between male and female is not justifiable. And in the place where a man's testimony is enough, a woman's testimony is also enough, without any difference between them. What we can deduce (*al-mustafad*) from the verse is that there is no difference between the testimony of a woman or that of a man. In some issues, it is necessary to have one witness, whether woman or man. In some matters, it is necessary to have two witnesses, women or men. This is my reading and understanding of the verse.[56]

Grand Ayatollah Saanei draws on science, but unlike the conservatives, he refers to science to assert that women's and men's minds are the same. In other words, although he did not cite specific scientific studies, his view of mental equality between the sexes was more akin to my own assumptions than were the views of some of the other Ayatollahs.

This excerpt highlights the most common method used by reformists to reinterpret the Qur'ān, which is to historicise its text. By asserting that particular verses and rulings apply to particular contexts, reformists are able to reinterpret these verses and rulings in light of changing circumstances. According to Grand Ayatollah Saanei, the verse was revealed at a time when women did not study arithmetic and go out of the house regularly. Even recently, he asserts, women were not educated in maths:

[55] Ibid., p. 113. [56] Yusuf Saanei, Personal Interview, Qom, Iran, 13 June 2011.

'I have seen a woman from my neighbourhood, and when her father came with the bill, if the sum came to three hundred thousand, she was not able to add it up. She said, "three hundred tomans!" She did not know three hundred thousand. That time was different from this time'.[57] This justification subtly reinforces the fact that social circumstances in Iran have changed even within his own lifetime. But we did not discuss whether his own personal opinion had changed through time; he simply used this personal anecdote as an example of why circumstances could require new laws. He explained further:

> There is not a change in the text of the Qur'ān, but there can be a change in the interpretation of the Qur'ān. Our understanding of the Qur'ān changes through time. Our derivation of laws changes through time. One example: women were at the time of the revelation of the verse ignorant of mathematical matters. But nowadays, women know about maths. Therefore, nowadays the testimony of one woman who is knowledgeable in maths can take the place of two men who know nothing about mathematics. In this case, one woman equals two illiterate men.[58]

Ayatollah Saanei is making the point that, although the Qur'ān is a constant, new laws need to be derived through time. In this case, knowledge about something determines the reliability of a witness. If a witness is not knowledgeable, then he or she will not remember something, and hence the statement in the verse that 'if one of the two women errs, the other will remind her'. Although grammatically the verse is clearly in the feminine and speaks about women, now it is not limited to women. He proposes a radical solution: the verse refers to knowledgeable people, so one knowledgeable woman's testimony could equal the testimony of two illiterate men.

When I asked him about the *ḥadīth*s that contradict this view, he rejected them. He asserted that God created men and women equal, so the idea that women could be deficient was absolutely false. But he does not reject all tradition. To back up his view, he cites pre-modern jurists who accept women's testimony in some matters. For instance, al-Shaykh al-Mufīd (Abū ʿAbd Allāh Muḥammad b. Nuʿmān, d. 413/1022) said that two women could testify to marriage. According to Ayatollah Saanei, that is because women are knowledgeable about marriage. He uses this ruling to support his view that it is knowledge, rather than gender, that determines the reliability of a witness, and it reinforces his argument that women's minds are equal to men's minds. But as I showed in Chapter 1,

[57] Ibid. [58] Ibid.

for pre-modern jurists, allowing women to testify in certain areas does *not* necessarily indicate that their minds equal men's minds. Ayatollah Saanei has a deep awareness of the pre-modern tradition and builds on it, but like the conservatives, his justifications for his rulings may differ from the original justifications in the pre-modern works of *fiqh*.

In the interview, I was given a clear and straightforward view of the reasons for women's testimony now being accepted on a par with men's, or in certain circumstances above men's: women and men are equal, and to say otherwise is false. However, in his book, his view of women's testimony was more nuanced. He had mentioned 'exceptions' in passing in the interview. A brief examination of the issue of fornication (*zinā*) in his book shows that sometimes he aligns himself with the near consensus of pre-modern schools, rather than accepting women's word on a par with men's absolutely.[59] In the interview, he used a common sense, rational argument to justify his position. He said, 'this is not because of any deficiency but because of concealing matters. This is why the testimony of two men is not acceptable, because the goal is to narrow the incidence, and not cover up lewdness (*lā yastur al-faḥshā'*)'.[60] He told me that the entire matter was discussed in the book and did not dwell on the point.

In the book, his method is to cite several views of the matter, to compare and analyse them. By looking at all of the views on women's testimony, he shows that the supposed pre-modern consensus on these matters was not absolute. He cites certain pre-modern *'ulamā'*, who accepted the testimony of three men and two women, or two men and four women in the case of *zinā*. Like these sources, he accepts women's limited testimony in *zinā*: two men and four women, or three men and two women.

In the case of homosexuality, including lesbianism, Grand Ayatollah Saanei rejects women's testimony entirely. He begins with many *ḥadīth*s, such as the following: 'On the authority of 'Alī, peace be upon him, "women's testimony is not permitted in *ḥudūd*, nor in retaliation (*qawad*)"'.[61] He then explains:

[59] There are also exceptions for more normal cases. The normal cases are summarized thus: 'With the elimination of personal affairs and the re-examination of the instances, the testimony of one woman, in these three instances, is like the testimony of one man; except if, in the instance, a proof is presented contrary to that, in which case the testimony of two women is equal to that of one man' (Fakhr al-Din Saanei, *Shahādat al-mar'a fī' l-Islām*, p. 202).

[60] Yusuf Saanei, Personal Interview, Qom, Iran, 13 June 2011.

[61] Fakhr al-Din Saanei, *Shahādat al-mar'a fī' l-Islām*, p. 220.

The law builds on lessening *ḥudūd*, and on not enforcing it in the case of the least doubt, so the Lawmaker does not make the paths of establishing *ḥudūd* easy, especially the *ḥudūd* of honour (*ʿirḍiyya*) which ... shatters the sanctity of the whole society....

With the comparison of the two sides together, we find that the stronger doctrine is non-acceptance of the testimony of women in lesbianism and gayness, and that is due to the sound narratives, with complete chains, that attest to that.[62]

There are two points to make here. The first is that Grand Ayatollah Saanei relies on *ḥadīth*s that reject women's testimony. Although he rejects some *ḥadīth*s, he accepts others: in this case, he argues, there is no proof for going against the narratives. His adherence to dynamic *fiqh* does not mean a complete abandonment of medieval *fiqh*; on the contrary, it means that in certain cases his views are predicated on the correctness of the medieval sources. For instance, his entire discussion of women's testimony in homosexual acts presumes that homosexuality is a crime punishable by death. This assessment of his relationship to medieval *fiqh* accords with Mir-Hosseini's assessment of Grand Ayatollah Saanei as a 'neo-traditionalist', rather than a 'modernist'.[63] The second point is that although he frames himself as a reformist, he uses pre-modern principles of law in his explanation. This recourse to traditional methods differentiates him from the Syrian al-Būṭī, who in his book relies on the principle of innate womanhood to justify his ruling. Ayatollah Saanei mentions a well-established notion in *fiqh*: testimony must not be accepted in case of doubt. This is the same reason cited by medieval jurists against women's testimony in *ḥudūd*.

While my interview with Grand Ayatollah Saanei included general, common-sense proofs and downplayed the exceptions, the book was more specific and detailed. That is, in part, because these are distinct genres, with distinct audiences. A verbal interview or sermon will not necessarily include the same level of detail and source citation as a written scholarly text. When I submitted this text to his office, they clarified the reason for these differences: 'it is worth mentioning that we believe an interview is more of a persuasive function rather than a detailed comprehensive reasoning and argument which you can come across reading the

[62] Ibid., pp. 220–1.

[63] Ziba Mir-Hosseini defined Ayatollah Saanei as a neo-traditionalist: in other words, a cleric who uses tradition but is open to reinterpretation. For Mir-Hosseini, this group is differentiated from the modernists, who represent a 'theoretical break from conventional wisdoms of Islamic feqh' (Mir-Hosseini, *Islam and Gender*, p. 19).

book. Thus, should one need to learn about Grand Ayatollah Saanei's views on women's testimony, certainly the book is the recommended source'.[64]

The persuasive function of the interview raises an important point about all of the interviews I conducted. Interviews between a Western female academic and an Eastern male Ayatollah had a particular function for each of us. In her interviews with Iranian clerics, Ziba Mir-Hosseini also noted that she stood in for 'the West', although she tried to resist assuming this role by presenting herself as an Iranian Muslim woman.[65] Unlike Mir-Hosseini, in some ways I played into this dynamic. My role as standing in for the West was especially pronounced in my interviews with conservatives. When speaking to clerics who argued essentially for the preservation of pre-modern laws, I argued as the token Western feminist, while they worked to convince me that biological differences between the sexes justify legal differences. The dynamic was subtly different in interviews with reformists and neo-traditionalists such as Grand Ayatollah Saanei. We began on more common ground. His emphasis was on convincing me that the Islamic system can be rational and that one's rational sense is an appropriate source for deriving laws and critiquing *ḥadīth*s.

SUMMARY AND CONCLUSION

Testimony is a topic that brings to the fore the question of deriving modern laws from medieval texts. It has practical and political implications, and it also cuts to the heart of the question of culture and religion: in the West, women and men have equal rights and duties to testify; so is the Qur'ān's statement on women's testimony culturally bounded, or is it a religious mandate? By writing about testimony, Ayatollah Saanei and other reformists such as Mr Mehdi Mehrizi are directly confronting the assumptions of those who say that pre-modern *fiqh* rulings must stand in all times and all places. They are declaring their belief that new laws may be derived when circumstances change. In so doing, they are responding not only to their intellectual heritage, but to the current intellectual situation in Qom. They are not alone in their beliefs; however, in 2011, when I conducted my Iranian interviews, very few people were willing to take such a public stand against current conservative legislation. In Ayatollah Saanei's words, 'I may be the only person who gives you these

64 Personal email communication from the office of Grand Ayatollah Saanei, 1 July 2014.
65 Mir-Hosseini, *Islam and Gender*, p. 19.

interpretations, but although my interpretation is less in terms of the number of people who subscribe to it, it is not less in terms of its quality'.[66]

It is clear that particular social and political contexts must exert some influence on the interpretations of the *'ulamā'*, what they are willing to say, and what determines conservatives' 'unchanging core' interpretations from the changing periphery. However, I would warn against a simple equation of 'reformist' or 'conservative' interpretations with political reform or conservatism. My Syrian experiences revealed a far more nuanced and complex picture.

When I interviewed him in 2004, Dr Muḥammad al-Ḥabash was a member of parliament. He explained to me that the religious ruling was that women's testimony differed from men's. However, he also asserted that certain types of ruling can change through time based on new circumstances. Thus, current Syrian legislation was acceptable:

> The verse is connected to the circumstances in which it was revealed. The expression of this verse is not applicable to all circumstances. The testimony of women in the law in Syria for instance is perfectly acceptable. When the parliament decided that a woman could be a complete partner in business, then there was no longer anything preventing the ruling from changing.[67]

Muhammad al-Ḥabash connects the current parliamentary laws with the Islamic permissibility of women's testimony. By drawing a direct link between governmental policy and his own opinion as an Islamic scholar, he highlights the tension that often exists in Middle Eastern countries between religious scholars and the state. At the time of my interview, al-Ḥabash was popularly perceived to be a state ally, and he clearly supported state reform in my interview with him. Yet he was forced to resign from all religious activities by the Minister of Awqāf in 2010.[68] It is unclear why he fell out of favour with the regime. It is possible that the move was a tactic on the part of the government designed to distance itself from reformist ideology in a time of increasing tension and conservatism in the country.

Al-Ḥabash's conservative colleague Muḥammad Sa'īd Ramaḍān al-Būṭī, whose work I cited earlier this chapter, met a much sadder fate:

[66] Yūsuf Saanei, Personal Interview, Qom, Iran, 13 June 2011.

[67] Muḥammad al-Ḥabash, Personal Interview, August 2004.

[68] This was reported in Syrian newspapers and was discussed by Joshua Landis in his blog 'Syria Comment'. See http://www.joshualandis.com/blog/muhammad-al-habash-resigns-from-all-religious-activities (accessed on 11 February 2014).

he was killed while preaching in his mosque in 2013. At the time of my Syrian interviews, I heard an anecdote from an acquaintance in the marketplace that indicated al-Būṭī's trustworthiness, while concurrently distancing him from the Syrian regime. The apocryphal tale was that in the days of the former Syrian president Hafez al-Asad, al-Būṭī had been offered a car as a 'gift' from the government. Al-Būṭī refused, and handed the keys back. But when he gave the keys back to the governmental official, it revealed a mistake. Al-Būṭī handed back the keys to a Lada, but he was supposed to have received the keys to a Mercedes. In refusing to be corrupted, al-Būṭī revealed the extent of the government's corruption: someone within their own ranks had switched al-Būṭī's bribe for an inferior one. For my market-stall acquaintance, this anecdote revealed al-Būṭī's trustworthiness and incorruptibility. However, was it true? Was he incorruptible, or did he have a more complicated relationship with the government? After civil war broke out in Syria, al-Būṭī did not condemn the government's actions, and according to some sources, he was an Asad supporter. When he was assassinated in his mosque in March 2013, it was widely speculated to have been the work of opposition groups, although opposition leaders denounced the killing.[69] In Syria, the ground was constantly shifting in the public's perception of which *ʿulamāʾ* were reliable and trustworthy, and it seemed that the state was also constantly shifting its alliances between reformist and conservative *ʿulamāʾ* to curry public favour. In the Syrian case, it is by no means clear that a relationship with the government determined the interpretation of the *ʿulamāʾ*. Instead, it may have been the other way around: an *ʿālim*'s position could attract attention, favourable or otherwise, from the government.

One of the reasons for the intellectual conservatism of the majority of the *ʿulamāʾ*, and their reliance on tradition, has been described aptly by Muhammad Qasim Zaman: 'the appeal of the ʿulama is … grounded in their guardianship of the religious tradition as a continuous, lived heritage that connects the past and the present'.[70] In other words, the *ʿulamāʾ* rely on tradition for their legitimacy and their appeal. Through the process of preservation of a core of that tradition, they forge the link between past and present. The importance of tradition might help to explain why those *ʿulamāʾ* who actively advocate for wholesale change and reform of medieval interpretations and laws are a minority. By asserting

[69] *Al-ʿArabiyya* newspaper online, 22 March 2013, http://english.alarabiya.net/en/News/2013/03/22/-Sheikh-al-Bouti-the-Syrian-Sunni-cleric-who-stood-by-Assad.html.

[70] Muhammad Qasim Zaman, *The Ulama in Contemporary Islam*, p. 180.

that the laws that were appropriate in the medieval period are no longer appropriate now, such reformists may undercut the basis for their own authenticity as *'ulamā'*.

So what makes tradition, and when is it all right to break from tradition? The following chapters discuss the relationship between *ḥadīth*s and interpretation, and show that on women's status 'tradition' is not as stable, or cut and dried, as it may seem.

CREATION

3

From a Single Soul: Women and Men in Creation

In the 14th century CE (8th Islamic century), ʿAbd al-Razzāq al-Kashānī (d. 736/1336) wrote a *tafsīr* that has been attributed to the mystic Ibn ʿArabī because of its philosophical and mystical elements. Kāshānī uses Q. 4:1, *fear your Lord, who created you from a single soul and from it created its mate*, to explain creation and the relationship of the universal rational soul to the bodily form. In this interpretation, the 'single soul' stands for Adam, father of humankind; 'its mate' stands for Eve, mother of humankind, and they in turn stand for deeper philosophical truths about the animal and the intellectual souls:

Who created you from a single soul[1] That is the universal rational intellect, which is the heart of the world, and that is the true Adam. He made *from it its mate*, i.e., the animalistic soul, which originates from [the intellectual soul, Adam]. It is said that she was created from his left rib, from the part which follows the world of generation and corruption, which is weaker than the part that follows the truth [God], and if it were not for her mate [the intellectual soul], then she [the animalistic soul] would not have been sent down to the world.[2]

For modern scholars and medieval interpreters alike, the question of equality between the sexes begins at the moment of human creation. But the manner of the creation of woman is not detailed in the Qurʾān, so the exegetes refer to other sources. In this account, the Aristotelian divisions

[1] Quoted references to Q. 4:1 in Chapters 3 and 4 are italicized but are not otherwise identified.

[2] ʿAbd al-Razzāq al-Kāshānī, attributed to Ibn ʿArabī, *Tafsīr al-Qurʾān al-Karīm lil-shaykh al-akbar … Muhyī al-Dīn Ibn ʿArabī* (Beirut: Dar al-Yaqẓa al-ʿArabīya, 1968), v. 1, p. 247–8. Thanks to Caner Dagli, who, many years ago, helped me to understand this passage.

into the universal rational soul and the bodily form are materialized, in the actual persons of Adam and Eve. Eve, he says, was created from Adam's left rib. The left is the side that follows the world of generation and corruption, and is weaker than the part that follows the truth, which is God, or the right side. He then explains that the intellectual soul came to the earth first, and was followed by the animalistic soul. As in many exegeses, Adam is the cause of Eve's existence. In this case, that is also because the spiritual exists in time before the physical embodiment, and there could be no physical world without the spiritual coming first. Eve causes Adam's downfall, his descent into the world.

The *tafsīr* of al-Kashānī ends up embellishing the text of the Qur'ān to such an extent that it has led one scholar to question whether there is necessarily any relationship between the Qur'ān and *tafsīr* at all.[3] The purpose of the exegesis, which is ostensibly to bring to light the meaning of the words of the text of the Qur'ān and to preserve earlier interpretations, becomes a tool for expounding on deeper truths that are suggested by the text. Commenting on Q. 4:1, *fear your Lord, who created you from a single soul, and from it created its mate*, some interpreters refer to the creation of Eve from Adam's rib, others to women's naturally physical, base nature as opposed to Adam's essentially spiritual nature, and still others cite the original marriage between Adam and Eve to justify their own legislation on marriage.

This chapter explores the Qur'ān's narratives on human creation and describes how medieval interpreters transform the fragmented and incomplete narrative of Eve's creation in the Qur'ān into a coherent story, a story used to argue against gender equality and to justify the gender hierarchy in legal and social norms. Aside from highlighting the gendered nature of interpretations of Q. 4:1, the underlying aim of this chapter is to examine the relationship of interpretation in the genre of *tafsīr* to its sources beyond the Qur'ān itself, particularly *ḥadīth*s. After a close reading of the Qur'ān on human creation, this chapter examines the medieval exegetical accounts of Eve's creation in detail, showing how interpreters use different hermeneutical strategies to build the Qur'ānic Eve into the archetypical woman, the nature of whose creation is the cause of many interpretations and rulings that grant men both privilege and power.

[3] Feras Hamza, '*Tafsīr* and Unlocking the Historical Qur'an: Back to Basics?', in *The Aims, Methods, and Contexts of Qur'ānic Tafsīr*, ed. Karen Bauer (Oxford: Oxford University Press, 2013), pp. 19–39.

Al-Ṭabarī listed several sources of interpretation in the introduction to his massive, multi-volume *tafsīr*; this list of sources has served as a kind of template for later authors (and for the basic diagram of the idealised sources of *tafsīr* presented in the Introduction). The first source on which he claimed to rely was the Prophet. He also said that he relied on *ḥadīth*s of the Prophet's Companions,[4] the Successors, and knowledge of the Arabic language.[5] One element against which al-Ṭabarī spoke strongly was the use of personal opinion in exegesis. It is his scheme of interpretation that has encouraged a view among some scholars that *tafsīr* is rooted in, and based on, *ḥadīth*s. *Tafsīr*, in this view, is a genre that essentially defines the meaning of the Qur'ān through the words of the Prophet and his Companions.[6] In subsequent centuries, *tafsīr* began to be judged as sound or unsound by the application of the labels *tafsīr bi'l-ma'thūr* (transmission-based *tafsīr*) and *tafsīr bi'l-ra'y* (opinion-based *tafsīr*).

But, as I outlined in the Introduction, all interpretation is influenced by a number of factors. Al-Ṭabarī does not limit himself to *ḥadīth*s; in many instances he does exercise his own judgment. The use of learned judgment is so widespread that scholars have questioned whether there is really such a thing as a *tafsīr* that is not in some sense opinion-based: they claim that all *tafsīr* is *tafsīr bi'l-ra'y*.[7] Even al-Ṭabarī is not against learned judgment: he is against whimsical, non-learned judgment; his claim is that his own judgment is based on the sources of Qur'ān and *ḥadīth*. But the question is: If all interpreters incorporate their opinions, to what

[4] Here I use the term *ḥadīth* as al-Ṭabarī used it, referring generally to sayings of trusted authorities, not just the Prophet.

[5] Al-Ṭabarī, *Jāmi' al-bayān*, v. 1, p. 92–3. See also Chase Robinson on the general question of the importance of Arabic in the 10th century in *Islamic Historiography* (Cambridge: Cambridge University Press, 2003), p. 15: 'Command of the Arabic language thus became the *sine qua non* for anyone with aspirations for work in the imperial administration or learning'.

[6] For instance, Brannon Wheeler says that 'Muslim exegesis relies first on the Prophet Muḥammad himself for understanding the context and meaning of the revelations'. *Prophets in the Qur'ān: An Introduction to the Qur'ān and Muslim Exegesis* (London: Continuum, 2002), p. 5.

[7] See, for instance, 'Tafsīr', *The Encyclopaedia of Islam* 2, by Andrew Rippin, and Ignaz Goldziher, *Schools of Koranic Commentators*, ed. & trans. Wolfgang H. Behn (Weisbaden: Harrasowitz Verslag, 2006), which has as its theme the subjectivity of the exegetical enterprise. Even al-Suyūṭī exercises interpretive choices in his entirely *ḥadīth*-based work *al-Durr al-Manthūr*. See Stephen Burge, 'Scattered Pearls: Exploring al-Suyūṭī's Hermeneutics and Use of Sources in al-Durr al-manthūr fī' l-tafsīr bi'l-ma'thūr', *Journal of the Royal Asiatic Society*, 3, 24, 2 (2014): pp. 251–96.

extent does approach matter? Are they all the same? In this chapter, I examine the effect of the hermeneutical approach of several different groups of interpreters: Sunnī traditionalists, Shīʿī traditionalists, Fāṭimid Ismāʿīlīs, and those who incorporated philosophy and mysticism. Each of these approaches has a significant effect on the content of interpretation. Yet each also reads the text of the Qurʾān according to common assumptions, and none relies solely on the words of the Prophet.

The interpreters had no choice but to read into the text of the Qurʾān. While the Qurʾān makes it clear that Adam and his spouse are the parents of humankind, the nature and manner of Eve's creation remain obscure. In her recent dissertation, Catherine Bronson discusses the possible sources for the Islamic image of Eve, including the Bible, para-Biblical accounts, and older myths.[8] This work gives insight into the mythical sources of the Biblical Eve, as well as the accounts about Eve that were circulating in the Islamic milieu which influenced the interpreters. The intertextual approach is particularly useful for a figure such as Eve, because the fragmented way that the Qurʾān tells her story implies that common knowledge can fill in the gaps. Most interpreters fill the gap by saying that Eve was created from one of Adam's ribs, following the Biblical account and that in a *ḥadīth* attributed to the Prophet. A minority Imāmī Shīʿī view says that she was created from the same clay as Adam. And one Muʿtazilite interpreter, Abū Muslim al-Iṣfahānī (d. 322/934), is credited with the interpretation that 'from' means 'of the same type'. Although the Qurʾān says that Eve is created 'from' Adam, it does not differentiate which 'from' is meant: from the rib, from the clay, or from the same type. Because of the Qurʾān's ambiguity, any of these interpretations is possible.

THE CREATION OF HUMANS IN THE QURʾĀN AND EARLIEST INTERPRETATIONS

Shorn of interpretation, and read apart from the rest of the Qurʾān's verses, Q. 4:1 is somewhat ambiguous. It reads: *fear your Lord, who created you from a single soul, and from it created its mate; and from the two of them spread forth many men and women.* What or who is the single soul, and what or who is the mate? What does it mean to say that the mate is created 'from' the single soul? Recently, some scholars have

[8] Catherine Bronson, 'Imagining the Primal Woman: Islamic Selves of Eve', PhD Dissertation, The University of Chicago, 2012.

argued that the exegetes' view of Eve as created from Adam's rib is not taken from the Qur'ān at all, and that interpreters were influenced by outside sources.[9] In the first part of this chapter, I examine all of the different Qur'ānic narratives of creation. I argue that these different types of creation are a part of the same story, and that, when all of the verses on the creation of Adam's mate are read together, it becomes clear that the first woman was created from (*min*) and for man (*lahu*). However, it is not entirely clear what 'from' (*min*) means. By examining various narratives of human creation from the Qur'ān, and comparing them with Biblical accounts, I argue that despite a certain fragmentation in the Qur'ān, it tells a story akin to the Biblical narratives of creation, and that some version of the Biblical account must have been well known and taken for granted in the Qur'ān's original milieu.

This section, then, follows recent trends in Qur'ānic studies to argue that ultimately the Qur'ān was not meant to stand alone in its original environment. It was meant to be heard or read with certain specific background knowledge. Bronson points to many para-Biblical traditions about Eve that were likely to have informed Muslim scholars. In order to take a full study of Eve's creation in the Qur'ān, I would follow her method of examining para-Biblical accounts; yet even the simple comparison between Qur'ān and Bible that I present here highlights key points of similarity. My analysis here sets the stage for the remainder of the chapter, in which it becomes clear that the exegetes took some form of the Biblical accounts of creation for granted, whether from the Bible itself or from para-Biblical and popular tales. Ultimately, I argue that the earliest interpretations may shed light on what the Qur'ān meant to its original audience.

The physical creation of humans is described along with that of the world in Q. 32:

> God created in six days, the heaven and the earth and all that is between them, then he mounted the throne; you have not, besides him, a protecting friend or mediator [32:5] … He who made all things good which he created, and who began the creation of man from clay [32:7]. Then he made his seed from a drought of despised fluid [32:8]. Then he fashioned him and breathed into him of his spirit, and appointed for you hearing and sight and minds [32:9].[10]

[9] Wadud, *Qur'ān and Woman*; Bronson, 'Imagining the Primal Woman', particularly pp. 85, 114, & 131.

[10] Qur'ānic translations in this chapter are Pickthall's; in some cases, I have made minor modifications. The Qur'ān includes many other references to the physical matter of

This passage bears a strong resemblance to the first Biblical account of man's creation; Genesis 2:7 reads: *And the lord God formed man of the dust of the ground, and breathed into his nostrils the breath of life; and man became a living soul.* Biblical stories were clearly known in the environment in which the Qur'ān emerged. The Qur'ān's creation stories do not replicate exactly the Biblical versions of the event of creation, but they do resonate with the Biblical narratives and with para-Biblical accounts. It seems clear that the creation story did not need to be told as a unified account in the Qur'ān, because the Biblical story, or a version of it, was already well known.

In the Qur'ān, as in the Bible, this first created human is the father of humankind, Adam.[11] There are numerous links among the verses

creation, and its verses are not uniform. Verses speak of man being created from water, dust, mud, a clot of blood, or God's word. They include: Q. 3:47, *[Mary] said: My Lord! How can I have a child when no mortal hath touched me? He said: So [it will be]. Allah createth what He will. If He decreeth a thing, He saith unto it only: Be! and it is*; Q. 3:59, *Lo! the likeness of Jesus with Allah is as the likeness of Adam. He created him of dust, then He said unto him: Be! and he is*; Q. 15:26, *We created humans (al-insān) from potter's clay, of black mud altered*; Q. 15:28–9, *And [remember] when thy Lord said unto the angels: Lo! I am creating a mortal out of potter's clay of black mud altered. So, when I have made him and have breathed into him of My Spirit, do ye fall down, prostrating yourselves unto him*; Q. 15:33, *[Iblīs] said: I am not one to prostrate myself unto a mortal whom Thou hast created out of potter's clay of black mud altered!*; Q. 17:61, *And when We said unto the angels: Fall down prostrate before Adam and they fell prostrate all save Iblīs, he said: Shall I fall prostrate before that which Thou hast created of clay?*; Q. 18:37, *His comrade, when he [thus] spake with him, exclaimed: Disbelievest thou in Him Who created thee of dust, then of a drop [of seed], and then fashioned thee a man?*; Q. 19:67, *Doth not man remember that We created him before, when he was naught?*; Q. 23:12–14, *Verily We created man from a product of wet earth; then placed him as a drop [of seed] in a safe lodging; then fashioned We the drop a clot, then fashioned We the clot a little lump, then fashioned We the little lump bones, then clothed the bones with flesh, and then produced it as another creation. So blessed be Allah, the Best of creators!*; Q. 24:45, *Allah hath created every animal of water. Of them is (a kind) that goeth upon its belly and [a kind] that goeth upon two legs and [a kind] that goeth upon four. Allah createth what He will. Lo! Allah is Able to do all things*; Q. 25:54, *And He it is Who hath created man from water, and hath appointed for him kindred by blood and kindred by marriage; for thy Lord is ever Powerful*; Q. 38:71–2, *When thy Lord said to the angels: Lo! I am about to create a man out of the mire, and when I have fashioned him and breathed into him of my spirit, then fall down before him prostrate*; Q. 40:67, *He it is Who created you from dust, then from a drop [of seed] then from a clot, then bringeth you forth as a child, then [ordaineth] that ye attain full strength and afterward that ye become old men – though some among you die before – and that ye reach an appointed term, that haply ye may understand*; and Q. 96:1–2, *Read: In the name of thy Lord Who createth, createth man from a clot.*

11 Adam also appears elsewhere in the Qur'ān – not in verses describing the creation of man, but in verses describing other events. The verses which mention Adam by name include:

describing the creation of the first humans, the parents of humankind, and those naming Adam. After breathing life into the man in Q. 32:7–8, God appointed 'for you [pl.]' the faculties of hearing, sight, and mind. By switching from the description of Adam in the singular to the description of human attributes in the plural, the text makes it clear that Adam was the model for all humans.[12] Other verses describe Adam's creation from the substances of the earth, which are often described as the materials of the creation of the first human; for instance, Q. 17:61 describes Adam's creation out of clay, and Iblīs's refusal to bow down to him. Humans are frequently referred to as the *sons of Adam*, presumably meaning the sons of the first man, who was created out of dust or clay.[13] Adam and his mate are, furthermore, described as the parents of humankind. Human beings are admonished not to disobey God in the manner of *your two parents* (*abawaykum*) – Adam and his spouse – at the conclusion of the story of the Garden of Eden.[14] And the creation of humankind is said to

Q. 2:31, 33, in which God teaches Adam the names of things and has Adam tell the creatures their names; Q. 2:34, in which the creatures prostrate themselves to Adam; Q. 2:35, in which Adam is commanded to dwell in the garden but not eat of the tree; Q. 2:37, in which Adam learns from the lord; Q. 3:33, in which God chose Adam and Noah; Q. 3:59, in which God created Adam from dust and said 'be' and he was; Q. 5:27, which is the story of the two sons of Adam; Q. 7:11, in which Iblīs refuses to bow down; and Q. 7:19–27 which tells of the garden of Eden. Adam is mentioned by name in Q. 7:19, Q. 17:61, in which Iblīs refuses to prostrate himself; Q. 18:50, in which Iblīs refuses to prostrate himself, and is one of the Jinn; Q. 19:58, in which God bestows his grace on Adam; Q. 20:115, which describes the covenant of Adam; Q. 20:116, in which Iblīs again refuses to prostrate himself before Adam; Q. 20:117, in which Iblīs is named as the enemy of Adam and his wife; Q. 20:120, in which Satan whispers to Adam about the tree; and Q. 20:121, in which Adam and his wife eat of the tree and see that they are naked.

12 Q. 22:5, 'O mankind! if ye are in doubt concerning the Resurrection, then lo! We have created you from dust, then from a drop of seed, then from a clot, then from a little lump of flesh shapely and shapeless, that We may make (it) clear for you. And We cause what We will to remain in the wombs for an appointed time, and afterward We bring you forth as infants, then (give you growth) that ye attain your full strength'; Q. 30:20, 'And of His signs is this: He created you of dust, and behold you human beings, ranging widely!'; Q. 35:11, 'Allah created you from dust, then from a little fluid, then He made you pairs (the male and female). No female beareth or bringeth forth save with His knowledge. And no-one groweth old who groweth old, nor is aught lessened of his life, but it is recorded in a Book, Lo! that is easy for Allah'.

13 Humankind is referred to as the 'sons of Adam' in the following verses: Q. 7:26, Q. 7:27, Q. 7:31, Q. 7:35, Q. 7:172, Q. 17:70, and Q. 36:60. Some verses speak of the creation of males and females: Q. 49:13, 'O people! We have created you male and female, and we have made you into tribes and nations in order to know one another'; and Q. 53:45, 'He created the spouses, male and female'.

14 Q. 7:27.

be from a man and a woman, in Q. 49:13: *O people, we created you from a male and a female.*

Another type of verse that speaks of human creation refers to a 'single soul' and (usually) 'its mate'.[15] This single soul and the mate are also Adam and Eve. Q. 4:1 begins with an admonition to the *people* (*nās*) to *fear your Lord.* This admonition defines the addressees of the verse, which goes on to read: *who created you from a single soul.* This seems to be an allusion to the creation of mankind; *you* is in the plural, and the verse addresses *people* – although there was a dispute over whether the verse addresses all people or just the Meccans, the majority view is that humankind is addressed. The word which I have translated as 'soul' here is *nafs*, which has many meanings; among them is 'self', or 'individual' (as in English, when 'soul' is used to mean 'person'). Not only did God create 'you' from the single soul/person, but *from it He created its mate.* This brings up the only linguistic difficulty of this verse: because of the feminine gender of the word 'soul', the pronoun 'it' is in the feminine. The feminine gender of the term 'soul' raises a doubt as to whether it can refer to a masculine being, namely Adam. That obscurity is clarified in Q. 7:189, where the 'single soul' is an unambiguous reference to a male being:

> It is He who created you [pl.] from a single soul, and created from it [him] its [his] mate so that he could find rest in her. When the man covered her, she bore a light burden, and went about with it, and when she grew heavy, they called upon God: We shall be truly grateful if you bestow upon us a healthy [child].

This verse makes it clear that the soul and the mate are not simply ethereal essence, but rather are two physical beings, capable of procreation.[16] The mate is a female being, which was created *for* the single soul, the male being, so that he could find rest in her. The verse at that point changes from the feminine, which is used to describe the 'soul', to the masculine, to show that this soul is Adam.[17] Q. 4:1 also emphasises the procreative power of the two souls, by describing how, after the mate was created, the two together created others: *fear your Lord, who created you from a*

[15] For instance, Q. 4:1, Q. 7:189, and Q. 39:6.

[16] If it were the case that the 'soul' referred to an ethereal essence, *Fear your Lord, who created you from a single [ethereal] soul, and from it created its mate*, the possessive 'its' would refer back to the ethereal soul, and so the mate is wedded to the insubstantial soul, which does not seem likely. I thus disagree with Bronson's reading of Q. 4:1. Bronson, 'Imagining the Primal Woman', p. 43.

[17] Cf. Bronson, 'Imagining the Primal Woman', pp. 83–5.

single soul, and from it created its mate, and spread forth from the two of them many men and women.

Does the Qur'ān support the Biblical version of creation from a rib, with the clear implication that women are a subsidiary creation? This is plausible, but there is an equally plausible argument that 'from' (*min*) means 'of the same type'. In three cases, the mates of the believers/humankind are described as *min anfusikum*, meaning 'of the same type': *God has made you mates of your own type* (*min anfusikum*) (Q. 16:72), *God has made for you mates of your type* (*min anfusikum*), *so that you may find rest in them, and He ordained between you love and mercy* (Q. 30:21), and *the creator of the heavens and the earth made mates for you of the same type* (*min anfusikum*), *and from among the cattle, mates* [*of their type*]; *He multiplies you in this way*' (Q. 42:11). However, these verses all differ syntactically from Q. 4:1, which does not mention *min anfusikum* (rather saying, 'from a single soul' *min nafsin wāḥidatin*). Given that women and men clearly are of the same type, it is possible to read: 'fear your Lord, who created you from a single soul [Adam] and created from [the same type] his mate, and spread forth from the two of them many men and women'. Equally plausible is the reading 'fear your Lord, who created you from a single soul [Adam] and created from [his rib] his mate'. Although the latter is the more popular explanation in the medieval period, a minority Shīʿī interpretation states that Eve was created from the same matter as Adam, and one exegete is credited with the interpretation that Eve was of Adam's type.[18]

The creation of Eve from Adam and the creation from the same substance as Adam each have a parallel in the Biblical accounts of creation. The creation of Adam and Eve is first described in Genesis 1:26–7: *And God said, Let us make man in our image, after our likeness ... So God created man in His own image, in the image of God created He him; male and female created He them.* In this creation account, significantly, male and female were created at the same time, seemingly as equal beings and seemingly from the same substance. A second creation story appears a few verses later, in Genesis 2:20–4. This story is much longer and more detailed, and specifies that the male and female were created differently:

> And Adam gave names to all the cattle, and to the fowl of the air, and to every beast of the field; but for Adam there was not found a help meet for him; and the

[18] Both views are described next. The interpretation that *min* means 'from its type' is the interpretation of the Muʿtazilī Ibn Baḥr (Abū Muslim al-Iṣfahānī); as discussed in the following, his view is cited by the Ḥanbalī Ibn al-Jawzī and the Shāfiʿī Fakhr al-Dīn al-Rāzī.

Lord God caused a deep sleep to fall upon Adam, and he slept. And He took one of his ribs, and closed up the flesh instead, thereof; and the rib, which the Lord God had taken from man, made he a women, and brought her unto the man. And Adam said: 'This is now bone of my bones, and flesh of my flesh: she shall be called Woman, because she was taken out of man'. Therefore shall a man leave his father and his mother, and shall cleave to his wife, and they shall be one flesh.

In this second account of Eve's creation, woman was created not only from man, but *for* him, as in Q. 7:189.

In sum, the Biblical story of Adam and Eve, or a version of it, must have been well known in the Qur'ān's original milieu, and the Qur'ān's story of human creation casts itself in the same vein as the Bible, although not precisely mirroring all of the Biblical details. Between the two texts, there is a basic shared outlook of Adam and Eve as the parents of humankind.[19] Although the story in the Qur'ān and that in the Bible apparently refer to the same protagonists, and some of the same events, the way these events are described differ in these two works. One prominent instance is that of the temptation in the Garden.

In the Bible, Eve is first tempted into eating the forbidden fruit, and then she tempts Adam, whereas in Q. 2:36 and 7:20 they are both tempted and they both eat, and in Q. 20:120–1 *Adam* is tempted and they both eat.[20] The Bible deals directly with the creation of the first woman, saying in one version that the Eve was created from Adam's rib; unlike the Bible, the Qur'ān does not go into any detail about the identity of Adam's spouse or about the exact manner of her creation. The question is whether the differences between these texts are significant and meaningful. It may be that the Qur'ānic account represents a real departure from the Biblical account and that the Qur'ān intentionally blames both parties. Yet it may be that, as in the view of the interpreters, the Qur'ān's account is shorthand for the Biblical (or a para-Bibilical) version. Perhaps the Qur'ān meant to tell the very same story, but told it in a slightly different manner.

It is also unclear whether the differences between Qur'ān and Bible on human creation are significant and meaningful. It is possible that, given the Qur'ān's use of *min nafs*, Eve was created from Adam's self or rib, as in the second Biblical account. It is also possible that *min* could refer to

[19] For more on Adam in the Qur'ān, see Roberto Tottoli, *Biblical Prophets in the Qur'ān and Muslim Literature* (Surrey: Curzon Press, 2002), especially p. 18 ff.

[20] For a more detailed analysis of these accounts, and their origins, see Bronson, 'Islamic Selves of Eve'.

the creation of Eve in the same type as Adam, as in the first Biblical account. And it is possible that in both the Qur'ān and the Bible, these types of creation are linked. This is not the place to solve these mysteries; rather, I raise them in order to understand the assumptions made by the medieval interpreters. From a modern perspective, these interpreters often seem to be reading into the Qur'ān in a completely unwarranted fashion, and indeed much modern secondary literature on the creation of woman starts from this assumption.[21] From their own perspective, however, medieval interpreters had a firm basis from which to make assumptions about the nature of creation, of temptation, and indeed of womankind as modelled on their primordial mother, Eve.

Before delving into the different hermeneutical approaches to interpretation in the period of al-Ṭabarī and beyond, I will present here two pre-Ṭabarī interpretations of Q. 4:1, that of Muqātil b. Sulaymān (d. 150/767) and Hūd b. Muḥakkam al-Hawwārī (d. 3rd/9th cy.). The content of the interpretations of Hūd and Muqātil represents certain important trends that are to continue throughout the history of the exegesis of this verse: the 'single soul' refers to Adam; 'its mate' refers to Eve, who was created from Adam, and specifically from his rib; and the creation of Eve reflects on the innate nature of all women. Eve's creation from a left rib, cited by Hūd, is also popular in later works of exegesis. But neither Hūd's nor Muqātil's work is a source for later texts. On the contrary, it is reputed that al-Ṭabarī believed Muqātil's *tafsīr* to be unreliable, while Hūd was an Ibāḍī who lived in North Africa, far from the centre of production of *tafsīr* in his time; neither of these exegeses were cited much by later exegetes. Thus, these two works are important not because they are sources for later works, but rather because they are examples of the type of interpretations and reports that may have been widespread in the pre-Ṭabarī period. They give us some idea of the widespread understanding of Q. 4:1 in the earliest period.

The *tafsīr* of Muqātil b. Sulaymān is the earliest reliably dated interpretation of the Qur'ān that we have.[22] He states that Eve was created

[21] See, for example, Zohar Hadrami-Allouche, 'Creating Eve: Feminine Fertility in Medieval Islamic Narratives of Eve and Adam' in *In the Arms of Biblical Women*, ed. John Greene & Mishael M. Caspi, (Piscataway, NJ: Gorgias Press, 2013), pp. 27–63. I only came across this article in the final stages of copy editing this book, and so have not included reference to its other findings here.

[22] Although the dating of the manuscripts is uncertain, it seems that they are not later reconstructions, and it has been argued convincingly that each of these texts preserves even earlier material. For Muqātil, see Kees Versteegh, 'Grammar and Exegesis: The Origins

from Adam's rib, and that this creation from a living being is reflected in her name: she was called Eve (Ḥawwāʾ) because she was created from a living being (*ḥayy*).[23] The implication is clear: Eve is a subsidiary creation, not created as Adam was, from the earth, but instead created from Adam himself. Although Muqātil does not cite *ḥadīth*s in this instance, his is a work that could be considered as a composite of his opinion, the prevailing view passed down through previous generations of exegetes, and common lore: the linguistic interpretation of the names Adam and Eve, both derived from the Hebrew, was also undertaken by Jewish exegetes. *Ḥadīth*s were probably taken for granted in this exegesis.

Hūd b. Muḥakkam al-Hawwārī (d. 3rd/9th century) has a much clearer citation of canon in his work, and also a much clearer statement about the implications of Eve's creation for the status of all women. The elements of his interpretation are repeated by many later *mufassirūn*, in particular the 'crooked rib *ḥadīth*', which he quotes in two versions:

> It is mentioned that al-Ḥasan [al-Baṣrī] said: the Messenger of God said: indeed woman was created from a rib, and if you wish to straighten her you break her; her crookedness lives with her. It is mentioned that Abū Hurayra said: the Messenger of God said: woman was created from a rib, do not attempt to straighten out the nature of one of them, for she is like the rib, and if you straighten her, you break her, and if you leave her you [may] enjoy her despite her crookedness.[24]

The 'crooked rib *ḥadīth*' and its variants imply that Eve's creation from a rib had direct consequences for all women's morals and dispositions. Men are naturally 'straight', while women – who are naturally crooked – cannot be 'straightened out'; as in the deficiency *ḥadīth*, men are the ideal human model. Women naturally deviate. The fact that Hūd includes two variants of this *ḥadīth* makes it seem likely that it was widespread in

of Kufan Grammar and the *Tafsīr* Muqātil' *Der Islam* 67.2 (1990): pp. 206–42, at pp. 206-9.

[23] The interpretation reads: '*O people! Fear your Lord* he puts fear into them, saying fear your Lord with awe *who created you from a single soul* meaning Adam *and created from it its mate* meaning Eve, from Adam's self (*nafs*), from his rib. And she is only called Eve (*ḥawwāʾ*) because she was created from the living Adam *and spread forth from the two of them many men and women* he says and He created from Adam and Eve many men and women, they are a thousand communities' Muqātil b. Sulaymān, *Tafsīr Muqātil*, v. 1, p. 355. Versteegh comments on Muqātil's use of 'folk etymologies' that do not derive from Jewish or Christian sources, as well as the elements in his interpretation that do derive from Jewish sources in *Arabic Grammar and Qur'ānic Exegesis*, p. 216.

[24] Hūd b. Muḥakkam al-Hawwārī, *Tafsīr Hūd b. Muḥakkam al-Hawwārī*, ed. al-Ḥājj b. Saʿīd al-Sharīfī (Beirut: Dār al-Gharb al-Islāmī, 1990), v. 1, pp. 345–6.

different versions in his time: it is likely that his work preserved earlier opinions. The editor of Hūd's *tafsīr*, al-Ḥājj b. Saʿīd al-Sharīfī, remarks on the great similarities between this *tafsīr* and that of Yaḥyā Ibn Sallām al-Baṣrī, who died in 199/815, nearly a century before Hūd. Ibn Sallām was born in Kūfa, lived in Baṣra, but then went to Qayrawān (in current-day Tunisia), where he stayed for a time and students listened to his *tafsīr*. After his stay in Qayrawān, Ibn Sallām went on *ḥajj* and then settled in Egypt, where he died; perhaps one of the students who heard this work in Qayrawān passed it to Hūd. Al-Sharīfī goes so far as to say that Hūd's text could be called an abridgement of the earlier work.[25]

This *ḥadīth* was further explained by a much later source, the exegete Abū Ḥayyān (d. 745/1353). Abū Ḥayyān's explanation may or may not represent the interpretation of earlier exegetes – it could well be an ex post facto explanation of the *ḥadīth*. He says that 'breaking' a woman is divorcing her, and that the 'crookedness' has both a literal and a metaphorical sense, in which the *ḥadīth* stands for 'women's unsteady morals, and their essence, which does not abide in one state; that is to say, their unruliness, which means that they are like a crooked rib'.[26] This exegesis, typically for the later period, goes much further than the early texts in assigning negative attributes to women.

Hūd transmits a report on the authority of Mujāhid, a variation of which is also cited by al-Ṭabarī and other interpreters. This report contains a word in Syriac that its transmitters, including Hūd, may not have understood; this could indicate the importance of transmitting the reports of early respected figures, even when the content of their interpretation was mysterious:

> *Fear your Lord who created you from a single soul* meaning Adam *and created from it its mate* that is to say Eve, from one of his short (*quṣayrā*) ribs, from the left side, while he was sleeping. Mujāhid said: he awoke and said '*Athā, athatī*', that is to say woman, my wife. *Athā* in Syriac is *ashā, ashatī*, that is to say woman, my wife; except that with a '*t*' it is Hebrew, and with an '*sh*' it is Syriac. And *ithā* is 'come here!'[27]

According to Ḥūd, Mujāhid cites Adam's words to Eve in their original language. But this interpretation does not stand up to linguistic scrutiny. Mujāhid's report says that Adam's first words to Eve were 'Woman, my

[25] Al-Ḥājj b. Saʿīd al-Sharīfī, 'Introduction', *Tafsīr Hūd b. Muḥakkam al-Hawwārī*, v. 1, pp. 21–2, n. 3, and pp. 23–4.
[26] Abū Ḥayyān, *al-Baḥr al-Muḥīṭ*, v. 3, p. 163.
[27] Hūd b. Muḥakkam, *Tafsīr*, v. 1, 345–6.

wife', which he quotes in Aramaic transliterated into Arabic as '*atha, athatī*'; he then quotes the words in languages he claims are Hebrew and Syriac (a dialect of Aramaic). However, the 'Hebrew' is actually Syriac, and vice-versa. Something has gone wrong at several stages of this transmission: at the very least, it seems that Hūd himself did not understand the report, or he might have corrected the mistake.[28] A variation of this interpretation, with similar mistakes, is attributed to Mujāhid by al-Ṭabarī in both his *tafsīr* and his *History of Prophets and Kings*. Rosenthal noted the linguistic implausibility of this interpretation.[29]

What do these examples tell us about women's status and about *tafsīr*? All of these interpretations imply that women are a secondary creation and of a lesser status than men, but none of them say so outright: such forthright statements of women's status come at a later time, when the genre was better developed. These examples also indicate that some interpreters believed themselves to be responsible for passing along what might be reliable transmissions from previous authorities, but not necessarily for verifying the facts of that transmission. Thus, Hūd cited two versions of the same crooked rib *ḥadīth* without criticising the chain of transmission of either of them, and also without commenting on the accuracy of either one; both he and al-Ṭabarī cite an interpretation on

[28] Nor is this interpretation consistent with Jewish interpretations of the verse: some Jewish commentators claim, contrary to Mujāhid's interpretation, that Adam spoke in Hebrew. In the *Midrash Rabbah*: 'She shall be called woman (*ishah*) because she was taken out of man (*ish*). From this you learn that the Torah was given in the Holy Tongue. R. Phineahas and R. Ḥelkiah in R. Simon's name said: Just as it was given in the Holy Tongue, so was the world created with the Holy Tongue. Have you ever heard one say, gini, ginia, itha, ittha, antropoi, pntropia, gabra, gabretha? But ish and ishah [are used]. Why? Because one form corresponds to the other'. *Midrash Rabbah, Genesis*, trans. Rabbi Dr H. Freedman (London: Soncinco Press, 1961), v. 1, p. 143. The editor's note clarifies that these interpretations mean Hebrew was the first language to be used; the other languages are Greek and Aramaic.

[29] 'Abū Jaʿfar al-Ṭabarī said: 'He means by His words *created from it its mate* from the single soul was created its mate. He means by "mate" the second [person] was [created] for him, and, according to what the interpreters have said, his wife, Eve'. An account of those who have said this: Mujāhid said, concerning His words *and created from it its mate*, 'Eve, from the shortest of Adam while he was sleeping, and he woke and said "Athā," which in Syriac is "woman"', al-Ṭabarī, *Jāmiʿ al-Bayān ʿan taʾwīl āy al-Qurʾān*, eds. al-Bakrī et al., (Cairo: Dār al-Salām 2007), v. 3, p. 2114. He gives the same tradition in his account of Eve's creation in his *History*. Rosenthal comments that 'The aspirated th indicated in the Ṭabarī text seems unlikely, as the Eastern Aramaic pronunciation of the word for "woman" was *attā* (*'ntt'*). However, the local origin of the Arabic tradition is, of course, uncertain. Modern Mandaic has *eththā*', al-Ṭabarī, *The History of al-Ṭabarī, General Introduction and From the Creation to the Flood*, trans. and annotated by Franz Rosenthal (New York: SUNY Press, 1989), p. 274, n. 671.

the authority of Mujāhid that seems to contain a linguistic mistake. In the following section, I undertake a further exploration of the interpretations in Sunnī traditionalist *tafsīr*.

CREATING CORE INTERPRETATIONS: SUNNĪ 'TRADITIONIST' *TAFSĪR*

This section examines the interpretation of Q. 4:1 in Sunnī *ḥadīth*-based[30] *tafsīr*, in which the narrative of Eve's creation from Adam's rib is universally accepted. The most popular question for these interpreters is: from which rib was Eve created? (The answer is usually a back or lower rib, on the left.) These interpreters are also interested in the substance of Eve's creation and the exact moment of creation: what happened, and what was said, which indicates the nature of Eve's creation and the spousal relationship as a whole. The implications are various. Eve is always a secondary creation, but some narrations emphasise Adam's loneliness without her, and thus value her as his helpmate and the object of his affections.

I begin with the work of al-Ṭabarī, whose massive *Jāmiʿ al-Bayān* is one of the earliest comprehensive *tafsīr* sources for the exegetical interpretations of the Prophet, his Companions, and early exegetes. Scholars have nevertheless challenged the overly simplistic view of al-Ṭabarī as the father of exegesis.[31] While later interpreters often seem to mine his work for early authoritative views, it is not often cited as a source in itself. Instead, the views attributed to early exegetical authorities such as al-Suddī, Mujāhid, al-Ḍaḥḥāk, and Ibn ʿAbbās become a part of 'common lore' and what is taken for granted about Q. 4:1 and the creation of Eve.

After describing his view of the larger implications of the verse, which is that there is a brotherhood of man by virtue of our creation from a single father and mother, al-Ṭabarī takes his first, and most basic, account of the verse's specific meaning from several early exegetes: al-Suddī (d. 127/744), Qatāda, and Mujāhid all say that the 'single soul' is Adam. He next explains the grammatical difficulty of saying that the grammatically feminine 'single soul' refers to a man. Al-Ṭabarī gives an example

[30] Here, as elsewhere in this book, I use *ḥadīth* in its broad sense, to mean sayings of early prominent authorities, not just the sayings of the Prophet.

[31] Two comparisons of the methods of al-Ṭabarī and Ibn Kathīr point out that although Ibn Kathīr claimed to rely on al-Ṭabarī, he actually introduced new methods. Jane McAuliffe, 'Qurʾānic Hermeneutics: the Views of al-Ṭabarī and Ibn Kathīr', in *Approaches to the History of the Interpretation of the Qurʾān*, ed. Andrew Rippin (Oxford: Clarendon Press, 1988), p. 61, and Calder, 'Tafsīr from Ṭabarī to Ibn Kathīr', p. 120.

from an exemplar poem in order to show that, in the pure Arabic of poetry, a feminine gendered word can be used to describe a man. The poem he cites says: 'your father is a caliph whom another bore (*abūka khalīfatun waladathu ukhrā*)'; in this case, the words 'caliph' and 'another' are grammatically feminine but refer to two men, the first and second caliph.[32] This explanation is cited by several later exegetes. He goes on to say that the word 'single' is only feminine because soul is feminine and 'if He had said from a single [masculine] soul (*min nafs wāḥid*), that would have been correct'.[33] The same explanation is given by his contemporary, the grammarian al-Zajjāj (d. 311/923).[34]

Finally, al-Ṭabarī states his opinion of the 'mate', saying that the second creation was Eve, created for the first; to back up his point, he cites several traditions on the authority of early exegetes. These emphasise Eve's creation for and from man. The first, on the authority of al-Mujāhid, has been described already: it says that Eve was created from Adam's shortest rib, and that when he woke, he spoke to her in Syriac, saying 'woman'; the second, on the authority of Qatāda, says that Eve was created from one of Adam's ribs; the third, on the authority of al-Suddī, describes a scene in the garden in which Adam is lonely and needs a companion, and Eve is created for him. In this last interpretation, Adam's life is not complete without Eve. Finally he cites an account on the authority of Ibn ʿAbbās, who cites the Jews:

> Ibn Ishāq said, He cast a slumber unto Adam, according to what has reached us on the authority of the people of the Book, from among the Jews and other learned people, on the authority of ʿAbd Allāh b. ʿAbbās and others, then He took one of his ribs from the left side and healed (*lāʾam*) the place while Adam was sleeping, and he did not awaken from his sleep while God created that mate Eve from his rib. He shaped her as a woman so that Adam could find rest in her. When the slumber was removed from him, and he awoke from his sleep, and he saw her in the Garden, he said, according to what they claim, and God knows best, 'My flesh, my blood, my wife!' And he found rest in her.[35]

It is unclear whether the 'left-rib' interpretation is really Jewish in origin; at least one prominent Jewish interpretation, Pseudo-Jonathan, says that Eve was created from the 'thirteenth rib of the right side'.[36] Al-Ṭabarī

32 al-Ṭabarī, *Jāmiʿ al-bayān*, v. 3, p. 2113. 33 Ibid., v. 3, p. 2114.
34 Al-Zajjāj, *Maʿānī al-Qurʾān*, v. 2, p. 1. 35 Al-Ṭabarī *Jāmiʿ al-Bayān*, v. 3, p. 2114.
36 Pseudo-Jonathan, *Targum Pseudo-Jonathan, Genesis*, trans. Michael Maher (Collegeville, MN: The Liturgical Press, 1992, series: The Aramaic Bible, The Targums), v. 1B, p. 24. The Palestinian Targum Neofiti in the same series has no mention of which rib was taken.

himself is unsure of the reliability of this interpretation, as he indicates by saying 'God knows best'. The point of this interpretation, however, is that it represents what Eve was to Adam: a kindred spirit and helpmate, in whom Adam could find rest. This echoes Q. 30:21, which describes the spousal relationship: *one of His signs is that He created mates from yourselves* (min anfusikum) *so that you could find tranquility in them, and he put between you love and mercy*. This interpretation, then, explains that the ultimate purpose of the first woman was to form a loving relationship with the first man.

Another early traditionist *tafsīr* is that of the Shāfiʿī Ibn Abī Ḥātim al-Rāzī (d. 327/938), who lived in Khurāsān, home of many prominent Shāfiʿī exegetes. Although Ibn Abī Ḥātim relied on some of the same sources as al-Ṭabarī (al-Suddī, Mujāhid, and Ibn ʿAbbās), they only have two of the same interpretations in common: al-Suddī saying that the 'mate' was Eve, and Mujāhid with the interpretation described previously, in which Adam says 'woman' in Syriac.[37] Whereas al-Ṭabarī had Ibn ʿAbbās giving the interpretation 'of the Jews' which is reminiscent of the Biblical account, Ibn Abī Ḥātim's Ibn ʿAbbās *ḥadīth* attributes men's and women's ultimate desires to the substance of their creation:

> My father told me, on the authority of Muqātil b. Muḥammad, that Wakīʿ said, on the authority of Abū Hilāl, on the authority of Qatāda, on the authority of Ibn ʿAbbās, the meaning of His words *and created from it its mate* is that woman was created from man, which made her crave for men, and man was created from the earth, which made him crave for the earth, so confine your women![38]

This *ḥadīth* justifies the laws that allow men to keep their wives indoors. Thus, this *ḥadīth* explains the implication of women's creation from men in terms of the necessary legal consequences of their moral dispositions. It could be that Ibn ʿAbbās gave both interpretations: the one credited to him by al-Ṭabarī and the one credited to him by Ibn Abī Ḥātim al-Rāzī; but it could also be that one or both of these interpretations was a later ascription.

Not all exegetes cite named authorities. After al-Ṭabarī and Ibn Abī Ḥātim, many give anonymous interpretations that vary the details of the story slightly. These unnamed variations probably represent common wisdom or taken-for-granted truths. One example is that of Abū 'l-Layth al-Samarqandī:

[37] In addition, he cites al-Daḥḥāk, a source that al-Ṭabarī did not cite, as saying that Eve was created from a back and lower rib.

[38] Ibn Abī Ḥātim al-Rāzī, *Tafsīr al-Qurʾān al-ʿAẓīm*, v. 3, p. 852.

Who created you from a single soul meaning Adam, *and created from it its mate* meaning He created from the self of Adam his mate Eve, and that is that God Almighty when He created Adam and put him to live in the garden, He delivered him unto sleep. While Adam was between sleep and wakefulness, He created Eve from one of his left ribs. And when he woke up, it was said to him, 'who is this, O Adam?' He replied, 'A women (*imra'a*) because she was created from a man (*mar'*)'. And it was said to him, 'What is her name?' He replied 'Eve (*ḥawwā'*) because she was created from a living being (*ḥayy*)'.[39]

Eve's secondary status is at the heart of this account. Her proper name, the name for women in general, and her essence as a woman are all derived from man. Adam knows who she is, and knows what she is, but Eve is silent in this text. This account is repeated nearly verbatim two centuries later by the Persian commentator Maybudī. Very little is known about this author except that he began writing his *tafsīr* in 520/1126.[40] Maybūdī's commentary includes three aspects: a translation of the Qur'ān's text into Persian (the first aspect), a description of its outward interpretation (the second aspect), and an esoteric interpretation (the third aspect). Esoteric and mystical interpretations have often been considered something of a separate genre within the umbrella of *tafsīr*. However, recent scholarly analysis of esoteric authors who write *tafsīr* works shows how they often use similar sources and methods to non-esoteric authors; esotericism is another layer added on to the outward, *ẓāhir* interpretations.[41] Maybūdī's *tafsīr*, with its three different aspects, is a particularly good example of the blending of techniques.

In his first level of interpretation, the translation, the significant point is that he translates 'soul' as 'individual' (*tan*); he does not understand it in the ethereal sense, but rather as a concrete person, as do other exegetes of his time.[42] The second level of his interpretation, the *ẓāhir* interpretation, tells the story of how Eve was created from Adam's rib, and bears a strong resemblance to that of Abū 'l-Layth:[43]

39 Abū 'l-Layth al-Samarqandī, *Tafsīr*, v. 1, p. 328.

40 Annabel Keeler, *Sufi Hermeneutics: The Qur'an Commentary of Rashīd al-Dīn Maybudī* (Oxford: Oxford University Press in association with the Institute of Ismaili Studies, 2006).

41 See for example, Keeler, *Sufi Hermeneutics*, chapter 2; and Martin Nguyen, *Sufi Master and Qur'an Scholar: Abū'l-Qāsim al-Qushayrī and the Laṭā'if al-Ishārāt* (Oxford: Oxford University Press, in association with the Institute of Ismaili Studies, 2012).

42 Rashīd al-Dīn Abū 'l-Faḍl Maybudī, *Kanz al-anwār fī kashf al-asrār*, ed. Muḥammad Kāẓim Busayrī (Qom: Daftar-i Nashr al-Hādī, 2001), v. 2, p. 401.

43 Maybudī's third level of interpretation, the esoteric, has little interest in terms of its gender discourse. Instead, he echoes the views of the earlier exegete al-Ṭabarī, by affirming that the creation from a single soul means that all humans have the same

Who created you from a single soul meaning Adam *and created from it its mate* meaning Eve, and the exegetes say: the Lord created Adam, and while Adam was sleeping, He created Eve from one of his left ribs. But Adam did not feel any pain from that, because if he had felt pain, he would not have felt kindly [towards her] and love would not have arisen between them, for God has said *and we have put love and mercy between you* [Q. 30:21]. When Adam awoke from sleep, it was asked of him: 'Who is this, Adam?' He answered: 'This is Eve (*ḥawwā'*) for she was created from something living (*ḥayy*)'. It was said to him: 'What is her type called?' He said: 'Woman, because she was created from man'.[44]

This account emphasises Eve's secondary status, but as in some of the accounts presented by al-Ṭabarī, it also stresses that Adam is meant to feel kindly towards Eve and to love her. This underlying notion of the original marriage, as hierarchical yet bounded by kindness, is one that persists in the interpreters' descriptions of the ideal marriage as described in Chapter 5.

Like the account of Abū 'l-Layth, Maybudī's interpretation is not attributed to a source. It may have been popular lore, the two authors may have had a common source, or Maybudī may have read Abū' l-Layth's account and may be citing him. It is typical of the genre not to cite. For instance, al-Māwardī's interpretation of Q. 4:1 is a kind of pastiche of earlier sources, but without the careful naming of individual reports: '*And created from it its mate* meaning 'Eve'. Ibn 'Abbās, Mujāhid, and al-Ḥasan said that she was created from one of Adam's ribs, and it is said "the left one", and because of that it is said of woman: the most crooked rib'.[45] The crooked rib *ḥadīth* that, in Hūd's work, was cited on the Prophet's authority, is here so taken for granted that it can be referred to in shorthand, rather than cited properly. Al-Tha'labī (d. 427/1035) does not cite anyone, simply saying that the 'single soul' is Adam, and 'its mate' is Eve, which for him was the most straightforward interpretation of the verse.[46] Al-Tha'labī's student al-Wāḥidī has three different works, but in none of them does he cite any immediate sources for his interpretation. In the simplest, the *Wajīz*, he just says that Eve was created from Adam's rib; in the 'middle' work, the *Waṣīṭ*, he cites the crooked rib *ḥadīth*' and in the comprehensive work, the *Baṣīṭ*, he cites the crooked rib *ḥadīth* and the grammatical caliph poem.[47] All of

essence. He then moves away from what al-Ṭabarī has said by affirming the importance of the unity of being.

44 Maybudī, *Kanz al-anwār*, v. 2, p. 405.

45 Al-Māwardī, *al-Nukat*, v. 1, p. 446.

46 Al-Tha'labī, *al-Kashf wa'l-Bayān*, v. 3, p. 241.

47 Al-Wāḥidī, *al-Wajīz fī tafsīr al-kitāb al-'Azīz*, ed. Ṣafwān 'Adnān Dāwūdī (Damascus: Dār al-Qalam, 1995), v. 1, p. 251; *al-Waṣīṭ fī tafsīr al-Qur'ān al-majīd*, ed. 'Adil Aḥmad 'Abd al-Mawjūd et al. (Beirut: Dār al-Kutub al-'Ilmīya, 1994), and *al-Baṣīṭ*, MS Nuru Osmaniye, 236.

these interpretations are either directly related to, or reminiscent of, the early interpretations on the authority of Hūd, al-Ṭabarī, and Ibn Abī Ḥātim, all of whom cite even earlier authorities. Yet in the *Basīṭ* these interpretations are not necessarily cited from specific authorities; they have become a part of the taken-for-granted, common knowledge about the verse. In this way, the genre is very much inward-looking.

Some new interpretations emerge in this period. Ibn al-Jawzī credits the Muʿtazilī exegete Ibn Baḥr (Abū Muslim al-Isfahānī) with the interpretation that 'from it' means 'of its type' (*minhā, ay min jinsihā*).[48] The interpretation, then, that Adam and Eve are of the same type, rather than that she was created from his rib, is not exclusively modern. This interpretation is also picked up by Fakhr al-Dīn al-Rāzī (discussed later in this chapter). Other exegetes, such as al-Zamakhsharī and Ibn ʿAṭīya, offer grammatical explanations of their own. In all of these cases, the exegetes consider the basic interpretation of the verse to be so commonplace that they do not cite their sources.

Both Ibn Kathīr and al-Suyūṭī cite the authors from within the genre whom they have consulted. A major source for their exegeses of Q. 4:1 is not al-Ṭabarī or al-Thaʿlabī, but rather Ibn Abī Ḥātim al-Rāzī. That is probably because Ibn Kathīr, al-Suyūṭī, and Ibn Abī Ḥātim are all Shāfiʿī exegetes. In this case, the school of law seems to play some role in which sources were deemed authoritative.

In his interpretation of Q. 4:1, Ibn Kathīr begins with an uncited interpretation: 'she was created from his left back rib while he was sleeping, and so he woke and saw her, and she pleased him and he liked her (*aʿjabathu faʾānasa ilayhā*), and she liked him'.[49] Again, the uncited interpretation probably represents common lore. He also cites interpretations from two works: Ibn Abī Ḥātim, from whom he takes the *ḥadīth* of woman's creation from man on the authority of Ibn ʿAbbās, and the *Ṣaḥīḥ* of Muslim, from which he takes the interpretation of the crooked rib (on the authority of the Prophet). It is noteworthy that he cites Muslim rather than other authors in the genre or the early exegetical authorities, and rather than simply presenting the *ḥadīth* with its chain of transmission. Ibn Kathīr's explicit citation of a *Saḥīḥ* work marks a change in the nature of authoritative sources for *tafsīr*.

[48] Ibn al-Jawzī, *Zād al-masīr fī ʿilm al-Tafsīr*, v. 2, p. 1.
[49] Ibn Kathīr, *Tafsīr al-Qurʾān al-ʿAẓīm*, ed. Muṣṭafā al-Sayyid Muḥammad et al. (Cairo: Muʾassasat Qurṭuba, 2000), v. 3, p. 333.

Al-Suyūṭī (d. 911/1505) wrote his innovative work over a century after Ibn Kathīr; in al-*Durr al-Manthūr*, he sought to use only *ḥadīth*s, with no commentary of his own on them. Like Ibn Kathīr, he cited 'intermediary' works, or the written works he consulted, rather than just the ultimate source of interpretation. Al-Suyūṭī cites five *ḥadīth*s about Eve's creation; most of these discuss which rib: back and left. Some of these are on the authority of several sources. In three of these cases, he cites Ibn Abī Ḥātim, and only once al-Ṭabarī, who is cited along with Ibn Abī Ḥātim as a source for the interpretation of al-Mujāhid.[50] One of the *ḥadīth*s cited by al-Suyūṭī speaks of the implications of women's creation: cited from Ibn Abī Ḥātim saying that, because of their creation from men, women's interest is in men.

Legal school, the views cited by prominent prior interpreters, and *ḥadīth*s on the Prophet's authority all seem to have some effect on later exegesis, but there is no one determinant for the course of interpretations: no one single iconic figure, nor one legal school. In all cases, the exegetes pick and choose from *ḥadīth*s, from *ḥadīth*-based works within their genre, and eventually from *ḥadīth* works outside of the genre, such as the *ṣaḥīḥ* works. And the most prominent form of interpretation for Q. 4:1 is the uncited reporting of what seems to be widespread, taken-for-granted knowledge. It seems likely that the content of interpretations affects their popularity. In the case of this verse, al-Ṭabarī is an acknowledged source for interpretation, but in actual practice Ibn Abī Ḥātim is drawn upon more frequently. Whereas al-Ṭabarī took a strand of interpretation that did not comment on women's intrinsic merit or their status, Ibn Abī Ḥātim cited a *ḥadīth*, widely cited by later authors, stressing women's status as a lesser creation and subject to male control.

FAṬIMID ISMĀʿĪLĪ INTERPRETATIONS[51]

This section analyses the esoteric interpretation of creation by the Fāṭimid Ismāʿīlī al-Qāḍī al-Nuʿmān, showing how he consciously took

[50] Burge says that al-Suyūṭī seems to have relied on four sources for his *tafsīr*, including al-Ṭabarī and Ibn Abī Ḥātim, who accounts for 25% of the *ḥadīth*s cited by al-Suyūṭī. See Burge, 'Scattered Pearls'.

[51] I would like to thank Husain Qutbuddin for his help with al-Qāḍī al-Nuʿmān's text. This section on al-Qāḍī al-Nuʿmān is partially reproduced from Bauer, 'Spiritual Hierarchy and Gender Hierarchy in Fāṭimid Ismāʿīlī Interpretations of the Qur'ān' *Journal of Qur'anic Studies* 14.2 (2012): pp. 29–46. The article gives a more complete explanation of Fāṭimid Ismāʿīlī attitudes towards gender hierarchy and spiritual hierarchy.

interpretation beyond the words of the Qur'ān. The narrative of the creation of the first humans is one essential point on which the Ismāʿīlī doctrine differs radically from that of the mainstream Sunnī and Imāmī Shīʿī doctrines. According to Fāṭimid Ismāʿīlī thinkers, the creation of Eve from Adam is a creation of spiritual hierarchy, not a physical creation. Al-Qāḍī al-Nuʿmān clearly states that the mainstream interpretation is false, and that the creation of Eve from Adam is not physical; instead, it is a spiritual fashioning of her as Adam's *ḥujja*, or his proof. In Fāṭimid Ismāʿīlī cosmology, each era has a prophet known as the *nāṭiq* (law-giving Prophet), followed by an executor (*waṣī*). In addition, each *nāṭiq* has several *ḥujaj*, who act as his representatives in the world. Al-Qāḍī al-Nuʿmān describes Eve as Adam's *ḥujja*. In his words:

God, blessed and almighty, created Ḥawwāʾ (Eve) from Adam, and that is known from His words *created from it its mate* [Q 4:1], and that is the creation of discipleship (*taʾyīd*), not a physical creation. That is to say God ordered Adam to undertake the discipleship (*taʾyīd*) of Eve, and her education, and her spiritual enlightenment; and he made her attached to him, and he made her his wife, and she was his *ḥujja* (proof), which God had given to Adam in place of Iblīs. [It is] not as the general [Sunnī] populace claims, that God Almighty delivered Adam unto sleep, and he slept, and then he extracted one of his ribs, and created from it Eve.[52]

In this passage, al-Qāḍī al-Nuʿmān explains that Eve is given to Adam as a replacement for Iblīs. The Qur'ān describes how Iblīs, alone of all of the angels, refuses to bow down to Adam because of his pride. Twice in the Qur'ān he is reported to say to God: *I am better than him* [*Adam*]: *you created me from fire, while you created him from clay* (Q. 7:12; 38:76). According to Ismāʿīlī thought, Iblīs had been designated as Adam's disciple (*waṣī*), but because of his refusal to bow down and accept Adam's authority, he is rejected by God.[53] Q. 2:34 describes this moment of Iblis's pride, and then says that Adam and his wife were sent to live in the Garden.[54] This is interpreted by al-Qāḍī al-Nuʿmān and other Fatimid Ismāʿīlī thinkers to mean that Eve was Iblīs's replacement in the spiritual hierarchy.

This interpretation shows that spiritual lineage is passed down not through physical descent, but through *taʾyīd*, a term that literally means

[52] Nuʿmān b. Muḥammad, known as al-Qādī al-Nuʿmān, *Asās al-Taʾwīl*, ed. Arif Tamer (Beirut: Dār al-Thaqāfa, 1960), p. 59.
[53] Ibid., pp. 55, 58.
[54] Q. 2:34: We said to the angels: Prostrate yourselves to Adam, and they did, except Iblīs, who refused and was proud, and became a denier.

'strengthening' but is translated here as discipleship, because it entails the passing on of specialised knowledge. Eve becomes Adam's *ḥujja* and his *waṣī* not because she is physically related to him, but because of the knowledge that he imparts to her. The discipleship of Eve to Adam entails shared knowledge: God imparts knowledge to Adam, which he then passes on to Eve through his mentorship and through accepting her *taʾyīd*. Knowledge creates the bond between them.

Significantly for the gender discourse, since Eve is a cipher for Adam's disciple, she is not necessarily a woman. Instead, expressions that refer to Adam's disciple or mate in the feminine indicate the relationship of the student to the teacher, in which the student is referred to as feminine, impregnated by the teacher's knowledge. This metaphor applies to many of the Qurʾān's references to women, both specifically and in general. The implication, though, is not that women have no place in the spiritual hierarchy; elsewhere, al-Qāḍī al-Nuʿmān mentioned women who acted as spiritual leaders. Fāṭimid Ismāʿīlī thinkers such as al-Qāḍī al-Nuʿmān upheld the outward, *ẓāhir* law on the gender hierarchy. But they also seemed to take a *bāṭin* interpretation: women could attain the ranks of the spiritual hierarchy that could be attained on account of learned knowledge (thus, those levels below Imām and *waṣī*). Women's spiritual abilities do not negate the *ẓāhir* of the text, the worldly gender hierarchy, but they seem to limit that hierarchy to the worldly realm. I shall return to this Ismāʿīlī metaphor of students in the female role, teachers in the male role, and its implications for the gender discourse in Chapter 5.

This particular Fāṭimid Ismāʿīlī interpretation was never mentioned in the works of *tafsīr* that I read for this study. That could be because there is no Ismāʿīlī work of *tafsīr* per se, and the interpretations of al-Qāḍī al-Nuʿmān are taken from his legal work. Although there are some works analysing individual *sūra*s of the Qurʾān, there is no Ismāʿīlī work that goes through the whole text line by line analysing its meaning. Since the genre of *tafsīr* relies heavily on the reports of specific, named exegetical authorities, and to a lesser extent on reference to other works within the genre, and since it is somewhat influenced by the Shāfiʿī–Ashʿarī orientation of its most prominent authors, reports like this one are excluded.

IMĀMĪ SHĪʿĪ *ḤADĪTH*-BASED INTERPRETATIONS

Eve's creation from a rib was by far the most popular view among the exegetes, but it was not the only interpretation that they took. The first mention of the alternative account is in the work of the Shī'ī al-'Ayyāshī (d. c. 320/932). He says, on the authority of Abū Ja'far, or Muḥammad al-Bāqir, the fifth Imām, that Eve was created from the clay left over after Adam's creation; since God could have created Eve from anything, why would he have created her from a rib? This interpretation reads:

On the authority of 'Amr b. Miqdām, on the authority of his father, he said: I asked Abū Ja'far 'From what thing did God create Eve?' He replied, 'What do they say regarding this creation?' I answered, 'They say: God created her from one of Adam's ribs'. So he said, 'They are wrong (*kadhabū*)! Was He incapable of creating her from anything other than a rib?' I replied, 'May I be your ransom, O descendant of the Messenger of God, from what thing was she created?' So he responded: 'My father told me, on the authority of his forefathers, that the Messenger of God said, "God Blessed and Almighty took a handful of clay, and mixed it with his right hand – and both of his hands are right – and created Adam from it. And there was some leftover earth, and from that he created Eve"'.[55]

This interpretation completely denies Eve's creation from a rib, and despite the clear statement that Eve is only created from Adam's leftover soil, might be understood these days as a basis for arguing the essential equality of the sexes. However, medieval Imāmī sources do not argue for gender equality. Furthermore, all of the Imāmī Shī'ī sources in this study that cite the 'leftover clay' interpretation *also* cite the interpretation of creation from a rib; al-Qummī (fl. 307/919) only cites the rib interpretation.[56] The rib *ḥadīth*s mirror Sunnī versions of the story. For instance, al-'Ayyāshī cites the following series of rib *ḥadīth*s:

On the authority of the Commander of the Faithful ['Alī b. Abī Ṭālib]: Eve was created from the *'quṣayra'* side of Adam, and the *'quṣayra'* is the smallest rib. God put flesh in its place. And on his chain of authorities, on his father's authority, on the authority of his ancestors, he said: Eve was created from the side of Adam while he was sleeping. On the authority of [...] Abū 'Abd Allāh, that God Almighty created Adam from water and clay, so the sons of Adam are interested in water and clay. God created Eve from Adam, so women are interested in men, so confine them in the house (*faḥaṣṣanūhunna fī l-buyūt*).[57]

These *ḥadīth*s, which echo the Sunnī versions cited previously, are on sound Shī'ī authority: two are on the authority of 'Alī b. Abī Ṭālib (Amīr al-Mu'minīn), and one on the authority of Abū 'Abd Allāh, in other words Ja'far al-Ṣādiq, the sixth Imām. Like its Sunnī counterpart on the authority of Ibn 'Abbās, this *ḥadīth* justifies the legal position that

[55] Al-'Ayyāshī, *al-Tafsīr* (Qom: Mu'assasat Ba'tha, 2000), v. 1, p. 363 at Q. 4:1.
[56] Al-Qummī, *Tafsīr al-Qummī*, v. 1, p. 130 (at Q. 4:1).
[57] Al-'Ayyāshī, *al-Tafsīr*, v. 1, p. 361–2 (at Q. 4:1).

women's husbands have the right to keep them indoors by explaining one of the implications of creation: men have been created from the earth, and therefore they are interested in matters of the earth. But because the first woman was created from a man, women's interests lie in men alone; thus, they may fall prey to sexual temptation and must be kept indoors. As mentioned in the Sunnī case, this *ḥadīth* justifies laws that allow husbands to confine their wives.

ʿAyyāshī's selection of *ḥadīth*s shows that *ḥadīth*s on the authority of the infallible Imāms support two irreconcilable views of creation: that Eve was created from Adam's rib, and that Eve was not created from the rib, but that she was created from the same clay as Adam. These contradictory views are preserved, without further comment, in a number of subsequent Imāmī sources.[58] Although different Imāmī factions may have taken different sides on this issue from an early period, no Imāmī commentators that I studied express their own opinion on the matter until Muḥsin al-Fayḍ al-Kashānī (d. 1091/1680), who judges between them.

Muḥsin al-Fayḍ was a prominent Akhbārī. As I mentioned in the Introduction, the Akhbārīs are a division of Shīʿī Muslims who rely on the reports (*akhbār*) of the Imāms for their interpretations. They are sometimes referred to as 'literalists', deriving their interpretations directly from *ḥadīth*s.[59] However, Gleave argues that the Akhbārīs are as 'innovative and intellectually complex' as other schools of law.[60] The adherents of this 'literalist' approach, although supposedly relying solely on *ḥadīth*s, actually dispute with each other as to the proper sources of law and interpretation.[61] As Gleave shows, Muḥsin al-Fayḍ goes beyond simple citation of *akhbār* and includes his own interpretations.[62] The Akhbārī movement is, therefore, somewhat parallel to the Sunnī traditionalists that I examined earlier: there is variation between works and methods, development through time, and picking and choosing from the sources. And, just as Ibn Kathīr drew on *Saḥīḥ* works in a way that previous authors did not, Muḥsin al-Fayḍ cites *ḥadīth*s from collections outside of the genre of *tafsīr*, thereby expanding the genre itself.

[58] Imāmī commentators who faithfully reproduce the *ḥadīth*s present in al-ʿAyyāshī's commentary include al-Ṭūsī, al-Ṭabrisī, and al-Baḥrānī.

[59] Robert Gleave, *Scripturalist Islam: The History and Doctrines of the Akhbārī Shīʿī School* (Leiden: Brill, 2007), p. 228.

[60] Ibid., p. xxiii.

[61] Ibid., especially in chapter 7: 'Akhbārī Qurʾānic Interpretation', pp. 216–44.

[62] Ibid., p. 232.

Muḥsin al-Fayḍ begins with the account that Eve was created from Adam's rib, citing al-Qummī and al-'Ayyāshī, whose report rests on the interpretation of the Commander of the Faithful, 'Alī b. Abī Ṭālib. He then cites al-Shaykh al-Ṣadūq (Ibn Babawayh al-Qummī, d. 381/991) and al-'Ayyāshī for the interpretation that Eve was created from the clay left over from Adam's creation, a report that ultimately rests on the authority of another Imām, Ja'far al-Ṣādiq. As he reports it, this *ḥadīth* is more elaborate than the versions found in other works of *tafsīr*. It explains why women are subservient to men, as well as justifying specific laws on marriage. It recreates the moment of Eve's creation complete with a conversation between her and Adam:

God, Blessed and Almighty, when He created Adam from clay, ordered the angels [to prostrate themselves before him,] and they prostrated themselves before him. Then God cast a deep sleep upon him, and created Eve for him, making her from the hollow of his abdomen. That is so that women are subservient to men. Eve began to move, and Adam paid attention to her, until she was called upon to go away from him. When he looked at her, he beheld a fair creation, which resembled him except in its being female. He spoke to her, and she spoke to him in his language. He asked her, 'Who are you?' And she said, 'A creation which God has made, as you can see'. Adam then asked, 'O Lord, who is this fair creation who has kept me company, who I gaze upon?' God replied, 'O Adam, this is my servant, Eve. Would you like her to remain with you, being your companion, and obeying your orders?' Adam responded, 'Yes, my Lord, and because of this I owe you thanks and praise'. God said to him, 'Ask me for her hand in marriage, for she is my servant, and she is suitable for you also as a mate for your sexual desires', and God bestowed upon him sexual desire. Before that, he had made him know everything [else]. Adam said, 'O Lord, I ask you for her hand in marriage, so what would you like for that [as a dower]?' God replied, 'I would like you to teach her about my religion'. Adam said, 'If you wish it, I owe you that, O Lord'. God responded, 'I wish it, and I give her to you in marriage, and join you to her'. Adam said to her, 'Come to me'. Eve responded, 'No, you must come to me!' [So] God Almighty ordered Adam to go to her, and he did. If he had not done that, then women would go out, and even ask for men's hand in marriage by themselves. This is the story of Eve, may God's blessings be upon her.[63]

As in other versions of the creation story, the method of Eve's creation has implications for the relations between the sexes and for women's status. In this case, women are naturally subservient to men because Eve was created from the hollow of Adam's abdomen. She was created for Adam, spoke his language, and was pleasing to his eye.

[63] Muḥsin al-Fayḍ al-Kashānī, *Kitāb al-Ṣāfī fī tafsīr al-Qur'ān*, ed. Muḥsin al-Ḥusaynī al-Amīnī (Tehran: Dār al-Kutub al-'Ilmīya, 1998), v. 2, pp. 176–7.

But after these details, the account veers in an unexpected direction: towards the laws and customs governing an Islamic marriage – a practical aspect of the Garden scene that was not covered in other exegeses. God acts in the role of Eve's marriage guardian, telling Adam, who is quite at a loss on beholding Eve's beauty, to ask for her hand. God then acts as her representative during Adam's proposal of marriage, setting the price of the dowry, joining them in marriage, and explaining to Adam the steps he must take. Adam's role as Eve's teacher acts as his dower, given to God rather than to Eve herself. This account seems to be influenced by both custom and law: the marriage takes place with the consent of the guardian, with the 'payment' of a dower, consisting of Adam's agreement to teach Eve, which, as I describe in Chapter 5, is a recognized duty of husbands towards their wives.

Early on, Eve defies Adam. When he asks her to come to him, she refuses, and God takes her side. This is why, Muḥsin al-Fayḍ explains, men ask for women's hand in marriage, and women do not ask for men's. Again, the events in the Garden bear a direct relation to current practice and law.

In each part of this story, men's superiority over women is asserted, but in the telling of it, Eve comes across as wiser than Adam. After all, despite the fact that he is supposed to teach her about God's law, she is the one who understands it first, knowing that Adam must come to her. Furthermore, she is not shy about defying Adam, despite God's assurances to him that she will obey. In her defiance she is correct, and God agrees with her, not taking Adam's side. Unlike the earliest versions of the story, Adam does not name Eve, and he does not say 'woman, my wife!' Instead, he must ask God about her, and God informs him of Eve's identity.

After this involved tale, Fayḍ moots the possibility of reconciling the interpretation of creation from a rib and creation from clay. He cites al-Ṣadūq as saying that the best interpretation is that Eve was created from one of Adam's left ribs, and the meaning is that she was created from the clay that was left over after his creation. This is why, explains al-Ṣadūq, men have one rib fewer than women.[64] Although his assertion may have represented the state of scientific knowledge in the time of al-Ṣadūq, it is not true: both sexes have twelve pairs of ribs. From today's perspective, instead of being a proof of the truth of his interpretation, this is an example of how common understandings of science and biology can shape – or be shaped by – Qur'ānic interpretation.

[64] Ibid., v. 2, p. 178.

Muḥsin al-Fayḍ agrees with the view that women have fewer ribs because it reconciles the seemingly irreconcilable positions in al-ʿAyyāshī's exegesis. He goes on to explain the deeper significance of this interpretation: men have a natural propensity towards the spiritual world, represented by the right side, and women incline towards the physical world, represented by the left side.

I say, what has been transmitted to us to the effect that Eve was created from one of Adam's left ribs is an indication that the bodily, animalistic tendencies are stronger in women than in men, and the spiritual, angelic (*malakīya*) tendencies are the other way around. That is because 'right' is among those terms which alludes to the spiritual, heavenly world (*ʿālam al-malakūt al-rūḥānī*), and the 'left' is among those terms which allude to the world of the physical realm (*ʿālam al-mulk al-jismānī*). The 'clay' is the substance of the body, while the 'right' is the substance of the spirit, and there is no physical without spiritual (*lā mulk illā bi-malakūt*). This is what is meant by the saying of the Imam, 'both of His hands are right'. The left hand rib missing (*manqūṣ*) from Adam alludes to some of the desires that originate from the dominance of the bodily [realm] (*ghalabat al-jismīya*), which is a characteristic of the created [physical] world (*ʿālam al-khalq*). These desires are the 'leftover clay' extracted from Adam's interior which then became the substance of Eve's creation. The Imam draws attention, in his *ḥadīth*, to the heavenly and commanding tendencies that are stronger in men than the tendencies towards the worldly (*mulk*) and the physical (*khalq*). It is the other way around in women.[65]

According to Muḥsin al-Fayḍ, the differences in the natures of men and women all come down to the fact that Eve was created from a left rib, removed from Adam. The right is the side of the spiritual realm, so men, missing the left rib, are naturally more spiritual. Meanwhile, the left is the side of the bodily physical realm, and so women, created with material taken from Adam's left rib, are naturally inclined towards the physical world.

This interpretation takes into account the rib mentioned in one *ḥadīth*, and it takes into account the clay mentioned in another, but it does not take into account the fact that, in the original *ḥadīth*, the Imām Abū Jaʿfar said that the interpretation of the rib was incorrect. In this interpretation, Muḥsin al-Fayḍ reconciles two positions that are actually irreconcilable. He then claims to have secret knowledge because of his adherence to the words of the Imāms.

Thus the outward appearance is a sign of the inner [truth] (*al-ẓāhir ʿunwān al-bāṭin*),[66] and this is the secret behind the omission in men's bodies, in relation to

[65] Ibid., v. 2, p. 178.

[66] This could mean one of two things (or it could mean both). The outward appearance of the missing rib could be a sign of the intrinsic differences between men and women. Or

women's. The secrets of God are only attained by the initiated (*asrār Allāh lā yanāluhā illā ahl al-sirr*). And disbelief in the words of the infallible [Imāms] is represented by the understanding of the Sunnīs (*al-ʿāmma*), which is based on the apparent meanings and not the origin of the *ḥadīths*.[67]

The story of creation becomes a vehicle for a polemical attack against the Sunnīs who are not initiated into the true ways of the Imāms and, through them, to the truth behind the *ḥadīths*. In other words, instead of being solely a tale of creation, this passage indicates points of Sunnī–Imāmī divide, with Muḥsin al-Fayḍ claiming superior understanding because of adherence to the inner truth (*bāṭin*) of the *ḥadīths*. By looking beyond the literal sense of texts and delving into their inner significance, he controverts the superficial understanding that he believes is entailed in a solely literal reading of the texts. The non-literal meaning, the hidden meaning, is revealed to only a few, the initiated (*ahl al-sirr*). This approach may be a justification for his going against the literal sense of the words of the Imām Abū Jaʿfar.

This interpretation is one example of the way that an exegete committed to an interpretive stance that adheres strictly to *ḥadīths*, an Akhbārī Shīʿī, can nevertheless go well beyond those *ḥadīths* and even contradict them in his work. Muḥsin al-Fayḍ's work takes certain strands of interpretation and elaborates on them, creating something that had not existed before. There is also development in the interpretations of other Akhbārīs. Al-Baḥrānī (d. 1107/1695) and al-Ḥuwayzī (d. 1112/1700) include many *ḥadīths* in their work, from various sources including al-ʿAyyāshī, but they do not replicate these sources exactly. Like their Sunnī counterparts, they exercise choice and discretion when picking their *ḥadīths*, and this shapes their interpretations.

Although Fayḍ's case is an extreme one because of the notion that, as an Akhbārī, he should be guided only by the literal sense of the *ḥadīths*, the pattern that he displays, of being able to interpret away the sense of *ḥadīths* and even the Qurʾān itself, is one displayed repeatedly in exegetical works by authors from diverse schools of law and thought.

THE NATURE OF CREATION: PHILOSOPHICAL AND ESOTERIC INTERPRETATIONS

If *ḥadīth* is understood in its broadest sense, as the interpretations of reliable early sources, then all works of *tafsīr* are *ḥadīth*-based. They all

the outward appearance of the text of the Qur'ān (the *ẓāhir*) represents inward truths (*bāṭin*) only understood by Imāmīs.

67 Muḥsin al-Fayḍ al-Kāshānī, *Kitāb al-Ṣāfī*, v. 2, p. 178.

rely on previous interpretations, preserving them and reinterpreting them. However, some exegetes consciously imported interpretations, concepts, and methods from other disciplines, such as philosophy, to answer larger questions about the nature of creation: Was Eve essentially the same as Adam, or different? How does her creation relate to deeper truths about the inherent nature of human existence? The first question is explored by the exegetes Sūrābādī (d. 494/1101) and Fakhr al-Dīn al-Rāzī; the second by ʿAbd al-Razzāq al-Kāshānī (pseudo Ibn ʿArabī, d. 736/1336).

Sūrābādī, who wrote the earliest extant Qurʾān commentary in Persian, focuses his interpretation of Q. 4:1 on the potential legal difficulties of Adam and Eve's marriage because of the question of whether Eve is Adam's kin or progeny, or a new creation. He explains that there are three different doctrines concerning Eve's creation that solve the problem of how she and Adam could have lawful sexual relations, since she was created from him and is thus, in a sense, his progeny. Sūrābādī's style is reminiscent of lessons in the mosque, in which the audience can ask questions, and the teacher explains the correct doctrine.

> Question: if Eve was created from Adam, then how could it be permissible (*ḥalāl*) [for] Adam to marry her? Answer: Some interpreters say, *and created from it its mate* means 'for its sake', and some interpreters say *and created from it its mate* means 'of its type' (*min jinsihā*)[68] just as God says *There hath come unto you a messenger, one of yourselves* (*rasūlun min anfusikum*) [Q. 9:128], which is to say, someone like you. A group of interpreters also say that Eve was created from Adam, but when she was created it was a new creation, thus the rules governing it were new, so that the rulings governing it are not the same as those governing progeny and close relations.[69]

Sūrābādī explains that three doctrines would make it legal for Eve to marry Adam: Eve was created *for* Adam; Eve was created *like* Adam/of the same type as Adam; or Eve was made from Adam, but as a new creation, not as a part of Adam. He says that the second doctrine, that Eve was like Adam (of his type), is supported by the Qurʾānic verse that says that prophets have been chosen 'from among you' (i.e., from among people like yourselves). Shīʿī sources discuss this, and the possibility of multiple Adams, at length; but this is not the place for a thorough examination of their doctrines on the matter.

[68] Although Sūrābādī's interpretation is in Persian, he includes this phrase in Arabic, probably because he is quoting from Arabic sources.

[69] Sūrābādī, *Tafsīr al-tafāsīr*, ed. Saʿīdī Sīrjānī (Tehran: Farhang-i Nashr-i Naw, 2002), v. 1, p. 380.

Fakhr al-Dīn al-Rāzī discusses the merits of the two accounts of Eve's creation, the first being that Eve was created from Adam's rib, and the second that she was created of his type. Supporting the first view is the Prophet's saying that Eve was created from a crooked rib. Fakhr al-Dīn is an Ashʿarī, and in the following passage he cites the opinions of the judge, probably the Ashʿarī al-Bāqillānī (d. 403/1013). One might expect him to agree with al-Bāqillānī, but it seems that he disagrees with this view,[70] and prefers the view propounded by the Muʿtazilī Abū Muslim al-Iṣfahānī that man and woman were created of the same type:

The second doctrine is that preferred by Abū Muslim al-Iṣfahānī, that the meaning of His words *created from it its mate* is from its type (*min jinsihā*), which is like the verse *God has made for you mates like yourselves* (*min anfusikum*) [Q. 16:72, 42:11] and as also in His words *when He has sent forth among them a messenger of their type* (*min anfusihim*) [Q. 3:164] and His words *He sent a messenger of your type* (*min anfusikum*) [Q. 9:128].

The judge [al-Baqillānī] says that the first doctrine is better, because it corroborates His words *created you from a single soul*. For if Eve had been created initially, then humans would have been created from two souls, not from a single soul. It is possible to answer him by saying that the word *from* is not used to implicate the initial point of departure (*ibtidāʾ al-ghāya*). If the beginning of creation consisted of Adam, then it is true that He *created you from a single soul*. Moreover since it is established that God Almighty was capable of creating Adam from earth, then He was also capable of creating Eve from the earth. And if this is so, what point would there be in creating her from one of Adam's ribs?[71]

Fakhr al-Dīn presents an interpretation previously only cited in Shīʿī sources, which is that since God is capable of anything, he would have no need to create Eve from Adam's rib. This interpretation is not, however, cited on the authority of Imām Abū Jaʿfar; it is given without reference.

After explaining that God is capable of creating Eve from the soil, Fakhr al-Dīn launches into an inquiry of the nature of her creation in a general sense, at the same time answering the different currents of thought about her creation:

Some scholars of the physical world (*ṭabāʾiʿīyūn*) use this verse as a proof, advancing the argument that *created you from a single soul* indicates that all people were created from a single soul, and His words *and created from it its mate*

[70] Ayman Shihadeh shows that Rāzī departs from certain elements of classical Ashʿarī thought. See Ayman Shihadeh, *The Teleological Ethics of Fakhr al-Dīn al-Rāzī* (Leiden: Brill, 2006), p. 7.

[71] Fakhr al-Dīn al-Rāzī, *al-Tafsīr al-Kabīr*, v. 9, p. 161.

indicate that its mate was created from it. Then He says, in describing Adam, *He created him from earth* [Q. 3:59] which indicates that Adam was created from earth, and then with regard to people, *from it, we created you* [Q. 20:55]. All of these verses are indications that what comes into being only does so from some pre-existing matter, from which [other] things are created, and that creating something from pure nothing, ex nihilo, is impossible. The theologians (*mutakallimūn*) respond by saying 'creating something from something else is rationally impossible, because this created thing, if it is the very thing which existed before, would not be *created* at all, and if it has not been created, it cannot have been created from another thing'. If we say that the created thing is distinct from that which existed before it, then the created thing and this new feature of it come out of pure nothing. But it is established that the creation of things out of other things is rationally impossible. As for the word 'from' in the verse, it is used for the initiation (*ibtidā' al-ghāya*) in the sense that the creation of these things originated with those things, not in the sense of any need or requirement, just in the sense that this is actually how it occurred.[72]

In this passage, which is quite confusing to a non-specialist, Fakhr al-Dīn responds to the arguments of the scholars of the physical world and theologians. These arguments, occurring for the most part outside of the genre of *tafsīr*, are brought into it as a way of highlighting the non-prosaic elements of the verse: everyone knows that this verse is about Adam and Eve, so what else can be said about creation? This passage indicates the manner in which Fakhr al-Dīn al-Rāzī replied to his peers and the intellectual context of his day.

Another type of philosophical *tafsīr* is represented by ʿAbd al-Razzāq al-Kāshānī, whose *tafsīr* I cited at the beginning of this chapter. After explaining that Adam and Eve refer to the spiritual and animalistic souls, al-Kāshānī goes on to explain that Adam's seduction was accomplished through Eve. Most strikingly for a modern reader, Eve is responsible for Adam's embodiment/downfall. This interpretation seems to contradict the Qur'ānic account of the fall.

It is well known that Iblīs enticed [Eve] first, so as to attain the seduction of Adam through her seduction, and there is no doubt that this attachment to the body would not have come about except through her. *And from them were spread forth many men* i.e., spiritual beings (*aṣḥāb qulūb*), who tend toward their father, *and women* beings of soul and nature (*aṣḥāb nufūs wa-ṭabā'iʿ*) who tend toward their mother.[73]

In the passage cited at the beginning of the chapter, al-Kāshānī said that the existence of the spiritual realm is a prerequisite for anything to be,

[72] Ibid., v. 9, pp. 161–2. [73] Ibid., v. 1, p. 248.

physically. In this passage he explains that Eve was made for Adam, yet the physical Eve causes the embodiment of the spiritual Adam by seducing him. This seduction was planned by Iblīs, who enticed Eve first in order for her to seduce Adam and cause his downfall into the physical realm. The incorporation of elements from the Biblical story of the creation and mankind's fall from grace emphasizes women's baser natures and their destructive effects on men; the implication in the final phrase, which speaks of men tending towards the father and women tending towards the mother, shows that these expressions indicate actual characteristics in men and women.

Although al-Kashānī mentions that Eve's temptation of Adam is 'well known', in asserting Eve's sole responsibility for the fall he seems, to modern eyes, to contradict the story of the Garden as told in the Qur'ān, in which both Eve and Adam are enticed.[74] As I noted in the introduction to this chapter, in the Qur'ānic account of the fall from the Garden, the sin of eating the fruit is both Adam's and his wife's; they are equally blamed for the sin when humans are admonished not to behave as their 'parents' did when disobeying God (Q. 7:27). ʿAbd al-Razzāq al-Kashānī's view is symptomatic of a much more widespread trend, starting from the earliest works of exegesis, to blame Eve for the fall.[75] In the Biblical and any number of para-Biblical accounts, Satan seduces Eve into eating from

[74] The Qur'ānic account reads: 'And [God said] (unto man): O Adam! Dwell thou and thy wife in the Garden and eat from whence ye will, but come not nigh this tree lest ye become wrong-doers. Then Satan whispered to them that he might manifest unto them that which was hidden from them of their shame, and he said: Your Lord forbade you from this tree only lest ye should become angels or become of the immortals. And he swore unto them (saying): Lo! I am a sincere adviser unto you. Thus did he lead them on with guile. And when they tasted of the tree their shame was manifest to them and they began to hide (by heaping) on themselves some of the leaves of the Garden. And their Lord called them, (saying): Did I not forbid you from that tree and tell you: Lo! Satan is an open enemy to you? They said: Our Lord! We have wronged ourselves. If thou forgive us not and have not mercy on us, surely we are lost! He said: Go down (from hence), one of you a foe unto the other. There will be for you on earth a habitation and provision for a while. He said: There shall ye live, and there shall ye die, and thence shall ye be brought forth. O Children of Adam! We have revealed unto you raiment to conceal your shame, and splendid vesture, but the raiment of restraint from evil, that is best. This is of the revelations of Allah, that they may remember. O Children of Adam! Let not Satan seduce you as he caused your (first) parents to go forth from the Garden and tore off from them their robe (of innocence) that he might manifest their shame to them. Lo! he seeth you, he and his tribe, from whence ye see him not. Lo! We have made the devils protecting friends for those who believe not' (Q. 7:19–27).

[75] Bronson, 'Islamic Selves of Eve', especially chapter 2 (but also see her Introduction), describes this trend.

the tree of knowledge, and she in turn encourages Adam to do so. Several elements in ʿAbd al-Razzāq al-Kashānī's exegesis relate to aspects of certain Jewish interpretations. For instance, in the *Midrash Rabbah*, Adam was described as being created with both higher, angelic, and lower, beast-like attributes.[76] Thus, while it is undeniable that his interpretation was an expression of his own personal interests and beliefs, in some respects ʿAbd al-Razzāq al-Kashānī was also expressing widespread, culturally taken-for-granted truths in his interpretation.

The interpretation that Eve tempted Adam seems to go against a literal reading of the Qur'ān, which uses the dual to say that Satan whispered to both Adam and Eve, and that they both ate of the tree. Yet for medieval interpreters, the Qur'ān's words were always read in light of existing knowledge and lore, and it was common knowledge in that time that Eve was tempted first. To use a modern term, medieval exegetes read the Qur'ān intertextually – with the background knowledge of their milieu of interpretations. It seems likely that medieval interpreters assume that the Qur'ān gives a shortened version of the story in which the exact timeline of the seduction is not specified (Eve, then Adam), only the end result (the two of them, eventually, were seduced). It is possible that in this case, the widespread understanding as reflected in exegesis sheds light on the meaning of the Qur'ān for its original audience. The author of the Qur'ān may indeed have intended to replicate the core of the Biblical story in his own terms, as the exegetes unanimously suppose, and so a literal reading of the Qur'ān's text on this incident may be misleading.

With its references to the rational and animalistic souls as well as the more widespread belief that Eve tempted Adam first, ʿAbd al-Razzāq al-Kashānī's interpretation of Q. 4:1 is a good example of how certain elements within the genre of *tafsīr* relate directly to the Qur'ān and its worldview, while other elements relate to a specific author's interests, concerns, milieu and taken for granted truths.

[76] *Midrash Rabbah*, v. 1, p. 61. Other Jewish exegetes described Adam as being created of 'upper and lower' elements; upper elements do not die, lower elements do die. 'R. Tifadi said in R. Aḥa's name: The Holy One, blessed by He, said: "If I create him of the celestial elements he will live [for ever] and not die, and if I create him of the terrestrial elements, he will die and not live [in a future life]. Therefore I will create him of the upper and of the lower elements; if he sins he will die, while if he does not sin, he will live"' (ibid., v. 1, p. 62). In one answer to a question posed to Rabbi Joshua, women were described as bringing death into the world: 'Why do they [women] walk in front of the corpse [at a funeral]? Because they brought death into the world, they therefore walk in front of the corpse . . . [and later it is said that] she extinguished the soul of Adam' (ibid, v. 1, p. 139).

SUMMARY AND CONCLUSION

Q. 4:1 is a test of the sources of interpretation, because the story of Eve's creation is not told there. All of the interpreters surveyed here adhere to the Qurʾān's text to the some degree, and to the extent that it tells the story of this creation: the original creation is held to be Adam and Eve in all but the Fāṭimid Ismāʿīlī case, when this story is understood to convey a deeper truth. But in the case of the nature of Eve's creation and the fall from the Garden, many interpreters use common, taken-for-granted truths to interpret the words of the Qurʾān, which, to modern eyes, gives the impression that they actually go against the Qurʾān's words. It may be that they were right to read into the Qurʾān: it may have given a shorthand version of a well-known story, rather than an alternate view of events. Whether or not they go against the text, most interpreters elaborate on Eve's creation in ways that go well beyond it. The examples in this chapter show how *tafsīr* relates to the text of the Qurʾān, to widespread, common understandings, and to individual interpreters' interests, particularly as it becomes more elaborate through time.

This chapter has focused on the role of narrations in shaping these interpretations. Although *ḥadīth*s influence *tafsīr*, none of the works surveyed here, whether *ḥadīth*-based or philosophical, relied solely on narrations of the Prophet or Imāms: early exegetical authorities played a far greater role in 4th/10th century works of *tafsīr*, which in turn influenced later works. At times exegetical authorities are held to have had conflicting views. I highlighted two such cases: one of Ibn ʿAbbās and one of the Shīʿī Imāms, who presented different and conflicting views of creation. These for the most part went unresolved by the exegetes, although later interpreters such as Muḥsin al-Fayḍ occasionally point to these discrepancies and attempt to reconcile them. In his work and others, some *ḥadīth*s and interpretations clearly justify legal and social norms, such as the husband's legal privilege in preventing his wife from going out of the house. Such *ḥadīth*s may have been post-facto justifications for widespread legal norms.

Although some of the early exegeses, such as that of Muqātil and al-Ṭabarī, spoke of Eve's creation from a rib without mentioning the implications of that creation, almost all other classical and post-classical accounts of Eve's creation were used by the exegetes to emphasise the secondary, dependent, and imperfect nature of women, and therefore the naturalness of the sexual hierarchy. Some interpreters emphasised that caring and kindness were an important part of the original spousal relationship. Others were far more interested in emphasising women's inferior nature.

In the modern period, some interpreters agree with the pre-modern interpretation that Eve's creation was from a rib, while others say that both Adam and Eve were created from a single ethereal soul. Modern interpreters nevertheless unanimously agree that the creation of the first man and woman from the same substance, whether the flesh of Adam or the universal soul, indicates that men and women are of equal status in this world. This volte-face in interpretation is described in Chapter 4.

4

Contemporary Interpretations of the Creation Narrative

I came to Iran steeped in the medieval tradition described in Chapter 3, and interviewed Mr Zibaei Nejad, Ḥujjat al-Islām wa'l-Muslimīn, the day after my arrival. He is tall and distinguished. He wears a turban over his dark hair, a light cloak over his shoulders, and has a short beard. He is also the director of the Women's Studies Resource Center in Qom, the conservative think tank where I met Dr ʿAlasvand. As I mentioned in Chapter 2, the key marker of conservatives is that they seek to preserve a core of interpretations from the medieval period. Thus, in response to my questions about Q. 4:1, *fear your Lord, who created you from a single soul and from it created its mate*, I expected a familiar litany drawn from medieval texts. As I described in Chapter 3, most medieval interpreters have a similar underlying interpretation of Q. 4:1: the verse refers to the creation of Eve from and for Adam, and that makes woman a secondary and lesser being in this world. *Ḥadīth*s on the authority of the Prophet and Imāms seem to have a strong influence on these interpretations: Sunnī and Imāmī Shīʿī *ḥadīth*s imply or state that women are secondary to, dependent on, and inferior to men. But when I heard what Mr Zibaei Nejad had to say, I was surprised. He took pains to emphasise that all modern interpreters agree on women's innate equality with men from the moment of the creation of the first woman:

According to the Shīʿīs there is a difference of opinion. There are ones who accept that Eve was taken from the rib, and others who say that Eve was created from the same substance as Adam.... Whichever one of these interpretations you accept, it does not interfere with the underlying message which is that there is absolute equality between Adam and Eve. Many verses of the Qur'ān prove the equality of men and women.[1]

There is no modern consensus on the exact manner of Eve's creation. But the notion that women are inherently equal to men is so common in modern interpretation that it amounts to a changing of consensus from the equally widespread medieval notion of inequality.

This Chapter examines the modern debate on Q. 4:1 and the nature of the original human creation, and how today's interpreters reconcile their ideals with *ḥadīth*s that contradict those ideals. In Chapter 2, I outlined a divide between the methods of conservatives and reformists which cut across confessional boundaries, but the conservative–reformist divide was less pronounced on the question of Eve's creation. Instead, in both textual sources and interviews, there was a strong Sunnī–Shī'ī divide on the acceptance of *ḥadīth*s. While most Sunnī sources in this study accepted the 'sound' *ḥadīth*s and negotiated within the boundaries of this basic acceptance, both conservative and reformist Imāmī Shī'īs engaged in vigorous *ḥadīth* criticism, with the result that many Shī'īs discounted *ḥadīth*s as inauthentic. These *ḥadīth*s are rejected not because of an argument for modern scientific theories of evolution, but rather because the *ḥadīth*s contradict the interpreters' basic moral outlook on the equality of human creation. The story of Eve's creation in the modern period, therefore, is one of both conservatism and reform: Eve's place as the mother of all humans, created by God, is usually carried over from the medieval period, but the significance of her creation and its import for all women has been completely reinterpreted.

Any discussion of human origins today raises the question of the relationship of science to the Qur'ānic worldview, and the relationship between conservative religious discourses in West and East. In my research, it was rare for the *'ulamā'* to support the modern scientific consensus on human creation. For the *'ulamā'*, even reformists, the theory of evolution and natural selection may be problematic because it calls into question the worldview of the Qur'ān. Evolution is generally considered to be incompatible with the Qur'ān and Bible not only because it conflicts with the Biblical/Qur'ānic story of creation, but also because it conflicts with the notion of what it is to be human in these texts. Damian Howard describes it as 'a scientific paradigm that would appear to liquidate any worldview in which the humanum commands objective

[1] Zibaei Nejad, Personal Interview, Qom, Iran, 28 May 2011.

cosmic significance'.[2] Natural selection is devoid of purpose, and presumes that human life is 'a randomly produced event, unintended, unwilled'.[3] For many conservative Christians and Muslims, it is not only the creation story per se that is at stake in accepting evolution, but it is also the vision of God's purpose for human life on earth, the idea of humans as a special and chosen form of life. Marwa Elshakry shows that early Arab proponents of Darwinian theories in the 1860s found ways around this thorny issue; they even saw it is 'nothing new', but simply the continuation of 'the much older, historic challenge of a heterodox and materialist view of a divinely ordered world'.[4]

While the Arab elite of the 19th and early 20th century supported evolutionary theories, with the increase in literacy of the later 20th century, these theories did not find widespread acceptance among the general public. Recently, a new movement of 'Muslim Creationism', borrowed from Christian fundamentalist texts, has arisen. This movement asserts that the findings of Darwin have largely been discredited.[5] Today, many reformist-minded clerics, like the conservatives, adhere to the idea of creationism or of 'fixity of types', which means that although there might be a kind of evolution within species, there is no evolution from one to the other. Yet science is hardly ignored by the *ʿulamāʾ*: as a concept, 'science' is routinely called on to support their interpretations.

SUNNĪ INTERPRETATIONS OF HUMAN ORIGINS

According to many later commentators, Muḥammad ʿAbduh went too far in his reinterpretation of the Qurʾān. In his day, colonialism and imperialism forced scholars in the Middle East to come to terms with the military, technological, and economic ascendancy of Europe. ʿAbduh responded to these concerns by critiquing scholars of his day for their backwardness.[6] He was not afraid to go against the plain sense reading of the Qurʾān. For him, Q. 4:1 does not refer to Adam at all. According to ʿAbduh, the expression 'sons of Adam' found elsewhere in the Qurʾān

[2] Damian Howard, *Being Human in Islam: The Impact of the Evolutionary Worldview* (London: Routledge, 2011), p. 5.

[3] Ibid., p. 2.

[4] Marwa Elshakry, 'Muslim Hermeneutics and Arabic Views of Evolution', *Zygon: Journal of Religion and Science* 46.2 (June 2011): pp. 330–44, at pp. 333–4.

[5] Ibid., pp. 341–2.

[6] 'Muslims had no partner in [intellectual] life, and they became without a presence in it.... Perhaps they will return'. ʿAbduh, *Tafsīr al-manār*, v. 4, p. 266, n. 1 (at Q. 4:1).

does not prove that all humans were the sons of one man, Adam; interpreters only believe that the verse refers to Adam because of their preconceived notions.[7] He explains the verse by saying that humans were created from a 'single soul', but that soul is 'obscure' and purposefully in the indefinite.[8] Furthermore, for him the expression that 'many men and women' were spread forth from 'the two of them' indicates that not *all* men and women were spread forth from the two of them. This raises an ambiguity about whether Adam and Eve are the parents of all of humankind.

Leaving the nature of the soul obscure is a part of ʿAbduh's philosophy, which is not to go beyond the words of the Qur'ān: 'We do not argue about matters beyond the perception of feeling and thinking, except by the revelation with which our Prophet, peace be upon him, came, and we stop at this revelation, we do not add nor do we take away, as we have said many times'.[9] This method seems to discount the probative value of *ḥadīth*s for determining interpretation, which may be why ʿAbduh so readily dismisses the entire interpretative tradition of Q. 4:1. As Jansen explains, this is part of his mission: 'ʿAbduh tries to make his readers, laymen and theologians alike, realize the limited relevance of the traditional commentaries that do not contribute to the solution of the urgent problems of the day'.[10] Damian Howard claims that ʿAbduh tries to make the Qur'ān compatible with modern scientific views. Part of ʿAbduh's project was to reform Islam in the name of science.[11] He is against the received tradition precisely because, for him, the Qur'ān supports the current theory of evolution; to make it do so entails a radical restructuring of existing knowledge about the stories told in that text.

ʿAbduh's student Rashīd Riḍā seeks to mitigate these radical ideas, and to accommodate a compromise solution that does not entirely discard Muslim tradition. It seems that both ʿAbduh and Riḍā were proponents of

[7] ʿAbduh, *Tafsīr al-manār*, v. 4, p. 264 (at Q. 4:1).

[8] 'Here God Almighty has made the matter of the soul, from which people were created, obscure; and He put it in the indefinite, so we leave it as it is, obscure. So if what the European researchers say is established, that for each human race there is a father, then that is not mentioned in our book, as it is mentioned in their book, the Torah, in which there is an unambiguous statement about that. And it is that which pushes their researchers to argue against its existence [that is, the existence of the single soul] from God Almighty and His revelation'. Ibid., v. 4, pp. 263–4 (at Q. 4:1).

[9] Ibid., v. 4, p. 263 (at Q. 4:1). See also Jansen, *The Interpretation of the Koran in Modern Egypt*, p. 19.

[10] Jansen, *The Interpretation of the Koran in Modern Egypt*, p. 19.

[11] Howard, *Being Human in Islam*, p. 46.

the evolutionary worldview; Riḍā probably first learned of the evolutionary worldview from his teacher, Ḥusayn al-Jisr, a Syrian who wrote about the compatibility of evolution with the Qur'ān in 1887.[12] According to al-Jisr, natural selection 'in no way seemed to contain anything that could be said to go against either common sense or Muslim scripture and its canonical and ethical laws, the *sharīʿah*'.[13] Thus, Riḍā takes a less radical approach than ʿAbduh – rather than denying Adam entirely, he seeks to accommodate traditional knowledge along with new scientific theory. And in *al-Manār*, Riḍā asserts that people who believe that Adam is the father of humankind can still be considered believing Muslims. He then goes on to explain exactly what is meant by the 'single soul', which ʿAbduh had left ambiguous. It is thus not clear that the radical reformist teacher and his student agree entirely with one another. Instead, the student seems to have rejected some of the teacher's positions, actually responding to them in writing by describing ʿAbduh's position and then 'answering' him:

> The teacher and Imām [ʿAbduh] has, in this point, two opinions. The first of them is that the plain sense of this verse denies that the meaning intended by the 'single soul' could be Adam, that is to say regardless of whether he is the father of all humans or not, because of what he has mentioned regarding the contradictions of this in scientific and historical study and from the indefiniteness of what was spread forth from him and its mate. Although it is possible to answer this last by saying that the indefinite is for those who were born from the two of them directly, as though He had said 'there spread forth from the two of them many men and women, and there spread forth from those the rest of the people'.[14]

ʿAbduh argues that the intention of the 'single soul' is not Adam since the story of Adam has been contradicted by 'historical and scientific' study and by the grammar of the verse. But it appears that Riḍā wishes to rehabilitate Adam as the father of humankind. He enables ʿAbduh's ideas to become somewhat less radical and somewhat more compatible with the traditional Islamic worldview. In this, Riḍā seems to be aligned with the version of evolution propounded by Ḥusayn Jisr, cited previously, rather than with the actual theory of evolution and natural selection, which by its very nature calls the religious worldview into question.

One difference between this *tafsīr* and those that came before is that ʿAbduh and Riḍā spend relatively little time talking about the 'mate'. ʿAbduh's opinion is that the verse refers to the creation of humans from

[12] Elshakry, 'Muslim Hermeneutics and Arabic Views of Evolution', p. 338.
[13] Ibid., p. 334. [14] ʿAbduh, *Tafsīr al-manār*, v. 4, p. 265 (at Q. 4:1).

spouses: every human has two parents. For ʿAbduh, the verse refers to human origins, but those origins are not limited to Adam and Eve. Riḍā again disagrees with his teacher, saying that the interpretation of the majority is easier: the verse refers to Adam and Eve, the parents of humankind. He cites both the interpretation of Eve's creation from Adam's rib, and the interpretation of Abū Muslim al-Iṣfahānī cited in the *tafsīr* of Fakhr al-Dīn al-Rāzī, which says that 'from it' means of the same type, and therefore Eve is of the same type as Adam.[15] Neither ʿAbduh nor Riḍā discuss the implications for women as a whole.

ʿAbduh's interpretation is not a precursor for later Sunnī works. The mainstream modern Sunnī approach denies evolution, affirms the creation of Eve from Adam's rib, and yet emphasises equality between the sexes. This approach is epitomised by Sayyid Quṭb (d. 1966), an Egyptian Sunnī whose commentary was very influential but who, nevertheless, was not a traditionally trained *ʿālim*. He says that the important point to remember from this verse is that everyone has the same source, the same ultimate father, by which he means Adam. If people were to remember this, he says, it would solve many of the world's problems, such as racism and the caste system.[16] Adam's mate was created from him and for him in order to propagate the species, which means that there is no inherent difference between them as humans, only a difference in 'abilities and roles'.[17] Here Quṭb voices the widespread modern perception that women and men are equal in humanity, but are each suited to different types of tasks and roles in this world. Whereas in the medieval period interpreters affirmed the sexes' spiritual equality but worldly inequality, in the modern period they are equal as humans too.

In order to support their interpretations, modern Sunnī exegetes cite pre-modern sources. By and large, they completely ignore ʿAbduh's views and the question of evolution. For instance, Muḥammad ʿAlī Ṭalḥa al-Durra, from Ḥoms, says: 'it is well known that the creation of Eve was from one of Adam's left hand ribs, which is what the exegetes (*mufassirūn*) have said'.[18] Saʿīd Ḥawwā, the Syrian member of the Muslim Brotherhood, cites several *ḥadīth*s, including the crooked rib *ḥadīth*, to prove that the Eve was created from the Adam.[19] The Damascene Wahba

[15] Ibid., v. 4, pp. 269–70 (at Q. 4:1).
[16] Sayyid Quṭb, *Fī ẓilāl al-Qurʾān* (Beirut: Dār al-Sharq, 2007), v. 1, p. 573–4 (at Q. 4:1). This interpretation is reminiscent of that of al-Ṭabarī at the beginning of Q. 4:1.
[17] Ibid., v. 1, p. 574 (at Q. 4:1).
[18] Al-Durra, *Tafsīr al-Qurʾān al-karīm*, v. 2, p. 304 (at Q. 4:1).
[19] Ḥawwā, *al-Asās fī 'l-tafsīr*, v. 2, p. 986 (at Q. 4:1).

al-Zuhaylī uses *ḥadīth*s to refute the 'same type' interpretation of Abū Muslim al-Iṣfahānī.[20] For the most part, the Sunnī sources that I read and the interviewees to whom I spoke seemed reluctant to break with tradition. In the words of Dr al-Būṭī, 'I do not have an interpretation other than the one that the exegetes (*mufassirūn*) have already given'.[21]

Most Sunnī *'ulamā'* simply ignored the issue of evolution; one exception is the Egyptian Muḥammad Maḥmūd Ḥijāzī, Shaykh of al-Azhar, whose book was published in 1964. His interpretation leaves open the possibility that the Qur'ān supports evolution, while at the same time asserting that the best interpretation is that of Adam and Eve. For him, the *ḥadīth*-based case for Adam and Eve is strong; science is interesting, but unproven. This interpretation is therefore a type of equivocation between a reluctant admission that modern science may have something to offer, and a steadfast commitment to the pre-modern science of *ḥadīth*s:

> It is said that this soul did not begin with a single Adam, but with many Adams before him, or with animals, so Adam is not the father of all humans. God knows best about all of this; while the matter is simple: the Qur'ān made the soul obscure, it did not make it known; therefore it can bear these meanings and more. If it were established scientifically that Adam was the father of humans, or that Adam was not the father of humans, that would not contradict the Qur'ān the way that it would contradict the Torah and other texts. Despite that, the first opinion is the best and that which is in harmony with many sound *ḥadīth*s, and the meaning intended is that He created you from a single soul, which he had formed from the earth, and He created from it its mate, and it is said from a rib of Adam as in a *ḥadīth*, 'indeed the intention is from the most crooked rib, and if you go to straighten her you will break her, while if you leave her crooked, you may enjoy her'.[22]

In this passage, the 'many Adams' tradition is used as a vehicle to carry the evolutionary theory back into traditional interpretations and knowledge. But ultimately, even though there is some way of accommodating modern science through a traditional interpretation, Ḥijāzī remains unconvinced. Ḥijāzī seems to have been heavily influenced by the *Tafsīr al-manār* of 'Abduh and Riḍā. Like 'Abduh, he asserts that the matter of the 'soul' has been left obscure intentionally, and that the Qur'ān does not contradict the theory of evolution in the same way as the Bible does. Nevertheless, according to Ḥijāzī, *ḥadīth*s win the day.

[20] Al-Zuhaylī, *al-Tafsīr al-munīr*, v. 4, p. 223 (at Q. 4:1).
[21] Sayyid Ramaḍān al-Būṭī, Personal Interview, Damascus, Syria, September 2004.
[22] Muḥammad Maḥmūd Ḥijāzī, *Tafsīr al-wāḍiḥ*, v. 4, p. 68.

Al-Ālūsī (d. 1854) was one early Sunnī source to cite the medieval Shī'ī interpretation, supported by several *ḥadīth*s, that there had been many Adams before 'our' Adam, the progenitor of humankind.[23] This interpretation was cited and rejected by ʿAbduh. Decades later, Saʿīd Ḥawwā confronts al-Ālūsī directly, accusing him of being a proponent of evolution:

> I say: these words [of al-Alūsī's] need an entire book to discuss the issue, so the reader should read with caution, for al-Alūsī has transmitted this for one reason, and that is that he accepts that the new theory of evolution is present in Islamic sayings, which indicates that our present human species was preceded by its like, or by something resembling it, despite the certainty that we are from our father Adam, and despite the certainty that Adam was created directly, and there is no trace of evolution, and despite the certainty that if there had been creations resembling the present humans before our Adam, peace be upon him, then there is no connection between them and our present human species from the point of view of reproduction and propagation, and despite the certainty that there are no sound or definitive texts concerning this matter.[24]

Ḥawwā's assertions against evolution are proven by the crooked rib *ḥadīth*. No effort is made to engage with the true parameters of the scientific debate. Instead, blanket assertions are backed up with reference to traditional sources of religious knowledge.

Although these Sunnī interpreters reject certain aspects of tradition by saying that women and men are actually equal, their methods and sources have continuity with the past interpretations, methods, and sources. Citing *ḥadīth*s such as the crooked rib *ḥadīth* is an indication of familiarity and conformity with past interpretations, even when those *ḥadīth*s seem to go against notions of fairness, equality, and justice that are common today. Instead of rejecting *ḥadīth*s, in works of *tafsīr* and interviews Sunnī interpreters were far more likely to uphold or reinterpret those *ḥadīth*s in a way that fits into their current ideals.

IMĀMĪ SHĪʿĪ INTERPRETATIONS OF ADAM, EVE, AND EVOLUTION

As I described at the beginning of this chapter, I went to Qom in 2011 with the assumption that I would encounter interpretations much like those in Syria, or indeed in the pre-modern texts. However, the Imāmī Shīʿī clerics

[23] Shihāb al-Dīn Maḥmūd al-Ālūsī, *Rūḥ al-maʿānī fī tafsīr al-Qur'ān al-ʿaẓīm wa'l-sabaʿ mathānī* (Beirut: Dār al-Qawmiyya al-ʿArabiyya Lil-Ṭibāʿa, n.d.), v. 4, p. 275.

[24] Saʿīd Ḥawwā, *al-Asās fī 'l-tafsīr*, v. 2, p. 986.

I interviewed veered away from the medieval interpretations and even rejected *ḥadīth*s that had been commonly cited to explain this verse. I had underestimated the profound influence of ʿAllāmah Ṭabāṭabāʾī (d. 1981).

Ṭabāṭabāʾī was born in 1904 in Tabriz and studied in Najaf before settling in Qom. He studied philosophy and the Qurʾān in depth, practiced mysticism, and authored a complete Qurʾān commentary, *al-Mizān fī tafsīr al-Qurʾān*. This Qurʾān commentary, which was traditional but which engaged with modern ideas and ideals, was to have a deep and lasting effect on Shīʿī thought; his influence is illustrated by the example of his interpretation of Q. 4:1.

Ṭabāṭabāʾī's interpretation of Q. 4:1 can be seen as a reaction to the interpretation of ʿAbduh. In a few areas he agrees with ʿAbduh, but in most aspects he seeks to refute ʿAbduh's views. One area of convergence is the nature of the *nafs* – the self or soul from whom all people were created. According to ʿAbduh, 'this is a strong indication that the expression "*nafs*", regardless of the narrations and the Muslim traditions, is the quality or reality with which the person becomes this being (*al-māhiyya aw al-ḥaqīqa allatī kān bihā al-insān huwa hadhā al-kāʾin*) differentiated from other types of being, that is, He created you from a single type and a single reality'.[25] Similarly, Ṭabāṭabāʾī asserts that *nafs* refers to a person's essence as a person, their humanity: 'the *nafs* of the person is what makes a person a person (*nafs al-insān huwa mā bihi al-insān al-insān*)'.[26] Ṭabāṭabāʾī uses this to argue against Eve's creation from Adam's rib; instead, he asserts that Adam and Eve were created of the same type. In comparison with previous Imāmī works of *tafsīr*, one striking element of Ṭabāṭabāʾī's interpretation of Q. 4:1 is the manner in which he refutes *ḥadīth*s:

> The clear meaning of the phrase *created from it its mate* is that it is a clarification of His bringing into existence the mate from the same type ... and what is in some of the works of *tafsīr*, that the intention of the verse is that the being of the mate of this soul is derived from it, and that she was created from part of it, is in agreement with some of the narrations, which is that God created the mate of Adam from one of his ribs. But there is no proof of this in the verse.[27]

Here Ṭabāṭabāʾī mentions that *ḥadīth*s are the cause and source of the rib interpretation. But nevertheless, he denies that the rib interpretation is supported by this verse or the others that he cites. For him, *ḥadīth* criticism is an important part of establishing the true interpretation: he

[25] ʿAbduh, *al-Manār*, v. 4, p. 265 at Q. 4:1.
[26] Ṭabāṭabāʾī, *al-Mīzān fī tafsīr al-Qurʾān*, v. 4, p. 139.
[27] Ibid., v. 4, p. 140 (at Q. 4:1).

confronts directly the issue of conflicting *ḥadīth*s, and rejects *ḥadīth*s that assert that Eve was created from Adam. After describing the *ḥadīth* about woman's creation from leftover soil, he describes the *ḥadīth*s that contradict this interpretation:

> I say: al-Ṣadūq narrated something like this on the authority of ʿAmr, and there are other narrations that indicate that she was created from the *khalaf* of Adam, which is the shortest rib on his left side. Something like this was mentioned in the Torah in the second Chapter of Genesis, and the meaning is not impossible in and of itself (*in lam yastalzam fī nafsihi muḥālan*) except that there is no proof of it in the Qur'ānic verses, as I have shown.[28]

Ṭabātabāʾī's overt rejection of *ḥadīth*s marks a turning point in the Imāmī Shīʿī interpretation of this verse. No longer do incompatible *ḥadīth*s need to sit side-by-side as in the interpretation of al-ʿAyyāshī and others, and no longer do they need to be somehow reconciled, as in the interpretation of Muḥsin al-Fayḍ. By rejecting *ḥadīth*s that were included in prior works of interpretation, Ṭabāṭabāʾī initiates a new wave of Imāmī interpretation about the nature of creation, and particularly Eve's creation. His interpretation, and methods, had a deep and lasting effect on later generations of Imāmī interpreters. As I describe later in this section, they too reinterpret the significance of the 'single soul' and overtly reject *ḥadīth*s.

Although Ṭabāṭabāʾī rejects certain *ḥadīth*s, he does not reject the entire corpus and he does not go against the plain sense of the Qur'ān, as did ʿAbduh. His work presents an example of current arguments against evolution among Imāmī *ʿulamāʾ*. He claims that Jewish interpretations put the earth's age at 7,000 years,[29] and in a chapter entitled 'The present human race begins with Adam and his wife', he explains that the Qur'ān's verses indicate 'that Adam was created from earth and that people are his sons, so the plain sense meaning of the verses indicates the origin of this race with Adam and his wife, about which there is no doubt'.[30] He also refutes ʿAbduh's assertion that the 'single soul' and 'mate' refer to human couples in general by saying that the intention of the verse is to say that all humans, despite their great diversity, come from a single 'branch and root'.[31] He argues against evolution from a separate

[28] Ibid., v. 4, p. 151 (at Q. 4:1, under the section heading *baḥth rawāʾī*).
[29] Ibid., v. 4, p. 144 (at Q. 4:1, under the section heading *kalām fī ʿumr al-nawʿ al-insānī wal-insān al-awwalī*).
[30] Ibid., v. 4, p. 147 (at Q. 4:1, under the section heading *kalām fī an al-nasl alḥādir yantahī ilā Ādam wa zawjatihi*).
[31] Ibid., v. 4, p. 146 (at Q. 4:1).

species as the origin of humans, but he seems to support the idea that after the creation of Adam and Eve, some evolution may have occurred within the human species:

> Scientific discussions nowadays are based on the theory of the evolution of species. If so, then how can we be sure that the difference in blood – and consequently in colour – is not caused by evolution or adaptation in a single species? They believe that there have been many changes in various animal species, e.g., horse, goat, sheep, elephant and many others.[32]

This modification of the theory of evolution allows Ṭabāṭabāʾī to maintain the sense of man as a distinct type of creation. Later, Ṭabāṭabāʾī asserts that his Qurʾān commentary is not the place to find a detailed discussion of the matter of evolution, but that perhaps there was a series of creations, in line with the Shīʿī *ḥadīth*s that mention many Adams before the current Adam. For him, this may indicate that there was evolution within the species: man was created, but then evolved into the current human race. This view differs from the theory of evolution because the basic premise of this view is that man was created as man, rather than evolving from other species.

Insofar as he disregards the natural selection aspect of evolution, he also disregards scientific consensus. But it is not immediately apparent whether he was exposed to the scientific tenets of the theory in the first place. For, according to what he wrote in his *tafsīr*, evolution was apparently not the only theory circulating in his time to explain the diversity of mankind. A second theory seems to have been that the western hemisphere was inhabited before it was discovered, and that the distance between the western and eastern hemispheres shows that there could have been no contact between people in each hemisphere; therefore, they must have a different origin. To refute this claim, he cites geological findings showing that 'oceans have turned into dry lands and vice versa'. Therefore, he says, the western hemisphere may have once been attached to the other continents. The careful use of some scientific knowledge, while ignoring or discrediting the main scientific consensus that evolution is the origin of the human species, is a method used by many religious scholars after Ṭabāṭabāʾī. This method may not, however, reflect a true engagement with the actual theory of evolution, but rather may reflect whatever mediated version of the theory was, or is, available to them at the time.

[32] Ibid., v. 4, p. 145–6 (at Q. 4:1).

Although on the whole Shīʿī *ʿulamāʾ* mention some version of the theory of evolution, not all of them use science as a way of refuting it. Using only the Qur'ān and *ḥadīth*s as proof against science is a common tactic for later commentators. The Lebanese thinker Muḥammad Jawād Maghniyya begins his attack by saying that ʿAbduh wishes to particularize the Qur'ān's statements about the 'sons of Adam': instead of Adam being the father of all humankind, he was only the father of some humans in Muḥammad's time. The response is twofold. First, he says that the Qur'ān is not only good for those who were present in its own time, but includes 'everything present until the last day', and instructions for people in all times and places. Second, he says that if the instructions to the 'sons of Adam' had been for a particular people, then we would not be bound by them, and nor would we need to be guided by them. For him, particularisation contradicts the principle that the Qur'ān and the *sunna* are the primary source for 'Islamic belief and law'.[33] He argues that everything in the Qur'ān is for all people and all times. Therefore, verses such as al-Aʿrāf (Q. 7:27), *O sons of Adam, do not be tempted by Satan*, are for all people, not just for specific people, so when the Qur'ān says that we created you from a single soul, it must be 'our father Adam, with no vagueness, or mistaking him for anyone else'.[34]

In his commentary published in 1972, Muḥammad Jawād al-Balāghī al-Najafī (d. 1982) cites verses of the Qur'ān to prove that Adam is the father of all humans, and that Adam was made from earth. He uses the traditional proof of grammatical analysis. If the 'single soul' and the 'mate' refer to the generic parents of people, rather than a specific couple, he asks: What is the meaning of 'spread forth from the two of them' in the dual? And if the 'single soul' is a universal soul, rather than a specific individual, what is the meaning of 'its mate'?[35] For al-Balaghī, the context of the Qur'ān proves that Adam and Eve are the progenitors of the human race. These examples show how the Qur'ān and *ḥadīth*s alone suffice for some Shīʿī commentators to refute scientific evidence.

Many clerics, both conservative and reform-minded, assert that the theory of evolution has no basis in the Qur'ān, and this was clear in the interviews I conducted. Although Grand Ayatollah Gerami was the most conservative and traditional cleric of those I interviewed, and regularly cited medieval sources verbatim, he did not take an entirely traditional

33 Maghniyya, *Tafsīr al-kāshif*, v. 1, p. 243 (at Q. 4:1).
34 Ibid., v. 1, p. 243 (at Q. 4:1).
35 Al-Najafī, *ʿAlāʾ al-raḥmān fī tafsīr al-Qur'ān*, v. 2, pp. 4–5 (at Q. 4:1).

view of this verse: he followed his teacher Ṭabāṭabāʾī. He pointed out that Q. 4:1 is not really concerned with the creation of Adam, but rather with the creation of Eve and the rest of the human population; to the extent that it deals with human creation, he said that the Qurʾān supports the idea of types, rather than evolution, and that no religious text offers proof for evolution.[36]

Ayatollah Mohaghegh Damad is a reform-minded cleric who trained in traditional sources in Qom, where he became an Ayatollah in 1970, and who received a doctorate in law from Louvain-la-Neuve University, Belgium.[37] He was prominent in the reformist government of Mohammad Khatami, prime minister of Iran from 2005–7. I met with Ayatollah Mohaghegh Damad in his grand office in the Iranian Academy of Sciences, Tehran, a complex of buildings surrounded by rose gardens. He believes in the use of reason to interpret the Qurʾān, rather than the use of *ḥadīths*, because of the numerous errors in transmission.[38] However, using the Qurʾān to interpret itself, rather than using *ḥadīths*, he reaches the same conclusion as the more conservative-minded Ayatollah Geramī:

AYATOLLAH MOHAGHEGH DAMAD: Some of the intellectuals believe that the Qurʾān does not contradict the theory of Darwin. But some of the greatest exegetes, for instance, ʿAllāmah Ṭabāṭabāʾī, God rest his soul, do not think in this way. He believes that a certain verse of the Qurʾān indicates a contradiction. That verse is: *The example of Jesus before God is like that of Adam. He created him from the soil and He said to him 'Be' and he was* [Q 3:59]. As Jesus did not have a physical existence before that, and just as Jesus was created without any evolution, so too was Adam created without any evolution, because Jesus is like Adam.

KAREN BAUER: And so there is no way to reconcile this with evolution?

AMD: Yes.

[36] Muhammad Ali Gerami, Personal Interview, Qom, Iran, 14 June 2011: 'We have not found a strong proof on the basis of the Qurʾān, the narrations and the rest of the texts of religion, for the theory of evolution'.

[37] See http://www.mdamad.com/Welcome.html, last accessed 24 March 2013.

[38] 'As I am a teacher of philosophy, I interpret the Qurʾān on a rational basis, rather than on the basis of transmission. And I do not believe in transmission as a basis, because the majority of narrations are weak; not all of them, but the majority of them do not have a strong chain of transmission. And I believe that the Qurʾān addresses all people, and due to that people must be able to understand it. If they think carefully then they will understand', Mohaghegh Damad, Personal Interview, Tehran, Iran, 23 June 2011.

KB: And so the rest of us, we are the *sons of Adam* [Q. 7:26 and others], and we are not the products of evolution?

AMD: Yes. We are *sons of Adam* which is against the theory of evolution.[39]

Although Ayatollah Geramī and Ayatollah Mohaghegh Damad have different views of the nature of interpretation, with the former relying on traditional sources and the latter supporting the idea of rational inquiry as a basis, they both agree that nothing in the Qur'ān supports evolution. On the question of evolution, my interviews did not reveal a black-and-white divide between 'reformists' and 'conservatives'.

A few *'ulamā'* see no contradiction between the Qur'ān and evolution. One of them is Sayyid Muḥammad 'Ali Ayazi, Ḥujjat al-Islam wa'l-Muslimīn, a professor of Qur'ānic knowledge at Mofid University. Mofid was founded by Grand Ayatollah Abdolkarim Ardebili, who is known for his moderate views. Many of the professors there are religious scholars with similarly moderate or reformist tendencies. It is a place where one can get a western-style university education while concurrently pursuing the traditional religious paths of learning at the *hawza*.

Sayyid Ayazi said that Q. 4:1 does not refer to the physical creation of Adam or Eve, but rather to their shared soul and spirit. The term 'soul' (*nafs*) does not refer to Adam at all; it refers to 'one shared reality, something that Adam and Eve have in common'. Although this verse does not refer to Adam and Eve, they are referred to in the Qur'ān. For Sayyid Ayazi, the references to Adam and Eve as the original parents do not contradict the theory of evolution:

KAREN BAUER: From what I understand, there is a contradiction between the belief in Adam and Eve, and the belief in evolution. Either you believe that there is evolution, or you believe in Adam and Eve. And that is what I would take for granted, it is my presupposition.

SAYYID AYAZI: Why? Why does it have to be a contradiction? There is evolution, even for Adam and Eve. Adam and Eve are the result of evolution, and so human beings are taken from Adam and Eve. Adam and Eve themselves evolved. It is the presence of rationality that distinguishes them from others.

KB: So there were original parents, but they evolved and were the result of evolution?

[39] Ibid.

SA: When the Qurʾān speaks of the *sons of Adam*, it refers to those people who have come to have rationality. Previous species before Adam and Eve didn't have the same rationality as Adam and Eve. They were the first ones to have rationality. The Qurʾān says *I am the maker of a vicegerent on earth* (*inni jāʿilun fī' l-arḍ khalīfa*) [Q 2:30], not 'I am the creator (*khāliq*)'. This proves that there were people before Adam and Eve, but that they did not have rationality, so God has chosen Adam and Eve as vicegerents. God gave some types of blessings to them, among them the knowledge of names. God says *we have blessed the sons of Adam* (*wa-qad karramnā banī Adam*) [Q 17:70]; the privilege is given to the sons of Adam and not anyone else. Even in Sūrat al-Aḥzāb [Q. 33], verse 72, God says *I have given a trust*. God offered it to all of the other creatures, but they feared to accept this trust; only human beings accepted it. Why did human beings accept this trust? The answer is rationality.[40]

For Sayyid Ayazi, the key marker of humanity is rationality, and references to the creation of humans are actually references to their rationality above and beyond that of other creatures. This rationality marks humans out as the true vicegerents of God on earth. Thus, for him, the Qurʾān is not incompatible with the theory of evolution.

Another professor at Mofid University, Dr Mohammad Sadegh Kamilan, Ḥujjat al-Islām wa'l-Muslimīn, asserted the Qurʾān's silence on the matter of evolution. For Dr Kamilan, while some verses of the Qurʾān refer to humans' physical creation, Q. 4:1 'refers to the ultimate spiritual reality, which is neither male nor female. The physical creation refers to the physical matter of people, not to the particular creation'.[41] The idea of creation from a rib, he says, reflects the notions of the interpreters rather than an objective 'truth'. They also believed that the sun moves around the earth rather than the earth moving around the sun. To look for science in the Qurʾān is a misapplication of its purpose:

The purpose of religion is not an explanation and interpretation of the scientific point of view regarding the creation of humans. This is not the purpose of religion. Rather, the verses are signs showing that you can see the earth, the physical world, and through the physical world you can come to know God. The physical world consists of such signs, for instance in verse 29:39, *indeed through the creation of*

[40] Muhammad ʿAli Ayazi, Personal Interview, Qom, Iran, 29 May 2011.
[41] Mohammad Sadegh Kamilan, Personal Interview, Qom, Iran, 30 May 2011.

the Heavens and the earth, are signs for those of understanding. All of these aspects of creation are signs for those who understand.[42]

According to Dr Kamilan, the purpose of religion is spiritual guidance, and that is not incompatible with a modern scientific understanding of the world; the realm of physical existence is one way to understand God. Thus, one could reconcile belief in scientific theories, such as the theory of evolution, with a religious understanding of the world. This view was echoed by Mehdi Mehrizi.

However, Mr Mehrizi focused more on the second part of the verse, *and spread forth from the two of them many men and women.* He used the dual form in the verse to assert that the ideal marriage in Islam consists of one single man and one single woman. Thus, for him, this verse is an argument against polygamy. He refers to an opinion that Q. 4:3, the polygamy verse, sanctions marriage to more than one woman only in exceptional circumstances. This argument states that among the Qur'ān's original audience, there was little or no protection for the weak and vulnerable in society, so men were permitted to marry more than once in order to protect women who might otherwise be vulnerable to exploitation. Now that the rule of law exists to protect women, the society can revert to the Qur'ānic ideal of a single man and wife.[43]

IMĀMĪ SHĪʿĪ RESPONSES TO DIFFICULT *ḤADĪTHS*

Although most Shīʿī scholars remain convinced of the traditional view of Adam and Eve as the parents of humankind, they do not accept the *ḥadīth*s that have been used since the medieval period to support this view. ʿAllamah Ṭabāṭabāʾī took a new interpretation of Q. 4:1, in the process of which he rejected *ḥadīth*s that had been cited through centuries of Shīʿī sources. Scholars after Ṭabāṭabīʾī followed his lead. In the interviews I conducted, I questioned the scholars extensively about how and why they could possibly reject *ḥadīth*s that had been so well accepted by previous generations. For them, *ḥadīth*s could be rejected on two grounds: on the basis of the chain of transmission (*isnād* criticism) and on the basis of reasoned judgment/rationality (*ʿaql*).

42 Ibid.

43 Mehdi Mehrizi, Personal Interview, Qom, Iran, 9 June 2011: 'Because of *created from it its mate*, and *spread forth from the two of them many men and women* – not from any man and woman, but from *the two of them*. This is the basis of the family in Islam, one single man and one single woman'.

Conservatives tended to favour the critique of chains of transmission. When I asked Grand Ayatollah Gerami to clarify whether *from a single soul* (*min nafsin wāḥidatin*) meant from the same clay, as in the pre-modern interpretations, he said that it had nothing to do with the clay, it meant of the same type. The 'single soul' was Adam, the 'mate' Eve, and 'from it' meant that Eve was created from the same essence as Adam, rather than from his rib. He rejected the *ḥadīth*s that said that Eve had been created from Adam's rib; the problem, according to him and to others, is that these *ḥadīth*s were probably *isra'īliyyāt* – in other words, *ḥadīth*s that had been transmitted from Christian or Jewish converts to Islam, but which were not authentic.[44]

Other scholars with traditional or conservative views of the roles of men and women also rejected *ḥadīth*s on the grounds of their chains of transmission. One example is Dr Zahiri, of the Jam'at Zahra, the women's seminary in Qom. The women's seminary is a bustling place, with mostly female teachers and all female students. Dr Zahiri, one of the teachers there, seemed to support the traditional view of the bodily creation of Eve from Adam's rib, unlike most other Imāmī interpreters I interviewed. Nevertheless, she did not stick entirely to pre-modern interpretations. Some *ḥadīth*s could be rejected on the basis of their chains of transmission. Like Grand Ayatollah Gerami, she says that these *ḥadīth*s were *isrā'īliyyāt*:

> There are several narrations concerning this verse. The first is that women were created from the left rib. The second is that woman belongs to man, she was created for him, and she is like a child. The third is that the woman was created after the man, and because of that she has a lesser degree than men. The fourth is that the woman comes from the leftover soil from Adam's creation. But we believe that women's and men's soul is the same. We believe that some of these *ḥadīth*s come from the *isrā'īliyyāt*, especially those that imply that woman is a secondary creation. Some of our Shī'ī *ḥadīth*s do say that woman was created from a rib. This *ḥadīth* may be acceptable from the point of view of bodily creation, rather than from the point of view of the spirit and soul.[45]

By describing *ḥadīth*s as *isrā'īliyyāt*, interpreters assert that Christian and Jewish ideas about the relations between the sexes, based in the Bible, infected Muslim interpretations of the Qur'ān. The implication is that the Qur'ān is essentially an egalitarian text.

[44] Mohammad Ali Gerami, Personal Interview, Qom, Iran, 14 June 2011.
[45] Masoumeh Zahiri, Personal Interview, Qom, Iran, 31 May 2011.

Dr ʿAlasvand, whom I introduced in Chapter 2, explained that in the Christian doctrine, women's biological fate – menstruation, pregnancy, and childbirth – is a consequence of Eve's part in the original sin. In the Islamic case, she says, the Qurʾān encourages men to be gentle with women in these times; women's state is natural, and not a punishment.[46] Dr Rahaei, professor of comparative law at Mofid University, insisted that the notion of original sin was present in Islam because of the interpretations of Jews who were false converts to Islam. Some of them were masters of *ḥadīth*.[47] Whether the *ʿulamāʾ* believed the influences to be Jewish or Christian, they emphasised that these foreign interpretations had influenced Muslim views of the Qurʾān.

But how could the medieval exegetes have gotten it so wrong? The *ʿulamāʾ* I interviewed had different explanations for why such unreliable *ḥadīth*s would have made it into books of *tafsīr*. Dr ʿAlasvand pointed out that the authors of works of *tafsīr* had varied aims and methods.[48] While some works, she said, were clearly *ḥadīth*-based, others were grammatical, or analytical. Dr Rahaei mentioned that many *ḥadīth*s came from Sunnī works, and were imported into Shīʿī works of *tafsīr* such as the *Tibyān* of al-Ṭūṣī and the *Majmaʿ al-Bayān* of al-Ṭabrisī, both of which rely heavily on the Sunnī tradition. He also mentioned that the purpose of works of *tafsīr* was different from that of works of jurisprudence (*fiqh*). Whereas works of *fiqh* take a particular position, the purpose of works of *tafsīr* was to elucidate all possible meanings of a verse. In the Akhbārī works of *tafsīr*, those based on transmitted opinions, they have 'no scientific facts, there is no proof'.[49] According to Dr Rahaei, many of the *ḥadīth*s contained in works of *tafsīr* are not authentic, and actually contradict the Qurʾān. 'In the works of *fiqh*', he says, 'where there is the need for proof the likes of these narrations are not seen, because they are weak *ḥadīth*s'.[50] Dr Rahaei's claim that the encyclopaedic nature of *tafsīr* accounts for the indiscriminateness of its authors in their inclusion of *ḥadīth*s, goes some way towards explaining why, if these *ḥadīth*s were so far removed from the true Islamic ideal, they were able to appear at all.

Some *ʿulamāʾ* admitted that culture plays a role in the production of religious knowledge. For them, it is important to take context into account when assessing the reliability of *ḥadīth*s. The professors at the reformist Mofid University were particular proponents of the use of

[46] Fariba ʿAlasvand, Personal Interview, Qom, Iran, 8 June 2011.
[47] Saeed Rahaei, Personal Interview, Qom, Iran, 7 June 2011.
[48] Dr ʿAlasvand, Personal Interview. [49] Saeed Rahaei, Personal Interview. [50] Ibid.

reason/rationality (ʿ*aql*) when assessing the reliability of *ḥadīth*s. In the Introduction, I referred to the Uṣūlī theory of interpretation, which admits the use of rationality in deriving the law. Dr Naser Ghorbannia is the dean of the Department of Law at Mofid; he teaches both law and Islamic law, and has degrees in law and in Islamic studies. He explained how and why he would use his rational ability to reject *ḥadīth*s:

KAREN BAUER: Some *ḥadīth*s say that Eve was created from the rib.

NASER GHORBANNIA: It is not correct in my opinion, and distinguished Islamic scholars say that this is not correct.

KB: But how do you know the *ḥadīth* is not correct? What is the proof that the *ḥadīth* is not correct?

NG: Because this is not reconcilable with the basis of Islamic law and the basis of the Holy Qurʾān. From the other verses of the Holy Qurʾān, we infer that men and women are the same. That's the first point. And you know that Islamic traditions have reached us from 1400 years ago. Today, it is possible that we hear of something happening in the United States but we don't know if what we have heard is correct or incorrect. How can it be that these traditions that we received from 1400 years ago are exactly correct? The Holy Qurʾān told us not to accept the traditions that are not compatible with it.

KB: So you can use your reason (ʿ*aql*) to deduce that?

NG: Yes, of course you can use rationality. In our traditions, our Imāms say to us, and the Prophet told us that God the Creator has sent two messengers to us. One is external, that is the Prophet, and the other messenger is internal, that is rationality and reason. Reason is our prophet ... so we are obliged to interpret the Holy Qurʾān by our reason, and with our intellect.[51]

Dr Ghorbannia's statement that 'reason is our prophet' was unlike anything that I had heard or read. His position marks a startling break from the focus on transmitted sources that characterises much modern discourse among the ʿ*ulamā*ʾ; I was shocked that he would put reason on a par with revelation. Yet, at its root, this idea goes back to earlier Shīʿī sources, as described in the Introduction. And not only reformists asserted that rationality should be used to interpret the Qurʾān: Mr Zibaei Nejad, the director of the Women's Study Resource Center, admitted that rationality is an independent source of interpretation, and named it as a

[51] Naser Ghorbannia, Personal Interview, Qom, Iran, 29 May 2011.

Shī'ī idea of interpretation.[52] He also explained that, although God's intention is constant in the Qur'ān and does not change, human understanding may change through time.[53] However, Dr Ghorbannia's analogy between human reason and the Prophet goes beyond the idea of evolving human understanding of revelation, and instead is a bold assertion that religious truth itself is a living, evolving construct that accommodates new realities.

SUMMARY AND CONCLUSION

All modern interpreters agree that Q. 4:1 indicates that the sexes have equal value, which represents a change from medieval interpretations. Most Sunnī interpreters nevertheless try to work with *ḥadīths* that were held to be true in the medieval commentaries, while most Imāmī Shī'ī interpreters reject such *ḥadīths*. Yet there is a divide even among Imāmī interpreters as to whether it is permissible to reinterpret the Qur'ān, and as to the correct bases of interpretation. Some *'ulamā'* believe *ḥadīths* may be rejected by critiquing their chains of transmission, while others believe that this is only one method of critique and that rationality is a basis of interpretation, so human intellect may be used to judge the validity of *ḥadīths*. Or, in a radical step, according to some, rationality has equivalence to *ḥadīths* as a source of interpretation.

Interpreters who advocate the use of rationality do not always advance reformist interpretations. Ayatollah Mohaghegh Damad believes that rationality is the correct basis of interpretation, but nevertheless rejects the possibility that the Qur'ān supports the scientific theory of evolution. And, although they rejected *ḥadīths*, conservatives maintained the idea of an unchanging core by speaking of the unchanging *ḥukm* of the verse. This nuanced picture of the scholars' attitudes towards *ḥadīths* belies the simplistic notion that *ḥadīths*, taken at face value, are the ultimate arbiter of the Qur'ān.

Most interpreters took a traditional view of human origins: the first two humans were Adam and Eve; God created them, and they did not evolve. However, a few interpreters said that the Qur'ān supports the theory of evolution, that the Qur'ān is silent about evolution, or that it is not the place of a religious text to address modern scientific theory. Instead, for the latter scholars, the Qur'ān should be seen as a text of

[52] Zibaei Nejad, Personal Interview, Qom, Iran, 28 May 2011.
[53] Zibaei Nejad, Personal Email Communication, 26 June 2014.

spiritual guidance. One scholar asserted that belief in Adam and Eve does not necessarily preclude belief in evolution: according to him, Adam and Eve themselves could have evolved.

My analysis of modern *ʿulamāʾ* has revealed different alliances along the lines of reformist, conservative, Sunnī, and Imāmī Shīʿī. In the case of women's testimony, I observed a clear divide between reformists and conservatives, but a negligible division between Sunnīs and Imāmī Shīʿīs. Those positions were reversed in interpretations of human creation: here the divide between conservatives and reformists was often negligible, while that between Sunnīs and Shīʿīs was stark. These different alliances are due, in part, to the nature of the verses and their import in the world of the *ʿulamāʾ*. The strict division between conservatives and reformists on women's testimony can be explained because women's testimony is a defining issue for reformists and conservatives. In both the Sunnī and Imāmī Shīʿī worlds, it is one of the areas on which they mark their position as to the reinterpretability of the Qurʾān, as well as indicating their attitude towards law and the state. The acceptance of modern scientific findings is much less charged politically, and is in many ways more complicated to assess in terms of its salience in the conservative–reformist divide. That is partially because of issues of schooling and translation: it is not clear how much of the scientific basis of evolution is taught in schools or widely understood through translated materials, where it has often been mediated or distorted. In the world of the *ʿulamāʾ*, evolution is not widely perceived as fact, but rather as a disproven theory or one of many potentially valid hypotheses. The modern Imāmī Shīʿī rejection of *ḥadīth*s on creation is therefore not due to widespread acceptance of scientific theories. Instead, it can be attributed at least in part to ʿAllāma Ṭabāṭabāʾī's attitude towards *ḥadīth*s.

The varied interpretations of human creation and the interpreters' attitudes towards *ḥadīth*s are indicative of the vibrant interpretive possibilities that emerge when medieval interpretations go beyond the boundaries considered fair, right, and proper today. These ethical considerations are put to the test in verses on marital hierarchy, which are discussed in the final section of this book.

MARRIAGE

5

Who Does the Housework? The Ethics and Etiquette of Marriage

A treatise on maintenance written by the early Ḥanafī jurist ʿUmar al-Khaṣṣāf (d. 261/874) describes the difference between a servant and a wife. It includes the statement that 'a wife's maintenance is obligatory because of her [sexual] availability, not because of her service'.[1] According to this early Ḥanafī legal source, a wife is obliged to make herself available to her husband sexually, but not to provide service in the house; on the contrary, her husband must maintain her servant, whether slave or free.[2] Some early *tafāsīr* reflect early *fiqh* by stating, overtly or implicitly, that women are owed servants in the house. For instance, Ibn Wahb lists service as a part of the maintenance that a man owes to his wife:

> *Women are owed* [3]rights and respect by their husbands like that which they owe to their husbands *bi'l-maʿrūf* in terms of companionship, and intimacy; *and men have a degree over them* superiority (*faḍīla*) in rationality (*al-ʿaql*), inheritance, blood wit, and witnessing; and what they owe in terms of maintenance [of their wives] and service (*khidma*).[4]

The Shāfiʿī al-Qushayrī states explicitly in his *tafsīr* that 'wives have a right to servants if their circumstances permit it'.[5] The wife's right to service was an early legal norm, possibly put in place as a consequence

1 As quoted by Ali, *Marriage and Slavery in Early Islam*, pp. 75–6. 2 Ibid., p. 76.

3 In Chapters 5 and 6, excerpts from Q. 2:228 and Q. 4:34 are italicized but not otherwise identified.

4 Ibn Wahb al-Dīnawarī (attrib.)., *Tafsīr ibn Wahb al-musamma al-wāḍiḥ fī tafsīr al-Qurʾān*, ed. Aḥmad Farīd (Beirut: Bār al-Kutub al-ʿIlmiyya, 2003)., v. 1, p. 75 (at Q. 2:228).

5 Abū ʾl Qāsim ʿAbd al-Karīm Al-Qushayrī, *Laṭāʾif al-ishārāt*, ed. Ibrāhīm Basyūnī (Cairo: Dār al-Kātib al-ʿArabī l [1968]).., v. 1, p. 193 (at Q. 2:228).

of the number of readily available slaves in the earliest period, plus the fact that in the period before mass conversion, Muslims were the political and military elite and could afford slaves. However, the ruling on service was not shared by all schools of law. The Ḥanbalī jurist Ibn Qayyim al-Jawziyya (d. 751/1350) clarifies the difference between legal schools:

> A group of jurists forbids making wives' service to their husbands in anything an obligation, and among those who hold to this opinion are Mālik, al-Shāfiʿī, Abū Ḥanīfa, and the Ẓāhirīs. They say that because the contract of marriage only stipulates enjoyment, not servitude, and [because it stipulates] spending freely for [the wives'] benefit, the *ḥādīth*s mentioned above only indicate that voluntary [service] is moral and noble, but not that it is a necessity.[6]

Ibn al-Qayyim explains that, according to the Ḥanafī, Shāfiʿī, Mālikī and Ẓāhirī schools of law, the wife should serve the husband, but this is only voluntary, not obligatory. For these schools of law, the marital contract stipulates 'enjoyment', meaning that the wife make herself sexually available to the husband. However, Ibn al-Qayyim's own view, as a Ḥanbalī, is that a wife should be required to provide service in the house:

> As for creating ease and relaxation for women, and their husbands' serving them by sweeping, grinding, kneading, washing, making the beds, and undertaking the service of the house; it is reprehensible (*min al-munkar*). God Most High says, *women's rights are equal to their duties in kindness* and He says, *Men are qawwāmūn over women.* So if women don't serve their husbands but rather their husbands are their servants, then the wife would be in charge of her husband (*al-qawwāma ʿalayhi*).[7]

By Ibn al-Qayyim's time, there were societies in which most people were Muslim, including those who were not rich. Perhaps as a consequence, he does not assume that there will be household servants, as do the earlier sources; instead, he assumes that either husband or wife must do the housework. And since one of the two must do it, he explains that women's performance of household duties is a part of men's authority over them: for men to undertake such work would make wives *qawwāmāt* over their husbands. In his view, men's doing such work would subvert their authority over women, overturning the gender hierarchy established in Q. 4:34.

[6] Ibn Qayyim al-Jawziyya, *al-Ḍawʾ al-munīr ʿalā al-tafsīr*, compiled and edited by ʿAlī b. Ḥamad b. Muḥammad al-Ṣāliḥī (Riyadh: Muʾassasat al-Nūr/Maktabat Dār al-Salām, 1999), v. 2, p. 211 (at Q. 2:228). This *tafsīr* is a modern compilation.

[7] Ibid.

As I showed in the case of women's testimony, the position of an exegete's legal school often influences his interpretation. It was, therefore, something of a surprise to me to find al-Zamakhsharī, a Ḥanafī, recommending that women should do the housework:

Their rights are like their obligations it is necessary that women have rights over men, like men's necessary rights over them. *Bi'l-ma'rūf* in a way that does not contradict the customs of the people (*'ādāt al-nās*) nor the law (*sharī'a*). Women should not ask men to fulfill duties that are not men's obligations towards them, nor should men ask women to fulfill duties that are not women's obligations; nor should either of the spouses treat the other harshly.[8]

In this passage, al-Zamakhsharī acknowledges that the Qur'ān, *sunna* of the Prophet, and previous exegeses are not the only determinants of interpretation. He interprets *bi'l-ma'rūf* to refer to social custom, which necessitates different household roles for men and women:

The parallelism [legislated in the verse with the words *women's rights are like their duties*] is in terms of duties in their proper essence, not in the type of deed. So if wives wash their husband's clothes, or bake for them, it is not necessary for husbands to do the same; it is acceptable for them to do things that men do.[9]

In siding with customary practice and common understanding, al-Zamakhsharī apparently goes against the ruling of his school of law on the matter, which was probably archaic by his time and did not make sense for his society. In other words, custom becomes normative over and above other authoritative sources, such as the established interpretation of al-Zamakhsharī's legal school. He is not the only exegete to adopt this interpretation.[10] Fakhr al-Dīn al-Rāzī provides a much fuller explanation of exactly why women should provide service in the house:

8 al-Zamakhsharī, *al-Kashshāf*, v. 1, p. 272 (at Q. 2:228). 9 Ibid.

10 Other exegetes who quote al-Zamakhsharī (without always mentioning him by name) are: al-Bayḍāwī (Shāfi'ī, d. 685/1286), al-Nasafī (Ḥanafī, d. 710/1310), Abū Ḥayyān (Mālikī/Shāf'ī, d. 745/1353), al-Biqā'ī, Muḥsin al-Fayd (Imāmī) and al-Qūnawī (Ḥanafī). Bayḍāwī's interpretation was very brief. He said: 'women have rights over men like men's rights over women, in terms of necessary duties and claims, but not in terms of type [of deed] (*jins*)' (al-Bayḍāwī and al-Qūnawī, *Ḥāshiyat al-Qūnawī 'alā tafsīr al-Imām al-Bayḍāwī*, ed. 'Abd Alāh Maḥmūd Muḥammad 'Umar (Beirut Dār al-Kutub al-'Ilmiyya, 2001), v. 1, p. 251, at Q. 2:228). Al-Nasafī quotes al-Zamakhsharī exactly. See 'Abd Allāh b. Aḥmad al-Nasafī, *Tafsīr al-Nasafī*, ed. Marwān Muḥammad al-Sha'ār (Beirut: Dār Nafā'is, 1996), v. 1, p. 180 (at Q. 2:228). Abū Ḥayyān explains that the law pays attention to customs, but does not explain further. Abū Ḥayyān, *al-Baḥr al-muḥīṭ*, v. 2, p. 200 (at Q. 2:228).

> The second possible interpretation [of the degree that men have over women] is [that] the desire for the benefits and pleasure [of marriage] is shared by both [husbands and wives], because the intention of marriage is tranquility (*al-sakan*), companionship, love (*mawadda*),[11] the intermeshing of lineage, increasing helpers and loved ones, and attaining pleasure (*al-ladhdha*). Both men and women share in these aspects of marriage; it is indeed possible to say that women get more out of it, and moreover that husbands alone [are responsible for] various kinds of rights of their wives: the dowry, maintenance, defending their wives, providing for their requirements, and keeping them from harm. So women's providing service to their husbands is more certainly obligatory in view of their extra duties towards their wives.[12] This is why God said: *Men are* qawwāmūn *over women* ... and the Prophet said 'if I had ordered anyone to prostrate themselves before anyone other than God, I would have ordered women to prostrate themselves before their husbands'.[13]

Fakhr al-Dīn states clearly that because women get more out of marriage, meaning that all of their financial needs, clothing, and food must be paid for by their husbands, they should serve in the household. He also says that housework is legally obligatory. As with al-Zamakhsharī, ideas about the common practice and the 'right' way to organise the household take precedence over older, established, authoritative sources. That is because the very notion of what is correct and right has changed through time along with changing social practices.

Why is this example important? In the medieval period, it can be difficult to contextualise jurists' and interpreters' debates in any kind of social setting, and particularly to know how social customs or historical trends may have influenced interpretation. It is equally hard to trace how these customary practices, and common sense about what is intuitively 'right' may have developed. In this case, social custom prevails even over an interpreter's school of law, because social custom supports the gender hierarchy, whereas a widespread application of the early laws might disrupt it, even though these laws were probably never intended to require husbands to do housework but rather referred to a wife's right to have servants. This example shows how, as social practice changed through time, law also slowly and subtly shifted to accommodate those changed social circumstances. It also sheds light on how the interpreters' sense of

[11] The terms *sakan* and *mawadda* relate directly to Q. 30:21: *And one of His signs is that He created mates for you from yourselves that you may find tranquility in them (li-taskunu ilayhā), and He put love (mawadda) and mercy between you.*

[12] *Fa-kāna qiyām al-mar'a bi-khidmati al-rajul ākad wujūban ri'āyatan li-hādhihi al-ḥuqūq al-zā'ida.*

[13] Fakhr al-Dīn al-Rāzī, *al-Tafsīr al-kabīr*, v. 6, p. 102 (at Q. 2:228).

what was socially or intuitively 'right' and 'wrong' guided their interpretations. It therefore serves as a key example for the remainder of this chapter, which examines the nature of marriage in the Qur'ān and medieval interpretations, with a particular focus on questions of what was considered to be just and fair in the marital relationship, and how these notions of justice and fairness developed through time.

It will not surprise many readers that hierarchy is at the heart of the medieval Islamic conception of marriage.[14] Most medieval interpreters agree on the following: spouses should be kind to one another, a husband is obliged to pay for the maintenance of his wife, and a wife is obliged to obey her husband (within certain disputed boundaries); he is in charge of her and responsible for disciplining her if she goes wrong, but such disciplinary measures should not be used without due cause, nor be taken too far. Medieval exegetes often quibble over the fine points of the marital bargain – how hard can a husband hit his wife? – but not its overall outline. Therefore, the underlying question here is not only what the exegetes said (which is, at times, entirely predictable), but why they said it. I argue that the interpreters' fundamental notion of marriage as a hierarchy, including each of the elements listed here, comes from the Qur'ān itself. But common understanding, ethical considerations, and common practice, which can be considered normative for interpretation, all inform the exegetes' elaborations on, and justifications of, the Qur'ān's basic description of the marital hierarchy.[15]

Much has been written on the marital hierarchy in medieval Islamic sources, particularly on the 'beating' aspect of Q. 4:34. These studies have been valuable in exposing the androcentric worldview of the interpreters and their general milieu, and in showing how this has affected the interpretation of the Qur'ān.[16] Moreover, a few seek to understand the ethical

[14] Cf. Kecia Ali: 'Hierarchy, tempered to a greater or lesser degree by affection, stood at the core of marriage. The jurists showed no hesitation in making analogies between wives and slaves or between marriage and commercial transactions. In fact, their central notion about marriage was that the marriage contract granted a husband, in exchange for payment of dower, a form of authority or dominion (*milk*) over his wife's sexual (and usually reproductive) capacity' (*Marriage and Slavery in Early Islam*, p. 6).

[15] Cf. Manuela Marín, 'Disciplining wives: a historical reading of Qur'ān 4:34', p. 29: 'Individual predilections did play a role in the varying interpretations given to Qur'ān 4:34, but exegetical authors were also reflecting the prevalent social and intellectual consensus of their times'.

[16] A few of these include Kecia Ali, 'The Best of You Will Not Strike: al-Shāfi'ī on Qur'ān, *sunnah*, and Wife-Beating', *Journal of Comparative Islamic Studies* 2.2 (December 2006):

tensions that arise from allowing husbands to beat their wives. Kecia Ali, for instance, shows how al-Shāfiʿī sought to reconcile the Prophet's *sunna* of not beating with the Qur'ānic verse; he recommended not beating. Ayesha Chaudhry asserts that the husbands' right to beat was the natural culmination of the interpreters' view of the relationship between wives, husbands, and God.[17]

I suggest that the interpreters sought to frame marriage within the context of common notions of just rulership. The exegetes' description of marriage as a hierarchy was predicated on the idealised vision that the stronger party (the man) should treat the weaker party (the woman) within acceptable bounds of propriety. This fundamental notion of just rule explains why it is common for the exegetes to compare the husband to a ruler and the wife to the ruled party, or the husband to a shepherd and the wife to the flock.[18] I would contend that beating as a consequence of disobedience was, for them, a natural corollary of the husband's rulership in a context in which corporal punishment for crimes was accepted or even presumed (and was also mentioned in the Qur'ān, as was the beating of wives). And as in statecraft, some rulership or rulings may seem arbitrary. In certain works, there seems to be a tension between the lists of justifications for male rule and the admission that wifely obedience may not be fair or easy for women. Yet the exegetes state repeatedly that the hierarchy and all that it entailed was the best way to achieve a state of fellowship, companionship, and harmony between the spouses.

The following pages explore each of the aspects of the marital hierarchy in turn: the duty of mutual kindness, the justification for male superiority in the hierarchy, the wife's duty to obey, and the consequences of her disobedience. This is a long and complex chapter; I have left it as a unit because I believe this is how the exegetes saw marriage. Each part of their interpretations was predicated on the other parts, and even

pp. 143–55; Ayesha Chaudhry, *Domestic Violence and the Islamic Tradition*; Hadia Mubarak, 'Breaking apart the Interpretive Monopoly: A Re-examination of Verse 4:34', *Hawwa: Journal of Women of the Middle East and Islamic World* 2.3 (2004): pp. 261–89; Manuela Marín, 'Disciplining Wives: a Historical Reading of Qur'ān 4:34'. New studies are appearing all the time. I regret that I have not been able to include references to all of the existing studies on Q. 4:34, and that references to some of the studies mentioned before, namely Chaudhry's *Domestic Violence*, are somewhat curtailed, as the book appeared after I had already written this chapter.

17 Ali, 'The Best of You Will Not Strike'; Chaudhry, *Domestic Violence*.

18 On hierarchy in governance, and women's place in the social order, see Patricia Crone, *Medieval Islamic Political Thought* (Edinburgh: Edinburgh University Press, 2005), pp. 332–57, esp. pp. 340–2, 'justifying social inequality'.

punishment for disobedience was supposed to be moderated by the repeated prescriptions for kindness. Thus, I go against the view that medieval interpreters only saw the Qurʾān in isolated bits and pieces, and that their fragmented interpretations do not take into account the Qurʾān's larger vision, or those who say that medieval exegetes were all entirely misogynist.[19] I believe that medieval authors took it for granted that certain parts of the Qurʾān related to others, telling a coherent story. They were not lacking in ethics, but their idea of justice differed from that of many of today's interpreters, who privilege notions of equality and egalitarianism over hierarchies, particularly in the marital relationship.

A. MARRIAGE IN THE QURʾĀN AND AN EARLY INTERPRETATION

The Qurʾānic spousal relationship involves some element of sharing, discussion, and reciprocity. For instance, in Q. 2:233, both spouses should agree when to wean their children. Mutuality is assured in other verses: in Q. 2:187 husbands and wives are described as 'garments' for one another; they are seen to complete one another and to be suited to one another. In Q. 30:21, God *created for you mates of your type, so that you may find tranquility in them, and he put love and compassion between you. Verily there are signs for those who reflect.* Reciprocity, kindness, and compassion are therefore part of the Qurʾān's conception of marriage.

But, as Kecia Ali has argued, control of basic aspects such as divorce and sexual intimacy lies in the hands of the husband. When describing marriage and divorce, the Qurʾān often addresses men, speaking to them about women.[20] As I noted earlier, Ali describes this as an androcentric perspective. Husbands are allowed more than one wife (Q. 4:3), men are allowed female concubines with whom sexual relations are permitted (Q. 4:3, Q. 4:24, and others), and husbands are put in charge of divorce proceedings (Q. 2:226–2:237). In Q. 2:223, wives are described not only as garments for the husbands, but as their tilth; the Qurʾān instructs husbands to *go into the tilth whenever you like.*[21] The implication is that men are considered to be in charge of sex within marriage.

[19] Cf. Ayesha Chaudhry, 'Pre-Colonial exegesis cannot easily be labeled as "atomistic" while post-Colonial and reformist interpretations are seen as "holistic"', in *Domestic Violence and the Islamic Tradition*, p. 203.

[20] Ali, *Sexual Ethics and Islam*, p. 112.

[21] For a more detailed treatment of these verses, see ibid.

Some modern readers view these two aspects of marriage as incompatible, or at least in tension with one another. But medieval exegetes saw both types of verse as a part of the larger picture of marriage. The verses at the heart of this chapter, Q. 4:34 and Q. 2:228, encapsulate much of what the exegetes see as the core elements of a marriage: affection and good conduct, mutual rights, the husband's financial support, his superiority, the wife's obedience, and the consequences of her disobedience.

Q. 2:228 speaks of the way that a husband and wives should behave in the case of divorce. The full verse, with the portion to be analysed here in bold, reads:

> Women who are divorced shall wait, keeping themselves apart, for three [monthly] courses. It is not lawful for them that they should conceal that which God has created in their wombs, if they are believers in God and the last day. And their husbands would do better to take them back in that case if they desire a reconciliation. **Women have rights like their obligations according to what is right, and men have a degree over them** (***lahunna mithlu 'lladhī ʿalayhinna bi'l-maʿrūfi wa-lil-rijāl ʿalayhinna darajatun***). God is Mighty, Wise.[22]

The part of Q 2:228 in bold consists of two elements: the statement that women have rights like their obligations 'according to what is right' (*bi'l-maʿrūf*), and the statement that men have a degree over them. Since the rest of the verse is about divorce, *women have rights like their obligations* is usually taken to be a prescription for how to behave during a marriage or divorce, rather than a general statement that women have rights. Thus, a better translation from the point of view of the exegetes might be: *wives have rights against their husbands like those that their husbands have against them.* A key point is the term 'like' (*mithl*), which has been interpreted in two ways: that women's and men's duties to one another are the same – women and men are each owed sex in marriage, for instance – or that women have rights just as their husbands have rights. In the latter case, the wives and husbands are not owed the same rights, but, for instance, husbands are obligated to maintain their wives and wives are obligated to obey their husbands. For many exegetes, particularly in the earliest period, the phrase *bi'l-maʿrūf* means that the mutual rights and obligations mentioned here encapsulate the moral obligation of good treatment in marriage; men's 'degree' consists of those elements that give men an edge over women.

While Q. 2:228 alludes to affection and good treatment in marriage, Q 4:34 completes the elements of the marital bargain: payment of maintenance, wifely obedience, and punishment for disobedience. The

[22] Trans: Pickthall, with my amendments.

following translation reflects the way that the majority of medieval exegetes would have understood the verse:

Men are in charge of women, because God has given the one more than the other, and because they maintain them with their property; so the good women are obedient, guarding for the absent what God has guarded, and if you fear misconduct (*nushūz*), admonish them, shun them in the beds, and strike them; and if they obey you, do not seek a way against them; surely, God is exalted, and great.

Every part of the verse is up for discussion by the exegetes. *Bi-mā*, which I have translated as 'because', could also be translated as 'with what'. 'The one ... the other' could also be 'some more than others'. But in the first part of this verse, three terms are particularly important: *qawwāmūn*, *faḍḍala*, and *anfaqū*. *Qawwāmūn*, the term translated here as 'in charge', could also be translated as 'supporters of', and indeed most exegetes understand that *qawwāmūn* entails men's support of *and* control over their wives. *Faḍḍala*, translated as 'given more than' could be 'made superior to'. Therefore, when the exegetes describe the ways in which men are superior to women, it is in part because they are reading this term as superiority. And finally, the term for 'spending', *anfaqū*, is from the same root as the term for 'maintenance', *nafaqa*. This verse could be read in conjunction with the verses that mention men's spending on women, such as *let the wealthy man spend* [in maintenance] (*li-yunfiq*) *according to his means* (Q. 65:7), *give the women their dowries as a gift, but if they, of their own desire, remit any of it to you, then take it and enjoy it* (Q. 4:4), and *do not covet that with which God has made some to excel others* (*faḍḍala Allāh bihi baʿḍakum ʿalā baʿḍin*); *for men there is a reward from what they have earned, and for women a reward from what they have earned* (Q. 4:32). The language of Q. 4:32, in particular, echoes that of Q. 4:34: both verses refer to God's preference for some over others/the one over the other (*baʿḍ ʿalā baḍ*); Q. 4:32 seems to be a direct reference to men's greater inheritance. Taken together, these verses indicate that men get more money in inheritance than women, but they must in turn spend this on maintaining their wives. Reading the terms *qawwāmūn*, *faḍḍala*, and *anfaqū* in the context of Q. 4:34 and other verses of the Qurʾān, the text itself seems to connect spending on women for their maintenance with control over them.

The second half of Q. 4:34 addresses wifely obedience. This portion of the verse reads: *and those women from whom you fear* nushūz, *admonish them, shun them in the beds, and strike them; and if they obey you, do not seek a way against them*. This part of Q. 4:34 specifies punishments for a woman who commits *nushūz*, which in exegeses of this verse is usually understood to mean women's disobedience and in particular their refusal to have sex. This part of the verse switches from a description (*men are...*) to a direct address (*if you fear...*). The verse is addressed to men, and the recipients of the three punishments are in the feminine plural. Thus, it cannot be reversed to say that wives should admonish, avoid, or beat their husbands.[23] Even though *nushūz* is a word that appears in the Qur'ān to describe the behaviour of both wives and husbands, it is treated differently in each case. The Qur'ānic verse regarding wives' *nushūz* (Q. 4:34) is directly addressed to husbands ('if you fear *nushūz*'), whereas the verse regarding the husbands' *nushūz* (Q. 4:128) is impersonal ('if a wife fears *nushūz*').[24] More to the point, the suggestions about dealing with *nushūz* in the Qur'ān are different for husbands and wives: whereas husbands confronting their wives' *nushūz* are advised to implement the three-stage punishment described previously, the suggestion for wives dealing with husbands' *nushūz* is that it is 'best' to reach an 'amicable settlement'. In Q. 4:34 *nushūz* and its consequences are directly related to the final phrase of the verse, *and if they* [f. pl.] *obey you, do not seek a way against them* [f. pl.]. Like the clauses before it on admonishment, shunning, and beating, this phrase is addressed to men, and speaks about women in the feminine plural. This final phrase makes it clear that, no matter what the exact definition of *nushūz*, disobedience is the cause of wives' punishment, and wifely obedience is the way to avoid such punishment.

For the medieval interpreters, both parts of Q. 4:34 work together to describe the spousal relationship. The husband must support the wife financially because he has been endowed with more than she, and the wife must obey the husband. If she does, he should not do anything against her, but if she does not, then he has the right to punish her in three stages. The following verse (Q. 4:35) addresses the consequences of a breach between the couple, and suggests getting an arbiter for each side.

Muqātil b. Sulaymān's interpretation is a good precursor to some of the main issues that arise in this chapter. He begins his interpretation with the verse's Occasion of Revelation (*sabab al-nuzūl*), a type of *ḥadīth* that describes the circumstances in which a verse was revealed. In this case, the Occasion establishes the extent of a man's rights over his wife, although these rights initially seem unfair to the wife, her father, and even the Prophet:

[23] Karen Bauer, '*The Male is Not Like the Female* (Q. 3:36): The Question of Gender Egalitarianism in the Qur'ān', *Religion Compass* 3/4 (2009): pp. 637–54, at p. 641.

[24] Q. 4:128 reads: *If a wife fears* nushūz *or reluctance* (i'rāḍ) *from her husband, there is no blame for them if they reach an amicable settlement, and such a settlement is best*'.

This verse was revealed concerning Saʿd b. al-Rabīʿ b. ʿAmr who was one of the Naqībs,[25] and his wife, Ḥabība bt. Zayd b. Abī Zuhayr. They were among the *Anṣār* of the Banū Ḥārith b. Khazraj. He slapped his wife, and she went to her family. Her father went with her to the Prophet and said, 'I married my daughter to him and gave her to his bed (*ankaḥtuhu wa-afrashtuhu karīmatī*), and he slapped her!' The Prophet ordered retaliation (*qiṣāṣ*), and she went to take retaliation from him, when the Prophet said, 'Come back! Gabriel has come to me and revealed this verse!'[26]

This Occasion portrays a time when the legal norms on husbands' rights had not yet been established, a time when Islamic practice is being distinguished from pre-Islamic practice. Ḥabība, her father, and the Prophet are all apparently outraged that her husband has dared to slap her. The Prophet orders that the slap be punished with *qiṣāṣ*, the legal response to a particular type of wrongdoing, involving either a monetary reward or punishment equal to the offence. However, Muḥammad's inclination to punish the husband is corrected by this verse allowing men to hit their wives.

The Occasion is given to establish a verse's historical context, and therefore to shed light on its true meaning and any laws to which it pertains. But in some cases such *ḥadīth*s are ex post facto explanations for a verse's interpretation that serve to justify the laws that were developed after the time of the Qurʾān. The Occasion of Q. 4:34 justifies later Islamic legal opinions that allow men to slap their wives without legal consequences; it is difficult to say whether the Occasion was the cause of those laws, or whether it is simply an ex post facto explanation for them.[27] In either case, however, this particular Occasion shows the tension that existed about notions of the correct, ethical behaviour towards wives, and the question of whether a husband's rights over his wife extended to physical chastisement.

Instead of finishing the story of the Occasion of Revelation, at this point Muqātil goes through the verse that was revealed, pausing to explain:

Men are qawwāmūn *over women.* They say it means that men are in authority over women (*musallaṭūn*). *With what God has given some more than others* that is that men have more rights than their wives *and with what they spend of their wealth*

[25] This term refers to the twelve representatives appointed by the Medinans who were negotiating with Muḥammad about the *hijra* from Mecca to Medina.

[26] Muqātil, *Tafsīr*, p. 370 (at Q. 4:34). In her article 'Disciplining Wives: A Historical Reading of Qurʾān 4:34', Manuela Marín describes several different versions of this *ḥadīth*.

[27] Cf. Ayesha Chaudhry, *Domestic Violence and the Islamic Tradition*, p. 33.

meaning, husbands have been given more because they pay wives the dowry. So they are in authority concerning moral guidance/discipline (*al-adab*) and managing them (*al-akhdh ʿalā yadayhinna*). There is no legal retaliation [when men beat their wives], other than when they kill or wound them. At that, the Prophet said, 'I wanted one thing, God wanted another, and what God wants is better'.[28]

In this interpretation, men's financial maintenance is directly linked to their control over women's behaviour and bodies. Muqātil first uses the term 'in authority over' (*musallaṭūn*) to describe men's relationship to women. *Sulṭa* is also used to describe political authority, a connection which is developed in later exegeses. Men are in charge of certain matters, including *adab* and 'holding their hands'. Both of these terms are somewhat difficult to translate. First and foremost *adab* as used here connotes moral guidance, and gaining praiseworthy discipline and training. Later exegetes used the term *taʾdīb*, which has a clearer connotation of disciplining, chastising, and punishing. I have translated 'holding their hands' as 'managing them', which conveys men's legal responsibilities for, and rights over, their wives.

Muqātil clarifies that men have more rights than women, and that this is because of the dowry. In turn, men have a measure of control over women's behaviour/morality: 'they pay wives the dowry, *so* they are in authority over women's moral guidance/discipline'. Thus, it seems that God has given men more wealth so that they will have the ability to pay their wives' dowries and maintenance, which in turn enables them to discipline them and restrain them from going astray. How far can this discipline and control go? Muqātil explains that there should be no legal retaliation – of the type sought by Ḥabība and her father – except in cases of wounding (*jurḥ*) or loss of life (*nafs*). This is one of several legal opinions about the limits beyond which men can be punished for beating their wives.[29] Through the Prophet's words 'I wanted one thing, and God wanted another', the Occasion portrays a time when the rules are being established, and explains the rulings in the verse when nobody – not even the Prophet – was entirely sure of what was correct.

Muqātil's interpretation offers the most expansive definition of men's authority in the early texts. And unlike other early commentators, Muqātil specifies that the 'obedient women' spoken of in this verse are obedient to God *and* to their husbands. 'Then God Almighty described women,

[28] Muqātil, *Tafsīr*, p. 370–1 (at Q. 4:34).

[29] On the legal limits of wife beating, see Chaudhry, 'Chapter 3: The Legal Boundaries of Marital Discipline', *Domestic Violence and The Islamic Tradition*, pp. 95–132.

saying *so the good women* in the religion *are obedient*, meaning obedient to God and to their husbands'.[30] In the exegesis of both Q. 4:34 and Q. 2:228, women's obedience to their husbands is linked to their obedience to God. As is clear from the commentary examined here, obedience to the husband becomes religious obedience; the husband becomes the context for the wife's salvation. Placing husbands between their wives and God cements the household hierarchy that the exegetes perceive to be fundamental to the nature of marriage. It is common for medieval exegetes and jurists to link God with the husband, and as Ali has noted, disobedience to husbands also becomes disobedience to God.[31] However, husbands do not *always* stand between their wives and God, for wives can disobey their husbands when the husband orders them to disobey God. The human-to-human marital hierarchy is, in such cases, secondary to the God-human hierarchy.

In the following sections, I outline each of the elements of marriage mentioned by the Qurʾān: marital kindness, the husband's position of authority, the wife's duty of obedience, and the consequences of her disobedience.

THE MUTUAL RESPONSIBILITY FOR KINDNESS[32]

Bi'l-maʿrūf is a key phrase that brings propriety into the discussion of human relations in the Qurʾān. This phrase is repeated many times in the Qurʾān. Michael Cook shows that the term is not necessarily technical or legal, but rather that it 'seems to refer to performing a legal or other action in a decent and honourable fashion'.[33] In Q. 2:228 it refers to women's rights in marriage or divorce: *women have rights like their obligations* bi'l-maʿrūf; this suggests common decency and morality in husbands' treatment of their wives, even when they are divorcing them.

30 Muqātil, *Tafsīr*, p. 370–1 (at Q. 4:34).
31 Kecia Ali, 'Religious Practices: Obedience and Disobedience', in *Encyclopedia of Women in Islamic Cultures*; also see Chaudhry, *Domestic Violence*, in numerous places, and Bauer, *Room for Interpretation* (PhD dissertation).
32 I have expanded this section into the following article: 'A Note on the Relationship Between *Tafsīr* and Common Understanding, with Reference to Contracts of Marriage', in *Islamic Cultures, Islamic Contexts*, ed. Asad Ahmed, Robert Hoyland, Behnam Sadeghi, and Adam Silverstein (Leiden: Brill, 2014) pp. 97–111.
33 Michael Cook, *Commanding Right and Forbidding Wrong in Islamic Thought*, p. 15.

Here, I compare *bi'l-ma'rūf* in the earliest works of *tafsīr* of Q. 2:228 and the documentary evidence from marriage contracts preserved from the earliest period, a period before works of *tafsīr* were commonly written. The similar language common to the sources could indicate that good treatment was a part of a widespread understanding of marriage, and that this popular understanding informed the scholarly works of *tafsīr*.

The nature of the genre of *tafsīr* means that supposedly early interpretations, from a time before interpretation was commonly written, or before it was commonly written in books, are only preserved in later works. An interpretation of Q. 2:228 attributed to al-Ḍaḥḥāk (d. 105/723) refers explicitly to the good treatment that the husband owes to his obedient wife, and is quoted in many later works of exegesis. Here, he explains the statement 'women have rights like their obligations *bi'l-ma'rūf*': "When a woman obeys God and obeys her husband, then her husband is obligated to give her good companionship (*yuḥsin ṣuḥbatahā*), refrain from harming her, and maintain her according to his means (*wa-yunfiq 'alayha min sa'atihi*)".[34] The term 'like' is not interpreted to mean that men and women have the *same* rights and duties. Men's duties are to support women, be companions to them, and refrain from harming them. Echoing the language of Q. 65:7, *let the man of means spend according to his means* (*li-yunfiq dhū sa'atin min sa'atihi*), Ḍaḥḥāk says that men must maintain women according to their wealth. Women's duty is obedience to their husbands and to God, who are put on the same plane. Women's rights are predicated on their obedience to God and to their husbands: if they do not obey, they may forfeit their rights to maintenance, companionship, and their husbands' refraining from harming them. However, when they do obey, he must give her 'good companionship (*yuḥsin ṣuḥbatahā*)'.

The notion of good companionship in Q. 2:228 has resonance with Q. 4:19, *live with them according to what is right ('āshirūhunna bi'l-ma'rūf) for if you hate them, you may hate a thing in which God has placed much good*. Good companionship and fellowship 'according to what is right' appears in about half of the interpretations of Q. 2:228 surveyed here. The language used varies, but the root words are often the same: *ḥ-s-n*, *ṣ-ḥ-b*, *'-sh-r*, and *bi'l-ma'rūf*. Some examples from the 4th/10th and 5th/11th century include: Ibn Wahb al-Dīnawarī

[34] Al-Ḍaḥḥāk (attrib.), *Tafsīr al-Ḍaḥḥāk*, compiled and edited by Muḥammad Shukrī Aḥmad Zāwītī (Cairo: Dār al-Salām, 1999), v. 1, p. 196 (at Q. 2:228). This has been compiled from sayings attributed to al-Ḍaḥḥāk in later sources.

(d. 308/920) uses the terms *iḥsan al-ṣuḥba wa'l-mu'āshara*,[35] while al-Jaṣṣāṣ (d. 370/981) cites Q. 4:19, *live with them according to what is right* (*'āshirūhunna bi'l-ma'rūf*).[36] Many exegetes cite al-Ḍaḥḥāk specifically, using variations on his terms: al-Ṭabarī cites the opinion, which he attributes to al-Ḍaḥḥāk and others, that women are owed good treatment, while their husbands are owed obedience in those matters in which God has commanded them to obey (*lahunna ḥusn al-ṣuḥba wa'l-'ishra bi'l-ma'rūf 'alā azwājihinna, mithl alladhī 'alayhinna lahum min al-ṭā'a fīmā awjaba Allāh*).[37] Al-Māwardī cites him as saying that women are owed good companionship and a living according to what is right (*ḥusn al-ṣuḥba w'al-'ishra bi'l-ma'rūf*).[38] Al-Ṭūsī (d. 460/1067) cites him as saying that women are owed pleasant fellowship according to what is right (*ḥusn al-'ishra bi'l-ma'rūf*).[39] There is some evidence that the prescription for good companionship and pleasant fellowship 'according to what is right' seen in works of exegesis represented a widespread understanding of the verse: the root words that appear in works of *tafsīr* are often included in marriage contracts preserved from the time.

Adolf Grohmann, who in 1934 published a trove of Arabic Papyri in the Egyptian Library, has a section on marriage contracts consisting of thirteen papyri. These range in date from 233/847, a period in which *tafsīr* (meaning, in this case, interpretation rather than the genre of text) was probably passed on orally, rather than in written form, to 461/1079, the period of the flourishing of the genre of *tafsīr* in Nīshāpūr. Six are complete marriage contracts, four are fragments of marriage contracts, and three are receipts and statements of marriage gifts, rather than marriage contracts as such. In this sample, all of the complete marriage contracts mention the need for good/pleasant fellowship and companionship (*ḥusn al-ṣuḥba wa'l-mu'āshara*) or some variation of that formula, using words found in both Qur'ān and *tafsīr*. For instance, document no. 38, dated Rabi' 1, 259/5 January to 4 February, 873 reads in part:

Ismā'īl, the freedman of Aḥmad b. Marwān, undertakes the obligation in respect of his wife 'Ā'isha to fear God most High, through good companionship and fellowship, as God – mighty and sublime – has ordered and according to the sunna

[35] Ibn Wahb al-Dīnawarī (attrib.), *al-Wāḍiḥ*, v. 1, p. 75 (at Q. 2:228).
[36] Al-Jaṣṣāṣ, *Aḥkām al-Qur'ān*, v. 1, p. 442 (at Q. 2:228).
[37] Al-Ṭabarī, *Jāmi' al-Bayān*, v. 4, p. 531 (at Q. 2:228).
[38] Al-Māwardī, *al-Nukat wa'l-'uyūn*, v. 1, p. 292 (at Q. 2:228).
[39] Al-Ṭūsī, *al-Tibyān fī tafsīr al-Qur'ān*, v. 3, p. 353 (at Q. 2:228).

of Muḥammad, may the blessing of God be upon him and may He preserve him, to *keeping them according to what is right, or dismissing them in kindness.*[40]

This contract uses terms found in the *tafsīr* of Q. 2:228, *ḥusn al-ṣuḥba wa'l-mu'āshara* and an almost verbatim quotation from the following verse, Q. 2:229, *imsāk bi-ma'rūf aw tasrīḥ bi-iḥsān* (the contract includes this phrase but with the definite articles: *al-imsāk bil-ma'rūf aw al-tasrīḥ bi'l-iḥsān*). Q. 2:228 and Q. 2:229 have to do with the treatment of women in marriage and divorce: exegetes use them to specify that men should not harm women, given the rights that they have over them. The 'no harm' clause in the contract is strengthened by the mention of specific responsibilities of the husband: he must allow his new wife to see her family and must not prevent her from doing so, and she must have control of dismissing any slave girl he may purchase. It is fairly clear that this wife, or her agnates, were well aware of the nature of her husband's rights over her, and that they believed that some of the imbalance could be rectified in the marriage contract with clauses reminding her new husband of his duty of care over her, and restricting his exercise of certain rights. Another contract also mentions men's responsibility not to harm.[41]

Some contracts refer to the 'degree' that men have over women from Q. 2:228. One from the 3rd/9th century reads:

And it is his obligation to fear God – He is mighty and sublime – in respect of her and to make companionship with her pleasant, as God – may He be blessed and exalted – has ordered in His book, and the example of Muḥammad, His messenger – may the blessing of God be on him and on his family . . . in what is incumbent upon him with regard to that, and one degree more, as God – may He be exalted – says: *but men have a degree over them and God is almighty, wise* [Q. 2:228].[42]

In this contract, the husband must make his wife's life pleasing because of his degree over her. This echoes the interpretation taken by al-Ṭabarī of the degree, discussed later in this chapter. The degree is also mentioned in one of three marriage contracts published by Geoffrey Khan from the Cambridge Geniza collection; the contract in question is from 419–27/

40 Adolf Grohmann, *Arabic Papyri in the Egyptian Library* (Cairo: Egyptian Library Press, 1934), doc. 38, v. 1, pp. 68–9.

41 Ibid., doc. 41, v. 1, p. 87 (Arabic), pp. 89–90 (translation, which I have used with minor modifications). The relevant part of document 41 reads: 'he must fear God alone – He has no associate – and make companionship and life with her [his wife] pleasant, and to do her no harm, and so do what God [and Muh. . .] ammad – May God's blessings and peace be upon him – has ordained, according to the ordinance of God as to keeping her according to what is right or dismissing her in kindness'.

42 Ibid., doc. 42, v. 1, pp. 92–3.

1028–36, in the middle of the Fāṭimid period.[43] These contracts have similar wording;[44] the clause was a standard part of the marriage contract for both Sunnīs and Shīʿīs at the time.[45]

I believe that the interpretation attributed to al-Ḍaḥḥāk, which includes the terms *ḥusn al-ṣuḥba*, reflects more than the personal opinion of the supposed author. Instead, it reflects a common understanding of the meaning of the verse, which was put into the formula for marriage contracts. The interpretation attributed to al-Ḍaḥḥāk and passed down through the ages as such was a way of incorporating the common understanding into the rarefied scholarly interpretation that is the genre of *tafsīr*.

The similar wording of works of *tafsīr* and marriage contracts raises the question of the relationship between *tafsīr*, *fiqh*, and common understanding. These preserved documents are legal contracts. But the language used in them seems more akin to that which is used in works of *tafsīr* than in works of law. Kecia Ali asserts that, in early works of *fiqh*, marriage is compared to a transaction and some jurists compare wives to slaves.[46] Ali's findings regarding the juridical discussions of the nature of marriage are significant for this study; yet in key elements, the discussion in *tafsīr* and contracts differs from that in *fiqh*. Neither exegetes nor contracts describe marriage as ownership, or compare wives to slaves. Both exegetes and contracts mention the ethics and etiquette of the marital bargain, including the kindness that each of the spouses owes the other. There are of course differences between contracts and works of exegesis: contracts include practical details such as the amount of the *mahr* payment from husband to wife; exegetes, but not contracts, describe the inherent qualities in men and women that justify a hierarchy in marriage. But on the whole, when describing the nature of marriage, the tone of many early exegeses seems similar to that in contracts: both use the same types of words to explain the Qurʾān's verses on marriage. The difference between the discourses in *tafsīr* and *fiqh* can be explained in part by genre constraints. While it was part of jurists' job description to draw analogies, exegetes seek to undertake linguistic analysis of the Qurʾān in a way that often explains, for them, the underlying ethical basis of the legal rulings. Since marriage contracts were in effect a part of the wedding

[43] Geoffrey Khan, *Arabic Legal and Administrative Documents from the Cambridge Geniza Collections* (Cambridge: Cambridge University Press, 1993), pp. 193–4.

[44] Ibid. [45] See Bauer, *A Note*, in which I cite a standard form of the contract.

[46] Kecia Ali, *Marriage and Slavery in Early Islam*, p. 6.

ceremony, it may have been important for them to include clauses that sounded nice to the bride or her family. *Tafsīr* may have also had a public function, as a genre that was read aloud in mosques and beyond.

ESTABLISHING THE HIERARCHY: MEN'S ROLE

Hierarchies were considered to be a natural and fair part of medieval Muslim societies. But hierarchies were only morally acceptable insofar as the superior person deserved his or her position. In explaining why the marital hierarchy made sense, exegetes focused on the nature of men's position, why they deserved it, and their responsibilities towards their wives. As I show in this section, ethical notions of just rule were central to these interpretations: men were expected to behave in a way that befitted their position of power.

But well-justified interpretations including the 'why' and 'how' of the hierarchy developed through time. In the earliest period, exegetes aimed to explain the hierarchy in terms of the meaning of the words of the Qur'ān and the laws connected with it, rather than the reasoning behind it. Works from the period of al-Ṭabarī and before focus on men's duties and rights: their financial maintenance of their wives, their control over their wives, and their responsibility for educating and disciplining them. For these interpreters, the main question is the nature of the *faḍl* that men have over women, mentioned in Q. 4:34, and the nature of men's 'degree' from Q. 2:228. These interpretations are the base point for the more complex, fuller, interpretations in later works.

Muqātil b. Sulaymān interprets Q. 2:228 by saying that men's superiority consists of husbands' having more rights, and of the rights that they give their wives.[47] In his view, a husband is in a position to give rights, like a political leader, while wives, like political subjects, receive them. ʿAbd al-Razzāq al-Ṣanʿānī (d. 211/826), says that men have a degree 'of superiority (*faḍl*) over women'.[48] The Ibāḍī Hūd b. Muḥakkam echoes Muqātil by saying that men have superiority (*faḍīla*) in rights – he then quotes Q. 4:34 to explain this advantage.[49] In his description of Q. 2:228,

47 'Muqātil says, women have rights over their husbands like those that their husbands have over them. *And men have a degree over them* He says, husbands have superiority (*faḍīla*) over wives in rights, and due to the rights the [husbands] grant them (*wa-bi-mā sāq ilayhā min al-ḥaqq*)', Muqātil, *Tafsīr Muqātil*, v. 1, p. 194 (at Q. 2:228).

48 ʿAbd al-Razzāq al-Ṣanʿānī, *Tafsīr ʿAbd al-Razzāq*, ed. Maḥmūd Muḥammad ʿAbduh (Beirut: Dār al-Kutub al-ʿIlmiyya, 1999), v. 1, p. 347 (at Q. 2:228).

49 Hūd b. Muḥakkam, *Tafsīr*, v. 1, p. 217 (at Q. 2:228).

the Imāmī ʿAlī b. Ibrāhīm al-Qummī (fl. 4th/10th c.) does not cite issues of men's authority or any innate differences between men and women. His exegesis of Q. 4:34 is similarly neutral on these questions.[50] He focuses on men's financial maintenance of women, but does not connect men's financial maintenance with their status, or position of authority over women. In all of these cases, the interpreters emphasise that the marital hierarchy consists of rights or maintenance, and do not delve into the reasons behind it. In short, pre-Ṭabarī interpreters discuss the exact application of the verse. To the extent that this is explained, it is in terms of its legal ramifications rather than inherent qualities in the sexes.

Unlike prior exegetes, al-Ṭabarī explains marriage as a coherent, bounded, system: husbands have control over their wives because of their rank, status, and monetary support; but they must exercise that control in a fair, ethical, and just manner. In his interpretation of Q. 4:34, he asserts that God has put men in a superior position to women because they pay the dowry and maintain women, both monetarily and in other provisions. On account of their payment, men are the 'executors of command' over their wives, responsible for disciplining and managing them.[51] In other words, al-Ṭabarī describes marriage as a contract in which men's part is to pay for women's maintenance and upkeep, and their wives' part is to obey their husbands 'in the matters in which God has commanded obedience', which, according to an early authority, means that a woman must 'be good to her husband's family and preserve her husband's wealth'.[52] There is a clear parallel with ideas of just governance. In his

[50] '*Men are* qawwāmūn *over women, with what God gave some of them more than others, and with what they spend of their wealth* meaning, God made it obligatory for men to maintain women monetarily. Then He praised women, saying, *so the good women are obedient* ... meaning they guard themselves when their husbands are absent. In the narration of Abū Jārūd, on the authority of Abū Ja'far, *obedient* means obedient', al-Qummī, *Tafsīr*, v. 1, p. 137 (at Q. 4:34).

[51] 'Abū Jaʿfar [al-Ṭabarī] says that by *men are* qawwāmūn *over women*, God means that men are women's guardians (*ahl qiyām ʿalā*) for they discipline them (*taʾdībihunna*) and manage them (*al-akhdh ʿalā yadayhinna*) in those matters that God has made obligatory for the women and themselves. *With what God has given some of them more than others* meaning, God has made men superior to women, in terms of payment of the dowry, spending on the wives from the men's property, and providing them with provisions. That is the superiority (*tafḍīl*) given by God Almighty to men over women, and because of it men have been made *qawwām* over women, executors of command over them, in that part of women's affairs that God has granted to men', al-Tabarī, *Jāmiʿ al-bayān*, v. 8, p. 290 (at Q. 4:34).

[52] Al-Ṭabarī says, 'And what we have said, so have the interpreters ... on the authority of Ibn 'Abbās, "His words *men are* qawwāmūn *over women* mean that men are commanders, and that it is women's responsibility to obey them in those matters that God has

interpretation of the second half of Q. 4:34, which I describe later in this chapter, he says that a woman's duty also includes having sex with her husband.[53] Therefore, like other early exegetes, al-Ṭabarī places limits on women's obedience: obedience is in certain realms, not in all realms. The marital bargain does not necessitate a husband's total control over every aspect of his wife's behaviour, but only over 'those matters that God made obligatory for her and for him'.[54] Al-Ṭabarī's interpretation is important because he explains men's ethical responsibilities towards women as an integral part of the marital hierarchy. He also places clear limits on the nature of the obedience owed by wives to their husbands.

In his interpretation of Q. 2:228, al-Ṭabarī emphasises the theme of just governance. He frames his discussion at the beginning of Q. 2:228 around the meaning of 'like', citing two groups of exegetes: the first takes the view that 'like' means 'just as' (in other words, men have rights and women have rights, but they are not necessarily the same rights); the second group, represented by Ibn ʿAbbās, takes the view that 'like' means 'the same as'.[55] The interpretation that men's and women's rights in marriage are the same relies on a *ḥadīth* of Ibn ʿAbbās's that has him saying both husbands and wives should take care of their physical appearance: 'I like to make myself beautiful for my wife, just as I like it when she makes herself beautiful for me, because God said, *women's rights are like their obligations*'.[56] Although he says that there is some evidence in the verse for this interpretation,[57] al-Ṭabarī's own view is that the verse refers to divorced women. It was a common provision in all legal schools to grant husbands unilateral divorce and the power to invoke their wives' 'return' to the marriage during a waiting period after having been divorced once or twice (a third divorce being final). For al-Ṭabarī, when they have been divorced once or twice, their husbands must not harm them in the waiting period. It seems that Ibn ʿAbbās's statement on beautification may be separate from his statement on the 'degree', which al-Ṭabarī does follow.

ordered them to". And this obedience is their being good to their husbands' families, and preserving their husbands' wealth. Men are superior because of their spending and their efforts' (al-Ṭabarī, *Jāmiʿal-bayān*, v. 8, p. 290, at Q. 4:34).

[53] That this is the wife's duty becomes clear in al-Ṭabarī's exegesis of the second part of Q. 4:34, described later in this chapter.

[54] Al-Ṭabarī, *Jāmiʿ al-bayān*, v. 8, p. 290 (at Q. 4:34).

[55] Ibid., v. 4, p. 531 (at Q. 2:228). [56] Ibid., v. 4, pp. 531–2 (at Q. 2:228).

[57] Ibid., v. 4, pp. 532–3 (at Q. 2:228).

Al-Ṭabarī has Ibn ʿAbbās saying that the 'degree' means that he likes to forgive his wife if she does not fulfil all of her duties towards him. For al-Ṭabarī, the degree is a 'rank and a status (*rutba wa-manzila*)' that men acquire when they manage women well. The marital hierarchy is the reason why men have power over their wives; but they are invited to use this power to be kind, generous, and forgiving towards them:

> The best interpretation, in my opinion, is that of Ibn ʿAbbās, which says that the degree which God Almighty gives to men over women is that He put the husband in a position to forgive his wife some of the duties enjoined upon her, disregarding them, while concurrently fulfilling all of his obligations towards her. And that is because God says *and men have a degree over them* following his statement that *women have rights like their obligations*, whereby He informed us that it is incumbent upon men not to harm women when they invoke their right of return after a revocable divorce, nor [should they harm them when fulfilling] their other rights. Likewise, it is women's responsibility not to harm men by hiding their pregnancy from them, or [in fulfilling] their other rights. Therefore, God invites men to manage women magnanimously (*al-akhdh 'alayhinna bi'l-faḍl*) if they fail to fulfil some of the obligations towards their husbands that God enjoins upon them. And this is what Ibn ʿAbbās meant when he said 'I do not like to take advantage of all of my rights over my wife, because God Almighty says this in His words, *and men have a degree over them*'. The meaning of degree is a rank and status. [Although] this statement from God, exalted is He, is overtly a factual statement, its meaning is that men are invited to manage women magnanimously, so that they will have superior ranking to them.[58]

For al-Ṭabarī, *men have a degree over them* is overtly factual and descriptive; but in reality it is prescriptive: certain behaviour (men managing women generously) is the substance of the degree. Because men have a higher rank and status than women, they are in the position to forgive their wives if the wives do not fulfil some of their duties. Al-Ṭabarī seems concerned that husbands not abuse their power over their wives. Although few interpreters took up al-Ṭabarī's view that the verse was prescriptive rather than descriptive, this is a clear example of the ethical consideration of just rulership that was important to al-Ṭabarī and other interpreters.

A sub-theme in interpretation of this verse is mentioned first by the Ḥanafī al-Zajjāj (d. 311/923), and that is men's sexual duties towards their wives.[59] He says 'its meaning is that the woman reaches pleasure

[58] Ibid., v. 4, pp. 535–6 (at Q. 2:228).

[59] Several subsequent exegetes cite his view that 'like' refers to the mutual sexual pleasure to be found in marriage, and al-Suyūṭī (d. 911/1505) cites two *ḥadīths* that focus on the wife's sexual satisfaction. Jalāl al-Dīn al-Suyūṭī, *al-Durr al-manthūr fī tafsīr bi'l-maʿthūr*, [no editor] (Beirut: Dār al-Maʿrifa, 1970), v. 1, p. 276 (at Q. 2:228).

from the man, just as the man reaches it, and he has superiority due to the maintenance and his guardianship, through which he corrects her'.[60] This interpretation crops up infrequently in later works of *tafsīr*. The *tafsīr* and non-*tafsīr* sources that speak of men's sexual duties towards their wives are referring to a moral duty that is also, according to some schools of law, a legal duty; however, men are not obligated by it to the same extent as women.[61]

Al-Ṭabarī and exegetes who died before him do not refer to men's and women's inherent qualities to explain Q. 2:228 or Q. 4:34. But his contemporaries and later exegetes explain why men are in a position to manage their wives by citing men's inherent superiority in body, mind, and religion. As I argued in Chapter 1, the change in discourse is not necessarily because there was a change in the way that women were perceived; rather, the genre of *tafsīr* was developing, and as the genre matured, the exegetes used more sophisticated arguments to explain the meaning of verses. *Ḥadīth*s such as the one mentioning women's deficient rationality, which were probably taken for granted by the earliest exegetes, increasingly became a part of post-Ṭabarī works, when explaining the 'why' of a verse became just as important as explaining what it meant. Still, in this case explaining the 'why' means a significant change in the tone of interpretations. In the first instances, men's innate superiority is mentioned as almost a side note. But over time, men's superiority and women's inferiority became a major theme. I describe this change through time in the following paragraphs.

In the interpretation of al-Zajjāj, men's superiority is mentioned only in passing, as a part of his general description of marriage. He compares the husband's role as caretaker of the wife's rights and the wife's role as caretaker of the husband's rights by using the same word (*qayyim/qayyimāt*) to describe them. This shows that the word *qayyim*, derived from the same root as *qawwāmūn*, may be interpreted in a gender-neutral way, as 'caretaker', or 'person responsible'. Legally, he places limits on men's responsibility for women. He says that men are responsible only 'in those matters that are obligatory. As for anything else, no'.[62] In limiting men's

[60] Al-Zajjāj, *Ma'ānī al-Qur'ān*, v. 1, p. 301.
[61] Kecia Ali has shown that, according to medieval Islamic law, women do not have the same right to sex within marriage that men do. See her 'Progressive Muslims and Islamic Jurisprudence: The Necessity for Critical Engagement with Marriage and Divorce Law', in *Progressive Muslims on Justice, Gender and Pluralism*, ed. Omid Safi (Oxford: Oneworld, 2003), pp. 163–89.
[62] Al-Zajjāj, *Ma'ānī al-Qur'ān*, v. 2, p. 48 (at Q. 4:34)

responsibilities, he is probably referring to the legal debate about whether a husband is responsible for maintenance beyond food and clothing, such as providing medicine when a wife is ill. Men are responsible for certain types of matters, according to al-Zajjāj, 'because of their superiority in knowledge (*ʿilm*) and judgment (*tamyīz*)'.[63] Men's superiority is not a major theme here: the focus is on their rights and duties.

Ibn Wahb al-Dīnawārī (d. c. 300/912–13) gives more pride of place to men's superiority. In his interpretation of Q. 4:34, he mentions that it is men's responsibility to discipline women in light of men's superior makeup and rights, and for Q. 2:228, men's degree is described in terms of legal and innate advantages: men have more inheritance than women, if they are killed, their blood-wit is more than women's, men can testify in cases where women cannot, and men have superior rationality (*ʿaql*).[64] The Ḥanafī jurist al-Jaṣṣāṣ (d. 370/981) also cites men's superior rationality as a key reason why they have been put in charge of women: because of their rationality, they are responsible for women's moral education and for managing them.[65] Whereas al-Ṭabarī simply says that men are responsible for managing women, al-Jaṣṣāṣ explains why they *deserve* to manage women; in this case, men's superiority is one of the first things to be spoken of in the interpretation. The discourse on marital relations was developing along with the development of the discourse in the genre of *tafsīr* and related genres, as in the *Aḥkām al-Qurʾān* written by al-Jaṣṣāṣ.

63 Ibid.

64 'Men are in authority (*musallaṭūn*) over women's discipline (*adab*). *With what God has given some of them more* meaning men, in rationality (*ʿaql*) and shares in booty and inheritance *than others* meaning women. *And with what they spend of their wealth* meaning that the dowry and maintenance is obligatory for men and not women. *So the good women* Ibn Wahb says, "the ones who are good to their husbands *are obedient* to God concerning their husbands"', Ibn Wahb, *al-Wāḍiḥ*, v. 1, p. 151 (at Q. 4:34) also see p. 75 (at Q. 2:228).

65 Al-Jaṣṣāṣ's interpretation reads: 'Men's control (*qiyām*) of women concerns disciplining them (*taʾdīb*), managing them (*tadbīr*) and protecting them, because God has made men superior to women in rationality (*ʿaql*) and judgment (*raʾy*), and because God has made it obligatory for men to spend on women. The verse has several implications, one of them being men's superiority over women in status. [Another is] that a husband is the one who undertakes his wife's management (*tadbīrihā*) and her discipline (*taʾdībihā*), which indicates that it is their responsibility to keep women in the house, and keep them from going out; it is women's responsibility to obey men and to accept their authority in those matters that are not sinful disobedience (*maʿṣiya*). The verse also indicates that their maintenance is men's responsibility, because of God's words *and with what they spend of their money* [Q. 4:34] and in light of His words *He shall bear the cost of their food and clothing on equitable terms* [Q. 2:233]' (al-Jaṣṣāṣ, *Aḥkām*, v. 2, p. 229, at Q. 4:34).

Another aspect of men's superiority, according to the exegetes, is their physical makeup. Explanations of men's physical superiority show how exegetes were not only influenced by religious knowledge in the form of Qur'ān and *ḥadīth*s. They also referred to ideas about the natural composition of the sexes that were current at the time. Abū 'l-Layth al-Samarqandī (d. 375/985) mentions two theories as to why men have been put in charge of women. One of these is a scientific analysis of men's and women's bodily makeup, which we briefly noted in exegeses of women's testimony:

> It is said that men are superior in rationality (*al-'aql*) and management (*al-tadbīr*), and God put them in charge of women because they have superior rationality to women. It is [also] said that men have strength in their selves and their natures which women don't have, because men's natures are dominated by heat and dryness, and in that there is strength and power, whereas women's natures are dominated by moisture and coldness, which means softness and weakness, and that is why men have been given the right to be in charge of women.[66]

Abū 'l-Layth seeks to explain Q. 4:34 using means other than just the canon or his own views: he cites what for him is a well-established scientific fact about the natural differences between men and women. In Abū 'l-Layth's interpretation, bodily humours affect men's and women's strength – since women are cold and weak, men are better suited to take care of them. The notion that men are hot and dry and women cold and moist goes back to the ancient Greeks, and this type of scientific explanation of the differences between men and women would have been current for a millennium before Abū 'l-Layth wrote of it in his exegesis (as mentioned in Chapter 1, the very same explanation was used by interpreters writing centuries later, such as Fakhr al-Dīn al-Rāzī and Abū Ḥayyān al-Andalusī, to explain women's forgetfulness in Q. 2:282). Although today's biologists have new theories about men's and women's natures, for Abū 'l-Layth this explanation is a known truth. By having recourse to objective truths, exegetes are attempting to guard against letting their own whims affect interpretation: rather than just venturing an opinion, they explain the verse by drawing on facts of which everyone in their world was aware. Those 'objective' facts help to explain the verse just as much as referencing elements of the canon such as Qur'ān and *ḥadīth*. From today's perspective, however, it is clear that their own cultural values influenced their interpretation of both Qur'ān and

[66] Abū 'l-Layth al-Samarqandī, *Tafsīr*, v. 1, p. 151 (at Q. 4:34).

science. The idea of the humours is a theory that reflects common cultural ideas, rather than testable hypotheses.

Another exegete who cited men's physical makeup as a part of their superiority was the Imāmī Abū Jaʿfar al-Ṭūsī. He cites another seemingly objective measure: linguistic analysis, specifically on the root consonants for the word 'man' (*r-j-l*). His interpretation focuses on the linguistic connection between masculinity and certain types of strength:

> You may say man (*rajul*) is distinguished by manliness (*rujūla*), i.e., strength (*quwwa*), and [one says] that he is the manlier of the two (*arjaluhumā*), i.e., the stronger or the two. A *rajīl* horse (*faras rajīl*) is [an expression which refers to] strength in walking, and the leg (*rijl*) is characterized by its strength in walking. [One says] a swarm of locusts (*rijl min al-jarād*) or a detached number, which resembles a leg (*rijl*) because it is part of the whole. The pedestrian (*rājil*) is the one who walks on his feet (*rijlayhi*). Extemporising a speech (*irtijāl al-kalām*) is called extemporising (*irtijāl*) because it means gaining the upper hand over those who can master neither their thoughts, nor their speech.[67]

Lexicology is a vehicle for expressing deeper truths. Men's strength is encoded in the very word for 'men'. In this way, al-Ṭūsī's linguistic analysis backs up his point about the nature of men and women. In these discussions, maleness and femaleness are inherent in both bodies and in language. Bodily and linguistically, men have the authority to interpret and to rule over those who do not possess such manly qualities. His argument is not isolated; it is echoed by his contemporary, the Sunnī al-Wāḥidī, who also cites the root of *r-j-l*.[68]

By having recourse to nature and grammatical analysis, the exegetes seem to be basing their interpretation on an objective measure. But even the nuances of words, and thus grammatical analysis, could be influenced by preconceived notions about the nature of the sexes. This is another example of how exegetes are influenced by factors other than the Qurʾān

[67] Al-Ṭūsī, *al-Tibyān*, v. 3, p. 354 (at Q. 2:228).

[68] According to al-Wāḥidī: 'It is said that man (*rajul*) is distinguished by going on foot (*al-rujla*), i.e., strength, and [one says] "he is the more manly of the two men (*arjal al-rajulayn*)" i.e., the stronger of the two. A *rajīl* horse (*faras rajīl*) is [an expression which refers to] strength in walking, and the leg (*rijl*) is characterized by its strength in walking. Extemporizing a speech (*irtijāl al-kalām*) means gaining the upper hand by mastery of thought and speech' (Al-Wāḥidī, *al-Basīṭ*, fol. 236, p. 307). Given that al-Ṭūsī and al-Wāḥidī were both from around Nīshāpūr (although al-Ṭūsī lived in Baghdād), and that they died only eight years apart, it seems likely that these two quotations have a common source in a lexicographical work. Indeed, a phrase from this passage (*wa-hādhā arjal al-rajulayn ay ashadduhuma*) is cited by Ibn Manẓūr under *r-j-l* in his dictionary *Lisān al-ʿArab*, indicating that they all may have gotten the interpretation from the same grammatical source. Part of this discussion is attributed to the grammarian Ibn al-Aʿrābī.

and *ḥadīth*s. Although these measures seem to be objective, they are heavily influenced by cultural ideas of what was correct and true.

Cultural ideas, and common notions of right and wrong, are readily apparent in the interpreters' discussions of the just rulership that men must undertake over the women in their care. Many exegetes state that men must behave in a way that merits their status. Al-Zamakhsharī likens the man's position in marriage to that of the governor over the people, and says that this governorship is due to men's superiority, not to their ability to subjugate women:[69]

> Men are the commanders [of right] and forbidders [of wrong], just as a governor guides the people.... The 'some' in *some of them* refers to all men and all women. It means that men are only in control over women because God made some of them superior, and those are men, to others, and they are women. This is proof that governance is only merited by superiority (*tafḍīl*), not by dominance, an overbearing attitude, or subjugation. Concerning the superiority of men over women, the exegetes mention rationality (*ʿaql*), good judgment (*ḥazm*), determination, strength, writing – for the majority of men – horsemanship, archery, that men are prophets, learned (*ʿulamāʾ*), have the duties of the greater and lesser imamate, *jihād*, the call to prayer, the Friday sermon, seclusion in the mosque (*iʿtikāf*), saying the prayers during the holy days (*takbīrāt al-tashrīq*); according to Abū Ḥanīfa they testify in cases of injury or death (*ḥudūd* and *qiṣāṣ*), they have more shares in inheritance, bloodwit (*ḥimāla*), pronouncing an oath 50 times which establishes guilt or innocence in cases of murder (*qasāma*), authority in marriage, divorce, and taking back the wife after a revocable divorce, a greater number of spouses, lineage passing through the male line, and they have beards and turbans.[70]

The obvious aspect of this interpretation is its development of earlier comparisons of marriage to politics: every state needs a leader to guide it correctly, as does every household. A more subtle aspect is that al-Zamakhsharī mentions that 'some of them' and 'others' indicates that *all* men are fit to exercise authority over women and that *all* women should be subject to this authority. Men's superiority is not a question of 'dominance and subjugation'. It is not merited purely because men are apt to dominate and women to be dominated; if that were the case, it could be that some strong women could dominate men. Rather, he explains, men deserve to be put in charge of women because of the qualities that he lists, which include personal attributes (rationality, judgment, strength,

[69] Al-Jishumī's *tafsīr*, which was an earlier Muʿtazilī *tafsīr*, does not have a similar discussion.

[70] Maḥmūd b. ʿUmar al-Zamakhsharī (known as Jār Allāh), *al-Kashshāf*, ed. Aḥmad b. al-Munīr al-Iskandarī (Beirut: Dār al-Kutub al-ʿArabī [1965]), v. 1, p. 505 (at Q. 4:34).

determination), skills (writing, archery), and legal rights (witnessing, blood-wit, authority in marriage, divorce, the privilege of waging the *jihād*, and so forth). This combination of qualities means that, even if women can match men in certain ways, they will never achieve every aspect of men's superiority over them, which is why, in his view, the verse refers to men collectively being in authority over women collectively. The implication is that men should not be overbearing, nor should they subjugate women, in their assertion of their rights. They should, in short, exercise just rulership.

Fakhr al-Dīn al-Rāzī goes further than al-Zamakhsharī in explaining why marriage is a good deal for both parties, men and women. He does this not just by giving old interpretations a new gloss: he incorporates older material into a cohesive argument. In other words, he does not simply list many, possibly conflicting, interpretations, nor does he re-gloss the interpretation of one single earlier exegesis. Instead, he makes a coherent argument, which involves reinterpreting some aspects of tradition, and ignoring others. Fakhr al-Dīn's discourse is much more sophisticated than that of others of his age. The Mālikī Ibn ʿAṭiyya (d. 546/1151), for instance, explains that men are better than women, but Fakhr al-Dīn explains the consequence of this superiority. And whereas most exegetes say that men have more rights, Fakhr al-Dīn connects men's rights with an increased level of responsibility towards women. Central to Fakhr al-Dīn al-Rāzī's conception of marriage is that husbands must act in a way that befits their position, which echoes the interpretation by al-Zamakhsharī cited previously. Husbands guide their wives like shepherds and, because of their status as rulers, they must uphold their wives' best interests. The parallel with statecraft is explicit: the ruler must secure the best interests of the people he rules, and the subjects must obey.[71]

Fakhr al-Dīn explains the degree that men have over women by outlining eight specific ways in which men are superior to women.[72] The eight

[71] He says: 'husbands are like rulers and shepherds, and wives are like the ruled and the flock; so it is necessary for husbands, because of their makeup as rulers and shepherds, to undertake to fulfill wives' rights and their best interests. [Likewise], it is necessary for wives, in exchange for that, to display obedience to husbands' (Fakhr al-Dīn al-Rāzī, *al-Tafsīr al-kabīr*, v. 6, p. 101, at Q. 2:228).

[72] 'Know that the superiority (*faḍl*) of men over women is a well-known matter, and its mention here admits two interpretations: the first, that men are superior to women in certain ways: first is rationality (*ʿaql*), second, blood money, third, inheritance, fourth suitability for the imamate, judgeship, and witnessing, fifth, that they may marry or take a concubine while already married, and women may not [marry again] when they are married [nor may they ever take a concubine]. The sixth is that the husband's share in

points are a combination of inherent qualities, such as rationality, with marital rights, such as the ability to take a concubine, and rights that entail power over others, such as the imamate, judging, or testimony. The culmination of his argument is that, because men have been made superior to women, and *ḥadīth*s tell men that they must take care of women, men who harm women are sinning:

> Thus the superiority of men over women is established in these matters, and it is clear that women are like helpless captives in men's hands. This is why [Muḥammad] said, peace and blessings be upon him, 'Treat women well, for they are your captives' and in another narration, 'Be God-fearing in your treatment of two weak ones: orphans and women'. The degree that God has given men over women in terms of ability is because men are recommended to fulfil more of women's rights [than women have to fulfil of men's]. The mention of that [degree] is like a threat to men when they set about to hurt and harm women, because whomever God bestows more blessings upon, their sinfulness is more detestable to God, and their liability for reprimand is greater.[73]

According to Fakhr al-Dīn, because God has given men so much more than women, in both natural abilities and rights, men have an added responsibility towards their wives. The tone of this passage is much the same as that in al-Ṭabarī, cited previously, even though it differs in important regards. Most striking here is the contention that the degree is a type of threat to men: they must take care of the people of lesser abilities, including women, and if they do not, then they are under greater liability than those who have fewer responsibilities.

In his interpretation of Q. 4:34, Fakhr al-Dīn explains the logic behind men's financial maintenance of women in a way that seems strikingly modern. He explicitly states that God has created a fair financial system for men and women. Such a system was alluded to in the early exegesis of Muqātil b. Sulaymān, who said 'husbands have been given more because they pay wives the dowry', but seems to have been left aside since that point.[74] Fakhr al-Dīn's argument is that one sex has not been made absolutely superior in monetary terms, because inheritance is a provision for the maintenance of families. To explain

inheritance from his wife is greater than the wife's share is from her husband, seventh, husbands are able to divorce their wives, and when they divorce them, they are capable of demanding that they return whether the woman wishes to return or not. As for women, they cannot divorce their husbands nor are they able to forbid their [divorced] husbands from demanding that they return. The eighth is that men's share in booty is greater than women's share' (ibid., v. 6, p. 101, at Q. 2:228).

[73] Ibid., v. 6, pp. 101–2, at Q. 2:228.

[74] Muqātil, *Tafsīr*, pp. 370–1 (at Q. 4:34).

this, he refers to the Occasion of Revelation of Q. 4:32, which, along with Q. 4:33, refers to men's inheritance.

Know that God Almighty said, *do not covet that which God gave some of them more than others* [Q4:32]. We have mentioned that the occasion of the revelation of this verse is that women were talking about the superiority (*tafḍīl*) given by God to men over them in inheritance. Thus God mentioned in this verse that when He gave men an advantage over women in inheritance, it is because men are *qawwāmūn* over women. God said that they share in [sexual] enjoyment, each of the other, then He ordered that men pay the dowry to women, and give them maintenance (*nafaqa*) so what was more for one of the two sides [in inheritance] is comparable with more for the other [in payment of dowry and maintenance]. He did not prefer anyone absolutely, and here He clarifies the method of [household] organisation.[75]

In the Occasion of Revelation cited by Fakhr al-Dīn, women asked the Prophet why men had been given more inheritance than women, and this verse was revealed showing that men's greater inheritance is because of their financial responsibilities. Fakhr al-Dīn thus explains Q. 4:34 in light of the preceding verses, as a system of social organisation in which men get more in order to be in a position to provide. This exegesis highlights the dual nature of men's responsibilities: on the one hand, protecting, and on the other, disciplining women. Fakhr al-Dīn does not just explain the various rights and abilities of the sexes, but also categorises them, putting earlier exegeses into a framework that explains how the disparate interpretations of the verse fit together and how the verse makes sense as a social and moral system.

The notion that men must treat women fairly, which was hinted at in the earliest work, became increasingly explicit through time. One *ḥadīth* cited by the exegete al-Baḥrānī (d. 1107/1795), which appears in the section on women's testimony, seems designed to remind men of their obligations towards women. It describes how a man who dealt poorly with his wife, treating her badly so that she was suffering, spoiled his own end.[76]

Both Fakhr al-Dīn al-Rāzī and al-Zamakhsharī emphasise that men must behave in a way that merits their position as rulers over women, but they do not entertain the possibility that husbands who do not fulfil their duties should not be considered to be in charge of their wives. This view is rarely expressed in *tafsīr*, even when an interpreter's legal school supports it.

[75] Fakhr al-Dīn al-Rāzī, *al-Tafsīr al-kabīr*, v. 10, p. 87 (at Q. 4:34).

[76] Hāshim Ḥusaynī b. Sulaymān al-Baḥrānī, *al-Burhān fī tafsīr al-Qurʾān*, ed. Qism al-Dirāsāt al-Islāmiyya, Muʾassasat al-Biʿtha (Qom: Muʾassasat al-Biʿtha, 1994), v. 1, p. 562.

According to Mālikī law, a man's non-payment of maintenance results in his wife's right to divorce. But not many Mālikī interpreters mention this legal maxim in their *tafsīr*, or even in their works of *Aḥkām al-Qur'ān*, works which were supposed to treat legal aspects of the Qur'ān. For instance, in his work of *Aḥkām*, the Mālikī Ibn al-ʿArabī omits any reference to women's right to divorce in the case of non-payment. Instead, he frames his argument around a husband's duty to teach his wives about proper religion and to seclude them.[77] Similarly, the Mālikī Ibn ʿAṭīya (d. 546/1151) ignores the consequences of men's non-payment when he discusses Q. 4:34. Instead, he defines *qawwāmūn* as 'having exclusive control' over something and 'concern' for it. Due to men's payment, he says, they have a type of ownership over women.[78] This language of ownership echoes the discussions in works of *fiqh* studied by Ali. Mālikī discussions of *qiwāma* in works of *Aḥkām al-Qur'ān* or *tafsīr* do not, therefore, anticipate the view of al-Qurṭubī (671/1273), who asserts that a man's failure to pay maintenance results in the loss of his position as *qawwām*, which in turn enables his wife to divorce him. He first explains the nature of men's management of women, and gives a list of reasons why they have been put in this position.[79] But after thoroughly detailing the numerous reasons why men have been given such control over their wives, he admits that if men do not uphold their financial end of the bargain, wives have the right to a divorce. In doing so, he is putting forth his school's view, but it is perhaps one that earlier exegetes of his school would prefer not to mention:

And with what they spend of their money when husbands are incapable of paying maintenance then they are not *qawwām* over their wives, and since they are not *qawwām* over them, then the wives have the right to annul the contract, due to the cessation of the intention for which marriage was legislated. In this is a clear proof as to the annulment of the marriage in cases of nonpayment

[77] Ibn al-ʿArabī, *Aḥkām al-Qur'ān*, v. 1, p. 416 (at Q. 4:34).

[78] Ibn ʿAṭiyya, *al-Muḥarrar al-wajīz*, ed. ʿAbd al-Salām ʿAbd al-Shāfī Muḥammad (Beirut: Dār al-Kutub al-ʿIlmiyya, 1993–95), v. 2, p. 47 (at Q. 4:34).

[79] He says: '[*Qawwām*] is that men are managers of women, they discipline them, and they keep them in their homes, preventing them from going out (*al-burūz*). Women must obey in those matters that are not sinful disobedience (*maʿṣiya*). The explanation for this ruling is in men's superiority, management, rationality, strength, that they have been ordered to fight *jihād*, that they have been given inheritance, and the [responsibility to] command right and forbid wrong. Some [exegetes] have the opinion that the superiority is due to men's beards, but this opinion is worthless (*laysa bi-shay'*)', Abū ʿAbd Allāh Muḥammad b. Aḥmad al-Qurṭubī, *al-Jāmiʿ li-Aḥkām al-Qur'ān* (Cairo: Dār al-Kātib al-ʿArabī, 1967), v. 5, p. 169, at Q. 4:34.

for maintenance and clothing, which is the opinion of the schools of Mālik and Shāfiʿī. Abū Ḥanīfa says it is not annulled.[80]

According to al-Qurṭubī, marriage is a legal contract that has a central point: the maintenance of women, in exchange for their [sexual] obedience. If the husband fails to pay, his wife can divorce him. Although dependent on payment, men's *qiwāma* is justified by their inherent qualities, both mental (rationality) and physical (men are hot and dry, while women are cold and moist).[81] The physical, intrinsic nature of their differences means that, while men's violation of the marriage contract can result in divorce, it is only men who may be *qawwām* over women: presumably, even exceptional women cannot reach the stature of men.

The idea that men's behaviour could affect their status as *qawwāmūn* over women is represented in different ways by other authors. Several express concern that men should act in a manner that befits their position as commanders of and supporters of women. Ibn al-Jawzī and Abū Ḥayyān (d. 745/1353) even go so far as to say that men are only *qawwāmūn* over women 'when they are men', which seems to indicate that they must fulfil their duties to their wives in order to justify their place in the marital hierarchy. He quotes a poem that references a 'fire at night', which may be a reference to men's sexual duty towards their wives, or may be a reference to their ability to provide for their needs:

> *Qawwāmūn* means that men are in control of disciplining women with regards to [their] rights [over them]. Hishām b. Muḥammad [al-Kalbī] narrated, on the authority of his father, concerning His words *men are* qawwāmūn *over women* that Muḥammad [the father of Hishām] said, 'when they are men.' And he recited: 'Is every man that you consider [really] a man? And is everything that you light at night [really] a fire?'[82]

Ibn al-Jawzī's interpretation is a clear rebuttal of the idea that all men are *qawwāmūn* over all women that was put forth by other exegetes, such as

[80] Ibid., v. 5, p. 169 (at Q. 4:34).

[81] He says: 'It has been said that men have superiority over women in rationality and education, and thus the right of guardianship over women was given to men. It is said that men have bodily and natural strength that women don't have, because the nature of men is dominated by heat and dryness, and in that there is strength and power, and the nature of women is dominated by moisture and coldness, and that means gentleness and weakness, so men were given the right of guardianship over women by virtue of those qualities, and by virtue of the words of God Most High, *with what they spend of their money*' (al-Qurṭubī, *al-Jāmiʿ li-aḥkām*, v. 5, p. 169, at Q. 4:34).

[82] Ibn al-Jawzī, *Zād al-masīr*, v. 2, p. 74, at Q. 4:34. '*A-kulla imriʾin taḥsibīnaʾmraʾan wa-nāran tuwaqqiddu biʾl-laylī nāran*?' This *bayt* is in Sībawayhī's *kitāb*.

al-Zamakhsharī. Thus, the question of whether individuals can defy the general characteristics of their sex represents a significant point of debate amongst the exegetes. Muḥammad b. al-Sāʾib al-Kalbī (d. 146/763), author of a *tafsīr* which was said to be the longest composed in its time, is the authority cited for this interpretation.[83]

The Mālikī Abū Ḥayyān modifies Ibn al-Jawzī's interpretation that only some men are eligible as *qawwāmūn* by saying that the verse refers to one sex over the other in general, and that it doesn't speak about specific cases.[84] In other words, some men might not be *qawwāmūn* over women.

> It is said: the meaning of 'men' here is someone who is discreet and trustworthy, it is not only people with beards. Some people with beards have no good [in them], nor harm, nor esteem; [they are of no consequence]. Thus it is said: a man between masculinity and manhood (*rujuliyya wa-rujūla*). Because of that an interpreter [namely Ibn al-Jawzī] comes to the conclusion that in the words the intended meaning is elided: men are *qawwāmūn* over women when they are men. [And he quotes the following lines:] 'Is every man you consider [really] a man? And is everything you light at night [really] a fire?' The clearest interpretation is that this verse only deals with the question of the whole sex; the question of individuals is not addressed. It as though it says, this type is *qawwām* over that type ... the meaning of the first 'some' is men, and the second is women, so the meaning is that men are *qawwāmūn* over women.[85]

Abū Ḥayyān describes what it is that constitutes a man: 'man' is a term that refers to attitudes and behaviour, such as discretion, trustworthiness, and esteem. He responds to the interpretation that the 'degree' that men have over women is merely physical – the beards that men can grow, and women can't. The beard interpretation was first cited by al-Ṭabarī, who gives five interpretations of men's 'degree': (1) inheritance, the *jihād*, and other matters in which God has given men privileges over women; (2) the 'command and obedience'; (3) the husband gives the wife the dowry, and if she accuses him, he performs *liʿān*, but if he accuses her, she is punished; (4) he confers benefit and favour on her, and forgives her if she fails to fulfil all of her duties; (5) 'That God gave him a beard, and prevented her from that'.[86] The last interpretation, that men's degree consists merely of the beard, is attributed to Ḥumayd. Several subsequent exegetes attack the notion that the real distinction between men and women is a matter of

[83] He was said to be an Imāmī, but was such an authority that 'even his detractors draw on him as a source' (W. Atallah, 'al-Kalbī', *Encyclopedia of Islam 2*, v. 4, p. 495).

[84] Abū Ḥayyān, *al-Baḥr*, v. 3, p. 249 (at Q. 4:34).

[85] Ibid., v. 3, p. 248–9 (at Q. 4:34).

[86] Al-Ṭabarī, *Jāmiʿ al-bayān*, v. 4, p. 533–5 (at Q. 2:228).

facial hair. In the passage just cited, Abū Ḥayyān asserts that, without masculine qualities, a 'man' has no right to be *qawwām* over women.[87] For him, the distinguishing factor between men and women is not merely physical – it is a matter of behaviour and attitude.

The previously cited exegeses hint that some exceptional women may equal men. But no exegete in this study states this outright until the Ḥanafī al-Qūnawī (d. 1195/1791). In his commentary on al-Bayḍāwī, he says that the verse legislates for men to be given authority over women, but that some individual women may surpass some men. Al-Bayḍāwī's commentary is in bold, and al-Qūnawī's commentary is in plain text.

Because of God's making men superior to women. Concerning the partitive 'some of them', it refers to the majority.

Due to their perfection in intellect, good management, and greater strength for pious deeds and religious ceremonies. The ruling here is with regards to the sex [as a whole] and it is not inconsistent [with the ruling] that the makeup of some individual women surpasses, in the matters mentioned, some individual men.[88]

This is the first time in these texts that the notion of women's absolute inferiority has been directly countered. By saying that certain exceptional women may reach men's level in both rationality and religious deeds, al-Qūnawī directly challenges the universal applicability of both parts of the 'deficiency' *ḥadīth*. This text demonstrates how, in glossing an older commentary, the later commentator can add his own opinions that may or may not reflect the original author's intent. From al-Bayḍāwī's text, it is impossible to tell if he would have agreed with al-Qūnawī's gloss that some exceptional women could surpass some men.

THE PERHAPS UNFAIR DUTY OF WIFELY OBEDIENCE

'By God, I will never marry!' declares one woman in a *ḥadīth* when she hears of the predominance of a husband's rights over his wife (the *ḥadīth* is described more fully in what follows). In a culture where

[87] The phrase he uses (namely, *rujliyya wa-rujūla*, between masculinity and manhood) is taken from the grammatical synopsis of the root *r-j-l*, which the lexicographer Ibn Manẓūr cites as coming from the grammarian Ibn al-Aʿrābī. Other words from this same entry are found in al-Wāḥidī's and al-Ṭūsī's exegeses of Q. 2:228. See Ibn Manẓūr, '*r-j-l*', *Lisān al-ʿArab*, v. 5, p. 155. In the matter of the beard interpretation and the *r-j-l* interpretation, Abū Ḥayyān is cross referencing his *tafsīr* of Q. 2:228 with his interpretation of Q. 4:34 – but of course without any attribution.

[88] ʿIṣām al-Dīn Ismāʿīl b. Muḥammad al-Qūnawī, *Ḥāshiyat al-Qūnawī*, v. 7, p. 145, at Q. 4:34.

disobedience to one's husband is regularly equated with disobedience to God and where a woman's piety consists in her obedience to her husband,[89] certain questions are raised about how this can be fair and just: Are there any limits on wifely obedience? How can women achieve the same heavenly rewards as men when they do not have the same opportunities, by virtue of being confined in the house? And how is it right that a morally good woman should have to obey her morally bad husband? The moral and ethical issues associated with obedience are captured in a number of *ḥadīth*s from both sound (*ṣaḥīḥ*) and non-*ṣaḥīḥ* sources in which women's and men's spiritual worth is addressed. The existence of such *ḥadīth*s in both major and minor collections seems to indicate that, despite its pervasiveness, the link between piety and wifely obedience raised ethical and practical dilemmas for some interpreters. *Ḥadīth*s give interpreters the ultimate sanction for this seemingly unfair situation. As I have remarked in previous chapters, *ḥadīth*s also seem to address common concerns through the voice of their female interlocutors, such as the woman quoted at the beginning of this section.

These *ḥadīth*s began to be quoted as a part of a subtle shift in tone from some early sources, which seem to limit wifely obedience, to later, post-Ṭabarī interpreters, who emphasise the necessity of total obedience. An interpretation attributed to ʿAlī Ibn Abī Ṭalḥa (d. 143/760) says 'women must obey in matters in which God has ordered their obedience'; next, it defines that obedience, saying that they 'must be good to their husband's family and preserve their husband's wealth', and finally it circumscribes men's superiority, saying 'men's superiority over women is due to their maintenance and efforts'.[90] The implication is that, although men are in the position of commanding women, the command and obedience are neither arbitrary nor unlimited. For Ibn Abī Ṭalḥa, the wife must behave in accordance with social norms by treating her husband's family well. Similarly, al-Ṭabarī seems to limit the wife's obedience to certain matters by citing the opinion that obedience is kindness to the husband's family. However, these limiting interpretations do not have a long shelf-life in the

[89] In the words of Kecia Ali: 'While *maʿṣiya* typically refers to sinful disobedience to God, through an interpretive maneuver, it is made to come full circle: God has ordained that women must obey their husbands, and thus disobedience (*nushūz*) to one's husband is sinful disobedience (*maʿṣiya*) to God'. Kecia Ali, 'Religious Practices: Obedience and Disobedience in Islamic Discourses' in *Encyclopedia of Women in Islamic Cultures*.

[90] ʿAlī ibn Abī Ṭalḥa, *Ṣaḥīfat ʿAlī b. Abī Ṭalḥa ʿan Ibn ʿAbbās fī tafsīr al-Qurʾān*, compiled and edited by Rashīd ʿAbd al-Munʿīm al-Rajjāl (Cairo: Maktabat al-Sunna, 1991), v. 2, p. 146 (at Q. 4:34).

genre of *tafsīr*. Particularly after al-Ṭabarī, it is far more common for interpreters to assert the necessity of total wifely obedience than it is to circumscribe that obedience. The interpretation of ʿAlī b. Abī Ṭalḥa dies out entirely after a few citations; later interpretations often take a broader view of the matters in which wives must obey.

The majority of *ḥadīth*s cited in *tafsīr* sources do not address the issue of wifely obedience as a moral dilemma. Instead, they simply state the facts. Some *ḥadīth*s cited in post-Ṭabarī sources not only link wifely obedience with piety, but also emphasise men's legal rights over women. For instance, in his *Aḥkām al-Qurʾān*, al-Jaṣṣāṣ cites the following:

> A woman came to the Prophet and said, 'O Messenger of God, what is the right of a husband over his wife?' He responded that she should not give alms with anything from his house without his permission, for if she did so, he would have the reward and she would be punished. [Or] she said, 'Oh Messenger of God, what is the right of a husband over his wife?' and he responded, 'She must not leave the house except with his permission, nor should she fast even for one day without his permission'.[91]

In the aforementioned *ḥadīth*, a version of which is cited in the *ḥadīth* collections of Muslim and Bukhārī, women's obedience to their husbands is more meritorious than supererogatory religious performance, and will result in their heavenly reward. Wifely obedience thus becomes a religious performance. Another version of this *ḥadīth*, cited by al-Wāḥidī, has the angels cursing a wife who refuses her husband.[92] Al-Jaṣṣāṣ goes on to cite more *ḥadīth*s in which a wife's salvation and standing in the afterlife are linked to her obedience to her husband. The following passage consists of a number of short *ḥadīth*s:

> It has been narrated on the authority of the Prophet ... 'it is not allowed for one human to prostrate himself before another, but if it were allowed, women would have to prostrate themselves before their husbands ...' The Messenger of God

[91] Al-Jaṣṣāṣ, *Aḥkām al-Qurʾān*, v. 1, p. 443.

[92] The following variant of the *ḥadīth* is cited by al-Wāḥidī: 'A woman from the tribe of Khathʿam came to the Prophet and said, "O Messenger of God, I am a widow. Tell me: what are the rights of husbands over their wives? If I am able to bear it, I will remarry; otherwise, I will remain as I am". He replied, "The right of husbands over wives is that if they ask to have sex with their wives, even if the wives are on the back of a camel, they must not refuse them access to themselves. Some of husbands' other rights are that wives must not undertake a voluntary fast except with their husbands' permission; if they do, the reward will not go to them, but instead they will be punished for it. It is among the husbands' rights that wives not leave the house without their permission, and if they do the angels of the sky, the angels of the earth, the angels of mercy and the angels of vengeance will curse them' (al-Wāḥidī, *al-Wasīṭ*, v. 1, pp. 334–5).

said, 'If a man calls his wife to his bed, and she refuses, and he remains angry at her, then the angels will curse her until morning . . .'

A woman came to the Prophet, who asked her if she was married. She responded, 'Yes', and he asked her, 'How are you with him?'

She answered, 'I will do anything for him, unless I am incapable of it'.

He said, 'Be aware of how you stand with him, for he will be your heaven or your hell'.[93]

In the first *ḥadīth*, a woman's relationship to her husband is likened to a man's relationship to God; because of husbands' God-like status vis-à-vis their wives, women must obey their commands just as men obey God's commands. In the second, women's refusal to come to bed results in their being cursed by angels: sexual availability is directly linked to piety. A final *ḥadīth* says that a husband's feelings about his wife will affect her fate in the afterlife; in this case the woman's actions are given less weight than the man's feelings.

Many of these *ḥadīth*s, or some version of them, were in major collections. Women prostrating themselves before their husbands, which is the most popular *ḥadīth* in subsequent works of exegesis, is in one major collection (Abū Dāwūd) and some minor collections; five subsequent exegetes cite this *ḥadīth*. That *ḥadīth* had twice the number of citations of the 'cursing angels' *ḥadīth*, despite the fact that the latter is in both Muslim and al-Bukhārī (the *Ṣaḥīḥayn*), and some more minor collections. The husband being his wife's heaven and hell is in Mālik's *Muwaṭṭa'*; it is not cited in the subsequent exegeses of this verse covered in this study.

Total wifely submission is, however, fraught. Some women are very pious and good, more so than their husbands. This difficulty is not addressed in the *tafsīr* sources that I reviewed, but it is highlighted by the Fāṭimid Ismāʿīlī interpreter al-Muʾayyad fī 'l-Dīn al-Shīrāzī (d. 470/1078) in his book of sermons. As mentioned in Chapter 3, Fāṭimid Ismāʿīlī interpreters wrote that references to men and women in the Qur'ān were references not just to a physical gender hierarchy, but to a spiritual hierarchy. In the following passage, al-Muʾayyad explains Q. 4:34 by saying that the word 'men' stands for the possessors of knowledge (teachers), while the term 'women' stands for the seekers of knowledge (students). The paradox of total wifely obedience can be explained with reference to the underlying meaning of the verse and the associated *ḥadīth*s. In the worldly realm, he says, some women can be better and

[93] Al-Jaṣṣāṣ, *Aḥkām al-Qur'ān*, v. 1, p. 445.

more pious than their husbands, whereas in the spiritual realm the teacher is always better than the student, hence the need for total submission:

> Exalted God has said *men are in charge* (qawwāmūn) *of women, with what God has made the one superior to the other* [Q 4:34], meaning that the possessors of knowledge (*al-ʿulamāʾ*) are in charge (*qawwāmūn*) of the seekers of knowledge (*al-mutaʿallimīn*). God has made their superiority over them manifest, and He has made the seekers of knowledge cleave to them with the attachment of a wife to her husband. The Messenger of God (peace be upon him) said 'If it were permissible for anyone to prostrate themselves to anyone other than God, I would have ordered that woman prostrate herself before her husband'. In its outward meaning (*ẓāhirihi*) this is an obligatory ruling, despite the weakness that enters into certain aspects of it: how many women are better than their husbands, more God-fearing, and are stronger preservers of the limits imposed by God? Thus the doctrine is taken according to the aspect of (inner) wisdom which secures it from its defectiveness and faults; for the being of the possessor of knowledge is superior to the seeker of knowledge in all aspects, and the Prophet said 'the possessors of knowledge are almost Lords (*kāda al-ʿulamāʾu arbāban*)'.[94]

In most Sunnī and Imāmī Shīʿī works of *tafsīr,* the exegetes seek to *confirm* the plain sense of Q. 4:34 by explaining the intrinsic mental and physical differences between the sexes. Al-Muʾayyad, however, admits to weaknesses and faults in the apparent meaning of the *ḥadīth* that implies the husband's spiritual superiority by saying that if women were ordered to bow down before anyone, they should bow down to their husbands. This is weak, he says, because many women are better than their husbands and more pious. The *bāṭin* of this verse, which refers to the hierarchical relationship between teachers and students, is thus more true and correct than its *ẓāhir* aspect. However, al-Muʾayyad is not antinomian. The verse and *ḥadīth* still indicate a ruling that is obligatory in its *ẓāhir* sense: women must be subservient to their husbands.[95] Al-Muʾayyad's interpretation is not taken up by authors within the genre of *tafsīr*. If one were to read solely within the genre of *tafsīr*, it would not be apparent that any such esoteric interpretation of Q. 4:34 existed. On the contrary, within the genre, exegetes such as al-Thaʿlabī refer directly to men's superior religious practice, including the points that men have surplus strength to worship, are more upright, may be prophets, go to Friday and communal prayers, and

94 Muʾayyad al-Dīn al-Shīrāzī, *al-Majālis al-Muʾayyadiyya*, 2nd edn., ed. Ḥātim Ḥamīd al-Dīn (Mumbai: Leaders Press Private Ltd., 2002), vol. 1, pp. 382–5.

95 This paragraph is duplicated from my article 'Spiritual Hierarchy and Gender Hierarchy', at pp. 39–40.

have the privilege of waging *jihād*. That is why, he explains, men must strive to educate and discipline their wives.[96]

Rather than taking an esoteric interpretation that resolves the issue, such as al-Mu'ayyad's, commentators within the *tafsīr* tradition are more likely to cite *ḥadīth*s that may present the answers to common concerns. Such *ḥadīth*s are instructive for women. If they choose to marry, they cannot expect equal treatment with men: they must be satisfied with getting less out of the deal. The repeated emphasis on the necessity of obedience, no matter how unfair it might be, seems to indicate that some, at least, found it unfair, as did the interlocutor in the following *ḥadīth*:

> While we were with the Messenger and a group of his Companions, a woman came so close that she nearly stood at his head, saying, 'Peace be upon you, O Messenger of God. I am a delegate to you from the women, and no woman heard of my coming to see you without being delighted by it, O Messenger of God. Indeed, God is the Lord of men and the Lord of women, and Adam is the father of men and the father of women, and Eve is the mother of men and the mother of women. So why is it that when men go out (*kharajū*) in the path of God and are killed, they will live with their Lord and be rewarded, and when they go out, the matter is as I say, but we women are confined by them, and we serve them (*nakhdumuhum*) – so do we receive any reward at all?'
>
> The Prophet said, 'Yes, greet the women and say to them that their obedience to their husbands and recognition of their rights will [earn them a reward] equal to the husbands' reward, although few of you do it'.[97]

There is a real sense of injustice in this woman's question to the Prophet. She reminds him first that men and women are spiritually equal: all sons and daughters of Adam and Eve, all followers of the Prophet. So why is it, she asks, that men are rewarded for going out of the house when women are ordered to stay indoors? The Prophet's answer is that women are promised a reward equal to that of their husbands for all of their hard work within the house. But the hierarchy between the sexes is re-established as the Prophet reminds her that most women are unlikely to

[96] Al-Tha'labī, *al-Kashf*, v. 3, p. 302–3 (at Q. 4:34). A passage in Jishumī's *Tahdhīb* is similar to this passage – while not all of the details are the same, the ways in which men are superior are listed in the same order as in al-Tha'labī's work, and most notably the mention of spending and trading (*taṣarruf*, *tijārāt*), which is quite unusual, is repeated in al-Jishumī. Al-Ḥākim al-Jishumī, *Tahdhīb*, MS Maktabat Muḥammad Qāsim al-Hāshimī, Private Library, Raḥbān, Sa'da. Al-Jishumī's *tafsīr* was not taken entirely from al-Tha'labī: the beginning of his discussion of 2:228 can be found in al-Ṭūsī's *tafsīr*.

[97] Al-Tha'labī, *al-Kashf*, v. 2, p. 173 (at Q. 2:228).

achieve this. A similar pattern is followed in other *ḥadīth*s stating that women's *jihad* consists of their obedience to their husbands.[98]

Al-Thaʿlabī also quotes several *ḥadīth*s in his interpretation of Q. 2:228 that, while affirming the need for the wife's obedience to her husband, nevertheless focus on her heavenly rewards, rather than her punishment. Again, these *ḥadīth*s address the tension inherent in rulings that reward men for doing things that women are not allowed to do. One remarkable *ḥadīth* addresses the questions that seem to be at the heart of the ethical dilemma of how men could be better than women in a religious sense, and gain more reward, even though their souls are the same:

> Maymūna, the wife of the Prophet, said the Messenger of God said, 'The best of men in my community (*umma*) are those who are best to their wives, and the best of women in my community are those who are best to their husbands. Every day and night the reward of a patient and God-fearing woman is that of a thousand martyrs killed in the path of God, and the superiority (*faḍl*) of one of them over the virgins of paradise is like my superiority over any man among you. The best women in my community are those who follow the path of their husbands in everything that they wish except if they ask them to do something that contradicts God's laws; the best of men in my community are those who are gentle towards their families with the gentleness of a mother to her son. Each day and night, the reward of one hundred martyrs killed in the path of God will be recorded for each patient and God-fearing man from among them'.[99]

In this portion of the *ḥadīth*, women and men are put on equal footing in one sense: women are able to gain access to the heavenly rewards reserved for martyrs. One aspect of men's heavenly reward is that they are given virgins of paradise, which is not among women's rewards. However, in this *ḥadīth* women are assured that they are superior to those virgins in the same way that Muḥammad is superior to normal men. Furthermore, even men's goodness is measured by using women as a yard stick: the best of men has 'the gentleness of a mother to her son'.

This initial statement of women's rights raises the anxieties of ʿUmar b. al-Khaṭṭāb in the second half of the *ḥadīth*, where he questions how a

[98] 'It is established (*thābit*) on the authority of Anas that he said: "The women came to the Messenger of God and they said, 'Oh Messenger of God, men achieve superiority (*al-faḍl*) by undertaking *jihād* in the path of God, and we do not have anything equivalent to this work in the path of God'".... "It was asked, 'is *jihād* obligatory for women?' And Muḥammad said, 'Yes. Their *jihād* is different, they strive within themselves, and if they are patient then they are *jihād* fighters (*mujāhidāt*). If they are patient then they are persevering (*murābiṭāt*), and they will have double the rewards'", (Ibid., v. 2, p. 173, at Q. 2:228). I could not find these *ḥadīth*s in any collection.

[99] Al-Thaʿlabī, *al-Kashf*, v. 2, p. 172 (at Q. 2:228).

woman could have more reward than a man. Here ʿUmar seems to represent the consummate patriarch, concerned that men should get a fair deal. Although the *ḥadīth* seems to appease both sides, the worried woman and the worried man, it highlights the tension around the issue of spiritual equality:

> ʿUmar b. al-Khaṭṭāb said, 'O Messenger of God, how will women's reward be that of one thousand martyrs and men's reward be that of [only] one hundred martyrs?'
>
> The Prophet responded 'Do you not know that [some] women will receive a greater reward than men, and a better hereafter, and that God, Blessed and Exalted, will raise a man up in paradise above his ranking [lit: degrees above his degrees] because of his wife's being pleased with him and because of her entreaties on his behalf? Do you not know that the greatest punishment after that for polytheism is for the woman who cheats on her husband? Are you not God-fearing in your treatment of the weak? For God will ask you about these two: orphans and women, and whoever is best to them has thereby reached God and pleased Him, and whoever is worst to them deserves God's displeasure.
>
> The rights of husbands over wives are like my rights over you [believers]; whoever causes me to lose my rights [through disobedience] has caused God to lose his; and whoever has caused God to lose his rights has brought upon himself the displeasure of God, and his end is Hell and his destiny is without hope'.[100]

In the second half of the *ḥadīth*, the Prophet explains that good women may receive greater rewards than men; in other words, rewards in the afterlife are not connected to a person's sex, but rather to their good deeds (cf. Q. 33:35). Yet despite his assertion that some women can receive even greater rewards than men, men still provide the context for women's rewards. It is obedience to the husband, regardless of his piety, that assures women a place above men in heaven. Whereas women in the first half of the *ḥadīth* are compared to the Prophet, in the second half, men are – their rights over their wives are as great as the Prophet's rights over his people. Any woman who disobeys her husband, 'causing him to lose his rights', has also disobeyed the Prophet and God. Women can expect dire results from failing to fulfil their husband's rights: hell and hopelessness. Thus, the *ḥadīth*, which started out by putting the 'best men' and the 'best women' on almost equal footing, ends up reinforcing the gender hierarchy.

By making obedience to her husband the sole path to a wife's salvation, this *ḥadīth* seems to place husbands between wives and any heavenly reward that the wives might eventually receive. Nevertheless, women need

[100] Ibid., v. 2, pp. 172–3 (at Q. 2:228).

not always obey their husbands. The beginning of this *ḥadīth* says that women may disobey when their husbands ask them to do something that contravenes God's laws. This indicates that women have some agency and some responsibility for knowing God's laws, and for obeying them above and beyond obedience to their husbands. If a good woman is married to a bad man, obeys him when necessary and disobeys his command to do things that contravene God's laws, then she presumably is rewarded and he is not. Husbands cannot come between their wives and God in this instance.[101] The marital hierarchy is subsumed to the greater God–human hierarchy. By marrying, women agree to an extra level of hierarchical duties (or, as in the case of some women, they vow never to agree to be married). Yet wifely obedience to husbands is limited; women's obedience to God is not.

Al-Thaʿlabī's work, conversational in style, relied on many unsound *ḥadīth*s, as well as some found in fragments in the sound collections.[102] By incorporating so many *ḥadīth*s on the Prophet's authority, he is shifting the balance of the authoritative sources commonly cited in *tafsīr* away from the early exegetical authorities, and towards the Prophet himself. This represents one trend in the genre of *tafsīr*, which in a way reached its culmination in the work of al-Baghawī (d. 516/1122), an exegete and *ḥadīth* scholar who removed all of the unsound *ḥadīth*s from al-Thaʿlabī's commentary, and, with some other minor changes, made it his own. Because the only *ḥadīth*s in this work are sound, the tone of al-Baghawī's commentary differs markedly from that of al-Thaʿlabī. He never mentions women's reward. The only *ḥadīth* on the Prophet's authority is the one which states 'if I were to order anyone to prostrate

101 *Pace* Ayesha Chaudhry, who suggests that the exegetes imagine husbands as being essentially between their wives and God ('men have direct, unfettered access to God, but women's relationship to God is mediated by men, who must oversee their wives' moral well-being'). She describes this as a 'patriarchal cosmology' and considers it central to Medieval Muslim conceptions of marriage. Chaudhry, *Domestic Violence and the Islamic Tradition*, p. 12 and elsewhere.

102 A fragment of the beginning of this *ḥadīth* ('the best of men is the best to his women') has a version in one major collection (al-Tirmidhī) as well as several minor collections; the remainder of the *ḥadīth*, both the first and second parts, is not in any *ḥadīth* collection that I searched. The full version as quoted is not cited by subsequent exegetes, except Abū 'l-Futūḥ-i Rāzī (d. 525/1131), an Imāmī whose Persian exegesis of Q. 2:228 is an almost exact translation of al-Thaʿlabī's *tafsīr* of the same verse, including at least one of the women's *jihād ḥadīth*s; quoting from Abū 'l-Futūḥ's text here would simply be redundant. The translation is so literal that at times it renders the Persian text unidiomatic. Walid Saleh has already noted that al-Thaʿlabī's *tafsīr* was used by Imāmī authors, and that this may be one reason for Ibn Taymīya's disapproval of him.

themselves before another, I would order a woman to prostrate herself before her husband'.[103] Here there seems to be less concern with justifying the unfairness of the marital hierarchy, and more concern with justifying its correctness as a religious practice.

The issue of spiritual equality and worldly inequality seems to have caused tension in Imāmī Shīʿī sources as well as Sunnī ones. The Imāmī exegete al-Ṭabrisī (d. 549/1153) cites a *ḥadīth* that paints a harsh picture of a married woman's fate:

> In the book *Man lā yaḥḍuruh al-faqīh* [by Ibn Babawayh] it is narrated on the authority of al-Bāqir (peace be upon him): a woman came to the Messenger of God, peace be upon him and his family, and she said, 'O Messenger of God, what is the right of a husband over his wife?' He said to her, 'That she obey him, and not disobey, that she not give alms from her house except with his permission, that she not undertake a supererogatory fast except with his permission, that she allow him to have sex with her, even if she is on the back of a camel, and that she not leave the house except with his permission, for if she leaves without his permission then the angels of the sky, the angels of the earth, the angels of anger, and the angels of mercy, will curse her until she returns to the house'.
>
> She said, 'Oh Messenger of God, what person has the greatest right over a woman?'
>
> He said, 'her husband'.
>
> And she said, 'I don't have any rights over him like those that he has over me?'
>
> He said, 'No, and for every hundred [of his rights] you don't [even] have one'.
>
> So she said, 'By God, no man will ever hold my neck [I will never marry!]'
>
> He said, 'If I were to order anyone to bow before another, I would order woman to bow before her husband'.[104]

As in *ḥadīth*s from Sunnī collections, in this Imāmī *ḥadīth* women's obedience is linked to their heavenly reward; the marital hierarchy is emphasised, as are men's superior rights. These *ḥadīth*s invoke the ultimate authority and sanction – that of the Prophet Muḥammad, the Imāms, or God – for a degree of wifely obedience that may otherwise seem unfair, and indeed is considered to be unfair by many of the women in the *ḥadīth*s.

The seeming unfairness of marriage is commonly justified by citing men's inherent religious superiority. Disagreement with the predominant

[103] Al-Ḥusayn b. Masʿūd al-Farrāʾ al-Baghawī, *Tafsīr al-Baghawī: maʿālim al-tanzīl*, ed. Muḥammad ʿAbd Allāh al-Nimr (Riyadh: Dār Ṭayba, 1993), v. 2, p. 208.

[104] Al-Ṭabrisī, *Majmaʿ al-Bayān*, v. 2, p. 134; although he is citing Ibn Bābawayh, his version differs slightly from that in the version of Ibn Bābawayh's book that we have. See al-Shaykh al-Ṣadūq, *Man lā yaḥḍuruh al-faqīh* (Najaf: Dār al-Kutub al-Islāmīya, 1378/1958), v. 3, p. 277.

view of men's bodily and spiritual superiority is only hinted at from within the *tafsīr* tradition. Al-Qushayrī (d. 464/1062) distinguishes between men's intellects and endeavours, which, he says, are a part of men's superiority over women, and their souls and bodies, which are not. 'Men are distinguished by their strength, so their burdens are greater [than women's], because one's burdens depend on one's strength. And this Qur'ānic phrase refers to intellects and endeavours (*al-qulūb wa'l-himam*), not souls and bodies (*al-nufūs wa'l-juthath*)'.[105] Al-Qushayrī specifies that men have been given more responsibilities than women because they are better able to bear them; their intellects and endeavours are greater than women's, but their selves, or souls, and bodies are not a part of this verse.

But the majority, whether Imāmī or Sunnī, say or imply that men are spiritually superior to women. In one *ḥadīth* cited by the Imāmī exegete al-Baḥrānī (1107/1695), God had to clarify the proper relations between the sexes after Adam obeyed Eve by eating the apple in the garden. It was because a man obeyed a woman that they were expelled from Paradise; this went against the natural order and the result was disastrous for Adam and, through him, for all of humankind.[106] Through Q. 4:34, God ensured that women would obey men.

The Sunnī exegete Ibn Kathīr seems to question the notion of equality in the hereafter. He writes that his method of interpreting the verse is to rely on the Qur'ān, the traditions of the Prophet, and finally on the exegesis of the Companions.[107] He composes his exegesis of this verse almost entirely of sound *ḥadīth*s. Norman Calder has noted his patent

[105] Al-Qushayrī, *Laṭā'if al-ishārāt*, v. 2, p. 25.

[106] 'A delegation of Jews came to the Messenger of God, and the most learned of them asked about several issues; among which was this question: "What is the superiority (*faḍl*) of men over women?" The Prophet said, "like the superiority (*faḍl*) of the sky over the earth, and like the superiority of water over the earth; for water brings life to the earth. If it had not been for men, God would not have created women, and God Almighty says: *Men are qawwāmūn over women, with what God has made some superior to others, and with what they spend of their wealth*". The Jew said, "In what way is that so?" The Prophet said, "Adam was created from earth, and from the surplus earth (*faḍla*) and the rest of it, Eve was created. In the beginning, Adam obeyed the woman [lit: women]. So God Almighty expelled him from Paradise, and He clarified the superiority of men over women in this world. Haven't you seen how women menstruate and are not able to worship, due to uncleanliness? Men are not afflicted by anything like menstruation". The Jew said, "We declare that you speak the truth, O Muḥammad"'. Al-Baḥrānī, *al-Burhān*, v. 2, p. 74.

[107] Jane McAuliffe, *Qur'ānic Christians: An Analysis of Classical and Modern Exegesis* (Cambridge: Cambridge University Press, 1991), p. 17.

lack of regard for the exegetical tradition of polyvalence; instead, he argues for a single, correct reading, which Calder blames on Ibn Taymīya.[108] In the case of verse 2:228, Ibn Kathīr takes an interpretation that has not appeared before in the exegeses of this verse, which is to say that men are superior to women in this world *and the next*. In other words, men's spiritual superiority has the result of a better reward in the afterlife. 'God's words, *and men have a degree over them* mean in superiority, creation (*khalq*), morals (*khuluq*), status, obeying the order, spending, upholding the good, preference in this world and the next, as He has said, *Men are* qawwāmūn *over women*'.[109] Ibn Taymīya's emphasis on the necessity of sticking close to the interpretations of the 'pious predecessors' might create an expectation that authors who were influenced by him, such as Ibn Kathīr, would go back to the earliest interpretations, *ḥadīth*s, and sayings of the Companions, and copy them verbatim. But, although Ibn Kathīr's exegesis includes many authenticated *ḥadīth*s, that does not stop him from including his own interpretation based on his understanding of these texts.

THE CONSEQUENCE OF DISOBEDIENCE, OR 'THE RULES OF DISCIPLINE TO BE OBSERVED IN THE EXERCISE OF FELLOWSHIP'[110]

In this chapter, I have argued that ethics and fairness matter to the interpreters: some take great care to explain why the marital hierarchy is fair and reasonable, and many show concern that husbands use their power over wives fairly, and seek to explain why a seemingly unfair situation is actually fair. But obedience is a wife's duty, even though it may seem unfair, and when wives disobey, ethical considerations are put to the test. Q. 4:34 gives the husband the right to punish his recalcitrant wife in various ways, including beating. How do the interpreters explain this? Al-Qushayrī, quoted in the section heading, says that the end of the verse instructs husbands to 'increase the punishment gently, by degrees, and if the matter is fixed after the admonition, do not use the stick to hit. For the verse comprises the rules of discipline to be observed in the exercise of fellowship (*adab al-'ishra*)'.[111] While the idea of a husband's

[108] Calder, 'Problems in the Description of a Genre', pp. 124–5.
[109] Ibn Kathīr, *Tafsīr al-Qur'ān al-'Aẓīm*, v. 2, p. 339 (at Q. 2:228).
[110] Al-Qushayrī, *Laṭā'if al-ishārāt*, v. 2, p. 25. [111] Ibid.

punishment of his wife is abhorrent to many modern readers, the medieval interpreters framed it as something that was necessary to preserve the proper fellowship between the spouses. In this section, I examine how interpreters attempt to reconcile the words of the Qurʾān with notions of correct and ethical behaviour.

In her analysis of legal sources, Kecia Ali notes that a wife's maintenance is predicated on her willingness to have sex with her husband, both at the commencement of the marriage and for its duration. Maintenance, Ali argues, is the payment for husbands' sexual enjoyment of wives and for the wives keeping themselves available for sex.[112] I would add that it is important to read *nushūz* and its consequences with the last part of the verse, which says *if they obey you, do not seek a way against them*; although the term *nushūz* is not defined, the link between punishment and disobedience is written into the verse itself.

In my study of sixty-seven pre-modern interpretations, I found that, in their interpretations of Q. 4:34, 50 per cent of all exegetes cite 'disobedience' as the meaning of the word, although many others did not give a definition at all. Seven interpreters mention that the basic idea of the word *nushūz* is 'rising up', like a hillock from the earth. Within the broad definition of 'disobedience' and 'rising up', exegetes have several variant views. I will review these first, and then examine definitions of *nushūz*, which are gender neutral or do not have to do with disobedience.

The variations on wifely disobedience are that wives: raise themselves up against their husbands (21 exegetes), takes their husbands' rights lightly (3 exegetes), rise up from bed, or disobey in bed (4 exegetes), or do not go willingly to the husband's bed as they used to. One exegete says that *nushūz* entails women's stubbornness.[113] Al-Wāḥidī quotes several unusual interpretations of every part of this verse; regarding *nushūz*, he says:

> *Nushūz* is wives' disobedience, according to the majority of the exegetes. ʿAṭāʾ says that it is that wives do not put on perfume for their husbands, and prevent them from having sex with them, and they stop doing the things that their husbands used to find delightful. The root of *nushūz* is to be raised up [so it entails a wife's raising herself up] against the husband, by contradicting his word.[114]

[112] Kecia Ali, 'Money, Sex, and Power: The Contractual Nature of Marriage in Islamic Jurisprudence of the Formative Period', PhD Dissertation, Duke University, 2002, pp. 169–210.

[113] Abū'l-Fayḍ al-Nakūrī, *Sawāṭiʿ al-ilhām fī tafsīr kalām Malik al-ʿallām*, ed. Murtaḍā al-Shīrāzī (M. Shīrāzī, 1996), v. 2, p. 29 (at Q. 4:34).

[114] Al-Wāḥidī, *al-Basīṭ*.

According to the sources cited by al-Wāḥidī, *nushūz* has to do with wives not making themselves ready for sex, by applying perfume and the like. In other words, wives are not just obligated to perform the act, but also to display enthusiasm, and to be agreeable. However, he also says that a wife must not contradict her husband's word. Thus, *nushūz* came to incorporate a variety of behaviours: it was not restricted to a wife's refusal to have sex.

A few exegetes offer definitions of *nushūz* that do not directly refer to disobedience. These include: that wives disturb their husbands, that the spouses dislike each other, that there is enmity between them, or that it is a wife's asking for a divorce in return for giving up her dowry (*khul'*).[115] One of the few sources that discusses men's *nushūz* along with women's *nushūz* is al-ʿAyyāshī. He defines a woman's *nushūz* as asking for *khul'* and then says that 'when the man commits *nushūz* along with the woman's *nushūz*, then this is discord (*shiqāq*)'.[116] *Shiqāq* is the term mentioned in the following verse (Q. 4:35), which calls for two arbiters.

There are two main interpretations of 'if you fear *nushūz*': 'if you know of women's *nushūz*', which is cited by seventeen exegetes, or 'if you strongly suspect their *nushūz*', which is cited by ten exegetes. The latter is the argument of the grammarian al-Farrā', who centres his discussion of this part of the verse on the word 'fear', saying that 'fear' is a strong suspicion, rather than positively knowing of the *nushūz*.[117] One exegete also says that to fear is to fear, or be afraid of. Another specifies that the husbands need proof of *nushūz* in the form of their wives' evil actions.[118]

In Q. 4:34, the first consequence of a wife's *nushūz* is an admonition.[119] Several exegetes specify that admonition should be the first step taken in the case of the wife's *nushūz*, and that all other measures can only be applied in order. The idea of minimal escalation is the view of al-Qushayrī, cited at the beginning of this section, who reminds

115 Ibn Abī Ḥātim, *al-Tafsīr*, v. 3, p. 942 (at Q. 4:34).

116 Al-ʿAyyāshī, *al-Tafsīr*, v. 1, p. 395 (at Q. 4:34). Al-ʿAyyāshī says: 'Abū Jaʿfar says, "When a woman commits *nushūz* against her husband, then she asks for *khul'*, and he should take what he can from her, but when the man commits *nushūz* along with the woman's *nushūz*, then this is discord (*shiqāq*)"'.

117 Al-Farrā', *Maʿānī al-Qur'ān*, p. 265 (at Q. 4:34).

118 ʿIzz al-Dīn ʿAbd al-Salām al-Sulamī, *Tafsīr al-Qur'ān ... Ikhtiṣār al-Nukat lil-Māwardī*, ed. ʿAbd Allāh b. Ibrāhīm b. ʿAbd Allāh al-Wuhaybī (Beirut: Dār Ibn Ḥazm, 1996), v. 1, p. 321 (at Q. 4:34).

119 For a different description of the admonition, particularly focusing on the warning of God's punishment for a disobedient woman, see Chaudhry, *Domestic Violence and the Islamic Tradition*, pp. 68–71.

husbands that they are undertaking to preserve the fellowship between themselves and their wives.

The earliest interpretations of 'admonish them' include the provisions that the admonition should be verbal, and that the admonition is to remind women of God and of husbands' rights, or the greatness of husbands' rights.[120] Less-cited interpretations of 'admonish them' include: telling wives to come back to bed;[121] admonishing them with religious knowledge,[122] or with the Qur'ān;[123] ordering them to be pious;[124] and making them fear God[125] or the punishment for their actions,[126] and the hitting that will result.[127] Some exegetes thus seemed to view the admonition as an opportunity for the husbands to spare their wives from further punishment, which would nevertheless be inflicted if the wives did not heed them.

The second of the three punishments for the *nāshiz* women is that their husbands shun them in the beds (*wa'hjurūhunna fī' l-maḍāji'*). As I mentioned at the beginning of the book, this part of the verse occasioned much disagreement among the exegetes: most define *nushūz* as the wife's refusal to have sex, and this punishment seems to entail her successful avoidance of it, which evidently does not make sense. It furthermore seems to require that men punish their wives' refusal by giving up their own right to sex, a right guaranteed to them in the marital contract.

Early interpreters have a variety of explanations for this phrase. Some take into account the plain sense of the words, others do not, and still others modify the words. Muqātil b. Sulaymān says that husbands should not go near their recalcitrant wives for sex.[128] His interpretation strays from the apparent meaning of *shun them in the beds* because the verse

120 This interpretation is taken by 'Alī ibn Abī Ṭalḥa, al-Ṭabarī, Ibn Abī Ḥātim al-Rāzī, and Abū'l-Layth al-Samarqandī.
121 Al-Qummī, al-Ṭabarī, and Ibn Abī Ḥātim.
122 This interpretation is taken by Ibn Wahb.
123 Ibn Wahb, al-Ṭabarī, Ibn Abī Ḥātim al-Rāzī, and al-Wāḥidī in *al-Basīṭ* and *al-Wajīz*.
124 Al-Sulamī, abridgment of al-Māwardī's *Tafsīr*, which actually includes some elements not found in al-Māwardī's *tafsīr*.
125 Al-Ṭūsī, al-Naḥḥās, al-Māwardī, *Nukat*.
126 Al-Naḥḥās, al-Māwardī, *Nukat*.
127 Al-Māwardī, *Nukat* and its abridgment, al-Sulamī, *Tafsīr*.
128 '*Those from whom you fear* nushūz, meaning, you know of your wives' disobedience ... *admonish them* by [mentioning] God, and if they do not accept *wa'hjurūhunna*. Muqātil says, don't come close to them for sex, and if they return to obeying their husbands with the admonition and leaving [don't pursue the matter], and if not, *hit them* without causing severe pain, meaning without blemishing them. *And if they obey you, then do not seek a way against them* meaning proof. Muqātil says, do not trouble them for love, you are not owed anything but obedience' (Muqātil, *Tafsīr*, v. 1, p. 371).

itself does not mention sex, and Muqātil does not mention beds. 'Abd al-Razzāq gives two different interpretations of this root, neither of which means avoidance. The first is that the husband speaks roughly to his wife, an opinion he attributes to Sufyān al-Thawrī. In this interpretation, the husband insults his wife verbally, and does not 'shun' her at all: he continues to have sex with her if he wishes.[129] The method of interpretation here is to change the form of the word: *hajara* is changed to *ahjara*, rendering it as 'speak roughly/harshly', rather than 'shun'. The second interpretation is attributed to al-Kalbī. He is credited with saying that *wa'hjurūhunna* means that the husband stays in bed and calls his wife to return to it.[130] This does not adequately explain how a word with the apparent meaning of 'shun' or even 'speak roughly' could mean 'order to return'.

Hūd b. Muḥakkam agrees with the interpretation 'speak roughly to them'; he clarifies that, since the entire matter of wifely *nushūz* is sexual, the husbands' response should take place entirely in the bed. Outside of the bed, the admonishing, speaking harshly, and hitting are not warranted: husbands cannot just hit their wives any time, for anything, but only when they have [sexual] need of them.[131] Although the early exegetes have radically different interpretations of this phrase, at one point most of these exegeses are left behind and 'avoid' becomes the most common explanation for the verse.

I described al-Ṭabarī's solution, and the reaction of his detractors, in the Introduction. One of the most interesting aspects of al-Ṭabarī's interpretation is that it shows that he was dissatisfied with the views of the earliest exegetes, and it was only because they did not answer the question properly that he had to seek the meaning of the phrase elsewhere. He lists several schools of thought on what husbands should do to punish recalcitrant wives, including the ones detailed in the early exegeses, namely: not have sex with them while lying with them; avoid speaking with them, but

[129] 'Abd al-Razzāq, *Tafsīr*, v. 1, p. 453, at. Q. 4:34, says 'al-Thawrī ... on the authority of Ibn 'Abbās says, concerning His words *wa'hjurūhunna* husbands should speak harshly to their wives (*yahjuruha bi-lisānihi*), being verbally rough with them; but they should not stop having sex with them (*jimā'ahā*)'.

[130] Ibid., v. 1, p. 452, at. Q. 4:34 has: 'Al-Kalbī says, the *hajr* in the beds does not mean to speak roughly to wives (*yaqūl la-hā hujran*). It is ordering them to come back, and return to their beds'.

[131] Hūd b. Muḥakkam, *Tafsīr*, v. 1, p. 378, at. Q. 4:34, reads: 'The admonishing is only in the bed, the cursing (*sabb*) is only in the bed, and the hitting is only in the bed. Husbands should not do this out of love, but only out of [sexual] need'.

lie with them and continue to have sex with them; avoid having sex with them; avoid talking to them during their absence from the bed; leave them [alone] on the mattress until they return to doing what their husbands like; and finally, speak harshly to them while they stay away from the bed. Al-Ṭabarī rejects three interpretations of the verse. The first is that *hajara* means to speak roughly. *Ahjara* means to speak roughly, but *hajara* does not.[132] Likewise, avoiding sex does not make sense as an explanation, because why would men avoid sex, when correcting their wives' refusal to have sex is the very purpose of the punishment? On similar grounds, he dismisses those who say that 'avoiding (*hajara*)' is 'avoiding words', or not speaking to recalcitrant wives: wives who are recalcitrant surely would not want to speak to their husbands.[133]

In his exegesis of the first part of Q. 4:34, he had hinted that wives' duty of obedience is not unlimited: it is in those matters that God requires. It is now clear that this is a reference to sex. But when it comes to this duty, wives must be made to comply. When words fail, they should be forced. Therefore, he takes the final interpretation:

> The likeliest interpretation concerning His words *wa'hjurūhunna*, and that which comes closest to its intention is securing with the *hijār*, according to [the sources] we have mentioned in which the Arabs say about the camel, when its owner has tied it up as we have described.... When this [is taken as] the meaning, then the interpretation of the verse is: those from whom you fear *nushūz*, admonish them concerning their rising up against you. And if they accede to the admonition, then you have no way against them.[134]

How could an interpreter who was so concerned with men's responsible use of power in his interpretation of Q. 2:228 and the earlier part of Q. 4:34, possibly demand that women be tied up and imprisoned when they refuse to have sex with their husbands? For he means this literally: in one summary, he mentions shackling women.[135] Al-Ṭabarī apparently sees no other way out of the linguistic and legal dilemma of the apparent order to 'shun' the wives in bed. He says that tying up is only to be taken as the last resort, after other measures have failed; it is not something that husbands can do arbitrarily. He supports his interpretation with recourse to *ḥadīth*s that have the Prophet saying that the husband's duty to his wife

132 Ibid., v. 8, p. 307 (at Q. 4:34).
133 Ibid., v. 8, pp. 307–8 (at Q. 4:34).
134 Ibid., v.8, p. 309.
135 Ibid., v. 8, p. 313, at Q. 4:34: 'Secure the [recalcitrant women] with shackles in their houses (*shaddūhunna wathāqan fī manāzilihinna*), and hit them, when they reject their duty to obey God concerning your rights [to sex]'.

is: 'That he feeds her, clothes her, does not hit her face, does not insult her, and does not shun her except in the house (*lā tahjuru illā fī' l-bayt*)'.[136] In this *ḥadīth* and another that he cites, the usual understanding of the word, 'shun', does not make much sense, especially since in the *ḥadīth*, the place of the *hajara* is the house (*bayt*), not the bed. These *ḥadīth*s seem to support al-Ṭabarī's view that the root *h-j-r* does not refer to avoidance.

The next two *ḥadīth*s are on exegetical authorities Ibn ʿAbbās and Ḥasan al-Baṣrī. The focus in these *ḥadīth*s is on the manner of forcing compliance from recalcitrant wives when admonishing does not work. One of these mentions imprisonment, and one advocates beating women into submission.[137] These *ḥadīth*s thus seem to support al-Ṭabarī's view that force is acceptable when dealing with non-compliant wives.

As I described earlier, al-Ṭabarī's interpretation is met with universal scorn, and the first of his detractors, al-Māwardī, attacked him precisely because of his use of *ḥadīth*s. This critique is echoed by Ibn al-ʿArabī, who was al-Ṭabarī's most vocal critic. Ibn al-ʿArabī's own solution to the linguistic conundrum is to undertake *ijtihād*, or independent reasoning, in order to glean the correct interpretation. The method he arrives at is an exact parallel to al-Ṭabarī's: he relies on Arab usage. But instead of the three meanings that al-Ṭabarī said were the only ones found in Arabic, he finds seven: (1) the opposite of coming together, (2) that which must not be said, (3) aversion to something, (4) the utterings of a madman, (5) being at the midpoint of a river, (6) a good youth, and finally, (7) the rope with which one ties the camel. Each of these meanings, he explains, really 'revolves around one single idea, and that is distance',[138] and he describes the ways in which each of the definitions encompasses the idea of 'distance'. Some of his descriptions are plausible: the midpoint of a river is equidistant from its two banks. However, some are not: a good youth, for instance, being far from defect.[139] This reasoning is vacuous because nearly everything is far from something.

Using the idea of 'distance', which he believes to be the basic sense of these root letters, Ibn al-'Arabī explains the meaning of the verse as 'to stay away from the recalcitrant wife'. He is quite clear that husbands should not have sex with their wives without speaking to them, for 'having sexual intercourse while not on speaking terms is a ridiculous thing to do'.[140] Thus, Ibn al-'Arabī consciously rejects the interpretations of certain early exegeses. I have documented 'picking and choosing'

[136] Ibid., v. 8, pp. 310–11 (at Q. 4:34). [137] Ibid., v. 8, p. 311 (at Q. 4:34).
[138] Ibn al-ʿArabī, *Aḥkām al-Qur'ān*, v. 1, p. 419 (at Q. 4:34). [139] Ibid. [140] Ibid.

elsewhere in this book: some early interpretations are left behind in later ages. Here, rather like al-Ṭabarī himself, Ibn al-ʿArabī believes that his methods allow him to arrive at a better understanding of the verse than earlier exegetes (in this case al-Suddī and al-Kalbī):

And since all of this is true, and the meanings all [go back to] the idea of distance, the meaning of the verse is (therefore): 'keep away from [the recalcitrant women] in the beds'. And it does not require all of this ado which everyone else has mentioned. Since it must not be as al-Suddī and al-Kalbī have mentioned, then how could it be what al-Ṭabarī has chosen?[141]

After rejecting the interpretations of early authorities, he explains that the law is a range, with a minimum and maximum extent. The minimum extent of the law is for husbands to turn their backs on their recalcitrant wives in bed, and the maximum extent is not to speak to, nor lie with, them.[142] By making the law into a range of acceptable possibilities, Ibn al-ʿArabī actually distorts the original sense of these texts, in which there was real disagreement. Instead of acknowledging the disagreements between earlier exegetes, he rejects the unacceptable interpretations and fuses the acceptable ones. This acceptable range is then put forth as the actual, correct interpretation of the verse. This stratagem enables Ibn al-ʿArabī to resolve yet another difficulty with the verse, which is the irreconcilable difference between the views of early exegetes.

'STRIKE THEM'

The final punishment of recalcitrant wives is the most controversial today, and that is the command to 'strike them'.[143] The sources allow for various levels of physical punishment, ranging from hitting with an object about the size of a forefinger to 'not breaking bones'. All sources that mention hitting (31 in all) also qualify it by saying 'without inflicting injury' (*ghayr*

[141] Ibid., v. 1, p. 419 (at Q. 4:34).

[142] Ibid., reads: 'Those who say "turn your backs on recalcitrant wives", have made the bed into the place [lit: adverbial noun denoting place] of separation. They have taken the doctrine according to the clearest of the clear meanings. It is [furthermore] the interpretation of Ibn 'Abbās (*ḥabr al-umma*), which carries out the minimum extent of the law.... And whoever says to avoid speaking to [recalcitrant wives] carries out the maximum extent of the law, and his doctrine is not to speak to [recalcitrant wives] nor lie with them'.

[143] For a discussion focused particularly on the permissible extent of the beating and its procedure, see Chaudhry, *Domestic Violence in the Islamic Tradition*, pp. 80–93, and also her third chapter, on the legal limits of wife beating. I disagree with Chaudhry's contention that the beating is the 'central focus' of interpretations of this verse (p. 81).

mubarriḥ).[144] Nine of these cite the interpretation that husbands should not break bones; eleven say that the hitting should be without blemishing (*ghayr shā'in*) and two say that it should not leave any mark (*ghayr mu'aththir*).[145] Six cite the interpretation that the beating should be with a *siwāk*, which is either a tooth-stick (a small stick used for cleaning teeth) or a branch from the tree called Arāk,[146] and one says that the beating should not seriously wound. Others say that it should not be too intense (*shadīd*) or gruelling. Two exegetes quote a *ḥadīth* which states that the Companion al-Zubayr used to hit his wives with a stick.[147]

Most exegeses focus on the extent of the beating, but do not question the man's right to beat. However, as mentioned previously, several exegetes specify that the beating must be the third and last measure in the series. A few seem uncomfortable with the notion altogether. Al-Wāḥidī cites a *ḥadīth* which says: 'The Messenger of God said, "Do not hit God's female servants", thereby forbidding the hitting of women, until those women turned their backs on their husbands, and the husbands complained to the Prophet, so the verse was revealed regarding hitting them'.[148] This interpretation hints at another Occasion of Revelation to the effect that the verse was revealed when some husbands complained of not being able to discipline their unruly wives. This *ḥadīth* exemplifies the attitude in many of these sources: beating is a necessary measure to keep women in line, but it is not an agreeable duty. Three authors (al-Ṭabarī, al-Jaṣṣāṣ, and Ibn Abī Ḥātim al-Rāzī) assert that if women obey their husbands, then God has forbidden striking them.[149] In other words, according to these exegetes, hitting is actually not legally permissible when women do their duty.

Other exegetes *recommend* not hitting, but they do not deny that men have the right to do so; they base their opinions on those of prominent

144 Kazimirsky says that *mubarriḥ* is: 'very harsh, very painful, causing intense pain (*très sensible, très-pénible, qui cause une douleur violente*)'.

145 Al-Ṭabarī, *Jāmi'* and al-Jaṣṣāṣ, *Aḥkām*.

146 Chaudhry suggests 'switch' for the *siwāk* (*Domestic Violence and the Islamic Tradition*, p. 83). She also points out that some interpreters preferred hitting with a handkerchief, but denies that this is an attempt to mitigate the extent of the beating, since these interpreters also recommended the use of a hand, which might be injurious (pp. 83–4).

147 Al-Tha'labī, *al-Kashf* and al-Zamakhsharī, *al-Kashshāf*.

148 Al-Wāḥidī, *al-Basīṭ*.

149 Al-Ṭabarī says, 'It is not permitted to strike women until after admonishing them for their *nushūz*, nor is admonition permitted to husbands unless [their wives are] disobedient. Then their husbands give them an order, or an admonition, according to what is right (*bi'l-ma'rūf*) according to what God has ordered' (al-Ṭabarī, *al-Jāmi'*, v. 8, p. 312, at Q. 4:34).

jurists. Fakhr al-Dīn al-Rāzī quotes al-Shāfiʿī as saying that 'hitting is permissible, but not doing it is better'.[150] And Ibn al-Jawzī quotes Aḥmad Ibn Ḥanbal as recommending that men delay hitting until the other measures have been taken, although he claims that al-Shāfiʿī allows the hitting at the commencement of women's *nushūz*. Other exegetes explain why the hitting should occur: three exegetes specify that it is intended to dissuade women from their evil actions.

Perhaps the most interesting case of imposing limits on men's hitting has already been discussed by Manuela Marín. She points out that al-Qurṭubī makes a class distinction in his recommendation to hit women who do not do the housework: lower class women may need to be beaten, while upper class women may not.[151] This may imply that upper class women could not be expected to do housework, as they would have had servants to do it. By citing class differences, al-Qurṭubī explicitly avows that circumstance can affect the implementation of law: special circumstances produce special limits on men's behaviour. Marín connects this with court cases from Mālikī regions (broadly, the Islamic West), which she uses to show that wives were granted divorces by Mālikī judges on the evidence that they had been beaten too hard.[152]

The Ḥanafī al-Ḥaddād (d. 800/1397) seems concerned that husbands not go too far with any of the measures specified in this verse. His interpretation reads much like an instruction manual, describing to men exactly what they should say, how they should say it, and why. If the situation gets to the point that hitting must occur, the blow should be 'as a man hits his son', in other words, to discipline wives, not to injure them. Because this interpretation seems to be motivated by such an earnest desire not to harm the wife, it is a particularly good example of how the boundaries of acceptable behaviour and attitudes vary according to time and place. By the norms of many societies today, hitting *itself* is considered to be seriously harmful. For al-Ḥaddād, hitting is acceptable *if* it does not seriously harm the wives. So, although al-Ḥaddād seeks to limit men's behaviour, he does not go beyond the norms of the society in which he lives:

> The intention is that the admonition, the *hujr*, and the hitting specified in this verse should be done in the order in which they are mentioned, because this is in the category of commanding right and forbidding wrong, and if correction

[150] Fakhr al-Dīn al-Rāzī, *al-Tafsīr*, v. 10, p. 90 (at Q. 4:34).
[151] Qurṭubī, *Jāmiʿ*, v. 5, p. 174 (at Q. 4:34); Marín, 'Disciplining Wives', p. 26.
[152] Marín, 'Disciplining Wives', especially pp. 29–34.

[of the disobedience] is possible with the easiest and lightest [measure], there is no need to go on to the heaviest. The first is that husbands say to their recalcitrant wives, 'Fear God and come back to bed!' If they obey, [that is acceptable], and if not, the husbands insult them (*sabbahā*), for Ibn 'Abbās says that the *hujr* is foul language. It is said a man commits *hujr* when he speaks irrationally.... Qatāda and al-Ḥasan say that *wa'hjurūhunna* is from avoidance, and that is that husbands should not come close to the bed, nor should they sleep with their wives, because God Almighty has joined the word 'shun' with the words 'in the beds'. When the admonition does not have any effect on recalcitrant wives, then husbands avoid them in bed, and if they love their husbands this will be unbearable for them. But if they loathe them, their agreement to the separation will be proof of *nushūz* on their part, at which point the husbands may hit them as long as they do not inflict serious injury, nor mark them, just as a man punishes his son. The [extent of the beating] will be entrusted to the husbands' reasoned opinion and their independent judgment (*ijtihād*), according to what they see as being helpful. Because of this, it is said that this blow is restricted by the condition of well-being (*muqayyad bi-sharṭ al-salāma*), and the best thing is to hit [recalcitrant wives] with a sandal, and the blow should be twice or three times.[153]

Among the texts examined for this book, this one is particularly limiting for men's behaviour: he says that the husband should really only hit two or three times, with a sandal. This is a good example of the patriarchal power dynamic that informs the understanding of marital relationships in most or all of these texts. Al-Ḥaddād's comparison of the husband-wife relationship with that of a father and son is particularly revealing. Fathers discipline their sons not because they wish to harm or injure them, and not because of an arbitrary wish for power, but because they love them and think that they will benefit from some discipline. Sons grow up, but women never outgrow the need for their husbands' loving but stern authority. They are permanently in a state of dependence and obedience. This interpretation is typical of the worldview pervading these texts of just rulership of husbands over wives: hitting is not done arbitrarily but rather because it is perceived to be in some way beneficial to the proper spousal relationship.

I have described how several exegetes in this study express concern regarding men beating their wives. They recommend that men not beat too hard or say that it is better not to beat or that beating must only occur after exhausting other options. Nevertheless, men's right to beat *at all* is not seriously questioned. The pre-modern exegetes reviewed here do not break out of the straightforward reading of the verse in

[153] Fakhr al-Dīn al-Ḥaddād, *Tafsīr al-Ḥaddād*, ed. Muḥammad Ibrāhīm Yaḥyā (Beirut: Dār al-Madār al-Islāmī, 2001), v. 2, p. 250 (at Q. 4:34).

order to take an interpretation which would exclude beating altogether, the way that some modern exegetes do.

The final part of Q. 4:34 reads *and if they obey you, do not seek a way against them*. For some exegetes, this phrase encapsulates the essence of the verse, and the trickiness of putting ethical boundaries on an ethically difficult situation. They take it to mean that wives owe the husbands obedience, but nothing more. When wives disobey, the husbands can seek measures against them – but not for any other reason.

At least seven exegetes cited the interpretation that the husband should not seek love from his wife, but only obedience. According to al-Ṭabarī, God has ordered wives to obey, whether they want to or not. The act of their obedience, despite their own wishes, is proof of their piety. If a wife does not love her husband, but she obeys him, that is all that the husband is owed in terms of rights; he cannot ask for her love, because nobody can control her feelings:

> O men, when your wives, from whom you fear *nushūz*, obey your admonition, then do not tie them to the beds. When they do not obey you, then tie them to the beds and beat them. If they resume obedience to you at that point, and return to doing what they are obligated to do, then do not seek a path towards harming them and being hateful to them. Nor should you seek a way to what is not lawful to you in terms of their bodies and their property on any pretext, such as one of you saying to his obedient wife, 'You do not love me – you hate me!' and hitting and harming her because of that. For God Almighty has said to men, *when they obey you*, meaning [that they obey] even when they hate you. So [when they are obedient despite their hatred of you] do not become angry with them, hitting them and harming them, and do not oblige them to love you, for that is not in their hands.[154]

Interpretations that speak of the necessity of obedience but not love are another example of how these texts are informed by the law. It is clear from al-Ṭabarī's interpretation that men are likely to want their wives to love them; this exegesis bids them to control this desire and to remember that in fact the contract of marriage legislates for wifely obedience but says nothing about love.

SUMMARY AND CONCLUSION

This chapter began with an examination of the Qur'ān's verses, in which I argued that there is a clear prescription for a marital hierarchy, but

[154] Al-Ṭabarī, *Jāmiʿ al-Bayān*, v. 8, p. 316 (at Q. 4:34).

equally a command for husbands (the stronger party) to behave ethically and fairly towards their wives, and for the marital relationship to include love and mercy. I showed that the prescription for 'good companionship' found in an early interpretation attributed to al-Ḍaḥḥāk is reflected in actual marriage contracts preserved from the time of these interpretations. The inclusion of this clause in marriage contracts may indicate that marriage was commonly understood as an institution of fellowship and companionship, rather than one akin to slavery, even though legal works sometimes compare wives to slaves. To that end, Ibn ʿAbbās's interpretation of men's 'degree' over women, which is followed by al-Ṭabarī, is that men should forgive their wives if they are derelict in some of their duties. Husbands, as the superior members of the hierarchy, are expected to treat their wives justly. Other early interpreters, such as ʿAlī b. Abī Ṭalḥa, stressed the limits on women's obedience; but such interpretations were not taken up by later commentators, who instead focused on the necessity for total wifely obedience. Thus, as in previous chapters, there was a change between early, pre-Ṭabarī interpretations, and post-Ṭabarī interpretations. Pre-Ṭabarī commentators said that men were in charge of women and that they had more rights than them, but did not say why. Post-Ṭabarī interpreters list various aspects of men's inherent makeup to justify their status in the marital hierarchy, whether it be physical, mental, spiritual, or a combination of these factors.

The exegetes' descriptions of men's physical, mental, and moral superiority to women were tempered with admonitions to husbands that such superiority carried responsibility. While not many post-Ṭabarī interpreters limited the extent of women's obedience, many of them stressed men's moral responsibility to treat their wives justly, in accordance with common ideas of just rulership. A few stressed the importance of behaving as men, in order to merit their ascendency over women. Thus, it is common to cite ethical considerations in works of *tafsīr*, and to say that men must act in ways that befit their status as *qawwāmūn* over women. However, it is rare to say that a man's failure to fulfil his duties results in loss of his status. Even interpreters from the Mālikī school, which holds that a woman can divorce her husband if he fails to pay maintenance, usually did not mention this ruling in their works. In the interpretations of Q. 4:34 and Q. 2:228 the rarest interpretation of all is that some exceptional women may equal men mentally. It was taken by one late Ḥanafī source, al-Qūnawī.

Wifely obedience is the crux of married women's religious performance. Although wifely obedience is almost unlimited according to some interpreters, all agree that wives could disobey if their husbands ordered them to do something unlawful. The husband could not come between his wife and God in this instance, and therefore the marital hierarchy is not absolute as is the God–human hierarchy. Yet the wife could not attain salvation if she was disobedient in the matters where her obedience was required. Several post-Ṭabarī Sunnī and Imāmī Shīʿī authors referred to *ḥadīth*s on the Prophet's authority that addressed the tension around the necessity of wifely obedience. Some *ḥadīth*s had women questioning the fairness of laws that rewarded men for activities that were normally forbidden to women, such as *jihād*. Others simply emphasised that women must obey, even though it may not seem fair. Such *ḥadīth*s seem to perform the function of both answering women's concerns, and also admonishing them, putting them in their place should they complain about the unfairness of their lot. These *ḥadīth*s were perpetuated in a male-dominated religious milieu, and may shed light on the common concerns associated with the extent of husbands' legal leeway over their wives.

The flourishing of these *ḥadīth*s in the post-Ṭabarī period indicates the shift in the genre of *tafsīr* away from the early exegetical authorities and towards the Prophet as the highest source of authority, a position he had always enjoyed in theory, but not in practice. This shift in the actual sources cited brought exegetical practice closer to its theoretical sources, although exegetical theory did little to account for the effect of social milieu or the interpreter's own reasoned judgment, and the interpretations of the early exegetical authorities continued to exert a strong influence on the genre. Gradually, a divide emerged between those interpreters who, in addition to the views of the early exegetes, cited only sound *ḥadīth*s on the Prophet's authority, and those who cited unsound *ḥadīth*s.

A wife's obedience as religious practice carries the strong implication that men have superior religious understanding. Only one author, the Ismāʿīlī al-Muʾayyad fī' l-Dīn al-Shīrāzī, addressed the possible paradox of the necessity of a wife's obedience to a husband who may not be as good as she. Many more authors implicitly denied that such a paradox could arise – around 30 per cent of the exegetes in this study mentioned that men had a surplus of religion in comparison to women, and many more exegetes gave men responsibility for women's moral education and discipline; furthermore, the term 'rationality' could have encompassed some moral sense, so saying that men had a surplus rationality may have implied a superior moral understanding. All of this gives the impression that men were widely considered to have a better religious sense than women, which would seem to follow from the *ḥadīth* on women's deficiency in rationality and religion. It would also seem to justify women's obedience to their husbands' guidance and moral education, which was a key part of the husband's role.

This chapter gave examples both of picking and choosing, and of reinterpretation. Just because an interpretation came from a reliable early source did not guarantee it a place in later tradition. Furthermore, later interpreters sometimes reinterpreted early views, making them say something that they had not actually said, or reconciling divergent views. One example was when the Mālikī Ibn al-ʿArabī reconciled early views on *abandon them in the beds*, which in al-Ṭabarī's work and those of others had been considered as separate and distinct interpretations. Another example is the *ḥadīth* on beautification attributed to Ibn ʿAbbās ('I like to adorn myself for my wife just as I like it when she adorns herself for me, because God has said *women have rights like their obligations*'), mentioned in passing by several later exegetes. This *ḥadīth* was cited as one interpretation of the ways in which women's rights are like (in other words equal to) their duties. But several centuries later, the Mālikī al-Qurṭubī cites the *ḥadīth* and describes, in great detail, the sorts of 'beautification' that men can undertake, and why it is important to do so: so that wives do not stray and are kept satisfied.[155] In the modern period, the *ḥadīth* has been revived again by Mehdī Mehrizi, whose interpretation will be discussed in Chapter 6.

[155] Al-Qurṭubī, *al-Jāmiʿ li-aḥkām*, v. 3, p. 124 (at Q. 2:228).

6

The Marital Hierarchy Today

While the marital hierarchy was taken for granted in medieval interpretations, today it is hotly contested. In 2009, the Iranian parliament passed laws on issues that bear directly on the modern interpretation of Q. 4:34 and Q. 2:228. Now, a woman can apply for divorce from her husband if he beats her hard enough to leave a mark, if he does not have sex with her for more than four months, if he is addicted to drugs, and in a number of other cases. These rulings have formed a common base point for all Iranian interpreters: no interpreter now says that a husband can hit his wife enough to leave a mark (although according to some he may hit lightly or in a symbolic way). Sunnī interpreters also moderate the extent of the beating; the interpreters whose views I surveyed recommend that this be light, not enough to leave a mark, or with a tooth-stick. These laws have been shaped by the medieval tradition, but they have been made modern. For medieval commentators, the Occasion of Revelation for Q. 4:34 was used to justify the view that that the husband was not liable 'except in cases of death or wounding', while qualifications such as 'lightly' or 'with a tooth-stick' represented the recommended limits, rather than what was legally enforceable. What was once considered to be the moral limit has now acquired legal force.

In another modern recasting of medieval tradition, the laws on housework have now been resuscitated and augmented: according to the same 2009 Iranian legislation, husbands cannot expect their wives to do housework and wives are entitled to be paid for doing it. Medieval laws did not require women to do housework, but they did not pay them for doing it. Such revival and recasting is a potent tool for connecting modern mores with the medieval tradition, and many of my Iranian interview subjects insisted that their wives were not obligated to cook or clean.

Since moral and actual laws mitigate against abject subjugation or bodily harm as a result of discipline, for interpreters the main question is now about the power structure of the household: should husbands be put in the position of being in charge of their wives, able to discipline them verbally or even with a light slap? If so, why? If not, why not? The basic lines of argument to answer these questions will be familiar by now. Conservatives support hierarchical and inflexible roles in the family based on their view of the inherent nature of the sexes; reformists and neo-traditionalists allow for modifications in the law in light of changing circumstances. In this chapter I investigate the roots of these interpretations, and delve into the hermeneutics of their proponents. I highlight the differences among conservatives and the recasting of traditional methods undertaken by reformists. Tradition and reform, the use of reason, revelation, and science, are themes for both conservatives and reformists writing on the ideal Islamic marriage today.

This chapter is, perhaps, the most personal chapter of the book. In it, I investigate how women themselves interpret the marital hierarchy, and why some of them support it. In these interviews and others, I was drawn in to discuss my own views of the ideal marriage, or my own marriage. It was sometimes difficult to answer conservative interpreters. Ziba Mir-Hosseini says, about her interview with one conservative *ʿālim*, 'Our conceptions of gender and rights were so different that we were simply talking about two different realities'. She also talks of him being 'kind and tolerant', and says that he 'spoke with such certainty, honesty, and integrity that my objections seemed flat and irrelevant'.[1] These words resonated with me after having interviewed conservative *ʿulamāʾ* for myself. I was always welcomed, treated with great solicitude, and taken seriously. But we believe in different truths and begin from different assumptions, both about the nature of the sexes and about the nature of the law. To me it is not clear why the marital hierarchy was necessary at all, given that the core rulings could change so much from the medieval period that men are no longer allowed to beat their wives and that women could be paid for housework. While reformists and neo-traditionalists readily admit that there can be negotiation of roles within a marriage, and development and change in the law, conservatives do not. Sometimes the conservatives' explanations of the unchanging law came a bit close to home, as, for instance, when one

[1] Mir-Hosseini, *Islam and Gender*, p. 30.

of my interview subjects asked me why, if women were as intelligent as men, the majority of great composers, philosophers, artists, and mathematicians were men; or when another asked why, since European legislation guarantees women equality, they had not achieved it; or a third warned me that perhaps I had better not spend too much time away from my husband doing my research.

At times I was simply struck speechless. When a Grand Ayatollah cited fishy statistics, was I allowed to challenge him? What was the etiquette? And how could I challenge him, when I had not come armed with statistics or prepared to justify my own assumptions? Such was not my purpose, I told myself: I was there to talk about the Qurʾān, not to defend my culture or to speak about neuroscience, sociology, history, statistics, or indeed my own relationship with my husband. But in some ways the 'intrusion' of these elements, whether cultural, historical, or scientific, sheds light on the interpretation of the Qurʾān in the modern world, and on the subtle manipulations of the tradition among both conservatives and reformists. As I went through the interviews later, I could see that what seemed like blanket similarities hid variations within their core interpretations, and especially in their attitudes towards the permissibility of reinterpretation.

THE MARITAL HIERARCHY ACCORDING TO THE CONSERVATIVES

Conservatives' justifications for the marital hierarchy have much in common with their justifications on women's testimony. According to conservatives, husbands are in charge of the marital relationship, and have the right to discipline their wives because, for them, the Qurʾān's references to a marital hierarchy indicate a universal truth about the nature of the sexes: women's and men's natural capacity differs to such an extent that it requires them to have fixed roles in the family, and to some extent different roles in life. Conservative rulings echo pre-modern rulings in the key point of advocating a fixed marital hierarchy. But, as in the case of women's testimony, while pre-modern *'ulamā'* justified their rulings by saying that women were inferior to men, the idea of women's inferiority is no longer an acceptable justification. To prove that these roles are indeed justified today, modern conservatives use arguments and proofs that are largely different from the ones used in the pre-modern period but which still refer to intrinsic, natural differences between the sexes. The basic interpretation remains; justifications for it have evolved over time.[2]

Their approach is illustrated in the interpretation of Grand Ayatollah Naser Makarim Shirazi, who has been mentioned in passing earlier in the book.[3] Rather than being innovative or unusual, the ideas expressed, methods used, and contexts drawn upon in his work exemplify the most widespread current doctrine on the relationship between the sexes in the modern Middle East. Although his text is by no means the progenitor of patriarchal interpretations, I believe that the keys to the contemporary resonance of patriarchal interpretations can be found in Grand Ayatollah Makarim's interpretation. In what follows, I compare his interpretation with that of other conservatives, in order to give a general picture of the marital hierarchy and the nature of the sexes according to the conservative view.

Makarim Shirazi was born in 1924 in Shīrāz, Iran. He began his formal religious studies at the age of fourteen, and concentrated on *fiqh* and *uṣūl al-fiqh*. In 1950, he travelled to Iraq, where he studied with Abū' l-Qāsim al-Khuʿī and Muḥsin al-Ḥakīm. Lacking the means to stay in Iraq, he returned to Iran in 1951. He was politically active in the time preceding the Iranian revolution, and during that time was jailed and exiled. He played a role in writing the first Iranian constitution, and, as recently as 2006, issued a *fatwa* on women's attendance at stadiums. His work of *tafsīr* was written originally in Persian; the earliest publication that I could find of the Persian *Tafsīr-i-namūneh* was in 1974. It was translated into Arabic as *al-Amthal fī tafsīr al-Qur᾽ān*, published in 1992. *Al-Amthal* is in some ways a typical work of Qur᾽ān commentary. It goes through the Qur᾽ān verse by verse, explaining the meanings of the verses, and making reference to past authorities. However, his *tafsīr* is essentially modern in its approach and methods of interpretation.

Grand Ayatollah Makarim's writing style is popular, rather than scholarly, which may reflect his desire to appeal to an increasingly literate mass audience. His arguments are often general, rather than specific. For instance, he speaks of 'Islam' rather than the views of any specific school of law. He virtually ignores grammar, which is a major component of

[2] Cf. Chaudhry, 'Traditionalist scholars frame their arguments in particularly modern ways', *Domestic Violence and the Islamic Tradition*, p. 141.

[3] Parts of this section were presented in January 2009, at the Modern Arabic Texts Workshop, Mansfield College, Oxford University. I would like to thank my colleagues there for their helpful comments, particularly Ronald Nettler, who convened the conference, Joseph van Ess, who suggested I find the ultimate source of these interpretations, and Leonard Wood.

most pre-modern exegeses. He does not refer to named authorities, and, perhaps most importantly, he does not give multiple, conflicting interpretations of a verse. For Grand Ayatollah Makarim, as for many other modern interpreters, religion is monolithic, and history is idealised.

Grand Ayatollah Makarim's methods are apparent in the explanation of his view of the nature of the sexes, which lays the basis for all following arguments. In his interpretation of Q. 2:228, *women have rights like their duties* bi'l-maʿrūf, he says first that all duties are accompanied by rights – so nobody has a duty without having a corresponding right. According to him, this is the case of the rights and duties in every area of life, including the rights of men and women. He then asserts that, because women's nature differs from men's, their rights cannot be equal. This patriarchal interpretation has great resonance as a response to contemporary concerns about gender roles and human rights. By using the discourse of human rights and women's rights, and by arguing that only the Islamic system truly guarantees these rights, he answers the pressing concerns of the day in a style appealing to the casual reader, rather than the scholar.

> Is it necessary that the two sexes be exactly equal in all duties, and, consequently, in all of their rights? If we were to take a look with respect to the large differences between the two sexes, in the field of bodily and spiritual strength, it would provide an answer to the question. The woman – by nature of her sensitive responsibilities in bearing children, and raising them – is blessed with a stronger capacity for tender emotions and feelings, and this superiority in feeling necessitates that we have entrusted men with all of the duties of society, which require, more than other things, strength of thought and distancing from the tender emotions and personal sensitivities. If we want to maintain justice, it is necessary that the responsibility of governing, judging, and guiding the family falls on the shoulders of the man, and that, in these matters, the man has been made superior. And, of course, this does not prevent some women, by virtue of superior upbringing, knowledge, and piety, from being far superior to men.[4]

In this excerpt, Makarim Shirazi explains that women are emotional and sensitive, while men are distanced from their emotions and are thus capable of 'governing, judging and guiding the family'. He finishes by asserting that some women can be superior to men. These exceptional women are not distinguished by their minds or innate characteristics, but rather by their upbringing, knowledge, and piety. Thus, women and men are equal, but different. As was apparent in interpretations of women's testimony, this is the most widespread conservative view of the nature of the sexes.

[4] Makarim Shirazi, *al-Amthāl fī tafsīr kitāb Allah al-munzal*, v. 3, pp. 98–9 (at Q. 2:228).

While equal-but-different is the most common conservative view, some conservatives, both Sunnī and Shīʿī, closely replicate views common in the medieval tradition: the sexes are unequal and men are superior. Grand Ayatollah Mohammad ʿAli Gerami explained that in aspects of the will, such as piety, women may be better than men; but in all natural and physical aspects, men are better:

AYATOLLAH GERAMI: In what way should she obey? Willingness with regards to the matter of his sexual desire, yes. Her acceptance is a duty! Even in a house in which the husband was a sinner (*fāsiq*), it is still the wife's duty to accept his advances. It's known. In the contract of marriage, [sexual] willingness is a duty for the wife with regards to the husband. This is an accepted matter. However, with regards to guardianship in the eyes of God, and in piety, and towards other people, this obedient woman is better than that sinning man. It's known. This is the aspect of will, rather than nature. With regards to the natural aspect, and the essence (*dhat*), in essence the man is superior (*bi'l-dhātin wa-ṭabīʿiyyatan al-rajulu afḍal*). But there is another aspect, the secondary aspect, and in this way, it is possible for a woman – for instance, Fāṭima al-Zahrā, the daughter of the Prophet, peace be upon him, is more noble than all men other than the Infallibles.[5] Than all men, it's known, and not just Fāṭima al-Zahrā, but also Zaynab al-Kubrā, the daughter of Fāṭima. Did any man bear same burden of responsibility that was borne by Zaynab at Karbala? Some women are much, much better than men, as is well known.

KAREN BAUER: Hm. But these are exceptions.

AG: Yes, but even with all of this, the Prophet did not make Zaynab or Fāṭima a judge. And he did not make them commanders of the army. And he did not make them governors of a city. Even when the Prophet went on a raid, he appointed ʿAlī as his deputy. And when he left Mecca for Medina, he made Maʿāẓ his governor. Not any of the women. How was that? And so when we speak about the essence, men are superior, but if we speak about the historical period, then there is no doubt that some women were many times better than men, because they stayed in their houses. Even the Prophet said that proper obedience of a wife to her husband is equal to *jihād* in the path of God.

I have one last thing to say. This has an effect on the makeup of the society in the country. Meaning that if there is a man who is free and

[5] By which he means the Imāms.

has an obedient wife, he will easily be able to resolve problems outside of the house. But if the woman is in the house and is not obedient, then neither the woman nor the man will be good members of society.[6]

In this passage, Ayatollah Gerami explains that even the most pious, holy, noble, and exceptional women, who were better than all men, were still not put in positions of leadership or authority. That is because, in his view, men are inherently better than woman in this regard. For a woman to be good is for her to stay in her house. Grand Ayatollah Gerami is implicitly referring to Q. 33:33, *stay in your houses, and do not display yourselves as in the time of ignorance*, a verse addressed to the Prophet's wives, also referenced in medieval interpretations of Q. 4:34, and he refers to the women's *jihād ḥadīth*s cited by al-Thaʿlabī (described in Chapter 5). He concludes this speech by asserting that the entire structure of a functioning society rests on the wife's obedience: if she is obedient, then men will not be violent and will cause fewer problems. Disobedience in the home causes social disruption outside of it. The woman who does not wish to engage in sexual activity with her husband must weigh these consequences. Thus, not every contemporary cleric engages in a rereading of tradition. In this instance, Ayatollah Gerami replicates the substance, as well as the core rulings, of the medieval tradition.

In both Grand Ayatollah Makarim's and Grand Ayatollah Gerami's interpretations, the differences between men's and women's minds mean that men have the ultimate authority in any dispute between the couple. Mr Zibaei Nejad draws an explicit parallel with political systems. He says that the democratic system does not work for families because problems are not resolved: someone needs to have the final say. Hierarchies are therefore natural and fair. The general idea of the fairness of hierarchies is certainly present in medieval sources. However, the formulation of Mr Zibaei Nejad's argument is entirely modern. If the family does not have a head, someone who can have the final word, then it simply 'doesn't work'. In the interview, it soon became obvious that we had different conceptions of what 'works' and what 'doesn't work'. Fatemeh, my translator and research assistant, joined in this discussion:

MR ZIBAEI NEJAD: In Western societies, there is a kind of democracy – parents are just the counsellors of children. But in our society, there is a hierarchy – parents are above children. It's the same for men and

[6] Mohammad ʿAli Gerami, Personal Interview, Qom, Iran, 14 June 2011.

women. If there would be one person to be the boss of the family, who would you choose?

KAREN BAUER: You mean me or my husband? I really can't answer that.

FATEMEH MUSLIMI: Why?

KB: I don't know, we discuss everything together.

ZN: No. If we suppose that there should be one person to be the boss of the family, then what are the criteria for choosing that person?

KB: Whoever is more level-headed, or smarter, or better at making decisions, I guess.

ZN: No. If the woman says that she can decide better, and the man says that he can decide better, then what do you do?

KB: You discuss it. You have a conversation together like adults. The man and the wife can have a conversation like two adults together, not like one is the parent and the other is the child.

ZN: But what if they discuss and they don't come to any conclusion, they debate and discuss, and then what shall we do?

KB: You just disagree. That's it. What kind of decision are you talking about? If you're buying a house, both people have to like it. If you're buying a car, both people have to like it. If you're going to have a baby, both people [need to] want to have it.

ZN: If you and your husband disagree with one another, it doesn't work. You won't come to any conclusion. And here Islam gives us the conclusion.[7]

In the patriarchal relationship described by Mr Zibaei Nejad, the husband assumes the role of parent over his wife in a case when there is disagreement between them. Whereas I assume that consensus is possible, or that it is possible to live with disagreement, he assumes that one person should be given the responsibility for making the final decision in disputes. When I asked about the husband's making bad decisions, for instance, gambling away the family wealth or doing things that were not right for the household, Mr Zibaei Nejad clarified that if the husband made decisions that were not in accordance with the religion, then his leadership was no longer valid.[8]

When Mr Zibaei Nejad saw what I had written about this interview, he wrote an email to clarify his position. He emphasised the communal and ethical aspect of family relations. 'When considering Islam's position on

[7] Mohammad Rezar Zibaei Nejad, Personal Interview, Qom, Iran, 28 May 2011.

[8] He reemphasised this point in his follow-up email communication: 'in the case of individual disqualification or when an individual avoids taking responsibility, the men are deposed from the leadership position' (Mr Zibaei Nejad, email communication, 26 June 2014).

man as a leader, Islamic evidence which encourages ethical behaviour must be taken into account. For instance, the verse that encourages men's good behaviour towards women, *live with them according to what is right* [Q. 4:19]. According to this verse, men should behave well towards their wives'.[9] He acknowledged that, if one were to have a purely individualistic perspective, rather than a communal perspective, then men's leadership role might seem unfair.[10] But in certain cases, he says, consensus is not possible, and nor is it possible to avoid making any decision at all. That is when the man has to assume his role as leader and manager of the family, not in his own interests, but in the interests of communal harmony. 'In these infrequent cases, the family members' agreement to the leader's (i.e., the man's) decision is not to submit to his selfishness, but to find a practical solution to the problem'.[11] For Mr Zibaei Nejad, fixed family roles are the most practical way of dealing with family problems. He explained to me that while the ultimate purpose of men and women is the same – worshipping God – their specific roles or abilities might differ.

Grand Ayatollah Makarim explains that to disregard the proper roles of the sexes is to disregard the tenets of nature and religion. He first cites Q. 2:228 and Q. 4:34 as Qur'ānic proofs of men's and women's roles. Second, he refers to 'the law of administration' as proof that men, since they are less emotional than women, should have charge of administration. It is important to note that he does not actually give any examples of the negative consequences of disregarding this rule – his argument here is not founded on science, but on his interpretation of the Qur'ān.

If we disregard these issues, and we wish to create equality between the two sexes in all rights and duties, then we will have disregarded the general ruling *men are qawwāmūn over women* [Q. 4:34], but, more than that, we will have nullified the justice established by the word of the Sublime *women have rights like their obligations* [Q. 2:228].

So that the truth may prevail, it is necessary for all men and women to fulfil their duties depending on ability, strength, instincts, and bodily makeup. The woman aids the man in what he is not able to accomplish, and the man takes over assisting the woman, in that for which she has not the strength. Since the law of administration is that it must be stripped from emotional individuals, who are under the administration of the individuals who have a superior ability to think, the guidance of the family is entrusted to men, and women fulfil the role of helper in the administration of the family matters.[12]

[9] Zibaei Nejad, Personal Email Communication, 26 June, 2014.

[10] Ibid. [11] Ibid.

[12] Makarim Shirazi, *al-Amthal fī tafsīr kitāb Allah al-munzal*, v. 3, p. 99 (at Q. 2:228).

The basic message is that the sexes are complementary, rather than equal: neither men nor women are capable of doing everything, but in partnership they can fulfil all roles in life. Makarim Shirazi contextualises Q. 2:228 by telling the story of women in human history and Islamic history. The idea behind these historical examples is that the difference between men and women is innate and cannot be changed. His conception of the gender hierarchy in human history is that women have always and everywhere been in a subservient place to men, even in areas of the world where they supposedly have rights equal to men's. The idea that the roles of the sexes have been roughly fixed and unequal everywhere throughout time bears up his assertion that women's nature differs from men's. The urge towards equality is fairly newfangled, and, according to Makarim and others who hold his opinion, has little or no basis in women's and men's natures. In his depiction, Islam came as a positive force for women, enhancing and solidifying women's rights, or granting them new rights where there were none before.

Within the genre of *tafsīr*, the roots of the discourse put forward by Grand Ayatollah Makarim and others go back to the work of Muḥammad ʿAbduh, who in turn was part of a trend in his own time: the idea that Islam came as a positive force for women was prominent in the late 19th century.[13] ʿAbduh himself was said to have influenced the prominent feminist Qasim Amin. The emergence of the discourse of feminism in the *Tafsīr al-Manār* is probably due to its primarily oral transmission: since it was originally a record of popular preaching, he brought in ideas and methods that had not been used previously in the genre.

In his interpretation of both Q. 2:228 and Q. 4:34, ʿAbduh describes a system in which men and women are in complementary roles, but in which they work to help the other; they are supposed to take care of one another in their complementary spheres. In the following passage, he summarises his view of the ideal relationship between the spouses. It contains many elements familiar from the medieval discourse, yet could also be considered the blueprint for modern commentators such as Grand Ayatollah Makarim, Grand Ayatollah Gerami, and Mr Zibaei Nejad.[14]

[13] Booth, 'Before Qasim Amin'.

[14] Compare the following passage by Grand Ayatollah Makarim Shirazi with the passage by ʿAbduh: 'Is it possible with this great difference to call for sexual equality in all jobs and the two sexes sharing equally in all matters? Is not justice to convey to each being his essential requirements according to his talents and special abilities? Is it not against justice to burden the woman with work which does not accord with her bodily, spiritual makeup? From this we see that Islam, with its emphasis on justice, makes men superior

This passage ends with a critique of his fellow Muslims who have misinterpreted the Qurʾān in order to grant wholesale power to men:

Marital life is social life, and it is necessary for every society to have a head, because the members of the society will have different opinions and desires in some matters, and their interests will not be served except when there is a head whose opinion is reverted to in case of difference. That way, each will not work against the other … and the man is more deserving of the headship because he knows best about the interests and is more capable of performing the duty with his strength and his money. Therefore, he has been required by the law to protect the woman and to maintain her, and she is required to obey him in what is right, and if she disobeys him (*nashazat ʿan ṭāʿatihi*) then he may discipline her with the admonition, leaving, and non-injurious hitting that is required as a disciplinary measure. That is permitted to the head of the house because it is in the best interests of living together and good fellowship (*maṣlaḥat al-ʿashīra wa-ḥusn al-ʿishra*), just as the like is permitted to the commander of the army and the head of the state, the Caliph or the ruler, in order to protect the interests of the society. As for the assault on women due to authoritarianism or revenge, or as a cure for anger, it is a type of oppression, which is not permitted at all.[15]

As in medieval commentaries, ʿAbduh draws a parallel between the husband and the head of state; to describe the marital relationship, he invokes the same term used in both medieval commentaries and marriage contracts, *ḥusn al-ʿishra*; and he says that the husband is granted priority because of his innate characteristics. However, unlike medieval commentaries, he uses modern terminology, such as calling the family a 'society', and he critiques his fellow Muslims for not enacting the spirit of caring mentioned in the verses. He therefore upholds the rulings: men must still pay maintenance and women must still obey them; but the justifications for these rulings have changed. The family structure is now justified by saying that the spouses are complementary. Notably, ʿAbduh does not say

in certain matters, for instances directing the family, and gives woman her place as a helper in it. The family and society each need a director, and the matter of administration, in its final stages, necessarily ends with one person, so as not to descend into confusion and chaos. So is it better to delegate this responsibility to the woman or to the man? All of the accounts which are not fanatic say: the man's makeup requires that the responsibility of administering the family be in his hands, and the woman is his helper. The perseverance of the determined, and the obstinacy of the fanatics, is a rejection of reality. For indeed the real situation of life in our world today and even in countries which permit women complete freedom and equality – according to their claims – indicates that the issue in the field of work is as we have mentioned, even if the claims are contrary to that' (Makarim Shīrāzī, *al-Amthal*, v. 3, p. 102).

15 Muḥammad ʿAbduh, *Tafsīr al-manār*, v. 2, p. 319 (at Q. 2:228).

that women are innately inferior to men. He denies explicitly the notion that men's minds are superior:

> The two of them are similar in essence (*dhāt*), feelings, desires, and mind (*ʿaql*), i.e., each of them is a complete human, who has a mind with which to think of his best interests, a heart that loves that which agrees with him and delights him, and which hates that which does not agree with him and to which he has an aversion. It is unjust that one of the two sexes should dominate the other.[16]

ʿAbduh thus recognises the shared human qualities of each of the sexes in a way that marks a change from the medieval commentaries, which focused on difference. Part of this interpretation becomes the norm. Most subsequent commentators say that women and men are equal in essence. However, equality in mind is another matter: most modern conservatives assert that women's emotions overpower their rational minds.

ʿAbduh says that although a woman's spiritual duties are fixed, her duties with regards to housework, raising the children, and so forth 'differ according to time and place'.[17] Therefore, in principle, rulings can change when new situations arise; he draws a parallel with modern warfare techniques, which have changed the nature of *jihād*. In the end he comes down on the side of 'some of the Ḥanbalīs' who assert that a woman should do housework, but adds that the spouses should help one another and should not apply rules so strictly as to be inhumane.[18] In his justification, he cites traditional sources such as Ibn Taymiyya, and he rails against those in his society who mistreat women in the name of Islam. This is one example of how ʿAbduh draws on tradition in order to implement reform: while not reversing past laws or a widespread cultural practice of women doing housework, he nevertheless tries to encourage a flexible approach to the law. His focus on morality and ethics is typical of *tafsīr*.

The colonial encounter looms large in ʿAbduh's interpretation of Q. 2:228, and his discourse of equality is heavily peppered with references to Europeans' dismissive attitude towards Islam. Much of ʿAbduh's interpretation of Q. 2:228 is a detailed explanation of the way in which Islam gave women rights that they had never had in the West or in any other culture or religion. For him, the colonial encounter is close at hand, immediate. At one point, ʿAbduh recounts a conversation that he ostensibly had with a European visitor to a mosque, who was astonished to see a woman there:

[16] Ibid., v. 2, p. 315. [17] Ibid., v. 2, p. 316. [18] Ibid., v. 2, pp. 316–18.

These Europeans (*Ifranj*) – whose cities fall short of our *sharīʿa* in the elevation of women's affairs – hold themselves above us. Rather, they accuse us of savagery in dealing with women, and those who are ignorant of Islam claim that what we are doing is the vestige of our religion. The Imam [ʿAbduh] in his lesson mentions one of the European tourists who visited al-Azhār, and while the two of them were walking in the mosque, the European saw a girl walking in it. He was astonished, and said 'What is this!? A woman enters the mosque!!!' The Imam said to him, 'What is so strange about that?' He replied, 'We believe that Islam has decreed that women do not have souls, and they do not have any worship'. The Imam explained his mistake and interpreted some of the verses concerning women. He said [to his students]: 'So look at how we have become proof of our religion, and at the ignorance of these people concerning Islam, to the extent of the likes of this man, who was the president of a large university, so how much less [knowledge] among their common people?'[19]

Here, ʿAbduh's main concern is to exonerate Islam from the false charges levelled against it by ignorant Europeans. In the struggle against cultural imperialism, a woman's presence highlights the egalitarian elements of Islamic practice while showing up the European for his ignorance of Islam. In light of this defence of Islam against the West, ʿAbduh's chastisement of his fellow religionists for their lack of respect towards women is all the more striking, and shows the extent to which this *tafsīr* is written to address immediate, pressing social concerns. It is a work for the people of his day, and more particularly the people of his occupied nation. He uses the example of the European in the mosque to show his fellow Muslims that they are living examples of the faith, and that their behaviour can change incorrect attitudes and beliefs. The speech about the rights of women is almost a call to social action.

Although they share similar themes and approaches, ʿAbduh and Grand Ayatollah Makarim differ in attitude. This is clear in their attitudes towards 'the West'. ʿAbduh's work is a defence of Islam; as I will show, Makarim's is an attack on the West. ʿAbduh asserts that Islam calls for the good treatment of women; for Makarim, the important point is to discredit the West, Western laws, and the very idea of egalitarianism. Each of these authors is arguing against a perceived threat to his religion and his way of life. But, although the threat is always in the guise of the West, its nature has shifted. In ʿAbduh's day, the Western threat was the force of colonialism: the West had entered into the very walls and mosques of Cairo. Today, the threat is one of legal norms and cultural

[19] Ibid., v. 2, p. 316. The punctuation (including the triple exclamation marks) is in the original.

imperialism. Ayatollah Makarim's attack on the West is his way of defending his cultural values against the ever-encroaching influence of outside ideas. There is a particular focus on the law in his description of the different stages of women's history:

The second stage: the stage of history, and during this stage women in many societies were not independent persons with regard to all of the economic, political, and societal rights, and in some sectors of societies this has lasted until the most recent centuries.

This type of thought concerning women's affairs is seen even in the famously progressive French civil law. By way of example, we will indicate some of its articles connected with matters of property in marriage.

It is deduced from the two articles 215 and 217 that the married woman is not able, without the permission of her husband and his signature, to undertake any legal matter, and she needs in every instance to have the permission of the husband. This then does not dissuade the man from deriving an advantage from his power, and from refusing permission without justification.[20]

Grand Ayatollah Makarim seeks to undermine the notion of equality between the sexes by asserting that there is no true equality in the West. His argument is not that women and men have equality and that this equality is wrong, but that the idea of equality is a myth. The references to history, then, provide a context for his interpretation of the verse: not only is Makarim's conception of the proper roles of the sexes true religiously, but it has held true throughout human history, in all times and places, even when and where there is supposed equality. His focus on the law is no accident; by discrediting Western laws, he discredits the very idea of universal human rights, the same for men and women everywhere. Yet his critique is not entirely accurate. While the French civil code did contain unequal laws, it is still not a straightforward denial of all of women's rights, as he would have it.[21] More to the point, however, is that the 1970s, when he wrote his book, was a period of transition in French law; although equality had not yet been reached, the French laws

[20] Makarim Shirazi, *al-Amthal*, v. 3, p. 100 (at Q. 2:228).

[21] He cites articles 215 and 217: Article 215 reads: 'The wife cannot plead in her own name, without the authority of her husband, even though she should be a public trader, or non-communicant, or separate in property'. Article 217 reads: 'A wife, although non-communicant or separate in property, cannot give, alienate, pledge, or acquire by free or chargeable title, without the concurrence of the husband to the act, or his consent in writing'. But these are not the full picture. For instance, Article 218: 'If the husband refuse to authorize his wife to plead in her own name, the judge may give her authority'; thus, the husband's control is not absolute. Other articles grant women certain economic rights: Article 226 says that women can make their own wills, without the permission of their husbands.

were aiming towards a more egalitarian system, and the laws cited by Ayatollah Makarim were among those that were reformed then.[22] Article 217 in the Napoleonic code had to do with the husband representing the wife in court, but in the revised code of 1965 it says that a spouse of either sex can represent an incompetent spouse of either sex. Furthermore, the law 'permits either spouse to give the other a power of general administration and disposition'. Most importantly in the reformed laws, the wife's earned income is considered reserved – it is hers alone. This directly contradicts Ayatollah Makarim's assertions of the wife's complete economic dependence on her husband.

It may be that Ayatollah Makarim was unaware of these contradictions, or that they do not matter to him. For him, the key point is to dismiss the Western system. He argues against holding up the West as a model, because, according to him, the model is flawed: even if the West does grant the sexes equal rights, there is no true equality. Thus, when I challenged his notion of unequal laws in my interview with him, he was dismissive:

KAREN BAUER: In the *Tafsīr namouneh* you have quoted the French Civil Code in order to say that the situation of women is not better than that of men. But nowadays, the situation of women in Europe has changed. Have you changed your ideas about the status of women in our days?

AYATOLLAH MAKARIM: We have heard that the situation has not changed. And according to what has been published recently, the majority of your women have been put in trouble (*muzāḥamat*) by their husbands, from hitting and other matters. And I believe that there is a number – that 90 per cent of women suffer from some kind of trouble (*muzāḥamat*), either beating or otherwise. That means that the situation has not changed, and it may have even gotten worse. If you have some contrary information, that is another matter.

KB: The law *has* changed.

AM: It may be that the law has changed, but the deeds have not changed. The practical situation does not agree with the law. We are speaking about the present situation over there, not about the laws. We are speaking about the actual reality.[23]

Although it would be difficult to claim that men and women have true equality in the West or anywhere else, in the interview, as in his written

[22] Alexandre Danièle, 'The Status of Women in France', *The American Journal of Comparative Law*, 20.4 (Autumn 1972): p. 649.

[23] Makarim Shirazi, Personal Interview, Qom, Iran, 25 June 2011.

interpretation, Makarim's statistics are greatly exaggerated. It is unclear where he heard that 90 per cent of women in the West are abused, or why he thinks that the situation of women in the West has not changed since the 1960s. His desire to demean the 'actual' status of women in the West, and to dismiss entirely their legal equality with men, reflects a certain nervousness about equality as an ideal. If equality were plausible, it would be a threat to the system that he wishes to promote; therefore, his aim is to prove that it is neither plausible nor possible. Such interpretations send a message to women: they should be happy to be living in the hierarchical system, which promotes their well-being, rather than wishing to live in a system of supposed equality that actually subjects them to abuse and exploitation.

For conservative interpreters, the medieval textual tradition is seen as representing true religious and cultural norms. Cultural practice is equated with religion. Whereas the West is decadent and individualistic, the East is family orientated, geared towards individual sacrifice, and therefore innately Islamic. Dr ʿAlasvand explains the reason for the patriarchal organization of the household. She says:

> The intention of these points is to preserve the unity of the family. But in the West, I believe that the place of the family is not connected with these issues. The wife is a person, the husband is a person, and they are both thinking, and mature. The basis of Western life is individuality. But in Islam it is communal.[24]

Dr ʿAlasvand equates the cultural practices of Iran with the true practice of Islam. In other words, the Western cultural idea of individualism is against the cultural but also religious ideal of sacrifice for the family. She equates her conservative cultural practices with the 'true' interpretation of Islam. In turn, the medieval textual tradition from which these interpretations are drawn represents an authentic cultural and religious expression of an Islam free from Western imperialism. For conservatives the Qur'ān's hierarchical precepts are based on nature and the dominant conservative culture is therefore also based on nature. In its plain-sense reading, therefore, the Qur'ān is a religious text, but it is also a cultural text: a depiction of past times, and a model for current times.

Nevertheless, as I noted earlier, Western scientific studies are freely (if selectively) cited by conservatives. After my interview with Mr Zibaei Nejad, he showed me the library on women's issues at the Women's Study Resource Centre, which includes books in English, Persian, and Arabic.

[24] Fariba ʿAlasvand, Personal Interview.

Some of these were works that I have on my own shelves, such as Saba Mahmood's *Politics of Piety* and Ziba Mir-Hosseini's *Islam and Gender*. In the interview, however, he quoted from popular, not academic, books. Just as the *'ulamā'* use Western conservative Christian and Jewish arguments against the Darwinian theory of evolution and natural selection, Western conservative Christian and Jewish books are also drawn on to support the notion of a marital hierarchy. Marwa Elshakry posits that the anti-evolution works popular since the 1970s in Egypt are a part of a worldwide creationist movement.[25] I would posit that the worldwide creationist movement may in turn be one symptom of a worldwide fundamentalism, with several basic tenets, including a 'traditional' family structure. Thus, the works of Dr Laura Schlessinger have been translated into Persian, and are freely available to Mr Zibaei Nejad. Here again, the 'West' is selectively called upon to prove that the Islamic/Eastern system is better:

> There is a really good book by an American author, Dr Laura Schessinger, called *The Power of Women.* She emphasises the importance of sexual matters. Regarding the power of women, if they take control of this matter, then they have power in the relationship, they can take control in every respect. Some women called Dr Laura to say: Has it ever occurred to you that when a man asks for sex you may not feel like it? What do you do in this case? And the answer that Schlessinger gave is that you imagine that you're in the house and your baby is crying, and you want to feed him or her. Do you say that you don't want to feed the baby? You care about the baby when the baby wants the milk, and so you should care about what your husband wants in the same way.[26]

According to Dr Laura, women must use the power of their sexuality to control their husbands. This infantilizes the husband, who is compared to a helpless baby, unable to survive without sex, and unable to understand or discuss it if his wife does not feel like having sex. And it involves personal sacrifice for women: the wife is urged to imagine her husband as a hungry, helpless, child; but in so doing, her own agency is subsumed into his needs. This view reinforces the idea that men are unable to control their sexual urges, while women's 'control' lies in their passivity. Reasoned communication is not the model here. Instead, each person is playing a set, biologically determined, role.

All of these arguments serve to justify the familiar interpretation of women's and men's duties and rights, culminating in the husband's right

[25] Marwa Elshakry, *Reading Darwin in Arabic*, 1860–1950. Chicago and London: University of Chicago Press, 2014. p. 310.
[26] Zibaei Nejad, Personal Interview, 28 May 2011, Qom, Iran.

to beat his recalcitrant wife, although the methods and justifications used are not traditional in the genre of *tafsīr*. What is modern here is not the notion that women have rights – men's and women's specific rights and duties are described in detail in pre-modern works of *tafsīr*. What is modern is the desire to elaborate on the subject of 'women's rights', 'human rights', the equal value of men and women, and to provide scientific and psychological proofs for these facts. The difference between the pre-modern interpretations and these ones is that in the pre-modern period inequality was perfectly acceptable. In the contemporary period, equality must be reckoned with as an ideal. Pre-modern interpretations were unapologetic about men's superior duties and rights, and they were unapologetic in their assertion that such legal superiority is based on innate superiority. Modern interpretations, whether conservative or reformist, use the language of equality; but ultimately conservative interpretations argue for a traditional hierarchical setup for the family, with the husband's duty of support corresponding to his right to his wife's sexual obedience and the right to punish her when she disobeys.

Most conservatives allow a light beating, one that does not leave marks, whereas reformists, as I will show, usually say that this part of the verse was set down in a particular time and place and is no longer applicable now. Conservatives differ in their presentation of the hitting and their justifications for it. In his written interpretation, Grand Ayatollah Makarim Shirazi outlines three points to mitigate the hitting. First, he says that corporal punishment is a common response worldwide when someone neglects their duties.[27] Second, he says that the hitting that is permitted here is light, without 'breaking, wounding, or even leaving a bruise',[28] and third, that some women these days like it:

> Psychiatrists today see that some women suffer from a psychological condition called 'masochism', which necessitates for the comfort of the woman that she be hit, and that this state has grown so strong in the woman to the extent that she feels deliciousness, contentment, and pleasure when she is lightly beaten. Despite this, it is possible that this measure can have a similar [psychological] effect on the likes of these individuals, as it does on those for whom light physical chastisement is like a spiritual pain.[29]

Here Ayatollah Makarim brings in psychology to justify the beating, by saying that some masochistic women may feel pleasure at being hit lightly. Thus, like other modern conservatives, he draws on science, or

[27] Makarim Shirazi, *al-Amthāl*, v. 3, p. 195 (at Q. 4:34).
[28] Ibid., v. 3, p. 196 (at. Q. 4:34). [29] Ibid.

pseudo-science and psychology to prove his point. In the interview, he did not deny the assertion that some women like to be hit, but he added an interpretation that '*ḍaraba*' could mean 'to depart', rather than 'to hit'.[30] In this interpretation, the husband does not beat his recalcitrant wife at all; he merely walks away.

Grand Ayatollah Gerami took a practical approach. He referred to laws that condone corporal punishment for moral crimes, and said that if someone had to hit a woman, it should be her husband rather than an agent of the state:

AYATOLLAH GERAMI: If a woman does not respect the rights of her husband, or if she betrays him, or if she is a sinner (*fāsiq*), or if the woman disobeys God, Blessed and Almighty, it is necessary for her to be punished. Who should punish her? Is the best person to punish the woman the husband himself, or should she be given to a stranger to be punished by him?

KB: They should go to court!

YOUSEFI: But if the court says that he should beat her, then what?

KB: Our courts do not say that – she can be jailed but not hit.

AG: But they do it! They do use physical punishment in British jails, so much so that even we know about it here.

KB: But it is against the law if it is done.

AG: But there is not a constitution in England, the majority of the law is common law.

KB: Yes, yes, but ... [everyone laughs, including me, as he takes a phone call].[31]

The evident misunderstanding between myself and Grand Ayatollah Gerami, which left me sputtering in the end, hinges on the differences between our assumptions. For everyone else in the room, including the reformists, it was evident that if corporal punishment was necessary, then a woman's husband was best suited to do it. In fact there was a legal debate in the medieval sources about the correct person to undertake wifely discipline.[32] I started from the assumption that corporal punishment is not necessary and that it is not practiced. In a later email communication with Grand Ayatollah Gerami I explained this, and told him that

30 Naser Makarim Shirazi, Personal Interview, Qom, Iran, 25 June 2011.

31 Muhammad Ali Gerami, Personal Interview, Qom, Iran, 14 June 2011.

32 Chaudhry refers to this debate, with the Mālikīs in particular referring matters to the judge and other schools preferring the husband (she quotes the Shāfiʿī al-Nawawī) (*Domestic Violence and the Islamic Tradition*, p. 123).

I saw the point he was making. He responded with a final clarification: 'if the wife has done something illegal, first she should be admonished, and then if she does not heed her husband's word then the punishment must take place, that is, when the unlawful and illegal deed requires some retribution. Needless to say, the right and best person to undertake such punishment is her husband'.[33] This response underlines the hitting as a final step in the case of a wife's persistent misbehaviour.

I interviewed Muhammad Ghazizadeh, Ḥujjat al-Islām wa'l-Mu'minīn, a teacher of law at the *hawza*, in his home office, around a large table. Many people attended this interview: not only my research assistant Fatemeh, but also Dr Hamid Shivapour, from the Qur'ānic Studies department of Mofid University, and Dr Shivapour's fiancée. The presence of a couple led to some giggling in the more pointed parts of our interview. Mr Ghazizadeh takes a typically medieval explanation of the verse, but the medieval phrases are given a modern gloss. He first explains the nature of the hitting: it must be *ghayr mubarriḥ*, an expression which was very common in medieval texts. As I showed in Chapter 5, in medieval times, *ghayr mubarriḥ* meant 'without causing severe injury', and was explained in a variety of ways by the interpreters: as meaning without breaking bones, without leaving bruises, and so forth. Mr Ghazizadeh explains the term as 'without leaving a mark', which was one medieval interpretation of the hitting. He justified the hitting by explaining that it should happen in a way that kept the spousal disagreement as a private matter, within the family. In this exchange, Dr Shivapour joined in to explain a term:

KB: My next question is about the hitting. First, does *wa'ḍribūhunna* mean 'to hit' and second, is this the best way for a husband to convince his wife that she really wants to be with him sexually?

MUHAMMAD GHAZIZADEH: Yes, it does mean to hit, and the works of *tafsīr* specify that this should be *ghayr mubarriḥ*, which means that the hitting should not leave a mark.

DR HAMID SHIVAPOUR: Meaning *ghayr mu'aththir* (without leaving a trace).

KB: So is this really a good way to convince his wife to sleep with him? Is she going to feel like doing it after this?

MG: The law of the family is very important in Islam, and it is very important that private matters not be spoken about publicly. These

[33] Muhammad Ali Gerami, Personal Email Correspondence, 8 July 2014.

things occur in the bedroom. The first is a discussion, and the second is to sleep in a way that the wife becomes upset, so he turns his back on her, which is something that even the children are not aware of. If this doesn't work, then you may hit, but something very light. This is all because of the importance of family and family issues, and keeping these issues within the family. If this doesn't work then you can go outside of the house and speak, for instance, to the mother and the father.[34]

Mr Ghazizadeh sidestepped my question. Rather than addressing whether it would be an effective tactic, he gave a justification for the husband's actions: he is allowed to hit if it is effective, in order to keep the disagreement within the family and not spread news of it about. Even the children must not know that such a disagreement occurs, he says. This sociological argument serves to justify his preservation of the medieval core interpretation.

As to my question of whether this would be an effective tactic, Dr ʿAlasvand explained that it might work for those women who did not listen to the 'admonition', which in her view is the husband saying kind and gentle words to his wife:

KB: Because you have said before that the sexual relationship for the woman is something special, and something emotional, is this hitting the best way to get to her heart? Is this the best way to – if she is emotional and sensitive in this regard, is this going to correct her? If my husband hits me, even just like this, it would be a shock to me. It would not make me feel . . .

DR FARIBA ʿALASVAND: This issue is solved in the Qur'an at the time of the admonition. The admonition is kind words, emotional words, the majority of women will return to the correct path after the admonition, which means kind, gentle words. This is the first stage. The majority of women love their husbands and would like to return to this correct path after the admonition or after the abandonment. But with this issue, there is a rational necessity (*lā-buḍdiyya ʿaqliyya*). If the woman does not like to live together, or to share in sexual matters, then the man and the woman do not both taste the deliciousness of the sexual relationship it can cause difficulties. The difference between women and men in this regard leads to many problems.[35]

[34] Mohammad Ghazizadeh, Personal Interview, Qom, Iran, 5 June 2011.
[35] Fariba ʿAlasvand, Personal Interview 8 June, 2011.

When I questioned Dr ʿAlasvand about whether a wife would have the right to beat her recalcitrant husband, she said that, because of the physical differences between the spouses, she would not have that right. Instead, the wife should go to court to force her husband to comply.[36] Her answer is typical of her approach, as in her justification of rulings on women's testimony, in that she uses physiological arguments to justify the continuation of medieval laws. But how could she, as a woman, make this argument? In the next section, I explore the possible reasons behind the conservatism of the *ʿālimas* I interviewed.

WOMEN'S INTERPRETATIONS OF THE MARITAL HIERARCHY

In the English speaking world, women are at the vanguard of feminist interpretations of the Qur'ān.[37] Interpreters such as Amina Wadud are prominent public figures whose work is well known in academic circles. But in the Middle East and Iran, reformists as a whole are in the minority; although many women are mosque leaders for other women, it is comparatively rare to find female reformists who advocate a reinterpretation of the gender hierarchy in the Qur'ān. Despite their own activities as religious leaders, most of the women I interviewed supported the male-dominated gender hierarchy and traditional household roles; even self-described reformists took a positive view of the marital hierarchy.[38] This section discusses two prominent learned women (*ʿālimas*), Dr Fariba ʿAlasvand and Hudā al-Ḥabash, whose views are representative of a much larger trend of conservatism among female religious leaders.

[36] Ibid.

[37] See, for instance, Aysha Hidayatullah, *Feminist Edges of the Qur'an*, which focuses on women writing in English, and primarily based in the United States: Riffat Hassan, Azizah al-Hibri, Amina Wadud, Asma Barlas, and Sa'diyya Shaikh (based in South Africa). Although Hidayatullah notes that these women's feminist insights sometimes grow out of their experiences in Muslim-majority countries, their main work is undertaken in the West and written in English (Hidayatullah, *Feminist Edges*, p. 7).

[38] Conservative interpretations have a long precedent among female interpreters. The Egyptian author Bint al-Shāṭi' speaks of women's liberation, and women's emancipation; but that type of emancipation does not question men's right to *qiwāma*. As Roxanne Marcotte points out, she must be viewed in her time and place; but that does not make her a feminist interpreter. Marcotte, 'Bint al-Shāṭiʿ on Women's Emancipation', in *Coming to Terms With the Qur'ān: A Volume in Honor of Professor Issa Boulllata*, ed. Khaleel Mohammed and Andrew Rippin, pp. 179–208.

Both Saba Mahmood and Hilary Kalmbach have noted the trend towards conservatism among female mosque preachers. Kalmbach, whose views are discussed further in what follows, sees women's conservatism in terms of authoritarian power dynamics. For her, if women questioned conservative norms, their standing as mosque leaders would be compromised.[39] Mahmood approaches the question from the perspective of gender theory, which she finds unable to explain women's agency when they subject themselves to gendered practices such as veiling and modesty.[40] For Mahmood, piety itself becomes agency: pious women embody patriarchal norms, rather than subverting them. One of the ways in which these women lay claim to the tradition is through the citation and appropriation of *ḥadīth*s. As she says, this retelling and reworking of the tradition 'do not represent a dilution of a pristine doctrine'; instead, such reworkings are 'precisely the means through which the discursive logic of a scholarly tradition comes to be lived by its ordinary adherents'.[41]

Both of these researchers take an experiential approach to the question of women's agency and interpretations, an approach grounded in women's lived realities. I would suggest that it is equally important to access their wider context as *ʿālimas* – female members of the *ʿulamāʾ* relating to a textual tradition. Mahmood stresses that through retelling tradition, female mosque leaders make that tradition their own, exercising authority over it. But this method is common among male *ʿulamāʾ* as well. Conservative *ʿālima*s are, like conservative *ʿālim*s, seeking to recast a textual tradition in modern language that makes sense to their audience. Although this is in a sense claiming ownership, I have suggested that the more important function of such retelling is to reproduce core knowledge. By reproducing this core knowledge, the *ʿulamāʾ*, male or female, assert that they are masters of the tradition, and that through their reproduction of it, they have become a part of that tradition. The reproduction of core elements of the textual tradition, therefore, is a key element in women's claim to be *ʿālima*s, and in turn the textual tradition also influences the

39 Hilary Kalmbach, 'Social and Religious Change in Damascus: One Case of Female Islamic Religious Authority' *British Journal of Middle East Studies* 35:1 (2008): pp. 37–57.

40 Saba Mahmood, *Politics of Piety: The Islamic Revival and the Feminist Subject* (Princeton, NJ: Princeton University Press, 2005), chapter 5: Agency, Gender, and Embodiment, esp. pp. 167 ff.

41 Ibid., p. 99. See also pp. 83–91, 'textual invocations'.

conservative culture to which they adhere. The importance of the textual tradition was clear in my interviews with Hudā al-Ḥabash.

When I visited Damascus in 2004 and again in 2005, Hudā al-Ḥabash was teaching lessons for women at the al-Zahra mosque, where her brother, Muḥammad al-Ḥabash, was the Imām. She was immensely popular among women who were looking for a moderately reformist outlook: Hudā acknowledges that it is appropriate to reinterpret the Qurʾān according to time and place, but does not undertake a wholesale reinterpretation of the textual tradition. In most mosques, the designated women's area is in the basement, but al-Zahra mosque had been constructed with a women's area at ground level and above. It was full of sunlight. From the balcony, women could listen to the main preaching in the larger men's area; in their own space, women would gather to hear Hudā's lessons. She held awards ceremonies for the most talented girls and women who attended her lessons, including those who had memorised all or part of the Qurʾān.

In 2004, I had a number of lessons with al-Ḥabash in her home, where we discussed her interpretations of women's role. She admitted the need for reinterpretation according to time and place.[42] For instance, she said, women can now travel without a male guardian. The laws preventing women from traveling alone had been implemented at a time when it was dangerous for women to travel, in the desert, without an escort. Nowadays, there is security for women who travel. For Hudā,[43] this reinterpretation of traditional law had practical implications in her daily life. She sometimes travelled alone to the Gulf to preach to women there, while her husband stayed home with their two older children, Muḥammad and Enas. Her daughter Enas also lived according to this reinterpretation: she went to university far from home, at the American University of Dubai, which she thought would give her better opportunities than a Syrian university.

Hudā supports reinterpretation, but within limits. So, although certain rulings such as that on women's travel can be reinterpreted, she supports a traditional view of men's and women's roles in the household. Over the course of our interviews, I wrote notes and she checked them; the result

42 In her words: 'Firstly, it is necessary that we understand that culture differs from age to age and for that reason the exegesis (*tafsīr*) of a verse will also differ from age to age. And this is as the society develops, and likewise the understandings of the Qurʾānic text develop, but the text itself naturally does not' (Hudā al-Ḥabash, interview notes, Damascus, Syria, 2004)

43 Note that I use her first name here so that she is not confused with her brother, discussed here and previously.

was a document that summarised her teachings on this issue. She listed the duties of wives and husbands; her views are clearly influenced by dominant conservative and pre-modern interpretations:

The duties of the wife:

1. She must follow the husband where he goes to live, and she must live well with him.
2. She should have children and raise them.
3. She must fulfil the specific marital duties, that she make herself beautiful for her husband and that she not refuse sex with him, unless she is sick or menstruating, and thereby the love will grow between them. She must strive for his happiness and take an interest in his affairs. ...
4. She must obey him, specifically in his rights over her, such as sex. Two *ḥadīth*s in particular show this: 'the best of women is one who pleases her husband when he sees her, obeys him when he commands her, and preserves herself and his wealth in his absence' and 'if a wife refuses her husband and he goes to bed angry with her, the angels will curse her until the morning'.
5. She has the duty of organizing the house, though not as a servant.
6. She has the duty of preserving the house, and ensuring the stability and happiness of her husband and children, and that may limit her leaving the house in some ways, but it does not prevent her from leaving the house in order to seek knowledge or for family ties, or work if she needs to or for some other necessity.
7. She must keep the *ʿidda* in times of separation (divorce or death).

These are the duties of the wife.

The duties of the husband:

1. The security of the house and the household needs.
2. Paying the dowry.
3. Spending on maintenance which includes clothing, food, and medicine, with legally earned money.
4. Protection of the family (defence), living together well, putting up with her, and being patient with her.
5. That he teach her the religion or enable her to go to a place of learning.
6. Consulting with his wife because they share together in building their household.

7. Fairness between them in cases of having more than one wife.

> It is important that the degree is in responsibility and that is the duty to maintain her. The meaning is not that he is better.[44]

In Hudā's interpretation, traditional elements are intertwined with today's language and concepts. Although the husband has control over the household, and the wife must obey him in those areas where he has rights over her, he should engage in consultation with her. There are key points on which she follows medieval law: she cannot move home without his permission; he may have more than one wife. There are other points on which she is quite modern: the husband cannot prevent his wife from leaving the house in order to attain learning, particularly religious learning. On the whole, however, Hudā does not question the gender hierarchy, or the conservative defences and explanations for that hierarchy. According to her, as for the conservatives described previously, the household hierarchy is based firmly in human nature. Equality, she says, is a myth: even individual humans differ in their strengths and abilities, and so there is no true equality between any human. The sexes have broad differences in terms of their physical strength, and in their natures. While women's minds equal men's minds, their natures differ.[45] She was not open to reinterpreting the fundamental nature of the marital hierarchy, as were the neo-traditionalists and reformists described later this chapter. When I asked her for written references, she directed me to the *tafsīr* of the conservative Egyptian cleric Muḥammad al-Ghazālī (d. 1996).

By implicitly or explicitly citing well-known interpretations, female religious leaders demonstrate their prowess as scholars; but by adopting aspects of that tradition without question, they reproduce norms that are structurally biased against women. Such was the case in my interview of Dr Fariba ʿAlasvand. Her description of the man's *qiwāma* bears striking resemblance to that of Hudā al-Ḥabash, as well as to common medieval interpretations: 'The ruling that is necessary in exchange for the husband's

[44] Hudā al-Ḥabash, interview notes, Damascus, Syria, 2004.

[45] Ibid. Also compare with the list provided by Kalmbach, based on her own interviews of al-Ḥabash: 'In marriage a woman must be attractive and sexually available to her husband, live in the house that he provides, and supervise the household; she must give birth to, breast feed and educate the children, and provide healthy food for her family, but she can hire a servant to clean the house if housework would take her away from the children' (Kalmbach, 'Social and Religious Change in Damascus', p. 49). The list of a wife's duties is based on medieval laws, although certain formulations (such as cooking 'healthy' food) are distinctly modern.

qiwāma is the sexual obedience (*tamkīn*) of the wife. *Tamkīn* has a specific meaning, the intimate relations between husband and wife. The man is *qawwām* over the woman in this regard, and over her leaving the house'.[46] Both Hudā al-Ḥabash and Dr ʿAlasvand assert that the wife owes the husband sexual obedience. al-Ḥabash is slightly more circumspect about the husband's control over his wife's leaving the house: she says that he should not prevent her from going to religious lessons, but that her household duties may prevent her from leaving the house. Despite such minor differences, both interpreters agree with one another on the whole, and neither questions the gender hierarchy or its bases. To do so would risk undermining their position as *ʿālima*s. Kalmbach argues that the primary reason for Hudā's conservatism, and that of other women who preach in mosques, is the fragile nature of women's authority, which requires them to uphold conventional interpretations.[47] The fragile nature of authority can explain why women tend towards conservatism; the textual tradition helps explain the precise nature of that conservatism, and the particular interpretations that these women uphold. Culture, in turn, dictates the ways in which tradition is accepted, reinterpreted, or rejected.

The pattern of either overt or implicit reference to the textual tradition was repeated in all of my interviews with female religious authorities. For some women, it was not even necessary to take an independent interpretation. Instead, it was enough to show that they were familiar with, and could reproduce, the well-known, widespread, and trusted interpretations from the genre of *tafsīr*. I almost did not obtain an interview with Dr Zahiri of the Jamiʿat Zahra, the women's *hawza*, because she simply said that I should read existing works of *tafsīr* on the subject. When I convinced her to engage in dialogue with me, she referred first and foremost to the interpretations of ʿAllāmeh Ṭabāṭabāʾī and Ayatollah Jawadi-Amoli. Her interpretation consisted of a summary of their views. She did not offer her own interpretation, and insisted that I only approach her after refreshing my memory as to the writings of those authors and ask her questions that arose after reading their texts.[48]

Although they support a gender hierarchy, many of the women I interviewed spontaneously told me of the support that their husbands

46 Fariba ʿAlasvand, Personal Interview.

47 'If she were to challenge this system, she would likely lose her teaching position; her performative adherence to "conventional" religious and social norms may actually increase her very unconventional religious authority' (Kalmbach, 'Social and Religious Change in Damascus', p. 39).

48 Interview with Masoumeh Zahiri, Jamaʿat-i Zahra, Qom, Iran, 31 May 2011.

showed for their religious activities. Dr ʿAlasvand emphasised her husband's encouragement of her work:

> My husband affirms the importance and necessity of my studies, my activities, and my knowledge, and he shares with me in all work, even though from one perspective he is not obligated to do any house work and he does not require anything from me, but rather allows me the freedom to choose what I wish to do. Of course I am interested in household matters, the children, and the husband's rights according to Islamic principles, but I am mentally free, and because of the strength of his knowledge, my husband is always helping me.'[49]

Dr ʿAlasvand's husband too is a scholar. Their life together, as she portrays it, is one in which he actively engages with her scholarly work and does not burden her with excessive duties around the house. She is 'mentally free', which she connects directly with her husband's support of her scholarly ambitions. Hudā's husband Samīr is not a scholar, but in a moving interview he told me how he was first attracted to her because he knew of her public piety.[50] It may be the case that their husbands were drawn to women who were already independent and scholarly, leading lives that the husbands considered 'exemplary'.[51]

Kalmbach argues that the nature of the interpretations that women reproduce is essentially conservative because of the 'norms that govern religious society', which are 'inherently structured against the participation of women as equals to men'.[52] It is crucial to acknowledge the importance of the textual tradition in shaping this cultural conservatism. Culture mediates the interpretation of texts, but the texts have also influenced the dominant conservative religious norms. Thus, in Hudā's list of women's duties, she refers to *ḥadīth*s cited in medieval texts that strongly indict the notion of women existing independently of men: one defines the 'best women' solely in terms of her appeal to her husband, while the second asserts that a wife's ultimate salvation is connected to her obedience to her husband. At the same time, she lives a full life outside of her home, she is internationally recognised for her religious teaching and public piety, and her husband was drawn to her precisely because of this deep piety combined with an independence of spirit. Each would insist that her activities and their dynamic relationship are grounded in a base of tradition.

49 Fariba ʿAlasvand, Personal Email Correspondence, 10 June 2014.
50 Samīr al-Khālidī, Personal Interview, Damascus, Syria, 2005; this interview was recorded and appears in the film *Veiled Voices*, directed by Brigid Maher, 2009.
51 Ibid. This is the word that Samīr used to describe Hudā as a wife and a religious leader.
52 Kalmbach, 'Social and Religious Change in Damascus', p. 49.

Although there are reformist women scholars in the Middle East and Iran, none of the women I interviewed went as far as the male neo-traditionalists or reformists in this study.

THE MARITAL HIERARCHY ACCORDING TO THE NEO-TRADITIONAL APPROACH

Reformists take varied approaches to the question of the marital hierarchy. Some reinterpret the sense of the words themselves, to say, for instance, that the 'beating' means leaving; or that the beating is not in the hands of the husband, but rather in the hands of the court; some say that Q. 4:34 expresses a preference, but not an order; others that it is partially abrogated, or that it is completely abrogated. Many reformists and neo-traditionalists explain that the system stipulated by Q. 4:34 is basically fair: the husband has a responsibility towards his family in terms of payment of maintenance, and therefore he also has the final say in disputes. But if for some reason the hierarchical approach does not work for the couple, reformist interpreters granted that the couple had choice over the power structure in their marriage. If the husband and wife choose to do things differently, they may. The key point that differentiates neo-traditionalist and reformist *ʿulamāʾ* from conservatives is this flexibility of roles.

While reformist interpretations of the marital hierarchy allow for flexibility of roles, conservative interpretations, for which conservatives claim a natural basis, are ultimately inflexible. For conservative interpreters, the husband is the breadwinner, and the wife owes him sexual obedience, which puts him in a position to discipline her if she fails to obey. Those taking the conservative approach generally assert that the roles in the family are fixed: men are always the breadwinners; women must always be sexually obedient. If the husband does not fulfil his role as breadwinner, the wife may take him to court and obtain a divorce. If the wife does not fulfil her obligation to sexual obedience, the husband may discipline her. Although reformist interpretations differ from one another in details, they agree on the broad outline that there is room for negotiation and reinterpretation on all of these points: the breadwinning, the sexual obedience, and the discipline. That is because, for them, the differences between the sexes do not necessitate set and inflexible roles in the family: women can be breadwinners, and decisions about family life and sex can be made through discussion and consultation. Shīʿī reformists' overt willingness to accommodate reinterpretation is indicative of their acceptance of time, place, and reason (*'aql*) as sources of interpretation. They use these tools to reinterpret the plain sense, or binding nature, of the Qur'ān's verses.

I begin by describing the views of Grand Ayatollah Yusuf Saanei. In the following excerpt from our interview, Ayatollah Saanei makes several points in which he applies the neo-traditional approach to the marital hierarchy. As is typical among both conservative and reformist *'ulamā'*, he acknowledges the plain sense reading of the verse. But he mitigates the traditional interpretation of it in several ways. The crux of his argument is that Q. 4:34 is descriptive, not prescriptive: it describes a common style of ordering the household, rather than prescribing the only valid arrangement of the household:

The problem with this verse is that it has made man the commander of woman (*muṣallaṭan 'alā al-mar'a*). The meaning of *qawwām* is that they are their guardians, and they are their commanders. And this command is contrary to justice. How is it possible for men to be commanders over women?

The answer is that *qawwāmīn* means those who undertake the affairs. It is management (*tadbīr*). But management in the verse is connected solely with marriage, and not with other matters. It does not mean that women cannot have a place in parliament, or that they cannot make mutual decisions. It does not give [men] the right to leadership (*riyāsa*), mastery (*salṭana*), guardianship (*wilāya*), and other matters. The verse is, firstly, connected with marriage. This is the first point. The second point is that the verse is not an indication of a ruling that is incumbent and necessary for [obedience to] God (*laysa madlūl al-āya ḥukman al-wujūb wa'l-ilzām al-ilāhī*). We cannot infer from this verse that God has made man *qā'im* over his wife, as He made the Prophet *qā'im* over the people. Rather, the indication of the verse is that it is an indicative statement (*jumlatun khabariya*), telling about reality (*ikhbār lil-wāqi'iyya*). The visible reality, as it was in many societies today and in the past. In the small kingdom that is the house, it is necessary to have a director (*mudīr*) and a manager (*mudabbir*). And so people have given the role of manager and director to the husband. This is information about the real situation.[53]

Ayatollah Saanei connects justice with the ideals of equality between the sexes and individual autonomy. Here he displays the prominent reformist characteristic, described in previous chapters, of contextualising the verse in its time and place. Explaining that the verse is descriptive, rather than prescriptive, sets the stage for allowing a change, because circumstances have changed since the time of the Qur'ān. Because it is not a command for all times and places, it is possible to do things differently. Ayatollah

[53] Grand Ayatollah Saanei, Personal Interview, Qom, Iran, 13 June 2011.

Saanei said to me: 'If a man wants to make his wife the director of the house, it does not contradict the revelation, and it does not constitute disobedience to God. Because this verse is not a legal verse, but information about reality. The information has been renewed'.[54] He grants that women may manage the household, and that this does not constitute disobedience to God. Because it is an informative verse rather than a legal verse, the information it imparts is not static: it may be renewed, which is why, although the verse clearly says that men are *qawwāmūn* over women, it is not a binding law.

In the cited passage Ayatollah Saanei still puts the power to decide who manages in the hands of the husbands: a man may 'make his wife director of the house'; the implication is that if she wants to have a say but he does not want her to, then his word is final. Among the *ʿulamāʾ*, it is such a commonly-held belief that the household needs a director that this may have come into his speech unconsciously. Later in the interview he gave far more agency to women, saying that if they wanted to be the household director then there would be 'no harm in it'.

Throughout my interview with Ayatollah Saanei, he walked the fine line between the adherence to traditional interpretations and advocating the possibility of new household roles. Although he insisted repeatedly that the verse is descriptive and not legislative, nevertheless he still said that it serves the purpose of expressing a preference: it is good if men assume the position of caretaker of the family, providing for their wives financially and being the directors of the household. He stated that there is no harm in not doing this if the spouses wish to do things differently, but the verse's underlying message is that men should be willing to undertake this role and that it is preferable for them to do so. If the husband does not undertake the role of caretaker, and the wife wishes for him to undertake it, then she has grounds for divorce. Couples have choice, but the traditional roles are still preferred.

The tension between Ayatollah Saanei's traditionalism and his reformist tendencies was apparent in his views on the necessity of the wife's obedience, and the consequences of her disobedience. He explained that 'the good women are obedient' was a natural corollary of the man's payment of maintenance; however, like the beginning of the verse, this second part is not a legal order:

[54] Ibid.

AYATOLLAH SAANEI: If a man is responsible for paying the maintenance and he takes care of her, then our rationality tells us that she should be obedient to him in marital matters and not go against him. He bears the responsibility of maintaining her and of management. Therefore, in this case, should the wife be obedient in marital matters, or should she be recalcitrant? [silence] Obedient! *The good women are obedient* indicates the thing with which the mind also agrees, which is that the wife should be obedient in sexual matters. *Preserving for the absent* is preserving themselves for them. And then *if you fear their nushūz* in other words, *nushūz* in sexual matters.

KB: Well what about when he does not pay the maintenance?

AS: Then it is her right to leave the marriage. She can go to court and obtain a divorce.

KB: And in our day, many women work –

AS: That is what I explained before! It is not a legal order! It is a statement about reality! If the woman wants to be the director, then there is no harm in it. If she wants to be *muqayyima* and pay maintenance to the man, there is no harm in it. It is not an obligatory ruling![55]

Thus, for Ayatollah Saanei, if a couple chooses the traditional way, then they are bound by the traditional arguments and rules: the wife must be sexually obedient, the husband has the right to insist on this because of his financial maintenance of her, and the consequences of her disobedience are admonition, turning his back in bed, and then beating. The beating, however, is with a toothbrush, and is a type of joke. It is not a serious beating in order to scare the wife, or harm her:

AS: Not beating them with a sword! But rather beating them in a way that is appropriate between a man and his wife in specific circumstances. And this is clarified on the authority of [Imām] al-Bāqir, peace and prayers be upon him. Al-Bāqir said that the hitting is with a toothbrush. Have you seen the *siwāk* (traditional toothbrush)? A blow with that is nothing but a game (*la'b*), a joke (*mizāḥ*), in order to bring the woman round. It is not a beating of power and might. It is on the authority of al-Bāqir, peace be upon him, in the *Tafsīr majma' al-bayān*.

KB: And now – in the present time, now, in our day, is this the best way? Beating?

AS: It's a joke, a joke. There is no harm in a joke.

55 Ibid.

HEDAYAT YOUSEFI: Do you mean to ask if now we can still follow this verse?

KB: Yes.

AS: If a man follows this verse, there is no harm in it. If he goes against it, there is no harm in that (*la ba's 'alayhi*).

KB: Hm.

AS: The problem is strong beating. But this beating is not strong or violent! It is a beating of love. The admonition is done from love, the abandoning in the beds is done from love, and the beating is with a toothbrush. These English![56]

In this exchange, Ayatollah Saanei could not understand why I refused to admit that a joking beating might bring a recalcitrant wife around. For him, it was clear that a husband could admonish, abandon his wife, and jokingly hit her with a toothbrush, all from love for her. For him, this was an obvious point. But for me, such joking represented the hierarchy between husband and wife, and I had trouble expressing my own consternation that he should suggest that such a joke was an appropriate way of communicating between spouses. When I wrote to his office before publication of this book, they wished to clarify this point:

> Concerning the beating with a toothbrush, which has caused your 'consternation', it must be said that this is a cultural phenomenon and one needs to study the peoples and nations around the world to see how differently they act and react in different circumstances such as the expressing of love. The very fact that a toothbrush is the means by which you are allowed to beat someone indicates that the act is merely symbolic, meaning to convey a message to them rather than to harm them physically. Such lenient 'beating', pinching, and so forth are ways to show love and affection to your beloved wife and children about which you may learn by studying our culture.[57]

This point, made by one of the members of Ayatollah Saanei's office, is that interpretation must be culturally determined. This gives greater leeway for reinterpretation on cultural grounds. Ayatollah Saanei's reading relies on his particular hermeneutics. In his view, the possibility of reinterpretation is open, but he admits the plain sense reading of the verse. The tradition is not abandoned. Instead, traditional interpretation and the plain sense reading of the verse forms the base for all reinterpretation.

Ayatollah Mohaghegh Damad adopts a somewhat similar interpretive method to Ayatollah Saanei, and agrees that the verse is a description

[56] Ibid.

[57] Office of Grand Ayatollah Saanei, Personal Email Communication, 1 July 2014.

rather than an order. He says: 'There is a difference between an order and a description, *men are qawwāmūn over women* means that it is like this – but it does not mean that is necessary for it to be like this'. Some aspects of marriage are physical and natural: a husband cannot have children. But much of the verse refers to things that can be changed with agreement.

Ayatollah Mohaghegh Damad believes that the 'beating' part of the verse is an address that expresses a law or a norm. Other verses in the Qur'ān are similar – for instance, Q. 5:38, *the male thief and the female thief: cut their hands*, is a normative verse in the form of a command or address. For him, *nushūz* is adultery, and *if you fear* nushūz from Q. 4:34 intends to correct the woman who commits adultery. The question for Ayatollah Mohaghegh Damad is whom the verse addresses: who does the correcting? He says that because it is a normative verse in the form of a command or address, it is addressed not to husbands, but to the law-maker. Therefore, the correction is in the hands of the judge; punishment is not the responsibility of the husband.

> If a husband has a complaint about his wife, that she has a bad, non-acceptable relationship with a man who is not himself, he can complain to the judicial court. The judicial court will summon his wife, and ask her about it. If she confirms it, then the first stage – the admonition. The second stage is physical separation and the third stage is the lash. This is a lightening of the burden for women – but there is no lightening for men. The court undertakes this punishment like that for other crimes. The first stage is the lash. But lashes, *al-ta'zīr al-jismānī*, are connected to a particular time. The verse does not say that it is this only and there is no change. Types of punishment change in every time. Now, it may be solved with imprisonment.[58]

Ayatollah Mohaghegh Damad says that not only the matter should be resolved in court, not by the husband, but also that the punishments themselves can be moderated to fit this day and age: today, imprisonment is acceptable rather than the lash. The assertion that the matter may be resolved in court, rather than at home, is directly contradicted by some conservative interpreters, such as Grand Ayatollah Gerami, who said that a wife's disobedience is best corrected at home, by her husband. As I mentioned in the previous section, he firmly denied that the state was best suited to correct recalcitrant wives.[59]

Resolving the matter of adultery in court clearly requires a culture in which adultery is illegal. I asked Ayatollah Mohaghegh Damad about the

[58] Mohaghegh Damad, Personal Interview, Tehran, Iran, 23 June 2011.
[59] Mohammad 'Ali Gerami, Personal Interview, Qom, Iran, 14 June 2011.

issue of differences between societies. I pointed out that in England, adultery is a matter between husbands and wives, and is not for courts to decide. He responded that some interpreters say that *wa-ḍribūhunna* means 'to leave them'. It is based on Q. 4:101, *idhā ḍarabtum fī' l-arḍ*, meaning 'if you travel'.[60] Although reformists and conservatives usually differ, this reinterpretation of 'leave them' rather than 'beat them' was echoed by Grand Ayatollah Makarim Shirazi.

The neo-traditionalist approach adopted by Grand Ayatollah Saanei and Ayatollah Mohaghegh Damad allows that some aspects of the Qur'ān and law may be reinterpreted through time, with changing circumstances, while at the same time following the spirit of the verses in their plain sense reading. Neo-traditionalists admit that scientific advances might result in reinterpretation. For instance, Dr Kamilan, professor of philosophy and law at Mofid University, said that because of modern medical techniques for determining pregnancy, the *ʿidda* (waiting period after divorce) could be reinterpreted. At the time of the Qur'ān, he said, there was no reliable means of determining pregnancy, and so a three-month waiting period was initiated to see if the wife was pregnant after divorce. Now, because we can know of pregnancy much earlier through modern scientific methods, it is possible to re-interpret the need for the *ʿidda*.[61]

The concept of change through time is the most widespread justification for reinterpretation among both Sunnī and Imāmī Shīʿī interpreters. However, it is not universal in its application. While all reformists agree with change through time, not all of them agree on the exact implications; many conservatives agree that some laws change according to changing circumstances. Dr Kamilan cited Ayatollah ʿIraqī, a prominent conservative who agreed that the *ʿidda* could be reinterpreted in light of modern methods of pregnancy testing.[62] Dr Kamilan used this example to point out to me that change through time is not solely a reformist method.

60 Mohaghegh Damad, Personal Interview 23 June, 2011.

61 Mohammad Sadeq Kamilan, Personal Interview, Qom, Iran, 30 May 2011.

62 KB: Are the rules for this world something that can be reinterpreted through time, unlike the human relationship with God, which is constant? MK: Some of the exegetes and some of the *fuqahā'* have said that they can change through time. For instance, Ayatollah ʿIraqī, who is a conservative, says that if it is clear and diagnosed that a woman is not pregnant, and DNA can prove paternity anyway, so there is no reason to observe *ʿidda*. HS: Ayatollah ʿIraqī is a Grand Ayatollah. And very conservative. That opinion is very interesting, very wonderful. FM: Despite the fact that he is conservative, he believes in changing through time.

Dr Kamilan's colleague at Mofid University, Dr Rahaei, said that pregnancy was only one reason for the *'idda*, and it should not be reinterpreted these days.[63] Although Dr Rahaei accepted the notion of change through time, the exact details of which laws could and should change remain contested ground.

The contestation about the limits of reform was widespread. Several Syrian Sunnī clerics defined themselves as reformist, but they did not go as far as Ayatollah Saanei or Mohaghegh Damad in reinterpreting women's household roles. The most prominent of the reformists was Muḥammad al-Ḥabash, Hudā's brother. In our interview in 2004, he pointed out that in Syrian law, the *qiwāma* was only figurative, not literal: in Syria, a man could not be punished in court for not paying maintenance. However, for Muḥammad al-Ḥabash, *qiwāma* still stands as a religious duty for every man; and if there was no man to undertake this duty for a woman, for instance if she was widowed, then the state should intervene and pay her maintenance. He explained that the ruling of *qiwāma* was based on the natural inclinations of the sexes, and suggested that appropriate jobs for women would be those that would preserve a woman's beauty and femininity, such as being a music teacher. When I pressed him, he admitted that 'there is no final position for women. We can choose according to the situation'.[64] The idea of 'no final position' means that women's role can evolve according to circumstance. Ultimately, it is not limited to one set of rights and duties.

What marks Muḥammad al-Ḥabash out as being a reformist is not his particular interpretation of Q. 4:34; it is his willingness to admit that the Qur'ān can and should be reinterpreted, and that law is open to reinterpretation. Therefore, while he does not take a radical reinterpretation of the gender hierarchy, he admits that some amount of reinterpretation is necessary according to time and place:

> Renewal (*tajdīd*) is necessary, and there is no doubt that that requires a thorough study of these sources of law. Thus independent legal reasoning (*ijtihād*) is necessary. The jurists write the laws from the point of view of the best path for the people, and thus it is necessary to renew these laws according to time and place. The Quran is the very highest source, and yet even within the Quran there are 20 abrogated verses in view of the changing times. Ultimately when we work with the Quran we look for real laws that benefit life.[65]

[63] Rahaei, Personal Interview, Qom, Iran, 7 June 2011.
[64] Muḥammad al-Ḥabash, Personal Interview, Damascus, Syria, 22 August 2004.
[65] Ibid.

Al-Ḥabash's open approach to reinterpretation is distinct from the conservatives I cited previously. He himself contrasts his view with that of the Salafīs and the approach in Saudi Arabia. Conservatives tend to portray the laws as fixed, and to portray themselves as following a literal reading of the Qurʾān; al-Ḥabash speaks of 'working with' the Qurʾān, rather than of following it literally.

Grand Ayatollah Ardebili is another reformist whose interpretation of the gender hierarchy was somewhat conservative. Grand Ayatollah Ardebili was born in 1926, was a close associate of Ruhollah Khomeini, and was Chief Justice of Iran after the Iranian revolution. After Khomeini's death, he returned to Qom and subsequently founded Mofid University, which is the only reformist university in Qom. Grand Ayatollah Ardebili is reformist on many issues, but he sees Q. 4:34 as referring to men's and women's physical predispositions:

> We believe that, praise be to God, women have made a lot of progress. If we compare the past with the present, we see that the present is much better than the past. But when we consider carefully, we see that there is still a long way to go. The world is still in the hands of men. Sometimes we say that women have been oppressed, or that there is room for change. From this verse I understand that men are preferred over women. Men have more ability or power, or they have been created in such a way. Yes, in some cases, it may be that women are better than men, have more income, they may be able to handle property better than men. But in general, in matters related to running the world, how many are men, and how many are women? Even though there are many educated women. Wise women are not few in number. There are women ministers. They are mature. Why then are women in the minority? Can we say that someday this minority will become the majority? I have thought a lot about this. They say that men haven't given opportunities to women. But why did women give the opportunity to men? They could have refused to do so. This shows that men are more capable than women.[66]

Here Grand Ayatollah Ardebili shows that he is in favour of women taking up posts in the government and in professional life. As he says, there are many educated and intelligent women. However, despite the number of women in prominent posts, the majority of leadership roles are held by men. This, he says, is due to women's innate nature. However, he clarified that in a case where the man is incapable of exercising his duties as head of the family, then his responsibilities to do so are annulled. He related the story of a Muslim man living in England who had married

[66] Abdol-Karim Mousavi Ardebili, Personal Interview, Qom, Iran, 27 June 2011. I would like to thank Dr Salimi, head of the English department of Mofid University, for translating and transcribing this interview for me.

a Bahai woman many years ago, when he was not religious. Now, the man was disappointed that his children were not Muslim. Grand Ayatollah Ardebili laid the blame for this squarely at the man's own feet:

> This man told me 'My wife is Bahai, I married her about 30 years ago when I was not a practicing Muslim. She brought up my children as Bahai. I want to expel them from the home'. I said 'why did she make them Bahai, why didn't you bring them up as Muslims?' I asked: 'Do your children prefer their mother or their father' He said 'Their mother'. I told him 'This shows that you are not a capable person. You should not do anything. You should not kick them out of the house'. He said 'They do not let me do my supplications' I told him: 'that is all right'. Whatever he said, I simply replied that you must only observe the obligatory religious rituals. Ask them to leave you to yourself, but do not try to impose anything on them, because you are incapable of doing it.[67]

Although Grand Ayatollah Ardebili believes that men and women have different natural capabilities, through this anecdote, he is explaining that he is open to reinterpretation depending on circumstances. In this case, although the husband was a Muslim, he was also foolish and was unable to relate to his family. Such a man should not try to control the household arbitrarily, according to Grand Ayatollah Ardebili. Instead, he should recognise his own limitations, practice his religion himself, and leave his family to practice theirs.

INTERPRETING AGAINST A HIERARCHY: THE ABROGATION OF Q. 4:34

Some reformist reinterpretations of Q. 4:34 involve abrogating the verse in whole or in part. The method of the abrogating interpreters, like the neo-traditionalist reformers described previously, is to situate the verse in its historical context. However, they contest the limits of reinterpretation: because the context has changed so much, the verse is now no longer applicable in whole or in part. Interpreters who call for abrogation, therefore, do not dispute the methods of neo-traditionalist reformists; they only contest the limits of reinterpretation.

Dr Mahdi Meghdadi is a cleric and the director of the legal clinic at Mofid University. He says that the hitting has been abrogated (*naskh shode*). This is based on the time and place in which the verse was revealed: 'At the time when this verse was revealed, it was a time of ignorance for the Arabs. It is possible to remove rulings that once existed'.

[67] Abdol-Karim Mousavi Ardebili, Personal Interview, Qom, Iran, 27 June 2011.

For Mahdi Meghdadi, *nushūz* differs between a man and a woman, but 'if he is *nāshiz* then she can go to court and obtain a divorce without his consent'.[68]

Mehdi Mehrizi says that Q. 4:34 has been entirely abrogated. This is also based on the time and place of its revelation. In the interpretation of Mehrizi, the Occasion of Revelation is different from the story that is typically told. The most common story, which I described in Chapter 5, involves a woman who goes to the Prophet because her husband has slapped her, the Prophet orders retaliation, and then the verse is revealed allowing husbands to beat their wives. Mehdi Mehrizi says that the verse was revealed between battles, when there was a crisis. The men needed to fight in battle and needed to feel strong, so they were allowed to hit their wives at that moment. Later, the women complained and then the Prophet said that nobody could hit women 'except in cases of manifest lewdness'. He also says that the purpose of the verse was to remove a prohibition:

> There is another point: the hitting is in the order of a command: beat them! But no exegete says that it is necessary to hit women; they only say that it is permissible. Therefore, the verse was only to remove a prohibition, and it was for a specific time and place, and now it has been abrogated.[69]

Here Mehrizi is saying that the command 'beat them' is in that form as a way of removing the prohibition against beating; this command to men was given in a particular circumstance, and today it has been abrogated.

Mehrizi took an equally radical interpretation of the 'degree' that men have over women. He pointed out that Q. 2:228 contains two statements that seem to contradict one another: the statement that *women have rights like their obligations*, and the statement that *men have a degree over them*. The first statement implies that women's rights are equal to their obligations, while the second gives men an advantage over them. In order to remove the seeming contradiction between the first and second parts of the verse, he turns to the interpretation of Ibn ʿAbbās in al-Ṭabarī's *tafsīr*:

> He says that *men have a degree over women* does not mean that men have more rights than women, but rather that men have an obligation to forgive women with regard to some of the rights that women owe to them. And in exchange for this is a degree. 'Degree' is only used in a figurative sense in the Qur'ān; the word is never used with a material meaning. ... The husband has, in exchange for giving up these rights, a degree with God, in the figurative sense. And I believe that Ibn

[68] Mahdi Meghdadi, Personal Interview, Qom, Iran, 8 June 2011.
[69] Mehdi Mehrizi, Personal Interview, Qom, Iran, 9 June 2011.

ʿAbbās was the one who interpreted the verse in the way that was the closest to solving this problem. He says, 'I like to adorn myself for my wife, just as I like it when she adorns herself for me, because God has said *women have rights like their obligations*. And I do not like to take advantage of all of my rights over her, because God has said, *and men have a degree over them*'.[70]

The modern Imāmī Shīʿī Mehrizi uses a traditional argument, but not in the same way that it was used by the medieval Sunnī al-Ṭabarī. When al-Ṭabarī cited this view, as described in Chapter 3, he stated clearly that men have more rights than women; but Mehrizi cites it in order to say that women and men can have equal rights. Through such reframing, he has found an element in the tradition that enables him to resolve the seeming contradiction in the verse itself between the statement that *women have rights like their obligations* and the statement that *men have a degree over them*, and to bring the verse's meaning into line with current ethical standards.

Another trend in interpreting against the hierarchy is to interpret the Qur'ān against its plain sense reading, but this is more likely among 'modernists' than those who classify themselves as *ʿulamāʾ*. Modernists are Islamic reformists who may not have received a traditional education, and who do not need to base their reinterpretations on tradition. In these formulations, the Qur'ān is read as an egalitarian text; although some scholars may acknowledge the 'beating' in the verse, it is dismissed as a non-intrinsic part of the Qur'ān's message.

The Sunnī modernists Naṣr Ḥāmid Abū Zayd and Muḥammad al-Ṭalbī do not use the term 'abrogated' to describe the verse, but they situate it in its historical context and argue against beating by saying that the Qur'ān is essentially egalitarian in nature. Although they differ in their precise formulations, they have key points in common. Among these is the assumption that the Qur'ān has two types of verse, the unchanging ethical and the historically bound, and the notion that the historically bound verses are open to reinterpretation. I will give a brief summary of the interpretation of Naṣr Ḥāmid Abū Zayd as an example.

Naṣr Ḥāmid Abū Zayd does not give the verse much attention, but he does mention it in his autobiography.[71] He says that *qiwāma* is

[70] Ibid.

[71] This is the conclusion of Nadia Oweidat, who has studied all of the writings of Naṣr Ḥāmid Abū Zayd, including his book on women, which did not mention this verse. (Oweidat, 'Nasr Hamid Abu Zayd and Limits of Reform in Contemporary Islamic Thought', PhD thesis, Oxford University, 2014).

purely financial, and because of this, when a woman supports her family financially she is *qawwāma* over her husband.[72] For him, beating was a historical solution to a historical problem.[73] He cites the verses on inheritance to argue that the Qur'ān was moving from a situation in which men had unlimited rights (before Islam) to the situation in which men's rights were limited under Islam. While the idea that men had unlimited rights is implausible, he uses this tendentious history to argue that the Qur'ān was moving in the direction of egalitarianism.[74] Abū Zayd puts the locus of conservative interpretation firmly in the realm of cultural practices. He gives two examples of men's normal, everyday sexism: in one case, a lawyer is against a female judge, in another case, an acquaintance treats his wife in a domineering way. For Abū Zayd, cultural resistance has led to the stagnation of reinterpretation of the Qur'ān. In his other writings on women, he focuses on the egalitarian elements of the Qur'ān.[75]

Like Abū Zayd, Muḥammad Ṭalbī projects notions of equality and feminism into the Qur'ān; he speaks of Muḥammad's reforms as 'feminist'. This type of projection raises some of the problems with the modernist approach. Scott questions whether 'applying the concept of "feminism" to Muḥammad' is anachronistic.[76] Nettler speaks more pointedly: 'the unstated assumption which plays a key role in the logic of Ṭalbi's method is that God wants only the "good" and "progressive"'; he questions whether *ijtihād* could 'yield more than one *valid* conclusion'.[77] Nettler echoes conservatives' main critique of modernist and reformist interpretations: these interpretations are seen as arbitrary and inauthentic, while the conservative view is portrayed as authentic and sound. This raises the question of their sources of interpretation, which I address in the next section.

[72] Naṣr Hāmid Abū Zayd and Esther Nelson, *Voice of an Exile: Reflections on Islam* (Westport, CT: Praeger Publishers, 2004), p. 176.
[73] Ibid., p. 177. [74] Ibid., pp. 177–8.
[75] Oweidat, 'Nasr Hamid Abu Zayd and Limits of Reform in Contemporary Islamic Thought'.
[76] Rachel M. Scott, 'A Contextual Approach to Women's Rights in the Qur'ān: Readings of 4:34', *The Muslim World* 99 (January 2009): p. 72.
[77] Ronald Nettler, 'Mohammad Talbi's Commentary on Qur'ān IV:34: A "Historical Reading" of a Verse Concerning the Disciplining of Women', *The Maghreb Review*, 24.1–2 (1999): pp. 28–9. (as quoted by Scott, ibid., p. 71).

CONCLUDING, PART I: CONSERVATIVE ATTITUDES TOWARDS TRADITION AND CHANGE

Despite a shared commitment to preserving aspects of the tradition, conservatives' approach to law and tradition varies: some are open to reinterpretation to a certain extent, while others are not; furthermore, they pick and choose different aspects of the established tradition to include in their works. This section describes four conservative approaches to the question of reinterpretation: those who say that, once established, a law is eternal and abiding and cannot change in any circumstance; those who claim that the interpretation can change as our understanding changes; those who assert that the underlying basis for the law cannot change, but the particulars and details may change; and those who assert that if a law is based on certain circumstance alone, then it may change when those circumstances change. There may be some overlap between these approaches, and indeed in some cases the *ʿulamāʾ* may have been trying to express similar ideas, but in different ways, yet it is nevertheless important to see how the expression of these fundamental points differs between interpreters.

Mr Ghazizadeh claimed in our interview that law could never change, even in changing circumstances. This was his response when I asked whether the ruling on hitting wives could be reinterpreted these days:

MUHAMMAD GHAZIZADEH: As for the question about whether the law on hitting is related to the particular time and place, the answer is no, it is for all time. It is not related to one particular time and place. You cannot conclude that it doesn't work in any family. Even if it works in two families out of 100 families, then you should keep the rule.

KB: Well if it only works in two families out of 100 families, then isn't it the exception rather than the rule?

MG: No, a law is a law. In all families and all people and in every time. But just because we are now living in a very civilised period, it doesn't mean that the rule is abrogated. The rule is the rule, for all people in all times. It worked for a long time, but if you think that it doesn't work now, it's because of the change through time, and because we are more civilised. But it may work even now. You can't say for sure that it doesn't work, it may work.

KB: There are other questions, for instance slavery. The Qur'ān talks about slaves a lot, but now we don't have slaves. So are those rulings of the Qur'ān still fixed?

MG: This example actually confirms that this is a rule for all time. In one period of time we may use the rule, and in other periods we don't use it, but the rule is fixed.[78]

For Mr Ghazizadeh, the law is fixed, even when the customs of the people change around it. On the face of it, Mr Ghazizadeh's assertion that the law is immutable seems simplistic. The black and white nature of his response may be due to my presence as interviewer. He may have felt that he had to simplify things for me, which may have led him to a slightly exaggerated portrayal of the nature of the law.

His basic hermeneutical stance, which is to preserve past interpretations, was backed up with reference to *ḥadīth*s that other interpreters might reject. For instance, he referred to the *ḥadīth* that says that the superiority of men over women is like that of the sky over the earth, which had been cited by medieval Shīʿī sources.[79] This caused my research assistant, Fatemeh Muslimi, some surprise:

FATEMEH MUSLIMI: You are not rejecting this *ḥadīth*?
MG: No, it has a meaning. We interpret it to say that because the earth is brought to life by the heavens, so if a man can control and supervise and manage his family in a good way, he can revive the women of the family.
FM: Is this a good justification?
HAMED SHIVAPOUR: Mrs Karen, is it clear?
KB: It is clear, but . . .[80]

As in my interactions with other conservatives, I was not quite sure how to respond to Mr Ghazizadeh's reinterpretation of the *ḥadīth*. It is a common conservative method to cite a *ḥadīth* but to give it an entirely different meaning than the one it would have had for a medieval audience, as Mr Ghazizadeh does here. For instance, Saʿīd Ramaḍān al-Būṭī of Syria supports the deficiency *ḥadīth* by saying that women are deficient in both mind and religion; but rather than simply taking the *ḥadīth* at face value as did medieval interpreters, he justifies it in entirely new ways that are more in line with modern sensibilities. He first says that this *ḥadīth* is

78 Muhammad Ghazizadeh, Personal Interview, Qom, Iran, 5 June 2011.
79 'Some narratives mention that the superiority of men over women is like the superiority of the sky over the earth, or like the superiority of water over the earth. And just as water brings the earth to life, so men bring women to life' (ibid.)
80 Ibid.

merely 'friendly banter'; at the same time, he asserts that educational psychology proves that women are more emotionally inclined, and less intellectually inclined, than men.[81] Neither al-Būṭī nor Mr Ghazizadeh simply cite tradition. They manipulate it – preserving the words, but shifting the meaning to fall into line with modern sensibilities.

Although Mr Ghazizadeh's view of law as immune from change represents the most widespread perception of the conservative approach, it was actually rare for an interpreter to take this view. According to Grand Ayatollah Makarim Shirazi, for instance, there is more than one correct interpretation of the Qur'ān. 'In the *Tafsīr namūneh*' he said, 'we have brought forth many different interpretations, and we say that all of them are correct'.[82] The idea of many correct interpretations goes back to the medieval period, when interpreters did not always wish to judge between interpretations. He also asserted that, sometimes, interpretation can change through time because of advances in human understanding:

KB: And are there any cases in which the interpretation can and must change through time?

AYATOLLAH MAKARIM: Some interpretations do change through time, and we have written about them in our work. *Innā khalaqnā al-insāna min nuṭfatin* [Q. 76:2].... For instance, according to recent scientific findings we can find a different interpretation for the verse, different from what we have offered in *Tafsīr namuneh*.

KB: Then can I ask if the Qur'ān could support the scientific theory of evolution?

AM: Some of the exegetes say that there is no contradiction between the theory of evolution and the Qur'ān.[83]

Here Grand Ayatollah Makarim asserts that scientific findings might influence the interpretation of the Qur'ān. The words of the Qur'ān are, of course, immutable, but a person's proper understanding of them might change.

Mr Zibaei Nejad put the question of fixed laws a different way. He said: 'The underlying *ḥukm* is fixed, but the particulars may change according to the subject (*mawḍūʿ*) or it may change according to circumstances (*maṣāliḥihā*)'. His interpretation allows for slightly more flexibility than does that of Mr Ghazizadeh, but still emphasizes the point that the ruling (*ḥukm*) is fixed and unchanging. Reformists might

[81] al-Būṭī, *Women: Between the Tyranny of the Western System and the Mercy of Islamic Law*, pp. 253–4.
[82] Makarim Shirazi, Personal Interview, Qom, 25 June, 2011. [83] Ibid.

interpret that *ḥukm* differently – they might say, for instance, that the true *ḥukm* is not in the husband's authority, but in the notion of kindness between the spouses.

Ayatollah Gerami, whose views of women are distinctly medieval, admitted that certain aspects of law might change with the times, as long as the law is based entirely on something that changes, such as social practice. The laws on women do not change, however, because they are based not only on social practice, but also on men's innate superiority. Here he explains the two different aspects of men's authority in the phrase of Q. 4:34 *because the one is superior to the other, and because they spend on their maintenance*:

AYATOLLAH GERAMI: Men have authority over women in two aspects: the first of them is constant: it is the superiority of the rational mind (*ʿaql*) over the tender emotions. And the other depends on the context, the time, the place, which differ. But from the time of Adam until now, the second aspect has been present. Except in the West recently. Recently, in this past century, women have entered into the financial affairs of the family. But this is the second aspect. With regards to the first aspect, it stands until now.

KB: But here in Iran, even –

AG: Yes, recently here in Iran. But that is in, perhaps, the past 50 years.

KB: But it is possible to change the ruling (*ḥukm*) because of the time –

AG: If it were down to this aspect only, we would accept that it would change. But there is the first aspect, and that is the aspect of ability and strength with which God made them superior.[84]

Ayatollah Gerami explains that men's superiority is in both matters that can change, such as payment of maintenance, and matters that cannot change, such as the superiority of men's rational minds. The unchanging aspects cause the ruling to remain, despite changing times.

Rather than being a monolithic group which unthinkingly reproduces tradition, conservatives reinterpret and reimagine medieval tradition, and take varied approaches to the question of reinterpreting medieval laws. Thus, while I have argued that much of the conservative discourse is shared between conservative Sunnī and Shīʿī *ʿulamāʾ*, to the point of there being conservative tropes, individual interpreters still have leeway to justify their interpretations with their own particular methods, and their

84 Muhammad ʿAli Gerami, Personal Interview, Qom, Iran, 14 June 2011.

justifications may involve varied hermeneutical strategies. This variation in interpretation, and the leeway for personal opinion and explanation of the law, leads me to conclude that there is not one uniform conservative hermeneutical approach.

CONCLUDING, PART 2: IMĀMĪ SHĪʿĪ REFORMIST HERMENEUTICS

Although the limits of reinterpretation are contested among reformist interpreters, all of the reformist interpretations described in this book rest on the idea that correct interpretation can change through time; for if correct interpretation were fixed and static, there would be no need for reinterpretation. There are two assumptions behind the 'change through time' approach. One is that ethics can also change through time, or differ according to time and place, and the second is that one's rationality (*ʿaql*) is an appropriate means through which to determine interpretation. Reformists and conservatives alike use their own individual reasoning in interpretation; but reformists are far more likely than conservatives to acknowledge their own role in reinterpretation, to admit their rationality as a means or basis for interpretation, and to speak openly about the ways in which ethical notions differ according to time and place. But how do they know for sure that their interpretation is correct, especially if they derive it from their own reasoning? What if human reason goes against the Qur'ān?

I framed my questions about 'correct' interpretation around the term *maʿrūf* in Q. 2:228 (*women have rights like their obligations bi'l-maʿrūf*). As described in Chapter 5, the term literally means 'what is right, or correct'. However, it is derived from the root for 'custom' (*ʿurf*). The question is how to determine what is right from what is merely customary. There were two broad trends among reformists who answered this question: those who said that reason conforms with revelation, and those who said that reason is something to be exercised in order to interpret the truth. The first approach is more closely correlated with the neo-traditionalists, while the second is the view taken by a number of reformists.

Grand Ayatollah Saanei is a proponent of the first approach. He says that when rationality (*ʿaql*) is used properly, it will agree with the sources of revealed law. In his view, *ʿaql* must be used in conjunction with revealed texts, and cannot constitute independent proof:

ʿAql, when it agrees with the Qurʾān and what the Prophet and the Imāms (*ahl al-waḥy*) have said, then it is understanding (*dark*). *ʿAql* in terms of understanding the Qurʾān is that which understands and does not go against what the Prophet has also said. It is like the student's understanding of the words of the professor. When he follows what the teacher has taught him, then his understanding is sound. And when he goes against the principles (*ʿuṣūl*) and the clarifications of the teacher, then his understanding is mistaken. *ʿAql* in reading and in deriving has the meaning of understanding, not of proof. *ʿAql* is understanding (*dark*). But some of them have more *ʿaql* than others, some of them understand everything, some of them only understand some issues. *ʿAql* means understanding (*dark, istinbāṭ, fahm*). I understand from the Noble verse that men and women are equal, and another person says that that this does not have proof. His understanding has not reached that point. Just as the understanding of a child has not reached the level of the understanding of the adult. . . . There is a principle of *ʿaql* is that which enables us to say this agrees with the order or this goes against the order. *ʿAql* is independent. As for uncovering the rulings, and uncovering what God Almighty wishes, it is necessary that our *ʿaql* is connected to the revelation, not independent of the revelation.[85]

In rejecting the *ʿaql* as an independent source of law, Ayatollah Saanei is rejecting the position of some Uṣūlīs. This position is a hallmark of his neo-traditionalism.

Some reformists, however, went further in their discussion of the role of place and time in the interpretation of scripture. Naser Ghorbannia, professor of Islamic law at Mofid University, explained that 'what is right' could change at different times and places. He explicitly connects the changing of moral rules with the changing of legal rulings:

Maʿrūf means what is right. And *maʿrūf* will change with place and time. One thing was *maʿrūf* and right 100 years ago. Today we can say that that's not right and *maʿrūf* today. We know that morality can change from time to time and from place to place. . . . But this is not an absolute principle. Islam does not condone non-moral behaviour such as violence against women, or torture. We can never say that because the custom, ethos, and morality of a particular country accepts those things, therefore Islam accepts that behaviour.[86]

Although Dr Ghorbannia allows room for different interpretations on the basis of customary understanding, and different interpretations according to time and place, he admits that there are ultimately moral rules that must be interpreted against customary practice, and along with what he terms 'humane' concerns. Therefore, in this view, customary understanding determines correctness to a certain extent, but there are limits beyond which customary understanding actually transgresses Islamic ethics and law.

[85] Yusuf Saanei, Personal Interview.
[86] Naser Ghorbannia, Personal Interview, Qom, Iran, 29 May 2011.

In an interview with many of his followers present, which resulted in a lively discussion between them, Grand Ayatollah Ardebili pointed out that certain things might be socially acceptable (*ma'rūf*) but they may not agree with reason (*'aql*). He explained the different considerations that might lead to actions:

ABDUL-KARIM AL-MUSAWI ARDEBILI: Human beings have two kinds of perception and understanding. Sometimes a person thinks about a topic, while sometimes outside factors influence his thinking. Material interest, social acceptability, being agreeable and nice, and so forth might influence him. Working things out with intellectual reasoning, thinking, and trying not to let outside influences interfere is the best way. Issues and problems should be considered in and of themselves to see if they are appropriate or good.

KB: What some people perceive as being a benefit in and of itself is different from what other people perceive as being a benefit in and of itself. The very question of what things are intrinsically, though it should be accepted by everyone, sometimes has cultural differences.

AKMA: We believe that the essence and reality does not change, what changes is the appearance. Cultures change. Now she [referring to KB] is from one region of the world. We are from another region. We may consider something as good, but such a thing may not be considered good in her view. But these things cannot change the reality. There are things which are clear: lies are considered bad by all, fraud is regarded as bad by all. But can we say here that this originates from the whims and desires of a person, or are they manifestations of an ultimate reality? This issue is a bit complicated because of the possibility of environmental influences. She is right. In such cases, it is very difficult to distinguish. The more a person knows, the more a person uses his intellect, the better equipped they will be to distinguish between good and bad. We should use our reason and our thinking. Then those things which we have acquired by imitation, desires, and whims will be fewer and fewer.[87]

Grand Ayatollah Ardebili sets human reason as the determining factor in a person's ability to tell right from wrong. He admits that some people are better able to exercise their reason than others; but if one is able to remove

[87] Abdul-Karim Musawi Ardebili, Personal Interview, Qom, Iran, 26 June 2011.

environmental factors, one is likely to arrive at a type of universal truth that is accepted by all. In a similar vein, Dr Kamilan, professor of philosophy at Mofid University, explained that 'what is right' is not determined by just anyone, but by the people who have certain expertise, and who can be considered to be the rational people. He made the distinction between people who were using their minds and the 'fundamentalists' such as the Taliban:

DR KAMILAN: By *bi'l-ma'rūf* we mean what is common among the experts who specify the rule.

FATEMEH MUSLIMI: This is a very different interpretation from the previous ones, very different. It was really interesting to me to hear that.

KB: What if the *'urf* is something that causes harm? What if it is something like what the Taliban say, for instance that women cannot go to school?

DK: No, we have said that it is the *'urf* of the *'uqalā'* (the customs of the thinking people), the people who use their minds. Not like the Taliban, or people like that. Not people who act on whim (*iḥṣaṣat*) or fundamentalism in religion at all. The *'urf* of rationality.[88]

According to Dr Kamilān, what is correct is not determined by social norms – instead, it is determined by the customs and decisions of the thinking, rational people. This approach guards against common practice determining law, but it also assumes that there is an objective criterion through which to establish who is rational.

I assumed in the interview that Dr Kamilan's concept of the 'thinking people' meant those who were educated in religious matters. But he assured me later that this was not the case. Dr Rahaei, who is a student of Grand Ayatollah Ardebili, asserted that there are principles that should be, and are, generally recognised in most legal systems, and explained the difference between customary practice (*'urf*) and what is right (*ma'rūf*) by saying that there is a 'universal *'urf*', by which he meant something like a universal moral code. If customary practice goes against the universal moral code, the custom should not take precedent. According to him, *'aql* is the viewpoint of the *'uqalā'*, the thinking people, and general principles of law are things that most thinking people could accept. 'Today most of the human rights rules, not all but most, we can say that these are things

[88] Mohamed Sadeq Kamilan, Personal Interview, Qom, Iran, 30 May 2011.

that the *'uqalā'* accept'.[89] This is a radical step in that, rather than being particularly Islamic, the correct law is understood to be universal. His approach opens the way to reinterpreting religious law in accordance with international human rights laws. It also presumes that there is a type of rational, non-personal truth to be gleaned, perhaps, from outside of the traditional sources of law.

It was difficult to draw him into the question of who determines the universal moral code, and how it is determined; but it was clear that certain types of religious interpretation went against such a code. He contrasted the retrograde cultural interpretations of those who refused to use their intellect with the possibility of interpreting according to reason. Representing the former group was Ibn Baz, who was the Grand Mufti of Saudi Arabia until his death in 1999. In the following exchange, I was attempting to ask about the effect of cultural practice on interpretation:

DR RAHAEI: What is right (*ma'rūf*) is not the custom (*'urf*) itself. Reasoning, rationality and logic must be taken into account.

KB: But my question is that if you were a Saudi Shaykh then you would say that this was the correct *ḥijāb* [covers face]. You would say that this accords with reason (*'aql*).

DR: But Ibn Bāz would reject the use of *'aql* entirely. He would only agree with the use of traditions. He would not accept the use of *'aql* in the derivation of laws, only a narration. … Ibn Bāz's *'aql* was on holiday. Ibn Baz went to Iraq and visited Ayatollah Hakim, who is a Shi'ī *marja'*, and asked him why he interprets the Qur'ān's verses. He said 'you should just obey the verses'. Ayatollah Hakim replied to him: 'whoever is blind in this world will be blind in the next' (*man kāna fī' l-ālam a'mā, fa-huwa fī' l-ākhirati a'mā*) [Q. 17:72]. Ibn Bāz was blind. He got really upset and got up and left. The Shī'a *marja*'s and experts open the way for *'aql* and logic.[90]

Dr Rahaei points to tensions in the modern world, in which modern groups exploit long-held principles regarding the derivation of the law. He says that for the Sunnī Ibn Baz, who was Salafi in his approach, tradition is the only source of law. One should not even interpret the texts, but should simply obey.

[89] Saeed Rahaei, Personal Interview, Qom, Iran, 7 June 2011.
[90] Ibid.

The real tension here is not between reformists and conservatives, but between moderate interpretations (reformist and conservative) and Salafi interpretations, which do not admit any human reasoning, and which are used to promote practices that are often considered to be unethical. In the cited exchange, the poverty of the Salafi view is laid bare and the most prominent proponent of Salfism is made to look ridiculous by an Imāmī Shīʿī interpreter, who is willing to use his mind to interpret. While the discussion of the sources of interpretation seems at first glance to be an intellectual endeavour, removed from practical considerations, in reality these arguments are shaped by their social and political circumstances.

Conclusion

One of the aims of this book has been to highlight the power of the textual tradition, and to show how certain interpretations that were widespread in the medieval period, whether adopted or adapted, have become widely accepted and normative today. In a recently published book of essays entitled *Muslima Theology: The Voices of Muslim Women Theologians*, Rahba Isa al-Zeera, a Bahraini interpreter, promises a 'new understanding of verse 4:34'. She assures the reader that this verse does not condone marital violence, and then proceeds to explain that its correct interpretation is that if a husband anticipates that his wife will be unfaithful, he can prevent her infidelity by using the three-step solution in the verse: admonishing, shunning in bed, and hitting.[1] She asserts that any violence against women is prohibited except in one particular instance, which is when the wife threatens the marital bond through infidelity. The same does not apply to husbands, she says, because his second partner could be his second wife.[2] There is no sense of irony in her assertion that this interpretation does not give husbands permission to beat their wives. The reason becomes clear at the end of the essay, in her section on 'recommendations', addressed to a non-specified governmental or religious body. She recommends that her interpretation be used to 'modify, amend, and change family law articles that contain an incorrect definition of

[1] Rahba Isa al-Zeera, 'Violence Against Women in Qur'an 4:34: A Sacred Ordinance?', in *Muslima Theology: The Voices of Muslim Women Theologians*, ed. Ednan Aslan, Marcia Hermansen, and Elif Medeni (Frankfurt: Peter Lang, 2013), pp. 217–30, at p. 224.
[2] Ibid., p. 225.

nushūz and legitimate the "beating" of women for any reason'.[3] It seems that there is little legal protection for women in her context. Her interpretation seems at first glance simply to perpetuate widespread norms, and to replicate medieval interpretations; however, it is actually a considered response to her particular social and political circumstances. She is arguing against specific laws that enable and allow marital abuse on a widespread scale.

It is difficult to overestimate the effect of what has come to be taken for granted among the populace, whether it be that Darwinian theory is discredited, or that hitting lightly does not constitute marital violence. In politically charged issues such as women's testimony and marital violence, one must understand what is said (and not said) as more than merely a representation of tradition: it is also a response to the current political and social milieu. Political circumstances shape conventional wisdom as well as the interpretation of medieval texts. This Conclusion takes up the question of how different milieux have affected the way in which medieval and modern *ʿulamāʾ* have interpreted the Qurʾān's verses on women's status.

MEDIEVAL INTERPRETATIONS OF GENDER ROLES IN CONTEXT

I began Chapter 5 with the issue of housework, which, perhaps surprisingly, raises the issue of how legal precedent and social mores affect interpretation. Around the world today, housework is still commonly considered to be a woman's domain; yet it was not one of the duties of a wife according to several of the schools of Islamic law. I argued that this omission was not due to any nascent gender equality in the law, but rather to the presumption by the earliest jurists that Muslim households would have had slaves or servants. By the 6th/12th century, when all classes of the populace had been Muslim for centuries, housework was considered a wife's duty, despite the legal rulings against it. Exegetes explained that wives should do 'women's work', particularly in light of the recommendations for husbands to do 'men's work' such as defending the family, providing maintenance for wives and children, and instructing them. The question of housework came up in the context of Q. 2:228, which speaks of men's and women's rights and duties, and which is commonly cited in

[3] Ibid., p. 229.

marriage contracts to remind men of their duties towards their wives. For al-Zamakhsharī and Fakhr al-Dīn al-Rāzī, who addressed the question of housework, their own presuppositions about appropriate behaviour and social roles outweighed the textual tradition and intellectual context of their legal schools, as well as precedent within the genre which stated that it was men's duty to provide for service.

This study has highlighted numerous other ways in which social context, milieu, and authors' expectations affected the way in which medieval *'ulamā'* interpreted the Qur'ān: the notions of just governance so common in descriptions of marriage emerge from particular circumstances; the interpretations of Eve's creation from a rib reflect widespread cultural understanding; and 'scientific' ideas of men's and women's bodily makeup had little to do with empirical evidence.

For the *'ulamā'*, social context extended into their methods of writing texts. Their intellectual milieu had much to do with how they wrote, which in turn affects what they wrote about women. The development of the genre of *tafsīr* through time had important consequences for the interpretation of verses on gender. Such changes may relate to the ways in which these texts were used by the *'ulamā'*, particularly with the increasing sophistication of the madrasa system. While the genres of *ḥadīth*, *fiqh*, and *tafsīr* were initially discrete, by the 5th/11th century, and particularly with al-Tha'labī, elements from *fiqh* and *ḥadīth* became incorporated into works of *tafsīr*. In the earliest period, only the genre of *ḥadīth* had spoken of women's innate inferiority when explaining the verses in question; but increasingly in the 5th/11th century, and particularly in the 6th/12th century, works of *tafsīr* included references to these *ḥadīth*s as well as lengthy descriptions of women's inferior nature. Ibn al-'Arabī included a list of the many points of men's superiority, in which *ḥadīth*s were listed alongside Qur'ānic verses and social arguments to explain why women could not testify in the same way as men.

It is difficult to know exactly what lies behind the increase in statements of women's deficiencies by classical authors of *tafsīr*. The attitudes of these authors may reflect changes in society towards a more conservative view of women, or towards a more restrictive stance in a context of Islam as the majority religion rather than the sect of the ruling elite. Yet these explanations of women's inferiority may reflect nothing more or less than a shift in the way that *tafsīr* was written, towards explaining the 'why' of a verse rather than simply explaining its meaning. As such, classical authors may be stating what the earliest authors took for granted, which there was no need to mention. It is likely that the growing number of statements of women's inferior nature reflects a combination of changes in society, with its increasingly elaborate social and legal code, and changes in the way that *tafsīr* was written, as an increasingly sophisticated genre that includes various types of explanation for the verse and the reasons behind it.

A subtle transformation in the sources of authority cited in works of *tafsīr* was part and parcel of the technical changes in the nature of the genre in the classical period. The Prophet had always been the stated source of authority for this genre, but interpretations were initially passed down by a specific group of interpretative authorities. Ten Companions were accorded the most authority; they were followed by Successors, mostly the disciples of Ibn ʿAbbas.[4] The *tafsīr* of al-Ṭabarī and that of Abū Futūḥ-i Rāzī rely quite heavily on these early authorities; in the verses on women, they are cited in chains of transmission that do not go back to the Prophet himself. In his *Aḥkām al-Qurʾān*, al-Jaṣṣāṣ incorporates law and *ḥadīth*s on the Prophet's authority into the format of a work of *tafsīr*, but without the grammar and lexicographical analysis that is characteristic of that genre. By the time of al-Thaʿlabī in the 5th/11th century, long narratives on the Prophet's authority take precedence, although many of these are not in authoritative collections. In the 6th/12th century, with al-Baghawī, the transition seems complete, in that when he cites *ḥadīth*s on the Prophet's authority, they are only 'sound' *ḥadīth*s from authoritative collections. Significantly, this is before Ibn Taymiyya wrote his treatise on *tafsīr* calling for just such a method, and before Ibn Kathīr wrote his work along the same lines. The eventual shift to sound *ḥadīth*s on the Prophet's authority was not uniform or universal: many exegetes after al-Baghawī and Ibn Kathīr cite unsound *ḥadīth*s.[5] Yet the incorporation of lengthy *ḥadīth*s on the Prophet's authority in some works, and the subsequent incorporation of only sound *ḥadīth*s in others, reflects an important transition in the nature of authoritative transmission in the genre. The early exegetical authorities are not neglected in the post-Ṭabarī period, but as time passes, it seems that their word alone is no longer enough to certify the correctness of an interpretation.

[4] Claude Gilliot, 'The Beginnings of Qur'anic Exegesis', pp. 7–9.

[5] Cf. Roberto Tottoli, 'Methods and Contexts in the Use of Hadiths in Classical *Tafsīr* Literature: The Exegesis of Q. 21:85 and Q 17:1', in *Aims, Methods, and Contexts*, pp. 199-215.

Although citation patterns change through time, not all interpretations were attributed: unattributed interpretations were almost always present in works of *tafsīr*. I have suggested that unattributed interpretations represent common understanding or taken-for-granted truths, which may or may not derive from the words of the Prophet or the early exegetical authorities. While the early interpreter Hūd b. Muḥakkam cited the 'crooked rib' *ḥadīth* on the authority of the Prophet, two centuries later al-Wāḥidī cited the same interpretation with no authority or chain of transmission. This interpretation had by that point entered common lore to the extent that it did not need citation. Similarly, the scientific explanation of Abū 'l-Layth al-Samarqandī, Fakhr al-Dīn al-Rāzī, and Abū Ḥayyān al-Gharnāṭī that women are cold and moist, whereas men are hot and dry, was given without attribution. The idea of the humours had been passed down from the ancient Greeks and was probably common knowledge for these authors, rather than being an opinion that had to be cited with a specific chain of transmission.

Interestingly, the profound changes in the citation of authoritative sources that I have described here receive little direct attention from the interpreters in their introductions, and they do not cast themselves in the role of experts in *ḥadīth*. In al-Thaʿlabī's introduction, he indicates some of the improvements that he will make to previous efforts in the genre: he claims, for instance, that he will incorporate rulings from *fiqh*. Saleh notes that he does so, always following the Shāfiʿī school.[6] This shows that some of what he says in the introduction proves to be the model for how he works in the actual *tafsīr*. However, he never says anything specifically about *ḥadīth*s – instead, he says that the work should 'discover things that were overlooked, collect that which was scattered, explain that which was obscure, organise and systematise'.[7] In common with other exegetes, *isnād* criticism (critique of the chains of transmission for *ḥadīth*s) is not prominent in his work; in many cases it is not mentioned at all. Saleh notes that although al-Thaʿlabī's tools were primarily philological, his work was doctrinal rather than philological in nature.[8] Thus it should come as no surprise that he used any available *ḥadīth*s, not just the sound ones, to make his point; it is nevertheless intriguing that he does not highlight his own contribution in bringing the Prophet's words to the fore in his analysis. Al-Baghawī, who bases his commentary on al-Thaʿlabī's but omits the unsound *ḥadīth*s, says that he must 'renew what has been

[6] Saleh, *Formation*, p. 86. [7] Ibid., p. 68. [8] Ibid., particularly pp. 95–7.

left aside for too long'. This 'renewal' does not consist of anything new, but rather consists in refining the techniques for incorporating existing material.[9] Although his mission with regards to al-Thaʿlabī's *tafsīr* was primarily about refining the *ḥadīth*s used therein, like al-Thaʿlabī he does not claim to engage in *isnād* criticism. Nor does Ibn Kathīr place any emphasis on *isnād*s.[10] All of these examples show that, while the increasing incorporation of *ḥadīth*s directly on the authority of the Prophet must have been a conscious choice on the part of the exegetes, they did not see *tafsīr* as a venue for the science of *ḥadīth* criticism. Instead, they focus on linguistic analysis, which goes back to the origins of the genre and also to its place in the madrasa system of the time. The incorporation of these *ḥadīth*s is probably a corollary of their increasingly systematised madrasa education and of increasingly widespread expectations about the necessary proof for an interpretation.

Authoritative sources are, of course, most needed when the exegete's opinion or ruling seems in some way questionable. In this regard, the wide array of *ḥadīth*s on women's obedience is telling. In *ḥadīth*s cited by al-Thaʿlabī, women are assured that their obedience will give them the same rewards as men. And in *ḥadīth*s cited by the Imāmī al-Baḥrānī, women are warned of the magnitude of the husband's rights against the wife. Some exegetes, such as Ibn ʿArabī and Fakhr al-Dīn al-Rāzī, admit that women's lot does not seem to be a fair one; but they say that God's word is to be obeyed, even when it is not understood. There is no doubt that the patriarchal context of pre-modern Muslim societies shaped their interpretations, but that does not mean that interpreters had no notion of fairness or justice. At times they, too, struggled to explain a system that might lead to abuses of power.

Outside of the genre, there is at least one critique of the idea that men always deserve to be in charge of women. The Ismāʿīlī al-Muʾayyad fī' l-Dīn al-Shīrāzī discusses the *ḥadīth* that says 'if any human being were to prostrate themselves before another, women should prostrate themselves before men', and asserts that many women are better than their husbands and more pious. Although he asserts the necessity of the *ẓāhir* law, he says that the *ḥadīth* and Qurʾānic verses on men and women are

[9] Bauer, 'Justifying the Genre: A Study of Introductions to Classical Works of *Tafsīr*', in *Aims, Methods, and Contexts of Qur'anic Exegesis*, pp. 39–66, at p. 45.

[10] McAuliffe describes his hermeneutical approach in 'Quranic Hermeneutics: The Views of al-Ṭabarī and Ibn Kathīr', pp. 56–8.

truly a reference to teachers and students, rather than men and women. In this case the *ẓāhir* law supports the norms of society, while the deeper esoteric interpretation relates to the spiritual hierarchy in Fāṭimid Ismāʿīlī doctrine. The existence of this interpretation outside of the genre raises the question of what other interpretations were omitted from the genre of *tafsīr*, and why. I would suggest that the contents of these works was affected by the particular regional, and to a lesser extent legal, affiliations of the authors of *tafsīr* from its emergence as a genre through the classical period.

From the earliest period, the authorities in *tafsīr* centred in Khurāsān, as has been well-documented in several articles by Claude Gilliot. By the classical period, Khurāsān, and particularly Nīshāpūr, was the main centre of exegetical activity in the Islamic East – with a smaller rival centre later emerging in Islamic Spain; this latter centre focused mostly on works of *aḥkām al-Qur'ān* written by Māikī authors. In order to assess the geographical concentration of exegeses in the post-Ṭabarī period, I have plotted the main locations of the authors of *tafsīr* (not including authors of grammar or *fiqh*, but including works of *aḥkām al-Qur'ān*) on two maps. Figure C.1, 'Production of *Tafsīr*, 4th/10th century–6th/12th century', shows that there was a remarkable geographical concentration of exegetes in the immediate post-Ṭabarī period around Nīshāpūr and in Khurāsān more generally, particularly in the period from al-ʿAyyāshī (d. c. 320/932) to Abū' l-Futūḥ-i Rāzī (d. 525/1131). Eight of the fourteen authors in this period either lived in Nīshāpūr or stayed there for some time. Other authors lived nearby: in Herat, Rayy, Mashhad, Maybud, or farther East in Samarqand. Only three authors, al-Jaṣṣāṣ, al-Māwardī, and al-Ṭūsī lived in Baghdad, and they also spent significant periods in or around Nīshāpūr. This selection of authors does not represent every extant *tafsīr* from the period under consideration, and this map cannot show the travels of those who are represented; but it does consist of a broad cross section of the most prominent works from the post-Ṭabarī period, and indicates the authors' main base (or bases) of activity. *Tafsīr* in this period was a strikingly Khūrāsānī–Nīshāpūrī activity.

However, no less striking is that after Abū 'l-Futūḥ-i Rāzī (no. 14 on the map), there is no further activity in Nīshāpūr itself.[11] Around the same time, al-Andalus emerges as a rival centre for Mālikī works of Aḥkām al-Qur'ān, home of exegetes Ibn al-ʿArabī (no. 16) and Ibn ʿAṭiyya

[11] This should be verified by checking all scholars' travels: it could be that authors of exegesis still visited Nīshāpūr, although they did not live there.

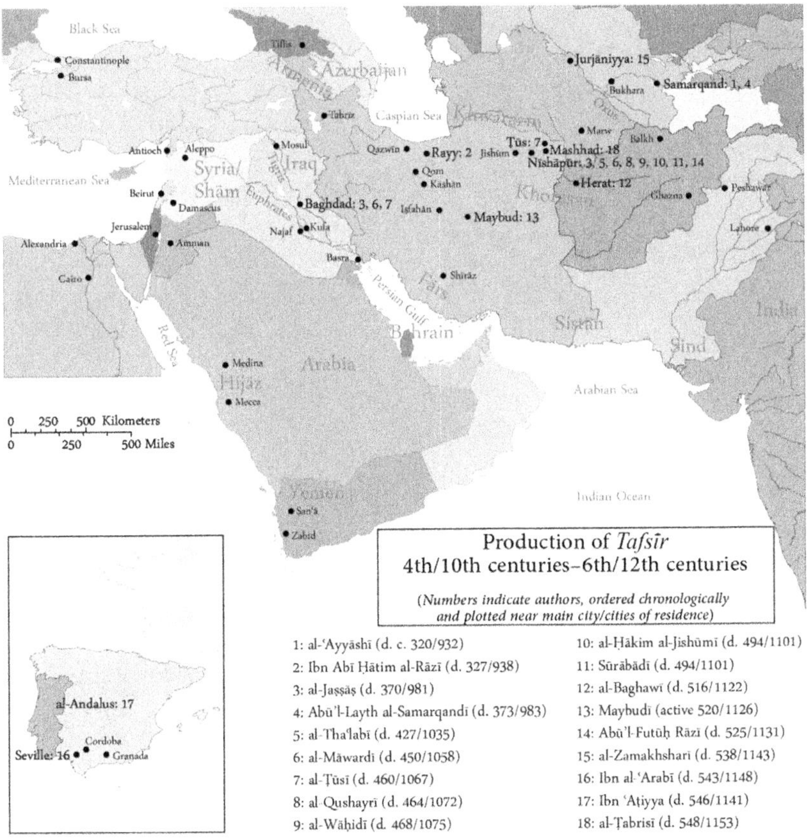

FIGURE C.1: Production of *Tafsīr*, 4th/10th century–6th/12th century

(no. 17). The dramatic decentralisation of the activity of exegesis from the middle of the 6th/12th century is clearly seen when one considers the second map, Figure C.2, showing the location of exegetes in the 7th/13th centuries–12th/18th centuries. In this period, exegetes are scattered from Zabīd in Yemen to Cairo, Damascus, Cordoba, Granada, India, and Constantinople. The broad geographical trends mapped here suggest that the genre of *tafsīr* in the classical period should, perhaps, be considered as a regional phenomenon.[12] In the 4th/10th–6th/12th centuries, *tafsīr* is not something that belonged to the Fāṭimid hub of Cairo, or the ʿAbbasīd

[12] This observation builds, of course, on the seminal work undertaken by Claude Gilliot, who was the first to observe that Khurāsān was an important centre of exegetical activity.

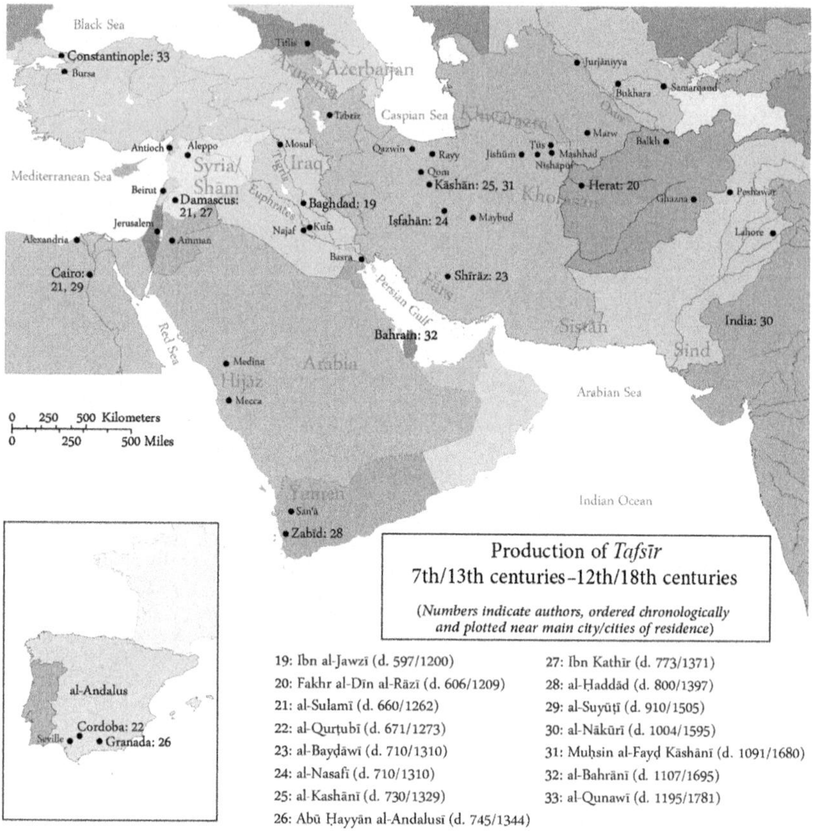

FIGURE C.2: Production of *Tafsīr*, 7th/13th century–12th/18th century

administrative centre of Baghdād, nor to the cities renowned as centres of variant readings, or variant legal interpretations. In short, *tafsīr* was not something done predominantly by Arabs. It was, rather, very much a Persian venture. Only in the mid-6th/12th century did it become mainstream elsewhere.

The regional element of *tafsīr* is all the more evident when one considers the range of legal schools involved in the venture. As depicted in Figure C.3, one-third of the classical and post-classical authors in this study were Shāfiʿī: eleven of thirty-three authors. Eight of the authors were Imāmī, seven were Ḥanafī, four Mālikī, and a mere two were Ḥanbalīs. The first Ḥanafīs in the study were both jurists: al-Jaṣṣāṣ and Abū' l-Layth al-Samarqandī; they were not known primarily as exegetes.

	Shāfiʿī	Imāmī	Ḥanafī	Mālikī	Ḥanbalī
4th/10th	1	1	2		
5th/11th	4	1	1		
6th/12th	1	2	1	2	2
7th/13th	2			1	
8th/14th	2		1	1	
9th/15th			1		
10th/16th	1				
11th/17th		2			
12th/18th		1	1		

FIGURE C.3: Exegetes' Legal Schools over Time

Particularly in the 5th/11th century, exegesis became largely associated with the Shāfiʿī school.

It may well be that the regional character of the venture of *tafsīr* to some extent determined its legal character, as the Shāfiʿī and later the Imāmī legal schools were dominant in Iran. The distribution through time shows that there was a clear peak in exegesis in the 6th/12th century, with all exegetical activity tailing off somewhat subsequently, and a definite lull in the 10th/16th century. That 6th/12th century peak followed the 5th/11th century peak in Shāfiʿī exegetes; subsequently, with the decrease in output by scholars of other schools there was a much smaller peak in Imāmī exegeses in the 11th–12th/17th–18th centuries, coinciding with the rise of the *Akhbārī* school of interpretation.

I would posit that the Nīshāpūrī school of *tafsīr*,[13] and to a lesser extent the Shāfiʿī law school, defined what it was to write a work of exegesis in the classical period, and that their output shaped much of what was to come thereafter. Recognising the underlying Khūrasānī–Shāfiʿī character of *tafsīr* as a genre might explain a number of points that impact on discussions of women's and men's rights within the genre. The Shāfiʿī flavour and Khūrāsānī locale of the genre might explain why, for instance, the esoteric interpretation of the Cairo-based author al-Muʿayyad never found its way into mainstream *tafsīr*, or why Imāmī

[13] I am using the term 'school' here in its broadest sense, to include all authors active in Nīshāpūr.

Shī'īs from Khūrāsān at the time of its Shāfi'ī peak, such as al-Ṭūsī and al-Ṭabrisī, echo its main Sunnī voices so strongly. Imāmī *tafsīr* came into its own with the much later *Akhbārī* works by authors such as Muḥsin al-Fayḍ al-Kāshānī and al-Baḥrānī. That classical *tafsīr* of the Islamic East was by and large the domain of the Shāfi'īs might go some way towards explaining why there were so few Ḥanafī scholars of *tafsīr* in the classical period, as opposed to law, which was dominated by the Ḥanafīs. The bias towards Shāfi'ī law in the genre had effects for the discourse on women, since the Shāfi'ī school opposed women's testimony in more cases than the Ḥanafī school.

While these findings are preliminary, I would suggest that they are nevertheless exciting in terms of their possible implications for the study of the genre as a whole.

GENDER DISCOURSES IN THE MODERN CONTEXT

Social, political, and intellectual contexts also deeply affect the writing of modern works, and particularly modern interpretations of gender. In the modern rhetoric within the Middle East and Iran, the issue of women has become a dividing line between the 'Western' way and the 'Eastern', and certain types of interpretation are portrayed as both culturally and religiously authentic. Yet global currents of thought have affected both reformists and conservatives, in different but interconnected ways. In addition to their own, indigenous discourses, reformists draw on global currents of rationalism, enlightenment thought, and more recently human rights legislation, and conservatives draw on religious fundamentalist answers to such rationalism emerging from the West. There is no denying the power of modern ethical considerations influenced by liberal ideals: all interpreters refer to equality to explain and justify their views, even if to refute the notion.

The interpreters' incorporation of global trends is apparent in their widespread references to science. To justify and explain legal differences between the sexes, conservatives such as Dr 'Alasvand and Mr Zibaei Nejad referred to brain science, Grand Ayatollah Makarim Shirazi cited statistics and 'common knowledge' about human nature, Muḥammad Sa'īd Ramaḍān al-Būṭī spoke of findings in psychology and medicine, and al-Ḥuwayzī referred to the weight of men's and women's brains. Reformists cited science to make a different point: Grand Ayatollah Saanei spoke about the scientific proof of the mental equality of men and women, and also based his judgment on their similar abilities to see, hear, and reason, while other reformists drew on theories of evolution. Modern scholars' references to science in some ways echo the use of physical and natural proofs in medieval interpretations, such as the notion that men are hot and dry, while women are moist and cold. Pre-modern *'ulamā'* cited such natural proofs to bolster their worldview, in the process of which they revealed their own presuppositions. In the modern period 'science' has, in some ways, become a new type of tradition to draw upon and be interpreted.

The parallel between science and tradition is clear when one considers the status that science has acquired as a rhetorical device. Brought in selectively to prove the truth of revelation, science performs the function of an objective witness to the innate correctness and naturalness of religious laws. Such arbitrary uses of science are common everywhere, as indicated by popular science books such as that by Allan and Barbara Pease, and in that sense the attitude of the *'ulamā'* is merely an indication of a global trend, with many commonalities between conservative movements in West and East. Popular science often reflects the widespread (but usually inaccurate) notion that objective measures can and do prove common sense. It was not the scientific method, but rather the idea of science as an objective witness that became global, and affected Qur'ānic hermeneutics as well as other areas of thought. Yet when it is used in this way, science is not objective, but is as subjective as tradition.

Just as the *'ulamā'* draw on tradition in ways that both resist and yet are defined by current sociopolitical realities, so too this attitude towards science is partially the product of social and historical circumstances. The reception of Darwin's ideas in Egypt was closely tied to the Arabic *nahḍa*, the movement of 'awakening' that seized the Arab world in the wake of the colonial encounter. Debates about the compatibility of evolution and religious ideals took place among the small numbers of the well-educated elites: literacy in Egypt was 5.8 per cent in 1897.[14] With the 20th-century rise in literacy, Darwin lost his appeal.[15]

According to some analyses, the *nahḍa* was not a movement of Arab chauvinism; instead, it was a co-opting of Western power and knowledge, undertaken by a narrow elite, which 'would enable the recovery of past glory'.[16] Yet popular works about women that were written in the late 19th century show that there was a much wider discourse responding to

[14] Marwa Elshakry, *Reading Darwin in Arabic*, p. 22.
[15] Ibid., p. 23. [16] Ibid.

Western liberalism and the colonial encounter by claiming that women's rights were culturally indigenous – that, for instance, Egypitian women had been liberated since Pharaonic times and had only recently come to be oppressed.[17] This reveals a *nahḍa* that was also nationalistic and responsive to popular concerns.

It is in this context that ʿAbduh's *tafsīr* represented a turning point in the way *tafsīr* was written and in the themes covered there. Responding to the 'West' and Western ideas of womanhood was of particular importance to him. In ʿAbduh's *tafsīr*, references to 'the West' and Western liberal ideals such as equality took the form of a conversation that he reported between himself and a Western visitor to the mosque, who was amazed to find women there. ʿAbduh in turn used this incident to warn his fellow Muslims to treat women with respect.

While ʿAbduh introduced an element of reinterpretability into the genre, after him the genre of *tafsīr* remained conservative; it became a venue in which traditional interpretations were replicated with new justifications. Yet it was not a genre immune from change, and the manner in which the exegetes considered gender was as modern as it was traditional. While post-ʿAbduh authors rejected the theory of evolution, which ʿAbduh had embraced, they began to incorporate references to egalitarianism and women's human worth that he had introduced into the genre. Authors after ʿAbduh had a no less complicated relationship with ideals such as feminism, which were widely associated with the West. The subject of women's rights became a point on which to express cultural and religious authenticity, and the ambivalence felt by many in society towards the West is reflected in the way that women's rights are treated in works of *tafsīr*.

Although post-ʿAbduh authors of *tafsīr* refer to the spiritual and human equality between men and women, on the whole they argue against any notion of legal equality. To bolster their claims that equality is a myth, they cite Western sources such as the Napoleonic Code of France. Yet in turn their protestations against equality may have been a conservative response, written in a conservative genre, to an increasingly liberal population in the Middle East of the 1950s, 1960s, and early 1970s. With the rise of political Islamism since then, and the concurrent rise of fundamentalist Christian political movements in the West, the pendulum has swung back. Now Western conservative writings, such as

[17] Booth, 'Before Qasim Amin'.

those of Laura Schlessinger, are appropriated by conservative clerics in the Middle East. And, although conservatives overtly reject liberal ideas, the very ideas that they reject are fundamental to their worldview.[18]

While the question of West versus East was a crucial focal point during the Arab *nahḍa* and the constitutional movement in Iran, more recent examples highlight the ways in which local and regional politics have also had a profound effect on the way that women's roles are described by the *ʿulamāʾ*. How can we explain, for instance, why reformists in Iran argue for complete gender equality, while those in Syria are more modest in their ambitions, and often resemble conservatives on gender questions? I would suggest that the Syrian trends in interpretation are deeply connected not just to a textual tradition, but also to current sociopolitical realities: the restrained nature of reformist interpretation by *ʿulamāʾ* in Syria when I visited in 2004 may be due to the undercurrent of Salafism there. Salafism is the main threat to the moderate range of interpretations preached by Hudā al-Ḥabash, Muḥammad al-Ḥabash, and Saʿīd Ramaḍan al-Būṭī. Rather than arguing for absolute equality, Syrian reformists were arguing against absolute inequality; rather than arguing for radical change to the tradition, they were arguing against a radical circumscribing of the tradition. While al-Būṭī and Muḥammad al-Ḥabash seemed to be at opposite ends of the interpretative spectrum (one being conservative and the other reformist), both were moderates, and they may each have been supported at different times by the secular Baʿthist Syrian government. It would have been in the government's interests to side with moderate *ʿulamāʾ*, whether reformist or conservative, against the Salafi influence; in turn, governmental support may have increased the prominence of these *ʿulamāʾ*. In this way, the prominence of particular interpreters and their interpretations, and therefore the parameters of the debates on women's status, is bound up in particular social, political, and intellectual contexts.

The Syrian example highlights the importance of taking into account audience and context when assessing the nature of interpretations, and particularly in trying to ascertain why certain interpretations are propagated by the majority of *ʿulamāʾ*, while others are marginalised. As this book has shown, both conservatives and reformists use new methods and approaches when interpreting the Qurʾān, and both pick and choose from tradition in important ways. But, in Damascus, conservatives are

[18] Marilyn Booth, 'Islamic Politics, Street Literature, and John Stewart Mill: Composing Gendered Ideals in 1990s Egypt' *Feminist Studies* 39.3 (2013): pp. 596–626, at p. 598.

undoubtedly viewed as more culturally authentic. This may be because of the popular perception that the conservative interpretation is a direct representation of medieval interpretations, and that such interpretations in turn represent the 'true' interpretation of Islam as both a cultural and religious phenomenon. Furthermore, the *'ulamā'* on the whole are a conservative group of people, particularly those *'ulamā'* who have received a traditional education, such as the ones I interviewed for this book.

The resonance of the conservative interpretations raises the question of the influence of the Qur'ān itself, and the medieval tradition, on conservative religious culture. Perhaps the most obvious argument for the popularity of conservative interpretations among the *'ulamā'* is that such readings often accord with the plain-sense reading of the Qur'ān's text and the basic thrust of certain elements of the medieval interpretative tradition. Modern conservatives have jettisoned unpalatable aspects of the pre-modern tradition: they no longer say that women are inferior, and use an almost entirely new set of justifications to explain the gender hierarchy. But they have retained a certain core: particular rulings that have been modified, but preserved in spirit (such as beating a wife lightly, or not allowing women to testify equally to men in court). Thus, perhaps it could be said that the Qur'ān and medieval tradition have influenced conservative religious society, notions of right and wrong, and correct interpretation. But the words of the text and tradition are never an absolute determinant of the nature of later interpretation: even conservatives radically reinterpret in a case such as the creation of Eve, which went from a story of ultimate inequality to one of ultimate equality. And the popular turn towards conservatism in recent decades may again be a reaction to the failed projects of liberalism and leftism in the 20th-century Middle East. As secular regimes proved to be corrupt and more allied with their own self-interests than the interests of the people, 'authentic' traditional interpretations became increasingly appealing to the disillusioned populace. The widespread impact of Salafism and well-funded educational programmes emerging from Saudi Arabia may have swung the whole Sunnī world to the right. And the very regimes that claimed to be secular often vehemently oppressed the secular opposition. A viable secular opposition would have been a greater threat to them than the Islamist opposition, which was often tacitly allowed and even fostered. Therefore, although it cannot be denied that conservative readings often agree, to some extent, with the plain sense of the Qur'ān, this is not the only, and may not be the main, reason for their current popularity.

Reformist *'ulamā'*, although in the minority, take a more self-aware and sophisticated approach to the text. They acknowledge that interpretation inevitably changes through time, and are well aware that social, cultural, and political circumstances influence the interpretation of texts. By acknowledging the impact of context on interpretation, they do not restrict the 'authentic' religious expression to one set of cultural practices, or to one reading of the text. But because they are *'ulamā'*, reformists still acknowledge the plain sense of the text, and the plain sense of the medieval interpretative tradition. The text, then, holds sway over them as well. And perhaps this agency that is granted to the text and medieval heritage is the defining feature of the *'ulamā'* as opposed to other groups of interpreters.

I would like to end with a few words on the function of gender in the sources for this study. In their descriptions of the gender hierarchy, both medieval and modern sources are constructing the categories of 'man' and 'woman' in particular ways that speak to their social, historical, and political circumstances. The medieval notion of manhood was epitomised in the person of the just ruler. Men, who had a type of guardianship over their wives, were supposed to enact the role of the just ruler, and wives, that of the obedient subject. Masculinity is therefore coded to include the attributes of justice, fairness, wisdom, and so forth, and is inscribed linguistically as well as physically in the many meanings of the root *r-j-l*. Some jurists explain that the paucity of these qualities is why women cannot hold positions of authority as leaders of the community, leaders of prayer, or judges. For Shī'īs, the ultimate just ruler is the Imām, and in Ismā'īlī writings, the gender implications of his headship of the community are brought to the fore: the male or female student is gendered as female, and the teacher as male. This continues up the hierarchy, with a person rising through the ranks being now female, now male (or a male to some members of the hierarchy and a female to others), until the highest rank, that of Imām, who can only be a man. In both Sunnī and Imāmī texts, the husband is the arbiter of his wife's salvation: she attains salvation through obedience to his authority. Authority itself, in both temporal and spiritual realms, is portrayed as inherently masculine. In medieval sources, the correct functioning of society hinged on these hierarchies, and upsetting them was akin to upsetting the natural, divinely ordained order between the sexes.

When male authors wrote about women, even when they wrote about women's liberation, women were still the subjects of the writing, not the active party in their own liberation. These texts were written primarily for male audiences.[19] Thus, although the idea of 'woman' is today a central metaphor for cultural authenticity and nationhood, women's own voices have remained marginalised.[20] However, in the 20th century, women themselves began to write works of *tafsīr*, and to participate as *ʿālima*s in the formation of this gendered discourse. On the whole, these women do not question the patriarchal assumptions of the dominant gender narrative, and it is important to pay attention to their words. They do not wish to challenge widespread interpretations, and they support the gender hierarchy. Yet might these women be shifting the discursive field subtly, through their very presence as interlocutors in the debate?

Throughout Islamic history, learned women taught men *ḥadīth*s: to name but one example, the famous 16th-century polymath al-Suyuṭī counted many women among his teachers. Thus, when today's women teach only other women (as do the vast majority), it is in some ways a step away from the status that their medieval counterparts enjoyed: their confinement within solely homosocial spaces makes it less likely that they will be recognised as authoritative sources of opinion for both men and women. These women have authority over other women, but men have authority over both men and women, and thus the final authority, as in the case of the Ismāʿīlī Imām, will always be male. In this way, limiting women's authority solely to other women serves to reify male dominance, and to reinforce the notion that ultimately authority is, by its nature, masculine. But some conservative women, like Fariba ʿAlasvand, do not restrict their activities solely to women's groups. Dr ʿAlasvand supports the gender hierarchy in both public and private spheres, saying that wives should be obedient to husbands, and that women should not testify equally to men in court. But that hierarchy does not necessarily extend to the realm of learning: both men and women can attain high levels of knowledge. By authoring her own texts and interpretations, by participating in gatherings with men and giving opinions that have been recognised by Grand Ayatollahs, and by teaching men 'when there is a preference and necessity' to do so,[21] Dr ʿAlasvand is entering into the male-dominated hierarchy,

[19] Booth, 'Before Qasim Amin'.

[20] On this point, see especially the work of Marilyn Booth and Afsaneh Najmabadi.

[21] Fariba ʿAlasvand, Personal Email Communication, 10 July 2014, told me 'yes, we predominantly teach women, except when there is a preference and necessity we teach men'.

which she so strongly supports. It remains to be seen whether the existence of ʿ*alima*s as recognised leaders for both women and men, who interpret the Qurʾān for both male and female believers, might, by their very presence, shift the widespread understanding of the inherent masculinity of traditional religious authority.

Works Cited

Primary Sources

ʿAbd al-Razzāq Ibn Ḥammām al-Ṣanʿānī, *Tafsīr ʿAbd al-Razzāq*. Ed. Maḥmūd Muḥammad ʿAbduh. Beirut: Dār al-Kutub al-ʿIlmiyya, 1999.

ʿAbduh, Muḥammad, and Rashīd Riḍā. *Tafsīr al-Qurʾān al-ʿaẓīm, al-maʿrūf bi-Tafsīr al-manār*. Ed. Samīr Muṣṭafā Rabāb. Beirut: Dār Iḥyāʾ al-Turāth al-ʿArabī, 2002.

Abī Dawūd al-Sijistānī. *Sunan*, in *Mawsūʿat al-ḥadīth al-Sharīf: al-kitāb al-sitta: Saḥīḥ al-Bukhārī, Saḥīḥ Muslim, Sunan Abī Dawūd, Jāmiʿ al-Tirmidhī, Sunan al-Nasāʾī, Sunan Ibn Mājah*. Ed. Sāliḥ b. ʿAbd al-ʿAzīz Āl al-Shaykh. Riyadh: Dār al-Salām lil-nashr wa'l-tawzīʿ, 1999.

Abū 'l-Fayḍ Ibn Mubārak. *Sawāṭiʿ al-ilhām fī tafsīr kalām Malik al-ʿallām*. Ed. Murtaḍa al-Shīrāzī. Iran: M. Shīrāzī, 1996.

Abū Ḥayyān al-Gharnātī al-Andalusī, Muḥammad b. Yūsuf. *Al-Baḥr al-Muḥīṭ*. Ed. ʿĀdil Aḥmad ʿAbd al-Mawjūd et al. Beirut: Dār al-Kutub al-ʿIlmīya, 1993.

Abū 'l-Layth al-Samarqandī, Naṣr b. Muḥammad. *Tafsīr al-Samarqandī al-Musammā Baḥr al-ʿUlūm*. Ed. ʿAlī Muḥammad Muʿawwaḍ, ʿĀdil Aḥmad ʿAbd al-Mawjūd, and Zakarīyā ʿAbd al-Majīd al-Nūtī. Beirut: Dār al-Kutub al-ʿIlmiyya, 1993.

Abū Zayd, Naṣr Hāmid, and Esther Nelson. *Voice of an Exile: Reflections on Islam*. Westport, CT: Praeger Publishers, 2004.

ʿAlasvand, Fariba. *Naqd konvansiyūn rafʿ kuliyya-i ashkāl tabaʿyiḍ ʿalayhi zanān*. Qom: Markaz-i Mudīrīyat Ḥawzah-yi ʿIlmīya, 1382/2004.

ʿAlī ibn Abī Ṭalḥa. *Ṣaḥīfat ʿAlī b. Abī Ṭalḥa ʿan Ibn ʿAbbās fī tafsīr al-Qurʾān*. Compiled and edited by Rashīd ʿAbd al-Munʿīm al-Rajjāl. Cairo: Maktabat al-Sunna, 1991.

ʿAlī b. Abī Ṭālib (attrib.). *Nahj al-balāgha ṭabʿa jadīda munaqqaḥa bimakhṭūṭa al-iskorīyal, jamʿahu wa nassaqa abwābahu al-Sharīf al-Rāḍī*. Ed. ʿAbd Allāh Anīs al-Ṭabbāʿ and Muḥammad Anīs al-Ṭabbāʿ. Beirut: Muʾassasat al-Maʿārif, 2004.

al-Ālūsī, Shihāb al-Dīn Maḥmūd. *Rūḥ al-ma'ānī fī tafsīr al-Qur'ān al-'aẓīm wa'l-saba' mathānī*. Beirut: Dār al-Qawmiyya al-'Arabiyya Lil-Ṭiba'a, n.d.

al-'Askarī (attrib.). *Tafsīr al-Imām Abī Muḥammad al-Ḥasan b. 'Alī al-'Askarī*. Ed. 'Alī Āshūr. Beirut: Dār Iḥyā' al-Turāth al-'Arabī, 2001.

al-'Ayyāshī. *al-Tafsīr*. Department of Islamic Studies, Mu'assasat al-Ba'tha. Qom: Mu'assasat Ba'tha, 2000.

al-Baghawī, al-Ḥusayn b. Mas'ūd al-Farrā'. *Tafsīr al-Baghawī: ma'ālim al-tanzīl*. Ed. Muḥammad 'Abd Allāh al-Nimr. Riyadh: Dār Ṭayba, 1993.

al-Baḥrānī, Hāshim Ḥussaynī b. Sulaymān. *Al-Burhān fī tafsīr al-Qur'ān*. Ed. Qism Dirasāt al-Islāmiyya, Mu'assasat al-Bi'tha. Qom: Mu'assasat al-Bi'tha, 1994.

al-Bayḍāwī and 'Iṣām al-Dīn Ismā'īl b. Muḥammad al-Qūnawī, *Ḥāshīyat al-Qūnawī 'alā tafsīr al-Imām al-Bayḍāwī*. Ed. 'Abd Alāh Maḥmūd Muḥammad 'Umar. Beirut: Dār al-Kutub al-'Ilmiyya, 2001.

al-Bukhārī. *Saḥīḥ*, in *Mawsū'at al-ḥadīth al-Sharīf: al-kitāb al-sitta: Saḥīḥ al-Bukhārī, Saḥīḥ Muslim, Sunan Abī Dawūd, Jāmi' al-Tirmidhī, Sunan al-Nasā'ī, Sunan Ibn Mājah*. Ed. Sāliḥ b. 'Abd al-'Azīz Āl al-Shaykh. Riyadh: Dār al-Salām lil-nashr wa'l-tawzī', 1999.

al-Būṭī, Muḥammad Sa'īd Ramaḍān. *Women: Between the Tyranny of the Western System and the Mercy of Islamic Law*. Tr. Nancy Roberts. Damascus: Dār al-Fikr, 2003.

Al-Ḍaḥḥāk (attrib.), *Tafsīr al-Ḍaḥḥāk*. Compiled and edited by Muḥammad Shukrī Aḥmad Zāwītī. Cairo: Dār al-Salām, 1999.

al-Durra, Muḥammad 'Alī Ṭāhā. *Tafsīr al-Qur'ān al-karīm wa-i'rābuhu wa-bayyānuh*. Damascus: Dār al-Ḥikma, 1982.

al-Farrā', Yaḥyā b. Ziyād. *Ma'ānī al-Qur'ān*. Ed. Aḥmad Yūsuf Najātī and Muḥammad 'Alī al-Najjār. Cairo: al-Hay'a al-Miṣriyya al-'Āmma lil-Kitāb, 1980.

Fayḍ al-Kashānī, Muḥsin. *Kitāb al-ṣāfī fī tafsīr al-Qur'ān*. Ed. Muḥsin al-Ḥusaynī al-Amīnī. Tehran: Dār al-Kutub al-'Ilmīya, 1998.

al-Ḥaddād, Fakhr al-Dīn. *Tafsīr al-Ḥaddād*. Ed. Muḥammad Ibrāhīm Yaḥyā. Beirut: Dār al-Madār al-Islāmī, 2001.

Ḥawwā, Sa'īd. *al-Asās fī' l-tafsīr*. Beirut: Dār al-Salām lil-Ṭabā'ī wa'l-Nashr wa'l-Tawzī', 1975.

al-Ḥijāzī, Muḥammad Maḥmūd. *Tafsīr al-wādiḥ*. Cairo: Maṭba'at al-Istiqlāl al-Kubrā, 1962–9.

Hūd b. Muḥakkam al-Hawwārī. *Tafsīr Hūd b. Muḥakkam al-Hawwārī*. Ed. al-Ḥājj b. Sa'īd al-Sharīfī. Beirut: Dār al-Gharb al-Islāmī, 1990.

Ibn Abī Ḥātim al-Rāzī, 'Abd al-Raḥman Muḥammad. *Tafsīr al-Qur'ān al-'Aẓīm*. Ed. As'ad Muḥammad al-Ṭayyib, Mecca: Maktabat Nizār Muṣṭafā al-Bāz, 1999.

Ibn al-'Arabī, Muḥammad b. 'Abd Allāh Abū Bakr. *Aḥkām al-Qur'ān*. Ed. 'Alī Muḥammad al-Bajawī. [Cairo]: 'Īsā al-Bābī al-Ḥalabī, 1967.

Ibn Āshūr, Muḥammad al-Ṭāhir. *Tafsīr al-taḥrīr wa'l-tanwīr*. Tunisia: al-Dār al-Tunisiyya lil-Nashr, [1900?].

Ibn 'Aṭiyya, *al-Muḥarrar al-wajīz*. Ed. 'Abd al-Salām 'Abd al-Shāfī Muḥammad. Beirut: Dār al-Kutub al-'Ilmiyya, 1993–5.

Ibn al-Jawzī, Abū' l-Faraj. *Zād al-masīr fī 'ilm al-tafsīr*. [No editor listed.] Beirut: al-Maktab al-Islāmī, 1964–8.

Ibn Kathīr. *Tafsīr al-Qur'ān al-'aẓīm*. Ed. Muṣṭafā al-Sayyid Muḥammad et al. Cairo: Mu'assasat Qurṭuba, 2000.

Ibn Māja. *Sunan*, in *Mawsū'at al-ḥadīth al-Sharīf: al-kitāb al-sitta: Saḥīḥ al-Bukhārī, Saḥīḥ Muslim, Sunan Abī Dawūd, Jāmi' al-Tirmidhī, Sunan al-Nasā'ī, Sunan Ibn Mājah*. Ed. Sāliḥ b. 'Abd al-'Azīz Āl al-Shaykh. Riyadh: Dār al-Salām lil-nashr wa'l-tawzī', 1999.

Ibn al-Nadīm. *Fihrist*. Tr. Bayard Dodge *as The Fihrist of al-Nadim*. New York: Columbia University Press, 1970.

Ibn Qayyim al-Jawziyya, Shams al-Dīn Abū 'Abd Allāh. *I'lām al-muwaqqai'īn 'an rabb al-'Ālimin*. Ed. Ṭaha 'Abd al-Ra'ūf Sa'd. Cairo: Maktabat al-Kuliyyāt al-Azhār, n.d.

al-Daw' al-munīr 'alā al-tafsīr. Compiled and edited by 'Alī b. Ḥamad b. Muḥammad al-Ṣāliḥī. Riyadh: Mu'assasat al-Nūr/Maktabat Dār al-Salām, 1999.

Ibn Qudāma, Abū Muḥammad 'Abd Allāh. *al-Mughnī*. Ed. Mahmūd 'Abd al-Wahhāb Fāyid. Cairo: Maktabat al-Qāhira, 1968.

Ibn Taymiyya, *Muqaddima fī 'uṣūl al-tafsīr*. [No named editor.] Kuwait: Dār al-Qur'ān al-Karīm, 1971.

Ibn Wahb al-Dīnawarī (attrib.). *Tafsīr ibn Wahb al-musamma al-wāḍiḥ fī tafsīr al-Qur'ān*. Ed. Aḥmad Farīd. Beirut: Dār al-Kutub al-'Ilmiyya, 2003.

al-Jaṣṣāṣ, Aḥmad b. 'Alī Abū Bakr. *Aḥkām al-Qur'ān*. Ed. 'Abd al-Raḥmān Muḥammad. Cairo: al-Maṭba'a al-Bahiyya al-Miṣriyya, 1928 (1347).

Javadi Amoli, Abd Allah. *Tasnīm tafsīr al-Qur'ān al-karīm*. Ed. Muḥammad Ḥusayn Alhā Zādeh. Qom: Markaz Nashr Asrā', 2007.

al-Jishumī, al-Ḥākim. *Tahdhīb*. MS Maktabat Muḥammad Qāsim al-Hāshimī. Private Library, Raḥbān, Sa'da.

Pseudo-Jonathan. *Targum Pseudo-Jonathan, Genesis*. Trans. Michael Maher. Collegeville, MN: The Liturgical Press, 1992.

Karamī, Muḥammad. *Al-Tafsīr li-kitāb Allāh al-munīr*. Qom: Al-Matba'a al-'Ilmiyya, 1982.

Kāshānī, 'Abd al-Razzāq (attrib. Ibn 'Arabī). *Tafsīr al-Qur'ān al-karīm lil-shaykh al-akbar ... Muhyī al-Dīn Ibn 'Arabī*. Beirut: Dar al-Yaqẓa al-'Arabīya, 1968.

Maghniyya, Muḥammad Jawād. *Tafsīr al-kāshif*. Beirut: Dār al-Malāyīn, 1968.

Mālik ibn Anas, *al-Muwaṭṭā'*. [No named editor.] Lichtenstein: Thesaurus Islamicus Foundation, 2000.

al-Māwardī, Abū 'l-Hasan. *al-Nukat wa'l-'ūyūn*. Ed. Sayyid b. 'Abd al-Maqṣūr b. 'Abd al-Rahīm. Beirut: Dār al-Kutub al-'Ilmiyya, 1992.

Al-Mawsū'a al-Fiqhiyya. [No named author or editor.] Kuwait: Wizārat al-Awqāf wa'l-shu'ūn al-Islāmiyya, 1992.

Maybudī, Rashīd al-Dīn Abū 'l-Faḍl. *Kanz al-anwār fī kashf al-asrār*. Ed. Muḥammad Kāẓim Busayrī. Qom: Daftar Nashr al-Hādī, 2001.

Mehrizi, Mehdi. *Mas'alat al-mar'a: dirāsāt fī tajdīd al-fikr al-dīnī fī qaḍiyyat al-mar'a*. Tr. (into Arabic from Persian) *'Alī Mūsawī*. Beirut: Markaz al-Ḥaḍāra li-Tanmiya Fikr al-Islāmī, 2008.

Midrash Rabbah, Genesis. v. 1. Trans. Rabbi Dr H. Freedman. London: Soncinco Press, 1961.

Mu'ayyad al-Dīn al-Shīrāzī. *al-Majālis al-Mu'ayyadiyya.* Ed. Ḥātim Ḥamīd al-Dīn. 2nd edn., Mumbai: Leaders Press Private Ltd., 2002.

Muqātil b. Sulaymān. *Tafsīr Muqātil b. Sulaymān.* Ed. 'Abd Allāh Muḥammad Shihāta. Cairo: al-Hay'a al-Miṣriyya al-'Āmma lil-Kitāb, 1979.

al-Naḥḥās, Abū Ja'far. *Ma'ānī al-Qur'ān.* Ed. Muḥammad 'Alī al-Ṣābūnī. Mecca: Umm Qurā University Press, 1988.

al-Najafī, Muḥammad Javād Balāghī. *'Alā' al-raḥmān fī tafsīr al-Qur'ān.* Qom: Maktabat al-Wijdān, 1971.

al-Nakūrī, Abū'l-Fayḍ, *Sawāṭi' al-ilhām fī tafsīr kalām Malik al-'allām*, Ed. Murtaḍā al-Shīrāzī, 1996).

al-Nasafī, 'Abd Allāh b. Aḥmad. *Tafsīr al-Nasafī.* Ed. Marwān Muḥammad al-Sha'ār. Beirut: Dār Nafā'is, 1996.

Nu'mān b. Muḥammad, known as al-Qāḍī al-Nu'mān. *Asās al-Ta'wīl.* Ed. Arif Tamer. Beirut: Dār al-Thaqāfa, 1960.

Da'ā'im al-Islām wa-dhakir al-ḥalāl wa'l-ḥarām wa'l-qaḍāya wa'l-aḥkām. Ed. Āṣif 'A. A. Fayḍī. Beirut: Dār al-Aḍwa', n.d.

Mukhtaṣar al-āthār lil–Dā'ī al-Ajall sayyidnā al-Qāḍī al-Nu'mān b. Muḥammad. [No named editor.] Surat, India: al-Jamī'a al-Sayfiyya, 2004) [1425 a.h.].

Pease, Allan and Barbara. *Why Men Don't Listen & Women Can't Read Maps.* London: Orion, 1999.

al-Qummī, 'Alī b. Ibrāhīm. *Tafsīr al-Qummī.* Ed. al-Ṭayyib al-Musawī al-Jazā'irī. Najaf: Maṭbar'at al-Najaf, 1996.

al-Qurṭubī, Abū 'Abd Allāh Muḥammad b. Aḥmad. *al-Jāmi' li-aḥkām al-Qur'ān.* Cairo: Dār al-Kātib al-'Arabī, 1967.

al-Qushayrī, Abū 'l Qāsim 'Abd al-Karīm. *Laṭā'if al-ishārāt, tafsīr ṣūfī lil-Qur'ān al-Karīm.* Ed. Ibrāhīm Basyūnī. Cairo: Dār al-Kātib al-'Arabī lil-Ṭibā'a wa'l-Nashr, [1968].

Quṭb, Sayyid. *Fī ẓilāl al-Qur'ān.* Beirut: Dār al-Sharq, 2007.

al-Rāzī, Fakhr al-Dīn. *al-Tafsīr al-Kabīr.* Ed. 'Abd al-Raḥmān Muḥammad. Cairo: Maṭba'at al-Bahīya, 1938.

Saanei, Fakhr al-Din. *Shahādat al-mar'a fī' l-Islām qirā'a fiqhiyya, 'arḍ li-naẓar-iyyāt al-marja' al-kabīr samāḥa Ayat Allāh al-'Uẓmā al-Shaykh Yūsuf al-Ṣāni'ī.* Qom: Manshūrāt Fiqh al-Thaqlayn, 2007 (1428).

al-Shāfi'ī, Muḥammad b. Idrīs. *Epistle on Legal Theory.* Ed. and tr. Joseph Lowry. New York: New York University Press, 2013.

al-Umm. Ed. Muḥammad Zuhrī al-Najjār. Beirut: Dār al-Ma'rifa, [198–?].

al-Shaykh al-Ṣadūq. *Man lā yaḥḍuruh al-faqīh.* Najaf: Dār al-Kutub al-Islāmīya, 1378/1958.

al-Shīrāzī, Abū Isḥāq. *Al-Muhadhdhab fī fiqh al-Imām al-Shāfi'ī.* Ed. Muḥammad al-Zuḥaylī. Damascus: Dār al-Qalam, 1996.

Shīrāzī (Shirazi), Nāsir Makārim. *al-Amthāl fī tafsīr kitāb Allah al-munzal.* Beirut: Mu'assasat al-Bi'tha, 1990.

al-Sulamī, 'Izz al-Dīn 'abd al-Salām. *Tafsīr al-Qur'ān … Ikhtiṣār al-Nukat lil-Māwardī.* Ed. 'Abd Allāh b. Ibrāhīm b. 'Abd Allāh al-Wuhaybī. Beirut: Dār Ibn Ḥazm, 1996.

Sūrābādī. *Tafsīr al-Tafāsīr*. Ed. Sa'īdī Sīrjānī. Tehran: Farhang-i Nashr-i Naw, 2002.
al-Suyūṭī, Jalāl al-Dīn. *al-Durr al-manthūr fī tafsīr bi'l-ma'thūr*. [No named editor.] Beirut: Dār al-Ma'ārifa, 1970.
al-Ṭabarī, Abū Ja'far Muḥammad b. Jarīr. *The History of al-Ṭabarī, General Introduction and From the Creation to the Flood*. Translated and annotated by Franz Rosenthal. New York: SUNY Press, 1989.
Jāmi' al-Bayān 'an tā'wīl āy al-Qur'ān. Eds. Maḥmūd Muḥammad Shākir and Aḥmad Muḥammad Shākir. Cairo: Dār al-Ma'ārif bi-Maṣr, 1950–60.
Jāmi' al-bayān 'an ta'wīl āy al-Qur'ān. Ed. al-Bakri et.al., Cairo: Dār al-Salām, 2007.
Ta'rīkh al-rusul wa'l-mulūk [Annales]. Ed. M. J. De Goeje. Leiden: Brill, 1964, prima series, v. 1.
Ṭabāṭabā'ī, 'Allāmah Sayyid Ḥusayn. *al-Mizān fī tafsīr al-Qur'ān*. Qom: Mu'assasat al-Imām al-Muntaẓar, 2004.
al-Ṭabrisī, Abū 'Alī al-Faḍl b. al-Ḥasan. *Majma' al-bayān li-'ulūm al-Qur'ān*. Ed. Muḥammad Wā'īẓzādeh al-Khurāsānī. Tehran: Mu'assasat al-Hudā, 1997.
al-Ṭanṭāwī, Muḥammad. *Tafsīr al-wasīṭ lil-Qur'ān al-karīm*. Cairo: Dār al-Ma'ārif, 1992.
Al-Tha'labī, *al-Kashf wa'l-bayān*. Ed. Abū Muḥammad b. Āshūr et. al. Beirut: Dār Iḥya' al-Turāth al-'Arabī, 2002.
al-Ṭūsī, Abū Ja'far Muḥammad b. al-Ḥasan. *Al-Tibyān fī tafsīr al-Qur'ān*. Ed. Mu'assasat al-Nashr al-Islāmī. Qom: Jami'a al-Mudarrisīn, 1992.
al-Wāḥidī, Abū' l-Ḥasan 'Alī b. Aḥmad. *Al-Basīṭ*. MS Istanbul, Nuru Osmaniye, 236.
al-Wajīz fī tafsīr al-kitāb al-'azīz. Ed. Ṣafwān 'Adnān Dawūdī. Damascus: Dar al-Qalam, 1995, v. 1.
al-Wasīṭ fī tafsīr al-Qur'ān al-majīd. Ed. 'Adil Aḥmad 'Abd al-Mawjūd et. al. Beirut: Dār al-Kutub al-'Ilmīya, 1994.
al-Zajjāj, Abū Ishāq Ibrāhīm b. al-Sārī, *Ma'ānī al-Qur'ān*. Ed. 'Abd al-Jalīl 'Abduh Shalabī. Beirut: Manshūrāt al-Maktaba al-'Asriyya, 1973–4.
al-Zamakhsharī, Maḥmūd b. 'Umar, known as Jār Allāh. *al-Kashshāf*. Ed. Aḥmad b. al-Munīr al-Iskandarī. Beirut: Dār al-Kutub al-'Arabī, [1965].
al-Zuhaylī, Wahba. *al-Tafsīr al-munīr fī 'l-'aqīda wa'l-sharī'a wa'l-manhaj*. Damascus: Dār al-Fikr, 1991.

Interview Subjects Cited

Dr Fariba 'Alasvand, Personal Interview, Qom, Iran, 8 June 2011. Follow up email correspondence 10 June 2014. Interview and follow-up correspondence conducted in Arabic.
Sayyid Muḥammad 'Alī Ayāzī, Ḥujjat al-Islam wa'l-Muslimīn, Personal Interview, Qom, Iran, 29 May 2011. Interview conducted in Persian with the assistance of a translator.
Muḥammad Sa'īd Ramaḍān al-Būṭī, Personal Interview, Damascus, Syria, September 2004. Interview conducted in Arabic.

Ayatollah Seyed Mostafa Mohaghegh Damad, Personal Interview, Tehran, Iran, 23 June 2011. Interview conducted in Arabic and English.

Grand Ayatollah Muhammad ʿAli Gerami, Personal Interview, Qom, Iran, 14 June 2011. Interview conducted in Arabic. Follow-up correspondence (with his student) conducted in English, 8 July 2014.

Mr Muhammad Ghazizadeh, Ḥujjat al-Islām wa'l-Muslimīn, Qom, Iran, 5 June 2011. Interview conducted in Persian, with translator.

Dr Naser Ghorbannia, Personal Interview, Qom, Iran, 29 May 2011. Interview conducted in English.

Hudā al-Habash, series of personal interviews, Damascus, Syria, 2004. Interviews conducted in Arabic.

Muḥammad al-Ḥabash, Personal Interview, Damascus, Syria, 22 August 2004. Interview conducted in English.

Dr Mohammad Sadegh Kamilan, Ḥujjat al-Islām wa'l-Muslimīn, Professor of Philosophy and Islamic Law, Mofid University, Personal Interview, Qom, Iran, 30 May 2011. Interview conducted in Persian, with translator.

Dr Mohammad Mahdi Meghdadi, Personal Interview, Qom, Iran, 8 June 2011. Interview conducted in Persian, with translator.

Mr Mehdi Mehrizi, Ḥujjat al-Islām wa'l-Muslimīn, Personal Interview, Qom, Iran, 9 June 2011. Interview conducted in Arabic.

Dr Saeid Rahaei, Ḥujjat al-Islām wa'l-Muslimīn, Personal Interview, Mofid University, Qom, Iran, 7 June 2011. Interview conducted in Persian, with translator.

Grand Ayatollah Yusuf Saanei (Yūsuf Ṣāneʿī), Personal Interview, Qom, Iran, 13 June 2011. Interview conducted in Arabic. Follow-up correspondence with his student, 1 July 2014.

Grand Ayatollah Makarim Shirazi (Mākārim Shīrāzī), Personal Interview, Qom, Iran, 25 June 2011. Interview conducted in Arabic.

Dr Masoumeh Zahiri (Zahīrī), Personal Interview, Jamat-e-Zahra, Qom, Iran, 31 May 2011. Interview conducted in Arabic.

Mr Zibaei Nejad, Ḥujjat al-Islām wa'l-Muslimīn, Personal Interview, Qom, Iran, 28 May 2011. Interview conducted in Persian, with translator. Follow-up correspondence 26 June 2014.

Secondary Sources

Alexandre, Danièle, 'The Status of Women in France', *The American Journal of Comparative Law* 20.4 (Autumn 1972).

Ali, Kecia. 'Money, Sex, and Power: The Contractual Nature of Marriage in Islamic Jurisprudence of the Formative Period'. PhD Dissertation. Duke University, 2002.

'Progressive Muslims and Islamic Jurisprudence: The Necessity for Critical Engagement with Marriage and Divorce Law', in *Progressive Muslims on Justice, Gender and Pluralism*. Ed. Omid Safi. Oxford: Oneworld, 2003, pp. 163–89.

Sexual Ethics and Islam: Feminist Reflections on Qur'an, Hadith, and Jurisprudence. Oxford: Oneworld, 2006.

'The Best of You Will not Strike: al-Shāfi'ī on Qur'ān, *sunnah*, and Wife-Beating', *Journal of Comparative Islamic Studies*, 2.2 (December 2006): 143–55.

Marriage and Slavery in Early Islam. Cambridge, MA: Harvard University Press, 2010.

'Religious Practices: Obedience and Disobedience', *Encyclopedia of Women in Islamic Cultures*.

Barlas, Asma. *'Believing Women' in Islam: Unreading Patriarchal Interpretations of the Qur'an*. Austin: University of Texas Press, 2002.

Bauer, Karen. *'Room for Interpretation: Qur'anic Exegesis and Gender'*. PhD Dissertation. Princeton University, 2008.

'*The Male is Not Like the Female* (Q. 3:36): The Question of Gender Egalitarianism in the Qur'ān', *Religion Compass* 3/4 (2009): 637–54.

'Debates on Women's Status as Judges and Witnesses in Post-Formative Islamic Law' *The Journal of the American Oriental Society* 130.1 (2010).

'I Have Seen the People's Antipathy to this Knowledge: The Muslim Exegete and His Audience 5th/11th – 7th/13th Centuries', in *The Islamic Scholarly Tradition: Studies in History, Law, and Thought in Honor of Michael Allan Cook*. Ed. Ahmed, Sadeghi, and Bonner. Leiden: Brill, 2011.

'Spiritual Hierarchy and Gender Hierarchy in Fāṭimid Ismā'īlī Interpretations of the Qur'ān', *Journal of Qur'anic Studies* 14.2 (2012): 29–46.

'Justifying the Genre: A study of Introductions to Classical Works of *Tafsīr*', in *Aims, Methods, and Contexts of Qur'anic Exegesis (2nd/8th – 9th/15th c.)*. Ed. Karen Bauer. Oxford: Oxford University Press in association with the Institute of Ismaili Studies, 2013, pp. 39–66.

'A Note on the Relationship Between *Tafsīr* and Documentary Evidence, with Reference to Contracts of Marriage', in *Islamic Cultures, Islamic Contexts: Essays in Honor of Professor Patricia Crone*. Ed. Asad Ahmed, Robert Hoyland, Behnam Sadeghi, and Adam Silverstein. Leiden: Brill, 2014, pp. 97–111.

Booth, Marilyn. 'Islamic Politics, Street Literature, and John Stewart Mill: Composing Gendered Ideals in 1990s Egypt', *Feminist Studies* 39.3 (2013): 596–626.

'Before Qasim Amin: Writing Gender History in 1890s Egypt', in *The Long 1890s in Egypt: Colonial Quiescence, Subterranean Resistance*. Ed. Marilyn Booth and Anthony Gorman. Edinburgh: Edinburgh University Press, 2014, pp. 365–98.

Bronson, Catherine. 'Imagining the Primal Woman: Islamic Selves of Eve'. PhD Dissertation. The University of Chicago, 2012.

Burge, Stephen. 'Scattered Pearls: Exploring al-Suyūṭī's Hermeneutics and Use of Sources in al-Durr al-manthūr fī' l-tafsīr bi'l-ma'thūr', *Journal of the Royal Asiatic Society* 24.2 (2014): 251–96.

Calder, Norman. 'Tafsīr from Ṭabarī to Ibn Kathīr: Problems in the Description of a Genre, Illustrated with Reference to the Story of Abraham', in *Approaches to the Qur'ān*. Eds. Hawting and Shareef. New York: Routledge, 1993, pp. 101–38.

Chaudhry, Ayesha. *Domestic Violence and the Islamic Tradition: Ethics, Law, and the Muslim Discourse on Gender*. Oxford: Oxford University Press, 2013.

Cook, Michael. *Commanding Right and Forbidding Wrong in Islamic Thought.* Cambridge: Cambridge University Press, 2000.

Crone, Patricia. *Medieval Islamic Political Thought.* Edinburgh: Edinburgh University Press, 2005

Elshakry, Marwa. 'Muslim Hermeneutics and Arabic Views of Evolution', *Zygon: Journal of Religion and Science*, 46.2 (June 2011): 330–44.

Reading Darwin in Arabic, 1860–1950. Chicago and London: University of Chicago Press, 2014.

Esack, Farid. 'Islam and Gender Justice: Beyond Simple Apologia', in *What Men Owe to Women: Men's Voices from World Religions.* Ed. John C. Raines and Daniel C. Maguire. Albany: SUNY Press, 2001, pp. 187–210.

Gadamer, Hans-Georg. 'The Universality of the Hermeneutical Problem', in *Hermeneutical Inquiry, Vol. 1: The Interpretation of Texts.* David E. Klemm, the American Academy of Religion Studies in Religion, No. 43. Atlanta, GA: Scholars Press, 1986, pp. 179–91.

Gilliot, Caude. 'The Beginnings of Qurʾānic Exegesis', in *The Qurʾān: Formative Interpretation.* Ed. Andrew Rippin. Aldershot: Ashgate, 1999, pp. 1–27.

'A Schoolmaster, Sotryteller, Exegete and Warrior at Work in Khurāsan: al-Ḍaḥḥāk b. Muzāḥim al-Hilālī (d. 106/724)', in *Aims, Methods and Contexts of Qur'anic Exegesis (2nd/8th – 9th/15th c.).* Ed. Karen Bauer. Oxford: Oxford University Press in association with the Institute of Ismaili Studies, 2013, pp. 311–92.

Gleave, Robert. *Scripturalist Islam: The History and Doctrines of the Akhbārī Shīʿī School.* Leiden: Brill, 2007.

Inevitable Doubt: Two Theories of Shīʿī Jurisprudence. Leiden: Brill, 2000.

Goldziher, Ignaz. *Schools of Koranic Commentators.* Ed. & tr. Wolfgang H. Behn. Weisbaden: Harrasowitz Verslag, 2006.

Grohmann, Adolf. *Arabic Papyri in the Egyptian Library.* Cairo: Egyptian Library Press, 1934.

Hadromi-Allouche, Zohar, 'Creating Eve: Feminine Fertility in Medieval Islamic Narratives of Eve and Adam' in *In the Arms of Biblical Women*, ed. John Greene & Mishael M. Caspi. Piscataway, NJ: Gorgias Press, 2013, pp. 27–63.

Hamza, Feras. '*Tafsīr* and Unlocking the Historical Qur'an: Back to Basics?', in *Aims and Methods of Qurʾānic Exegesis (2nd/8th – 9th/15th c.).* Ed. Karen Bauer. Oxford: Oxford University Press, 2013, pp. 19–39.

Hamza, Feras et al., *An Anthology of Qur'anic Commentaries, Volume 1: On the Nature of the Divine.* Oxford: Oxford University Press in association with the Institute of Ismaili Studies, 2008.

Hidayatullah, Aysha. *Feminist Edges of the Qur'an.* Oxford: Oxford University Press, 2014.

Howard, Damian. *Being Human in Islam: The Impact of the Evolutionary Worldview.* London: Routledge, 2011.

Jansen, J. J. G. *The Interpretation of the Koran in Modern Egypt.* Leiden: Brill, 1974.

Kalmbach, Hilary. 'Social and Religious Change in Damascus: One Case of Female Islamic Religious Authority', *British Journal of Middle East Studies*, 35:1, pp. 37–57.

Keeler, Annabel. *Sufi Hermeneutics: The Qur'an Commentary of Rashīd al-Dīn Maybudī.* Oxford: Oxford University Press in association with the Institute of Ismaili Studies, 2006.

Khan, Geoffrey. *Arabic Legal and Administrative Documents from the Cambridge Geniza Collections*. Cambridge: Cambridge University Press, 1993.

Madelung, Wilferd. 'Shi'i Attitudes towards Women as Reflected in Fiqh', in *Society and the Sexes in Medieval Islam*. Ed. Afaf Lutfi Sayyid-Marsot. Malibu, CA: Undena Publications, 1979, pp. 69–79.

Mahmood, Saba. *Politics of Piety: The Islamic Revival and the Feminist Subject*. Princeton, NJ: Princeton University Press, 2005.

Marcotte, Roxanne D. 'Bint al-Shāṭiʿ on Women's Emancipation,' in *Coming to Terms With the Qurʾān: a volume in honor of Professor Issa Boulllata*, ed. Khaleel Mohammed and Andrew Rippin, pp. 179-208

Marín, Manuela. 'Disciplining Wives: A Historical Reading of Qur'ān 4:34', *Studia Islamica* (2003): 5–40.

McAuliffe, Jane Dammen. 'Qurʾānic Hermeneutics: the Views of al-Ṭabarī and Ibn Kathīr', in *Approaches to the History of the Interpretation of the Qurʾān*. Ed. Andrew Rippin. Oxford: Clarendon Press, 1988, pp. 46–62.

Qurʾānic Christians: An Analysis of Classical and Modern Exegesis. Cambridge: Cambridge University Press, 1991.

'The Genre Boundaries of Qur'ānic Commentary', in *With Reverence for the Word: Medieval Scriptural Exegesis in Judaism, Christianity, and Islam*. Ed. Jane McAuliffe et al. Oxford: Oxford University Press, 2003.

Mir-Hosseini, Ziba. *Islam and Gender: The Religious Debate in Contemporary Iran*. Princeton, NJ: Princeton University Press, 1999.

Mubarak, Hadia. 'Breaking Apart the Interpretive Monopoly: A Re-examination of Verse 4:34', *Hawwa: Journal of Women of the Middle East and Islamic World* 2.3 (2004): 261–89.

Nettler, Ronald. 'Mohammad Talbi's Commentary on Qurʾān IV:34: A "Historical Reading" of a Verse Concerning the Disciplining of Women', *The Maghreb Review* 24.1–2 (1999), pp. 19–33.

Nguyen, Martin. *Sufi Master and Qur'an Scholar: Abū' l-Qāsim al-Qushayrī and the Laṭāʾif al-Ishārāt*. Oxford: Oxford University Press in association with the Institute of Ismaili Studies, 2012.

Oweidat, Nadia. 'Nasr Hamid Abu Zayd and Limits of Reform in Contemporary Islamic Thought'. PhD Dissertation. Oxford University, 2014.

Pregill, Michael. 'Methodologies for the Dating of Exegetical Works and Traditions: Can the Lost *Tafsīr* of al-Kalbī be Recovered from Tafsīr Ibn ʿAbbās (also known as al-*Wāḍiḥ*)?', in *Aims, Methods, and Contexts*, pp. 393–453.

Robinson, Chase. *Islamic Historiography*. Cambridge: Cambridge University Press, 2003.

Roded, Ruth. 'Jews and Muslims [Re]Define Gender Relations in their Sacred Books: *yimshol* and *qawwamun*', in *Muslim-Jewish Relations in Past and Present: A Kaleidoscopic View*. Studies on the Children of Abraham Series. Eds. Camilla Adang and Josef (Yousef) Meri. Leiden: Brill, forthcoming.

Jewish and Islamic Religious Feminist Exegesis of Their Sacred Books: Adam, Woman and Gender (forthcoming).

Rosen, Stanley. *Hermeneutics as Politics*. Oxford: Oxford University Press, 1987.

Sadeghi, Behnam. 'The Structure of Reasoning in Post-Formative Islamic Jurisprudence'. PhD Dissertation. Princeton University, 2006.

The Logic of Law Making in Islam: Women and Prayer in the Legal Tradition. Cambridge: Cambridge University Press, 2013.

Saleh, Walid. *The Formation of the Classical Tafsīr Tradition: The Qur'ān Commentary of al-Tha'labī (d. 427/1035).* Boston: Brill, 2004.

'The Last of the Nishapuri School of Tafsīr: Al-Wāḥidī (d. 468/1076) and His Significance in the History of Qur'anic Exegesis' *Journal of the American Oriental Society* 126.2 (2006): 223–43.

'The Introduction of al-Wāḥidī's Baṣīṭ: An Edition, Translation, and Commentary,' in Bauer (ed.) *Aims, Methods, and Contexts of Qur'ānic Exegesis*, pp. 67–100.

Savant, Sarah Bowen. *The New Muslims of Post-Conquest Iran: Tradition, Memory, and Conversion.* Cambridge: Cambridge University Press, 2013.

Scott, Rachel M. 'A Contextual Approach to Women's Rights in the Qur'ān: Readings of 4:34', *The Muslim World* 99 (January 2009): 60–84.

Shaham, Ron. 'Women as Expert Witnesses in Pre-Modern Islamic Courts', in *Law, Custom, and Statute in the Muslim World: Studies in Honor of Aharon Layish.* Ed. Ron Shaham. Studies in Islamic Law and Society Series, vol. 28. Ed. Ruud Peters and Kevin Reinhart. Leiden: Brill, 2007, pp. 41–65.

Shaikh, Sa'diyya. 'Exegetical Violence: *nushūz* in Qur'ānic Gender Ideology', *Journal for Islamic Studies* 17 (1997): 49–73.

'A Tafsir of Praxis: Gender, Marital Violence, and Resistance in a South African Muslim Community', in *Violence Against Women in Contemporary World Religions: Roots and Cures.* Ed. Daniel Maguire and Sa'diyya Shaikh. Cleveland, OH: Pilgrim Press, 2007, pp. 66–89.

al-Sharīfī, al-Ḥājj b. Sa'īd. 'Introduction', in *Tafsīr Hūd b. Muḥakkam al-Hawwārī.* Ed. al-Ḥājj b. Sa'īd al-Sharīfī. Beirut: Dār al-Gharb al-Islāmī, 1990.

Shihadeh, Ayman. *The Teoleological Ethics of Fakhr al-Dīn al-Rāzī.* Leiden: Brill, 2006.

Taji-Farouki, Suha. 'Introduction', in *Modern Muslim Intellectuals and the Qur'an.* Ed. Suha Taji-Farouki. Oxford: Oxford University Press in association with the Institute of Ismaili Studies, 2004.

Tottoli, Roberto. *Biblical Prophets in the Qur'ān and Muslim Literature.* Surrey: Curzon Press, 2002.

'Methods and Contexts in the Use of *Hadith*s in Classical *Tafsīr* Literature: The Exegesis of Q. 21:85 and Q 17:1', in *Aims, Methods, and Contexts*, pp. 199–215.

Versteegh, C.H.M. 'Grammar and Exegesis: The Origins of Kufan Grammar and the *Tafsīr* Muqātil', *Der Islam* 67.2 (1990): 206–42.

Arabic Grammar and Qur'ānic Exegesis in Early Islam. Leiden: Brill, 1993.

Vishanoff, David R. *The Formation of Islamic Hermeneutics: How Sunni Legal Theorists Imagined a Revealed Law.* New Haven, CT: The American Oriental Society, 2011.

Wadud, Amina. *Qur'an and Woman.* Kuala Lumpur: Penerbit Fajar Bakti, 1994.

Qur'an and Woman: Rereading the Sacred Text from a Woman's Perspective, Oxford: Oxford University Press, 1999 (reprint edition).

Wheeler, Brannon. *Prophets in the Qur'ān: An Introduction to the Qur'ān and Muslim Exegesis*. London: Continuum, 2002.

Zaman, Muhammad Qasim. *The Ulama in Contemporary Islam: Custodians of Change*. Princeton, NJ: Princeton University Press, 2002.

al-Zeera, Rahba Isa. 'Violence Against Women in Qur'an 4:34: A Sacred Ordinance?', in *Muslima Theology: The Voices of Muslim Women Theologians*. Ed. Ednan Aslan, Marcia Hermansen, and Elif Medeni. Frankfurt: Peter Lang, 2013, pp. 217–30.

Blogs and Online Newspaper Articles

Al-'Arabiyya Newspaper online, 22 March 2013. Accessed at: http://english.alarabiya.net/en/News/2013/03/22/-Sheikh-al-Bouti-the-Syrian-Sunni-cleric-who-stood-by-Assad.html

Landis, Joshua. Blog: Syria Comment. Accessed at: http://www.joshualandis.com/blog/muhammad-al-habash-resigns-from-all-religious-activities/

Ruling of the Supreme Court of Pakistan on the case of Mukhtar Mai, Criminal Appeals No.163 to 171 and S.M. Case No.5/2005, p. 41 (point 27), dated 19/4/2011. Accessed at: http://www.supremecourt.gov.pk/web/user_files/File/Crl.P.163_to_171&S.M.C5_2005.pdf

Website of Ayatollah Mohaghegh Damad: http://www.mdamad.com/Welcome.html

'Women Want Female Muftis', *Institute for War and Peace Reporting*, Syria Issue 16.2 (September 2008) [no author listed]. Accessed at: http://webcache.googleusercontent.com/search?q=cache:A4JB13qjAukJ:iwpr.net/report-news/women-want-female-muftis+&cd=1&hl=en&ct=clnk&gl=uk

Index

Other Titles in the Series:

Popular Culture in Medieval Cairo Boaz Shoshan
Early Philosophical Shiism: The Ismaili Neoplatonism of Abū Ya'qūb Al-Sijistānī Paul E. Walker
Indian Merchants and Eurasian Trade, 1600–1750 Stephen Frederic Dale
Palestinian Peasants and Ottoman Officials: Rural Administration Around Sixteenth-Century Jerusalem Amy Singer
Arabic Historical Thought in the Classical Period Tarif Khalidi
Mongols and Mamluks: The Mamluk–Īlkhānid War, 1260–1281 Reuven Amitai-Preiss
Hierarchy and Egalitarianism in Islamic Thought Louise Marlow
The Politics of Households in Ottoman Egypt: The Rise of the Qazdağlis Jane Hathaway
Commodity and Exchange in the Mongol Empire: A Cultural History of Islamic Textiles Thomas T. Allsen
State and Provincial Society in the Ottoman Empire: Mosul, 1540–1834 Dina Rizk Khoury
The Mamluks in Egyptian Politics and Society Thomas Philipp and Ulrich Haarmann (eds.)
The Delhi Sultanate: A Political and Military History Peter Jackson
European and Islamic Trade in the Early Ottoman State: The Merchants of Genoa and Turkey Kate Fleet
Reinterpreting Islamic Historiography: Hārūn al-rashīd and the Narrative of the 'Abbāsid Caliphate Tayeb El-Hibri
The Ottoman City between East and West: Aleppo, Izmir, and Istanbul Edhem Eldem, Daniel Goffman, and Bruce Masters
A Monetary History of the Ottoman Empire Şevket Pamuk
The Politics of Trade in Safavid Iran: Silk for Silver, 1600–1730 Rudolph P. Matthee
The Idea of Idolatry and the Emergence of Islam: From Polemic to History G. R. Hawting
Classical Arabic Biography: The Heirs of the Prophets in the Age of al-ma'mūn Michael Cooperson
Empire and Elites After the Muslim Conquest: The Transformation of Northern Mesopotamia Chase F. Robinson
Poverty and Charity in Medieval Islam: Mamluk Egypt, 1250–1517 Adam Sabra
Christians and Jews in the Ottoman Arab World: The Roots of Sectarianism Bruce Masters
Culture and Conquest in Mongol Eurasia Thomas T. Allsen
Revival and Reform in Islam: The Legacy of Muhammad Al-Shawkani Bernard Haykel
Tolerance and Coercion in Islam: Interfaith Relations in the Muslim Tradition Yohanan Friedmann
Guns for the Sultan: Military Power and the Weapons Industry in the Ottoman Empire Gábor Ágoston

Marriage, Money and Divorce in Medieval Islamic Society Yossef Rapoport
The Empire of the Qara Khitai in Eurasian History: Between China and the Islamic World Michal Biran
Domesticity and Power in the Early Mughal World Ruby Lal
Power, Politics and Religion in Timurid Iran Beatrice Forbes Manz
Postal Systems in the Pre-Modern Islamic World Adam J. Silverstein
Kingship and Ideology in the Islamic and Mongol Worlds Anne F. Broadbridge
Justice, Punishment and the Medieval Muslim Imagination Christian Lange
The Shiites of Lebanon Under Ottoman Rule, 1516–1788 Stefan Winter
Women and Slavery in the Late Ottoman Empire Madeline Zilfi
The Second Ottoman Empire: Political and Social Transformation in the Early Modern World Baki Tezcan
Non-Muslims in the Early Islamic Empire: From Surrender to Coexistence Milka Levy-Rubin
The Legendary Biographies of Tamerlane: Islam and Heroic Apocrypha in Central Asia Ron Sela
Law and Piety in Medieval Islam Megan Reid
The Origins of the Shi'a: Identity, Ritual, and Sacred Space in Eighth-Century Kufa Najam Haider
Politics, Law, and Community in Islamic Thought: The Taymiyyan Moment Ovamir Anjum
The Power of Oratory in the Medieval Muslim World Linda G. Jones
Animals in the Qur'an Sarra Tlili
The Logic of Law Making in Islam: Women and Prayer in the Legal Tradition Behnam Sadeghi
Empire and Power in the Reign of Süleyman: Narrating the Sixteenth-Century Ottoman World Kaya Şahin
Women and the Transmission of Religious Knowledge in Islam Asma Sayeed
The New Muslims of Post-Conquest Iran Sarah Bowen Savant
The Mamluk City in the Middle East Nimrod Luz
Disability in the Arab Ottoman World, 1500–1800 Sara Scalenghe
The Holy City of Medina: Sacred Space in Early Islamic Arabia Harry Munt
Muslim Midwives: The Craft of Birthing in the Premodern Middle East Avner Giladi
Doubt in Islamic Law: A History of Legal Maxims, Interpretation, and Islamic Criminal Law Intisar A. Rabb
The Second Formation of Islamic Law Guy Burak

CPSIA information can be obtained
at www.ICGtesting.com
Printed in the USA
LVOW04*0338231215
467588LV00008B/82/P

9 781107 041523